P9-EAY-098

Learning
Disabilities
SOURCEBOOK

Second Edition

DAVID O. MCKAY LIBRARY

3 1404 00745 7994

Gastrointestinal Diseases & Disorders
   Sourcebook
Genetic Disorders Sourcebook,
   1st Edition
Genetic Disorders Sourcebook,
   2nd Edition
Head Trauma Sourcebook
Headache Sourcebook
Health Insurance Sourcebook
Health Reference Series Cumulative
   Index 1999
Healthy Aging Sourcebook
Healthy Children Sourcebook
Healthy Heart Sourcebook for Women
Heart Diseases & Disorders
   Sourcebook, 2nd Edition
Household Safety Sourcebook
Immune System Disorders Sourcebook
Infant & Toddler Health Sourcebook
Injury & Trauma Sourcebook
Kidney & Urinary Tract Diseases &
   Disorders Sourcebook
Learning Disabilities Sourcebook,
   1st Edition
Learning Disabilities Sourcebook,
   2nd Edition
Liver Disorders Sourcebook
Lung Disorders Sourcebook
Medical Tests Sourcebook
Men's Health Concerns Sourcebook
Mental Health Disorders Sourcebook,
   1st Edition
Mental Health Disorders Sourcebook,
   2nd Edition
Mental Retardation Sourcebook
Movement Disorders Sourcebook
Obesity Sourcebook
Ophthalmic Disorders Sourcebook,
   1st Edition
Oral Health Sourcebook
Osteoporosis Sourcebook
Pain Sourcebook, 1st Edition
Pain Sourcebook, 2nd Edition

Pediatric C[...]
Physical & Mental Issues in Aging
   Sourcebook
Podiatry Sourcebook
Pregnancy & Birth Sourcebook
Prostate Cancer
Public Health Sourcebook
Reconstructive & Cosmetic Surgery
   Sourcebook
Rehabilitation Sourcebook
Respiratory Diseases & Disorders
   Sourcebook
Sexually Transmitted Diseases
   Sourcebook, 1st Edition
Sexually Transmitted Diseases
   Sourcebook, 2nd Edition
Skin Disorders Sourcebook
Sleep Disorders Sourcebook
Sports Injuries Sourcebook, 1st Edition
Sports Injuries Sourcebook, 2nd Edition
Stress-Related Disorders Sourcebook
Substance Abuse Sourcebook
Surgery Sourcebook
Transplantation Sourcebook
Traveler's Health Sourcebook
Vegetarian Sourcebook
Women's Health Concerns Sourcebook
Workplace Health & Safety Sourcebook
Worldwide Health Sourcebook

Teen Health Series
Diet Information for Teens
Drug Information for Teens
Mental Health Information
   for Teens
Sexual Health Information
   for Teens

WITHDRAWN

MAY 0 2 2024

DAVID O. McKAY LIBRARY
DAVID O. McKAY LIBRARY
REXBURG ID 83460-0405

Health Reference Series

Second Edition

Learning Disabilities
SOURCEBOOK

*Basic Consumer Health Information about Learning
Disabilities, Including Dyslexia, Developmental Speech
and Language Disabilities, Non-Verbal Learning
Disorders, Developmental Arithmetic Disorder,
Developmental Writing Disorder, and Other
Conditions That Impede Learning Such as Attention
Deficit/Hyperactivity Disorder, Brain Injury,
Hearing Impairment, Klinefelter Syndrome,
Dyspraxia, and Tourette Syndrome*

*Along with Facts about Educational Issues and Assistive
Technology, Coping Strategies, a Glossary of Related
Terms, and Resources for Further Help and Information*

Edited by
Dawn D. Matthews

Omnigraphics

615 Griswold Street • Detroit, MI 48226

Bibliographic Note

Because this page cannot legibly accommodate all the copyright notices, the Bibliographic Note portion of the Preface constitutes an extension of the copyright notice.

Edited by Dawn D. Matthews

Health Reference Series

Karen Bellenir, *Managing Editor*
David A. Cooke, MD, *Medical Consultant*
Elizabeth Barbour, *Permissions Associate*
Dawn Matthews, *Verification Assistant*
Laura Pleva Nielsen, *Index Editor*
EdIndex, Services for Publishers, *Indexers*

* * *

Omnigraphics, Inc.

Matthew P. Barbour, *Senior Vice President*
Kay Gill, *Vice President—Directories*
Kevin Hayes, *Operations Manager*
Leif Gruenberg, *Development Manager*
David P. Bianco, *Marketing Consultant*

* * *

Peter E. Ruffner, *Publisher*

Frederick G. Ruffner, Jr., *Chairman*

Copyright © 2003 Omnigraphics, Inc.

ISBN 0-7808-0626-3

Library of Congress Cataloging-in-Publication Data

Learning disabilities sourcebook : basic consumer health information about learning disabilities, including dyslexia, developmental speech and language disabilities, non-verbal learning disorders, developmental arithmetic disorder, developmental writing disorder, and other conditions that impede learning such as attention deficit/hyperactivity disorder, brain injury, hearing impairment, Klinefelter syndrome, dyspraxia, and Tourette syndrome; along with facts about educational issues and assistive technology, coping strategies, a glossary of related terms, and resources for further help and information / edited by Dawn D. Matthews.-- 2nd ed.
    p. cm. -- (Health reference series)
  Includes bibliographical references and index.
  ISBN 0-7808-0626-3
    1. Learning disabilities--United States--Handbooks, manuals, etc. 2. Learning disabled children--Education--United States--Handbooks, manuals, etc. 3. Learning disabled--Education--United States--Handbooks, manuals, etc. 4. Learning disabilities--United States--Diagnosis--Handbooks, manuals, etc. I. Matthews, Dawn D. II. Health reference series (Unnumbered)

LC4705 .L434 2003
371.92'6--dc21

2002192488

Electronic or mechanical reproduction, including photography, recording, or any other information storage and retrieval system for the purpose of resale is strictly prohibited without permission in writing from the publisher.

The information in this publication was compiled from the sources cited and from other sources considered reliable. While every possible effort has been made to ensure reliability, the publisher will not assume liability for damages caused by inaccuracies in the data, and makes no warranty, express or implied, on the accuracy of the information contained herein.

∞

This book is printed on acid-free paper meeting the ANSI Z39.48 Standard. The infinity symbol that appears above indicates that the paper in this book meets that standard.

Printed in the United States

Table of Contents

Part III: Academic Skills Disorders

Part IV: Other Conditions That Impede Learning

Part V: Educational Issues

Part VI: Accommodations and Assistive Devices

Part VII: Coping Strategies

Part VIII: Additional Help and Information

Preface

About This Book

Currently more than 2.8 million students with learning disabilities receive special education services. These students comprise 51% of the identified special education population and approximately 5% of all children in public schools. Unlike physical disabilities, such as paralysis or blindness, a learning disability is a hidden handicap. It does not disfigure or leave visible signs that would invite others to be understanding or offer support. The associated problems are real, however, and affect the ability of children to either interpret what they see and hear or to link information from different parts of the brain.

Learning Disabilities Sourcebook, Second Edition describes specific learning disabilities such as dyslexia, developmental speech and language disabilities, developmental arithmetic disorder, and developmental writing disorder, as well as other disorders that hinder learning, such as attention deficit/hyperactivity disorder (AD/HD), brain injury, hearing impairment, Klinefelter syndrome, and Tourette syndrome. It provides information about the diagnosis and assessment of learning disabilities, evaluations and individualized education programs, test-taking and workplace accommodations, and computer-based assistance for learning disabled people. A section on coping strategies, a glossary of related terms, information about financial aid for students with disabilities, and directories of additional resources are also provided.

The information about AD/HD in this volume offers a summary for people concerned about students with learning disabilities and attention problems. Readers seeking more in-depth information about AD/HD, however, may wish to consult *Attention Deficit Disorder Sourcebook*, a separate volume in the *Health Reference Series*.

How to Use This Book

This book is divided into parts and chapters. Parts focus on broad areas of interest. Chapters are devoted to single topics within a part.

Part I: Understanding Learning Disabilities provides an overview of learning disabilities. Individual chapters address specific issues related to gifted children, adults, and women with learning disabilities.

Part II: Language, Speech, and Processing Disabilities describes learning disorders that involve the ability to understand language or put words together in meaningful ways. It also includes facts about other disorders of spoken language including aphasia, motor-speech disorder, and auditory processing disorders.

Part III: Academic Skills Disorders offers information about disabilities in reading, writing, and mathematical calculation. The individual disorders are described and facts about related areas of academic concern are addressed.

Part IV: Other Conditions That Impede Learning describes various impairments and disorders that affect the ability to learn. These include attention deficit/hyperactivity disorder (AD/HD), autism, brain injury, hearing impairments, Tourette syndrome, and others.

Part V: Educational Issues gives practical advice for parents and educators about the diagnosis and assessment of learning disabilities. It also provides information about individualized education programs (IEPs), special education, alternative education programs, and other educational strategies that can be employed to promote successful learning experiences.

Part VI: Accommodations and Assistive Devices contains information about the various types of technical help available to those who are learning disabled. Examples include test-taking accommodations, workplace accommodations, and computer-based assistance in the classroom.

Part VII: Coping Strategies discusses the daily issues faced by learning disabled people and their families. It offers information about developing self-esteem, dealing with stress, and communicating with family members.

Part VIII: Additional Help and Information includes a glossary of important terms, resource directories, and information about financial aid for students with disabilities.

Bibliographic Note

This volume contains documents and excerpts from publications issued by the following U.S. government agencies: Educational Resources Information Center (ERIC); National Information Center for Children and Youth with Disabilities (NICHCY); National Institute of Child Health and Human Development (NICHD); National Institutes of Health (NIH); National Institute of Mental Health (NIMH); National Institute of Neurological Disorders and Stroke (NINDS); National Institute on Alcohol Abuse and Alcoholism (NIAAA); National Institute on Deafness and Other Communication Disorders (NIDCD); National Women's Health Information Center; and the Office of Special Education Programs (OSEP).

In addition, this volume contains copyrighted documents from the following organizations and individuals: American Speech-Language-Hearing Association; Association on Higher Education and Disability; Daniel J. Berkowitz, M.A.; Caroline Bowen; Childhood Apraxia of Speech Association/Michael A. Crary, Ph.D.; Coordinated Campaign for Learning Disabilities; Council for Learning Disabilities; Emily S. Fudge; Heath Resource Center; Lynne Anderson-Inman; International Dyslexia Association; Margaret J. Kay, Ed.D.; LD Online/WETA; Learning Disabilities Association of Canada; Learning Disabilities of Richmond; Rena Lewis, Ph.D.; Rosalyn Lord; Montana State University-Bozeman; National Center for Learning Disabilities; National Institute for Literacy; Regina Richards; Schwab Learning; and Taylor and Francis.

Acknowledgements

Special thanks go to the many organizations, agencies, and individuals who have contributed material for this *Sourcebook* and to the managing editor Karen Bellenir and permissions specialist Liz Barbour.

Note from the Editor

This book is part of Omnigraphics' *Health Reference Series*. The series provides basic information about a broad range of medical concerns. It is not intended to serve as a tool for diagnosing illness, in prescribing treatments, or as a substitute for the physician/patient relationship. All persons concerned about medical symptoms or the possibility of disease are encouraged to seek professional care from an appropriate health care provider.

Our Advisory Board

The *Health Reference Series* is reviewed by an Advisory Board comprised of librarians from public, academic, and medical libraries. We would like to thank the following board members for providing guidance to the development of this series:

Dr. Lynda Baker,
Associate Professor of Library and Information Science,
Wayne State University, Detroit, MI

Nancy Bulgarelli,
William Beaumont Hospital Library, Royal Oak, MI

Karen Imarisio,
Bloomfield Township Public Library, Bloomfield Township, MI

Karen Morgan,
Mardigian Library, University of Michigan-Dearborn,
Dearborn, MI

Rosemary Orlando,
St. Clair Shores Public Library, St. Clair Shores, MI

Medical Consultant

Medical consultation services are provided to the *Health Reference Series* editors by David A. Cooke, MD. Dr. Cooke is a graduate of Brandeis University, and he received his M.D. degree from the University of Michigan. He completed residency training at the University of Wisconsin Hospital and Clinics. He is board-certified in Internal Medicine. Dr. Cooke currently works as part of the University of Michigan Health System and practices in Brighton, MI. In his free time, he enjoys writing, science fiction, and spending time with his family.

Health Reference Series *Update Policy*

The inaugural book in the *Health Reference Series* was the first edition of *Cancer Sourcebook* published in 1989. Since then, the *Series* has been enthusiastically received by librarians and in the medical community. In order to maintain the standard of providing high-quality health information for the layperson the editorial staff at Omnigraphics felt it was necessary to implement a policy of updating volumes when warranted.

Medical researchers have been making tremendous strides, and it is the purpose of the *Health Reference Series* to stay current with the most recent advances. Each decision to update a volume will be made on an individual basis. Some of the considerations will include how much new information is available and the feedback we receive from people who use the books. If there is a topic you would like to see added to the update list, or an area of medical concern you feel has not been adequately addressed, please write to:

Editor
Health Reference Series
Omnigraphics, Inc.
615 Griswold Street
Detroit, MI 48226
E-mail: editorial@omnigraphics.com

Part One

Understanding
Learning Disabilities

Chapter 1

Learning Disabilities: The Basics

Introduction

Imagine having important needs and ideas to communicate, but being unable to express them. Perhaps feeling bombarded by sights and sounds, unable to focus your attention. Or trying to read or add but not being able to make sense of the letters or numbers.

You may not need to imagine. You may be the parent or teacher of a child experiencing academic problems, or have someone in your family diagnosed as learning disabled. Or possibly as a child you were told you had a reading problem called dyslexia or some other learning handicap.

Although different from person to person, these difficulties make up the common daily experiences of many learning disabled children, adolescents, and adults. A person with a learning disability may experience a cycle of academic failure and lowered self-esteem. Having these handicaps—or living with someone who has them—can bring overwhelming frustration.

But the prospects are hopeful. It is important to remember that a person with a learning disability can learn. The disability usually only affects certain limited areas of a child's development. In fact, rarely are learning disabilities severe enough to impair a person's potential to live a happy, normal life.

Excerpted from "Learning Disabilities," a brochure produced by the National Institute of Mental Health (NIMH), NIH Publication Number 93-3611, updated 1999.

3

Understanding the Problem

Susan

At age 14, Susan still tends to be quiet. Ever since she was a child, she was so withdrawn that people sometimes forgot she was there. She seemed to drift into a world of her own. When she did talk, she often called objects by the wrong names. She had few friends and mostly played with dolls or her little sister. In school, Susan hated reading and math because none of the letters, numbers or "+" and "-" signs made any sense. She felt awful about herself. She'd been told—and was convinced—that she was retarded.

Wallace

Wallace has lived 46 years, and still has trouble understanding what people say. Even as a boy, many words sounded alike. His father patiently said things over and over. But whenever his mother was drunk, she flew into a rage and spanked him for not listening. Wallace's speech also came out funny. He had such problems saying words that in school his teacher sometimes couldn't understand him. When classmates called him a dummy, his fists just seemed to take over.

Dennis

Dennis is 23 years old and still seems to have too much energy. But he had always been an overactive boy, sometimes jumping on the sofa for hours until he collapsed with exhaustion. In grade school, he never sat still. He interrupted lessons. But he was a friendly, well-meaning kid, so adults didn't get too angry. His academic problems became evident in third grade, when his teacher realized that Dennis could only recognize a few words and wrote like a first grader. She recommended that Dennis repeat third grade, to give him time to catch up. After another full year, his behavior was still out of control, and his reading and writing had not improved.

What Is a Learning Disability?

Unlike other disabilities, such as paralysis or blindness, a learning disability (LD) is a hidden handicap. A learning disability doesn't disfigure or leave visible signs that would invite others to be understanding or offer support. A woman once blurted to Wallace, "You seem so intelligent—you don't look handicapped!"

LD is a disorder that affects people's ability to either interpret what they see and hear or to link information from different parts of the brain. These limitations can show up in many ways—as specific difficulties with spoken and written language, coordination, self-control, or attention. Such difficulties extend to schoolwork and can impede learning to read or write, or to do math.

Learning disabilities can be lifelong conditions that, in some cases, affect many parts of a person's life: school or work, daily routines, family life, and sometimes even friendships and lay. In some people, many overlapping learning disabilities may be apparent. Other people may have a single, isolated learning problem that has little impact on other areas of their lives.

What Are the Types of Learning Disabilities?

Learning disability is not a diagnosis in the same sense as chickenpox or mumps. Chickenpox and mumps imply a single, known cause with a predictable set of symptoms. Rather, LD is a broad term that covers a pool of possible causes, symptoms, treatments, and outcomes. Partly because learning disabilities can show up in so many forms, it is difficult to diagnose or to pinpoint the causes. And no one knows of a pill or remedy that will cure them.

Not all learning problems are necessarily learning disabilities. Many children are simply slower in developing certain skills. Because children show natural differences in their rate of development, sometimes what seems to be a learning disability may simply be a delay in maturation. To be diagnosed as a learning disability, specific criteria must be met.

The criteria and characteristics for diagnosing learning disabilities appear in a reference book called the *DSM* (short for the *Diagnostic and Statistical Manual of Mental Disorders*). The *DSM* diagnosis is commonly used when applying for health insurance coverage of diagnostic and treatment services.

Learning disabilities can be divided into three broad categories:

- Developmental speech and language disorders

- Academic skills disorders

- "Other," a catch-all that includes certain coordination disorders and learning handicaps not covered by the other terms

Each of these categories includes a number of more specific disorders.

5

Developmental Speech and Language Disorders

Speech and language problems are often the earliest indicators of a learning disability. People with developmental speech and language disorders have difficulty producing speech sounds, using spoken language to communicate, or understanding what other people say. Depending on the problem, the specific diagnosis may be:

- Developmental articulation disorder
- Developmental expressive language disorder
- Developmental receptive language disorder

Developmental Articulation Disorder: Children with this disorder may have trouble controlling their rate of speech. Or they may lag behind playmates in learning to make speech sounds. For example, Wallace at age 6 still said "wabbit" instead of "rabbit" and "thwim" for "swim." Developmental articulation disorders are common. They appear in at least 10 percent of children younger than age 8. Fortunately, articulation disorders can often be outgrown or successfully treated with speech therapy.

Developmental Expressive Language Disorder: Some children with language impairments have problems expressing themselves in speech. Their disorder is called, therefore, a developmental expressive language disorder. Susan, who often calls objects by the wrong names, has an expressive language disorder. Of course, an expressive language disorder can take other forms. A 4-year-old who speaks only in two-word phrases and a 6-year-old who can't answer simple questions also have an expressive language disability.

Developmental Receptive Language Disorder: Some people have trouble understanding certain aspects of speech. It's as if their brains are set to a different frequency and the reception is poor. There's the toddler who doesn't respond to his name, a preschooler who hands you a bell when you asked for a ball, or the worker who consistently can't follow simple directions. Their hearing is fine, but they can't make sense of certain sounds, words, or sentences they hear. They may even seem inattentive. These people have a receptive language disorder. Because using and understanding speech are strongly related, many people with receptive language disorders also have an expressive language disability.

6

Of course, in preschoolers, some misuse of sounds, words, or grammar is a normal part of learning to speak. It's only when these problems persist that there is any cause for concern.

Academic Skills Disorders

Students with academic skills disorders are often years behind their classmates in developing reading, writing, or arithmetic skills. The diagnoses in this category include:

- Developmental reading disorder

- Developmental writing disorder

- Developmental arithmetic disorder

Developmental Reading Disorder: This type of disorder, also known as dyslexia, is quite widespread. In fact, reading disabilities affect 2 to 8 percent of elementary school children.

When you think of what is involved in the "three R's"—reading, 'riting, and 'rithmetic—it's astounding that most of us do learn them. Consider that to read, you must simultaneously:

- Focus attention on the printed marks and control eye movements across the page

- Recognize the sounds associated with letters

- Understand words and grammar

- Build ideas and images

- Compare new ideas to what you already know

- Store ideas in memory

Such mental juggling requires a rich, intact network of nerve cells that connect the brain's centers of vision, language, and memory.

A person can have problems in any of the tasks involved in reading. However, scientists found that a significant number of people with dyslexia share an inability to distinguish or separate the sounds in spoken words. Dennis, for example, can't identify the word "bat" by sounding out the individual letters, b-a-t. Other children with dyslexia may have trouble with rhyming games, such as rhyming "cat" with "bat." Yet scientists have found these skills fundamental to learning to read. Fortunately, remedial reading specialists have developed techniques that can help many children with dyslexia acquire these skills.

However, there is more to reading than recognizing words. If the brain is unable to form images or relate new ideas to those stored in memory, the reader can't understand or remember the new concepts. So other types of reading disabilities can appear in the upper grades when the focus of reading shifts from word identification to comprehension.

Developmental Writing Disorder: Writing, too, involves several brain areas and functions. The brain networks for vocabulary, grammar, hand movement, and memory must all be in good working order. So a developmental writing disorder may result from problems in any of these areas. For example, Dennis, who was unable to distinguish the sequence of sounds in a word, had problems with spelling. A child with a writing disability, particularly an expressive language disorder, might be unable to compose complete, grammatical sentences.

Developmental Arithmetic Disorder: If you doubt that arithmetic is a complex process, think of the steps you take to solve this simple problem: 25 divided by 3 equals?

Arithmetic involves recognizing numbers and symbols, memorizing facts such as the multiplication table, aligning numbers, and understanding abstract concepts like place value and fractions. Any of these may be difficult for children with developmental arithmetic disorders. Problems with numbers or basic concepts are likely to show up early. Disabilities that appear in the later grades are more often tied to problems in reasoning.

Many aspects of speaking, listening, reading, writing, and arithmetic overlap and build on the same brain capabilities. So it's not surprising that people can be diagnosed as having more than one area of learning disability. For example, the ability to understand language underlies learning to speak. Therefore, any disorder that hinders the ability to understand language will also interfere with the development of speech, which in turn hinders learning to read and write. A single gap in the brain's operation can disrupt many types of activity.

"Other" Learning Disabilities

The *DSM* also lists additional categories, such as motor skills disorders and specific developmental disorders not otherwise specified. These diagnoses include delays in acquiring language, academic, and motor skills that can affect the ability to learn, but do not meet the criteria for a specific learning disability. Also included are coordination disorders that can lead to poor penmanship, as well as certain spelling and memory disorders.

Attention Disorders

Nearly 4 million school age children have learning disabilities. Of these, at least 20 percent have a type of disorder that leaves them unable to focus their attention.

Some children and adults who have attention disorders appear to daydream excessively. And once you get their attention, they're often easily distracted. Susan, for example, tends to mentally drift off into a world of her own. Children like Susan may have a number of learning difficulties. If, like Susan, they are quiet and don't cause problems, their problems may go unnoticed. They may be passed along from grade to grade, without getting the special assistance they need.

In a large proportion of affected children—mostly boys—the attention deficit is accompanied by hyperactivity. Dennis is an example of a person with attention deficit hyperactivity disorder—ADHD. They act impulsively, running into traffic or toppling desks. Like young Dennis, who jumped on the sofa to exhaustion, hyperactive children can't sit still. They blurt out answers and interrupt. In games, they can't wait their turn. These children's problems are usually hard to miss. Because of their constant motion and explosive energy, hyperactive children often get into trouble with parents, teachers, and peers.

By adolescence, physical hyperactivity usually subsides into fidgeting and restlessness. But the problems with attention and concentration often continue into adulthood. At work, adults with ADHD often have trouble organizing tasks or completing their work. They don't seem to listen to or follow directions. Their work may be messy and appear careless.

Attention disorders, with or without hyperactivity, are not considered learning disabilities in themselves. However, because attention problems can seriously interfere with school performance, they often accompany academic skills disorders.

What Causes Learning Disabilities?

Understandably, one of the first questions parents ask when they learn their child has a learning disorder is "Why? What went wrong?"

Mental health professionals stress that since no one knows what causes learning disabilities, it doesn't help parents to look backward to search for possible reasons. There are too many possibilities to pin down the cause of the disability with certainty. It is far more important for the family to move forward in finding ways to get the right help. Scientists, however, do need to study causes in an effort to identify ways to prevent learning disabilities.

Once, scientists thought that all learning disabilities were caused by a single neurological problem. But research supported by National Institute of Mental Health (NIMH) has helped us see that the causes are more diverse and complex. New evidence seems to show that most learning disabilities do not stem from a single, specific area of the brain, but from difficulties in bringing together information from various brain regions.

Today, a leading theory is that learning disabilities stem from subtle disturbances in brain structures and functions. Some scientists believe that, in many cases, the disturbance begins before birth.

Errors in Fetal Brain Development

Throughout pregnancy, the fetal brain develops from a few all-purpose cells into a complex organ made of billions of specialized, interconnected nerve cells called neurons. During this amazing evolution, things can go wrong that may alter how the neurons form or interconnect.

In the early stages of pregnancy, the brain stem forms. It controls basic life functions such as breathing and digestion. Later, a deep ridge divides the cerebrum—the thinking part of the brain—into two halves, a right and left hemisphere. Finally, the areas involved with processing sight, sound, and other senses develop, as well as the areas associated with attention, thinking, and emotion.

As new cells form, they move into place to create various brain structures. Nerve cells rapidly grow to form networks with other parts of the brain. These networks are what allow information to be shared among various regions of the brain.

Throughout pregnancy, this brain development is vulnerable to disruptions. If the disruption occurs early, the fetus may die, or the infant may be born with widespread disabilities and possibly mental retardation. If the disruption occurs later, when the cells are becoming specialized and moving into place, it may leave errors in the cell makeup, location, or connections. Some scientists believe that these errors may later show up as learning disorders.

Other Factors That Affect Brain Development

Through experiments with animals, scientists at NIMH and other research facilities are tracking clues to determine what disrupts brain development. By studying the normal processes of brain development, scientists can better understand what can go wrong. Some of these studies are examining how genes, substance abuse, pregnancy problems, and toxins may affect the developing brain.

Genetic Factors: The fact that learning disabilities tend to run in families indicates that there may be a genetic link. For example, children who lack some of the skills needed for reading, such as hearing the separate sounds of words, are likely to have a parent with a related problem. However, a parent's learning disability may take a slightly different form in the child. A parent who has a writing disorder may have a child with an expressive language disorder. For this reason, it seems unlikely that specific learning disorders are inherited directly. Possibly, what is inherited is a subtle brain dysfunction that can in turn lead to a learning disability.

There may be an alternative explanation for why LD might seem to run in families. Some learning difficulties may actually stem from the family environment. For example, parents who have expressive language disorders might talk less to their children, or the language they use may be distorted. In such cases, the child lacks a good model for acquiring language and therefore, may seem to be learning disabled.

Tobacco, Alcohol, and Other Drug Use: Many drugs taken by the mother pass directly to the fetus. Research shows that a mother's use of cigarettes, alcohol, or other drugs during pregnancy may have damaging effects on the unborn child. Therefore, to prevent potential harm to developing babies, the U.S. Public Health Service supports efforts to make people aware of the possible dangers of smoking, drinking, and using drugs.

Scientists have found that mothers who smoke during pregnancy may be more likely to bear smaller babies. This is a concern because small newborns, usually those weighing less than 5 pounds, tend to be at risk for a variety of problems, including learning disorders.

Alcohol also may be dangerous to the fetus' developing brain. It appears that alcohol may distort the developing neurons. Heavy alcohol use during pregnancy has been linked to fetal alcohol syndrome, a condition that can lead to low birth weigh, intellectual impairment,

11

hyperactivity, and certain physical defects. Any alcohol use during pregnancy, however, may influence the child's development and lead to problems with learning, attention, memory, or problem solving. Because scientists have not yet identified safe levels, alcohol should be used cautiously by women who are pregnant or who may soon become pregnant.

Drugs such as cocaine—especially in its smokable form known as crack—seem to affect the normal development of brain receptors. These brain cell parts help to transmit incoming signals from our skin, eyes, and ears, and help regulate our physical response to the environment. Because children with certain learning disabilities have difficulty understanding speech sounds or letters, some researchers believe that learning disabilities, as well as ADHD, may be related to faulty receptors. Current research points to drug abuse as a possible cause of receptor damage.

Problems during Pregnancy or Delivery: Other possible causes of learning disabilities involve complications during pregnancy. In some cases, the mother's immune system reacts to the fetus and attacks it as if it were an infection. This type of disruption seems to cause newly formed brain cells to settle in the wrong part of the brain. Or during delivery, the umbilical cord may become twisted and temporarily cut off oxygen to the fetus. This, too, can impair brain functions and lead to LD.

Toxins in the Child's Environment: New brain cells and neural networks continue to be produced for a year or so after the child is born. These cells are vulnerable to certain disruptions, also.

Researchers are looking into environmental toxins that may lead to learning disabilities, possibly by disrupting childhood brain development or brain processes. Cadmium and lead, both prevalent in the environment, are becoming a leading focus of neurological research. Cadmium, used in making some steel products, can get into the soil, then into the foods we eat. Lead was once common in paint and gasoline, and is still present in some water pipes. A study of animals sponsored by the National Institutes of Health showed a connection between exposure to lead and learning difficulties. In the study, rats exposed to lead experienced changes in their brainwaves, slowing their ability to learn. The learning problems lasted for weeks, long after the rats were no longer exposed to lead.

In addition, there is growing evidence that learning problems may develop in children with cancer who had been treated with chemotherapy or radiation at an early age. This seems particularly true of children with brain tumors who received radiation to the skull.

Are Learning Disabilities Related to Differences in the Brain?

In comparing people with and without learning disabilities, scientists have observed certain differences in the structure and functioning of the brain. For example, new research indicates that there may be variations in the brain structure called the planum temporale, a language-related area found in both sides of the brain. In people with dyslexia, the two structures were found to be equal in size. In people who are not dyslexic, however, the left planum temporale was noticeably larger. Some scientists believe reading problems may be related to such differences.

With more research, scientists hope to learn precisely how differences in the structures and processes of the brain contribute to learning disabilities, and how these differences might be treated or prevented.

Getting Help

Susan

Susan was promoted to the sixth grade but still couldn't do basic math. So, her mother brought her to a private clinic for testing. The clinician observed that Susan had trouble associating symbols with their meaning, and this was holding back her language, reading, and math development. Susan called objects by the wrong words and she could not associate sounds with letters or recognize math symbols. However, an IQ of 128 meant that Susan was quite bright. In addition to developing an Individualized Education Plan (IEP), the clinician recommended that Susan receive counseling for her low self-esteem and depression.

Wallace

In the early 1960s, at the request of his ninth grade teacher, Wallace was examined by a doctor to see why he didn't speak or listen well. The doctor tested his vocal cords, vision, and hearing. They were all fine. The teacher concluded that Wallace must have brain damage, so not much could be done. Wallace kept failing in school and was suspended several times for fighting. He finally dropped out after tenth grade. He spent the next 25 years working as a janitor. Because LD frequently went undiagnosed at the time when Wallace was young, the needed help was not available to him.

Dennis

In fifth grade, Dennis' teacher sent him to the school psychologist for testing. Dennis was diagnosed as having developmental reading and developmental writing disorders. He was also identified as having an attention disorder with hyperactivity. He was placed in an all-day special education program, where he could work on his particular deficits and get individual attention. His family doctor prescribed the medication Ritalin to reduce his hyperactivity and distractibility. Along with working to improve his reading, the special education teacher helped him improve his listening skills. Since his handwriting was still poor, he learned to type homework and reports on a computer. At age 19, Dennis graduated from high school and was accepted by a college that gives special assistance to students with learning disabilities.

How Are Learning Disabilities First Identified?

The first step in solving any problem is realizing there is one. Wallace, sadly, was a product of his time, when learning disabilities were more of a mystery and often went unrecognized. Today, professionals would know how to help Wallace. Dennis and Susan were able to get help because someone saw the problem and referred them for help.

When a baby is born, the parents eagerly wait for the baby's first step, first word, and a myriad of other firsts. During routine check-ups, the pediatrician, too, watches for more subtle signs of development. The parents and doctor are watching for the child to achieve developmental milestones. Parents are usually the first to notice obvious delays in their child reaching early milestones. The pediatrician may observe more subtle signs of minor neurological damage, such as a lack of coordination. But the classroom teacher, in fact, may be the first to notice the child's persistent difficulties in reading, writing, or arithmetic. As school tasks become more complex, a child with a learning disability may have problems mentally juggling more information.

The learning problems of children who are quiet and polite in school may go unnoticed. Children with above average intelligence,

14

who manage to maintain passing grades despite their disability, are even less likely to be identified. Children with hyperactivity, on the other hand, will be identified quickly by their impulsive behavior and excessive movement. Hyperactivity usually begins before age 4 but may not be recognized until the child enters school.

What should parents, doctors, and teachers do if critical developmental milestones haven't appeared by the usual age? Sometimes it's best to allow a little more time, simply for the brain to mature a bit. But if a milestone is already long delayed, if there's a history of learning disabilities in the family, or if there are several delayed skills, the child should be professionally evaluated as soon as possible. An educator or a doctor who treats children can suggest where to go for help.

How Are Learning Disabilities Formally Diagnosed?

By law, learning disability is defined as a significant gap between a person's intelligence and the skills the person has achieved at each age. This means that a severely retarded 10-year-old who speaks like a 6-year-old probably doesn't have a language or speech disability.

He has mastered language up to the limits of his intelligence. On the other hand, a fifth grader with an IQ of 100 who can't write a simple sentence probably does have LD.

Learning disorders may be informally flagged by observing significant delays in the child's skill development. A 2-year delay in the primary grades is usually considered significant. For older students, such a delay is not as debilitating, so learning disabilities aren't usually suspected unless there is more than a 2-year delay. Actual diagnosis of learning disabilities, however, is made using standardized tests that compare the child's level of ability to what is considered normal development for a person of that age and intelligence.

For example, as late as fifth grade, Susan couldn't add two numbers, even though she rarely missed school and was good in other subjects. Her mother took her to a clinician, who observed Susan's behavior and administered standardized math and intelligence tests. The test results showed that Susan's math skills were several years behind, given her mental capacity for learning. Once other possible causes like lack of motivation and vision problems were ruled out, Susan's math problem was formally diagnosed as a specific learning disability.

Test outcomes depend not only on the child's actual abilities, but also on the reliability of the test and the child's ability to pay attention and understand the questions. Children like Dennis, with poor attention or hyperactivity, may score several points below their true level of ability. Testing a child in an isolated room can sometimes help the child concentrate and score higher.

Each type of LD is diagnosed in slightly different ways. To diagnose speech and language disorders, a speech therapist tests the child's pronunciation, vocabulary, and grammar and compares them to the developmental abilities seen in most children that age. A psychologist tests the child's intelligence. A physician checks for any ear infections, and an audiologist may be consulted to rule out auditory problems. If the problem involves articulation, a doctor examines the child's vocal cords and throat.

In the case of academic skills disorders, academic development in reading, writing, and math is evaluated using standardized tests. In addition, vision and hearing are tested to be sure the student can see words clearly and can hear adequately. The specialist also checks if the child has missed much school. It's important to rule out these other possible factors. After all, treatment for a learning disability is very different from the remedy for poor vision or missing school.

ADHD is diagnosed by checking for the long-term presence of specific behaviors, such as considerable fidgeting, losing things, interrupting, and talking excessively. Other signs include an inability to remain seated, stay on task, or take turns. A diagnosis of ADHD is made only if the child shows such behaviors substantially more than other children of the same age.

If the school fails to notice a learning delay, parents can request an outside evaluation. In Susan's case, her mother chose to bring Susan to a clinic for testing. She then brought documentation of the disability back to the school. After confirming the diagnosis, the public school was obligated to provide the kind of instructional program that Susan needed.

Parents should stay abreast of each step of the school's evaluation. Parents also need to know that they may appeal the school's decision if they disagree with the findings of the diagnostic team. And like Susan's mother, who brought Susan to a clinic, parents always have the option of getting a second opinion.

Some parents feel alone and confused when talking to learning specialists. Such parents may find it helpful to ask someone they like and trust to go with them to school meetings. The person may be the child's clinician or caseworker, or even a neighbor. It can help to have someone along who knows the child and can help understand the child's test scores or learning problems.

16

What Are the Education Options?

Although obtaining a diagnosis is important, even more important is creating a plan for getting the right help. Because LD can affect the child and family in so many ways, help may be needed on a variety of fronts: educational, medical, emotional, and practical.

In most ways, children with learning disabilities are no different from children without these disabilities. At school, they eat together and share sports, games, and after-school activities. But since children with learning disabilities do have specific learning needs, most public schools provide special programs.

Schools typically provide special education programs either in a separate all-day classroom or as a special education class that the student attends for several hours each week. Some parents hire trained tutors to work with their child after school. If the problems are severe, some parents choose to place their child in a special school for the learning disabled.

If parents choose to get help outside the public schools, they should select a learning specialist carefully. The specialist should be able to explain things in terms that the parents can understand. Whenever possible, the specialist should have professional certification and experience with the learner's specific age group and type of disability.

Planning a special education program begins with systematically identifying what the student can and cannot do. The specialist looks for patterns in the child's gaps. For example, if the child fails to hear the separate sounds in words, are there other sound discrimination problems? If there's a problem with handwriting, are there other motor delays? Are there any consistent problems with memory?

Special education teachers also identify the types of tasks the child can do and the senses that function well. By using the senses that are intact and bypassing the disabilities, many children can develop needed skills. These strengths offer alternative ways the child can learn.

After assessing the child's strengths and weaknesses, the special education teacher designs an Individualized Educational Program (IEP). The IEP outlines the specific skills the child needs to develop as well as appropriate learning activities that build on the child's strengths. Many effective learning activities engage several skills and senses. For example, in learning to spell and recognize words, a student may be asked to see, say, write, and spell each new word. The student may also write the words in sand, which engages the sense of touch. Many experts believe that the more senses children use in learning a skill, the more likely they are to retain it.

An individualized, skill-based approach—like the approach used by speech and language therapists—often succeeds in helping where regular classroom instruction fails. Therapy for speech and language disorders focuses on providing a stimulating but structured environment for heating and practicing language patterns. For example, the therapist may help a child who has an articulation disorder to produce specific speech sounds. During an engaging activity, the therapist may talk about the toys, then encourage the child to use the same sounds or words. In addition, the child may watch the therapist make the sound, feel the vibration in the therapist's throat, then practice making the sounds before a mirror.

Researchers are also investigating nonstandard teaching methods. Some create artificial learning conditions that may help the brain receive information in nonstandard ways. For example, in some language disorders, the brain seems abnormally slow to process verbal information. Scientists are testing whether computers that talk can help teach children to process spoken sounds more quickly. The computer starts slowly, pronouncing one sound at a time. As the child gets better at recognizing the sounds and hearing them as words, the sounds are gradually speeded up to a normal rate of speech.

Is Medication Available?

For nearly six decades, many children with attention disorders have benefited from being treated with medication. Three drugs, Ritalin (methylphenidate), Dexedrine (dextroamphetamine), and Cylert (pemoline), have been used successfully. Although these drugs are stimulants in the same category as speed and diet pills, they seldom make children high or more jittery. Rather, they temporarily improve children's attention and ability to focus. They also help children control their impulsiveness and other hyperactive behaviors.

The effects of medication are most dramatic in children with ADHD. Shortly after taking the medication, they become more able to focus their attention. They become more ready to learn. Studies by NIMH scientists and other researchers have shown that at least 90 percent of hyperactive children can be helped by either Ritalin or Dexedrine. If one medication does not help a hyperactive child to calm down and pay attention in school, the other medication might.

The drugs are effective for 3 to 4 hours and move out of the body within 12 hours. The child's doctor or a psychiatrist works closely with the family and child to carefully adjust the dosage and medication schedule for the best effect. Typically, the child takes the medication so that the drug is active during peak school hours, such as when reading and math are taught.

In the past few years, researchers have tested these drugs on adults who have attention disorders. Just as in children, the results show that low doses of these medications can help reduce distractibility and impulsivity in adults. Use of these medications has made it possible for many severely disordered adults to organize their lives, hold jobs, and care for themselves.

In trying to do everything possible to help their children, many parents have been quick to try new treatments. Most of these treatments sound scientific and reasonable, but a few are pure quackery. Many are developed by reputable doctors or specialists—but when tested scientifically, cannot be proven to help. Following are types of therapy that have not proven effective in treating the majority of children with learning disabilities or attention disorders:

- Megavitamins
- Colored lenses
- Special diets
- Sugar-free diets
- Body stimulation or manipulation

Although scientists hope that brain research will lead to new medical interventions and drugs, at present there are no medicines for speech, language, or academic disabilities.

How Do Families Learn to Cope?

The effects of learning disabilities can ripple outward from the disabled child or adult to family, friends, and peers at school or work. Children with LD often absorb what others thoughtlessly say about them. They may define themselves in light of their disabilities, as behind, slow, or different.

Sometimes they don't know how they're different, but they know how awful they feel. Their tension or shame can lead them to act out in various ways—from withdrawal to belligerence. Like Wallace, they may get into fights. They may stop trying to learn and achieve and eventually drop out of school. Or, like Susan, they may become isolated and depressed.

Children with learning disabilities and attention disorders may have trouble making friends with peers. For children with ADHD, this

19

may be due to their impulsive, hostile, or withdrawn behavior. Some children with delays may be more comfortable with younger children who play at their level. Social problems may also be a product of their disability. Some people with LD seem unable to interpret tone of voice or facial expressions. Misunderstanding the situation, they act inappropriately, turning people away.

Without professional help, the situation can spiral out of control. The more that children or teenagers fail, the more they may act out their frustration and damage their self-esteem. The more they act out, the more trouble and punishment it brings, further lowering their self-esteem. Wallace, who lashed out when teased about his poor pronunciation and was repeatedly suspended from school, shows how harmful this cycle can be.

Having a child with a learning disability may also be an emotional burden for the family. Parents often sweep through a range of emotions: denial, guilt, blame, frustration, anger, and despair. Brothers and sisters may be annoyed or embarrassed by their sibling, or jealous of all the attention the child with LD gets.

Counseling can be very helpful to people with LD and their families. Counseling can help affected children, teenagers, and adults develop greater self-control and a more positive attitude toward their own abilities. Talking with a counselor or psychologist also allows family members to air their feelings as well as get support and reassurance.

Many parents find that joining a support group also makes a difference. Support groups can be a source of information, practical suggestions, and mutual understanding. Self-help books written by educators and mental health professionals can also be helpful.

Behavior modification also seems to help many children with hyperactivity and LD. In behavior modification, children receive immediate, tangible rewards when they act appropriately. Receiving an immediate reward can help children learn to control their own actions, both at home and in class. A school or private counselor can explain behavior modification and help parents and teachers set up appropriate rewards for the child.

Parents and teachers can help by structuring tasks and environments for the child in ways that allow the child to succeed. They can find ways to help children build on their strengths and work around their disabilities. This may mean deliberately making eye contact before speaking to a child with an attention disorder. For a teenager with a language problem, it may mean providing pictures and diagrams for performing a task. For students like Dennis with handwriting or spelling problems, a solution may be to provide a word processor and software that checks spelling. A counselor or school psychologist can help identify practical solutions that make it easier for the child and family to cope day by day.

Every child needs to grow up feeling competent and loved. When children have learning disabilities, parents may need to work harder at developing their children's self-esteem and relationship-building skills. But self-esteem and good relationships are as worth developing as any academic skill.

Sustaining Hope

Susan

Susan is now in ninth grade and enjoys learning. She no longer believes she's retarded, and her use of words has improved. Susan has become a talented craftsperson and loves making clothes and furniture for her sister's dolls. Although she's still in a special education program, she is making slow but steady progress in reading and math.

Wallace

Over the years, Wallace found he liked tinkering with cars and singing in the church choir. At church, he met a woman who knew about learning disabilities. She told him he could get help through his county social services office. Since then, Wallace has been working with a speech therapist, learning to articulate and notice differences in speech sounds. When he complains that he's too old to learn, his therapist reminds him, "It's never too late to work your good brain." His state vocational rehabilitation office recently referred him to a job-training program. Today, at age 46, Wallace is starting night school to become an auto mechanic. He likes it because it's a hands-on program where he can learn by doing.

Dennis

Dennis is now age 23. As he walks into the college job placement office, he smiles and shakes hands confidently. After shuffling through a messy stack of papers, he finally hands his counselor a neatly typed resume. Although Dennis jiggles his foot and interrupts occasionally, he's clearly enthusiastic. He explains that because tape-recorded books and lectures got him through college, he'd like to sell electronics. Dennis says he'll also be getting married next year. He and his fiancé are concerned that their children also will have LD. "But we'll just have to watch and get help early—a lot earlier than I did."

Can Learning Disabilities Be Outgrown or Cured?

Even though most people don't outgrow their brain dysfunction, people do learn to adapt and live fulfilling lives. Dennis, Susan, and Wallace made a life for themselves—not by being cured, but by developing their personal strengths. Like Dennis' tape-recorded books and lectures, or Wallace's hands-on auto mechanics class, they found alternative ways to learn. And like Susan's crafts or Wallace's singing, they found ways to enjoy their other talents.

Even though a learning disability doesn't disappear, given the right types of educational experiences, people have a remarkable ability to learn. The brain's flexibility to learn new skills is probably greatest in young children and may diminish somewhat after puberty. This is why early intervention is so important. Nevertheless, we retain the ability to learn throughout our lives.

Even though learning disabilities can't be cured, there is still cause for hope. Because certain learning problems reflect delayed development, many children do eventually catch up. Of the speech and language disorders, children who have an articulation or an expressive language disorder are the least likely to have long-term problems. Despite initial delays, most children do learn to speak.

For people with dyslexia, the outlook is mixed. But an appropriate remedial reading program can help learners make great strides. With age, and appropriate help from parents and clinicians, children with ADHD become better able to suppress their hyperactivity and to channel it into more socially acceptable behaviors. As with Dennis, the problem may take less disruptive forms, such as fidgeting.

Can an adult be helped? For example, can an adult with dyslexia still learn to read? In many cases, the answer is yes. It may not come as easily as for a child. It may take more time and more repetition, and it may even take more diverse teaching methods. But we know more about reading and about adult learning than ever before. We know that adults have a wealth of life experience to build on as they learn. And because adults choose to learn, they do so with a determination that most children don't have. A variety of literacy and adult education programs sponsored by libraries, public schools, and community colleges are available to help adults develop skills in reading, writing, and math. Some of these programs, as well as private and nonprofit tutoring and learning centers, provide appropriate programs for adults with LD.

What Aid Does the Government Offer?

As of 1981, people with learning disabilities came under the protection of laws originally designed to protect the rights of people with mobility handicaps. More recent Federal laws specifically guarantee equal opportunity and raise the level of services to people with disabilities. Once a learning disability is identified, children are guaranteed a free public education specifically designed around their individual needs. Adolescents with disabilities can receive practical assistance and extra training to help make the transition to jobs and independent living. Adults have access to job training and technology that open new doors of opportunity.

Increased Services, Equal Opportunity

The Individuals with Disabilities Education Act of 1990 assures a public education to school-aged children with diagnosed learning disabilities. Under this act, public schools are required to design and implement an Individualized Educational Program tailored to each child's specific needs. The 1991 Individuals with Disabilities Education Act extended services to developmentally delayed children down to age 5. This law makes it possible for young children to receive help even before they begin school.

Another law, the Americans with Disabilities Act of 1990, guarantees equal employment opportunity for people with learning disabilities and protects disabled workers against job discrimination. Employers may not consider the learning disability when selecting among job applicants. Employers must also make reasonable accommodations to help workers who have handicaps do their job. Such accommodations may include shifting job responsibilities, modifying equipment, or adjusting work schedules.

By law, publicly funded colleges and universities must also remove barriers that keep out disabled students. As a result, many colleges now recruit and work with students with learning disabilities to make it possible for them to attend. Depending on the student's areas of difficulty, this help may include providing recorded books and lectures, providing an isolated area to take tests, or allowing a student to tape record rather than write reports. Students with learning disabilities can arrange to take college entrance exams orally or in isolated rooms free from distraction. Many colleges are creating special programs to specifically accommodate these students.

Programs like these made it possible for Dennis to attend and succeed in college. The Heath Resource Center, sponsored by the American Council on Education, assists students with learning disabilities to identify appropriate colleges and universities.

Public Agency Support

Effective service agencies are also in place to assist people of all ages. Each state department of education can help parents identify the requirements and the process for getting special education services for their child. Other agencies serve disabled infants and preschool children. Still others offer mental health and counseling services. The National Information Center for Children and Youth can provide referrals to appropriate local resources and state agencies.

Counselors at each state department of vocational rehabilitation serve the employment needs of adolescents and adults with learning disabilities. They can refer adults to free or subsidized health care, counseling, and high school equivalence (GED) programs. They can assist in arranging for job training that sidesteps the disability. For example, a vocational counselor helped Wallace identify his aptitude for car repair. To work around Wallace's language problems, the counselor helped locate a job-training program that teaches through demonstrations and active practice rather than lectures.

State departments of vocational rehabilitation can also assist in finding special equipment that can make it possible for disabled individuals to receive training, retain a job, or live on their own. For example, because Dennis couldn't read the electronics manuals in his new job, a vocational rehabilitation counselor helped him locate and purchase a special computer that reads books aloud.

Finally, state-run protection and advocacy agencies and client assistance programs serve to protect these fights. As experts on the laws, they offer legal assistance, as well as information about local health, housing, and social services.

What Hope Does Research Offer?

Sophisticated brain imaging technology is now making it possible to directly observe the brain at work and to detect subtle malfunctions that could never be seen before. Other techniques allow scientists to study the points of contact among brain cells and the ways signals are transmitted from cell to cell.

With this array of technology, NIMH is conducting research to identify which parts of the brain are used during certain activities, such as reading. For example, researchers are comparing the brain processes of people with and without dyslexia as they read. Research of this kind may eventually associate portions of the brain with different reading problems.

Clinical research also continues to amass data on the causes of learning disorders. NIMH grantees at Yale are examining the brain structures of children with different combinations of learning disabilities. Such research will help identify differences in the nervous system of children with these related disorders. Eventually, scientists will know, for example, whether children who have both dyslexia and an attention disorder will benefit from the same treatment as dyslexic children without an attention disorder.

Studies of identical and fraternal twins are also being conducted. Identical twins have the same genetic makeup, while fraternal twins do not. By studying if learning disabilities are more likely to be shared by identical twins than fraternal twins, researchers hope to determine whether these disorders are influenced more by genetic or by environmental factors. One such study is being conducted by scientists funded by the National Institute of Child Health and Human Development. So far, the research indicates that genes may, in fact, influence the ability to sound out words.

Animal studies also are adding to our knowledge of learning disabilities in humans. Animal subjects make it possible to study some of the possible causes of LD in ways that can't be studied in humans. One NIMH grantee is researching the effects of barbiturates and other drugs that are sometimes prescribed during pregnancy. Another researcher discovered through animal studies that certain prenatal viruses could affect future learning. Research of this kind may someday pinpoint prenatal problems that can trigger specific disabilities and tell us how they can be prevented.

Animal research also allows the safety and effectiveness of experimental new drugs to be tested long before they can be tried on humans. One NIH-sponsored team is studying dogs to learn how new stimulant drugs that are similar to Ritalin act on the brain. Another is using mice to test a chemical that may counter memory loss.

This accumulation of data sets the stage for applied research. In the coming years, NIMH-sponsored research will focus on identifying the conditions that are required for learning and the best combination of instructional approaches for each child.

25

Piece by piece, using a myriad of research techniques and technologies, scientists are beginning to solve the puzzle. As research deepens our understanding, we approach a future where we can prevent certain brain and mental disorders, make valid diagnoses, and treat each effectively. This is the hope, mission, and vision of the National Institute of Mental Health.

Chapter 2

Early Warning Signs of Learning Disabilities

Something's not quite right about Johnny. He seems bright enough, but often his performance or behavior falls short of expectations. He can do some things very well, but in other ways is behind his peers. Is he simply lazy? Does he just need to try harder?

When the development or academic performance of a healthy child falls short of what is expected for his or her age and intelligence, parents or teachers may suspect the child has a learning disability (LD). Being aware of the signs of learning disabilities will help parents determine if the child should be referred for evaluation. This chapter summarizes some of the common warning signs of learning disabilities for preschool, elementary, and secondary school children and youth. As the name implies, LD is a condition that affects learning, and sooner or later is manifested by poor school performance, especially in reading, mathematics, spelling, and writing. In addition, LD is a lifelong condition, and can significantly impact relationships, daily activities, and eventually work and careers.

Learning disabilities are presumed to arise from dysfunctions in the brain. Individuals with learning disabilities have significant difficulties in perceiving information (input), in processing and remembering information (integration) and/or in expressing information (output). Outward manifestations of any of these difficulties serve as indicators—or warning signs—of a learning disability.

"The Warning Signs of Learning Disabilities," by Susan Bergert, ERIC (Educational Resources Information Center) Clearinghouse on Disabilities and Gifted Education (ERIC EC), *ERIC EC Digest* E603, December 2000.

27

Warning Signs in Preschool Children

Although children's growth patterns vary among individuals and within individuals, uneven development or significant delays in development can signal the presence of LD. It is important to keep in mind that the behaviors in the following lists must persist over time to be considered warning signs. Any child may occasionally exhibit one or two of these behaviors in the course of normal development.

- Language
    Slow development in speaking words or sentences
    Pronunciation problems
    Difficulty learning new words
    Difficulty following simple directions
    Difficulty understanding questions
    Difficulty expressing wants and desires
    Difficulty rhyming words
    Lack of interest in story telling

- Motor Skills
    Clumsiness
    Poor balance
    Difficulty manipulating small objects
    Awkwardness with running, jumping, or climbing
    Trouble learning to tie shoes, button shirts, or perform other self-help activities
    Avoidance of drawing or tracing

- Cognition
    Trouble memorizing the alphabet or days of the week
    Poor memory for what should be routine (everyday) procedures
    Difficulty with cause and effect, sequencing, and counting
    Difficulty with basic concepts such as size, shape, color

- Attention
    High distractibility
    Impulsive behavior
    Unusual restlessness (hyperactivity)
    Difficulty staying on task
    Difficulty changing activities

Constant repetition of an idea, inability to move on to a new idea (perseveration)

- Social Behavior

  Trouble interacting with others, playing alone

  Prone to sudden and extreme mood changes

  Easily frustrated

  Hard to manage, has temper tantrums

Because early intervention is so important, federal law requires that school districts provide early identification and intervention services. The special education department of the local school district can direct families to the agency that provides these services. Families may also want to consult the child's doctor, who should also be able to refer the family to appropriate resources.

Warning Signs in Elementary School Children

It is during the elementary school years that learning problems frequently become apparent as disabilities interfere with increasingly demanding and complex learning tasks. Difficulties in learning academic subjects and emotional and/or social skills may become a problem. Warning signs for this age group may include any of those previously listed for preschool children in addition to the following.

- Language/Mathematics

  Slow learning of the correspondence of sound to letter

  Consistent errors in reading or spelling

  Difficulty remembering basic sight words

  Inability to retell a story in sequence

  Trouble learning to tell time or count money

  Confusion of math signs (+, -, x, /, =)

  Transposition of number sequences

  Trouble memorizing math facts

  Trouble with place value

  Difficulty remembering the steps of mathematic operations such as long division

- Motor Skills

  Poor coordination, or awkwardness

  Difficulty copying from chalkboard

      Difficulty aligning columns (math)

      Poor handwriting

- Attention/Organization

      Difficulty concentrating or focusing on a task

      Difficulty finishing work on time

      Inability to follow multiple directions

      Unusual sloppiness, carelessness

      Poor concept of direction (left, right)

      Rejection of new concepts, or changes in routine

- Social Behavior

      Difficulty understanding facial expressions or gestures

      Difficulty understanding social situations

      Tendency to misinterpret behavior of peers and/or adults

      Apparent lack of common sense

If teachers have not discussed the possibility of an evaluation already, the parents may request that the child's school conduct a formal evaluation. A request submitted to the school principal must be honored by the school system in a timely manner.

Warning Signs in Secondary School Children

Some learning disabilities go undetected until secondary school. Physical changes occurring during adolescence and the increased demands of middle and senior high school may bring the disabilities to light. Previously satisfactory performance declines. Inappropriate social skills may lead to changes in peer relationships and discipline problems. Increased frustration and poor self-concepts can lead to depression and/or angry outbursts. Warning signs of learning disabilities in secondary school students include the following, which again, should occur as a pattern of behaviors, to a significant degree, and over time.

- Language/Mathematics/Social Studies

      Avoidance of reading and writing

      Tendency to misread information

      Difficulty summarizing

      Poor reading comprehension

      Difficulty understanding subject area textbooks

      Trouble with open-ended questions

      Continued poor spelling

      Poor grasp of abstract concepts

      Poor skills in writing essays

      Difficulty in learning foreign language

      Poor ability to apply math skills

- Attention/Organization

      Difficulty staying organized

      Trouble with test formats such as multiple choice

      Slow work pace in class and in testing situations

      Poor note taking skills

      Poor ability to proofread or double check work

- Social Behavior

      Difficulty accepting criticism

      Difficulty seeking or giving feedback

      Problems negotiating or advocating for oneself

      Difficulty resisting peer pressure

      Difficulty understanding another person's perspectives

Again, parents have the right to request an evaluation by the public schools to determine if the student has learning disabilities.

Summary

Research has shown that the sooner LD is detected and intervention is begun, the better the chance to avoid school failure and to improve chances for success in life. When parents or teachers suspect a child has learning disabilities, they should seek evaluation.

References

Colarusso, R.P.; O'Rourke, C.M. (1999). *Special Education for All Teachers* (2nd ed.). Dubuque, IA: Kendall/Hunt Publishing Company.

Lerner, J.W.; Lowenthal, B.; Egan, R.W. (1998). *Preschool Children with Special Needs: Children at Risk: Children with Disabilities*. Needham Heights, MA: Allyn & Bacon. 800-666-9433.

Mercer, C.D. (1997). *Students with Learning Disabilities* (5th ed.). Upper Saddle River, NJ: Prentice-Hall, Inc. 800-282-0693.

National Center for Learning Disabilities. (2000). *Early Warning Signs.* [online]. Available: http://ld.org/info/early_signs.cfm.

O'Shea, L.J.; O'Shea, D.J.; Algozzine, R. (1998). *Learning Disabilities: from Theory Toward Practice.* Upper Saddle River, NJ: Prentice-Hall, Inc. 800-282-0693.

Schumaker, J.; Deshler, D.; Alley, G.; Warner, M.M. (1983). Toward the development of an intervention model for learning disabled adolescents: The University of Kansas Institute. *Exceptional Education Quarterly,* 4 (1), 45-74.

Silver, L. B. (1998). *The Misunderstood Child: Understanding and Coping with Your Child's Learning Disability* (3rd ed.). New York: Times Books, (a division of Random House). 800-733-3000.

Chapter 3

Drug and Alcohol Use during Pregnancy Linked to Learning Disabilities in Children

Alcohol and tobacco use during pregnancy have both been associated with a number of adverse effects on the growth, cognitive development, and behavior of the exposed child. Understanding the effects of prenatal tobacco exposure allows researchers to identify those characteristics that are uniquely related to tobacco and those that are affected by alcohol exposure. This research, along with studies on the effects of alcohol use during pregnancy, has implications for preventing various types of substance use during pregnancy and for treating children affected by prenatal substance use.

Women who smoke during pregnancy are also likely to drink alcohol. In one survey, conducted as part of the Maternal Health Practices and Child Development (MHPCD) project in Pittsburgh, Pennsylvania, 76 percent of adult women who reported smoking during their first trimester of pregnancy said that they also drank alcohol during that period.

Among pregnant teenagers surveyed, 61 percent of those who smoked during the first trimester also drank alcohol. In addition, tobacco and alcohol use are both prevalent among women who use illicit drugs

Excerpted from "The Effects of Tobacco Use During and After Pregnancy on Exposed Children, Relevance of Findings for Alcohol Research," by Marie D. Cornelius, Ph.D., and Nancy L. Day, Ph.D., from *Alcohol Research & Health,* Volume 24, Number 4, 2000 National Institute on Alcohol Abuse and Alcoholism (NIAAA); and an excerpt from "Drinking Moderately and Pregnancy," by Joseph L. Jacobson, Ph.D., and Sandra W. Jacobson, Ph.D., from *Alcohol Research & Health,* Volume 23, Number 1, 1999, National Institute on Alcohol Abuse and Alcoholism (NIAAA).

during pregnancy. In the National Pregnancy and Health Survey, 74 percent of women who used illicit drugs during pregnancy also reported either smoking, drinking, or both. The use of either one of these drugs is, in itself, a risk factor for poorer pregnancy outcome.

Although alcohol and tobacco are frequently used together during pregnancy, researchers studying the negative effects of prenatal exposure to tobacco and alcohol have generally examined the effects of each drug separately. Therefore, it is difficult to discuss the effects of the combined use of the two drugs.

Effects of Tobacco Use during Pregnancy

Smoking during pregnancy is more prevalent among Caucasian women compared with African-American or Hispanic women. Caucasian women also smoke at higher levels than do women of other ethnicities. Women who smoke during pregnancy are less likely to be married, have less education, have lower incomes, and attend fewer prenatal visits compared with women who do not smoke during pregnancy. Compared with alcohol, marijuana, and other illicit drug use, tobacco use is less likely to decline as the pregnancy progresses. In the National Pregnancy and Health Study, approximately two-thirds of the women who smoked prior to their pregnancy continued smoking into the last trimester.

In contrast, only one-fourth of the women who used alcohol prior to conception continued to drink into the third trimester. Women who smoke during pregnancy also continue smoking after the pregnancy. Therefore, children born to women who use tobacco during pregnancy are likely to continue to be exposed to tobacco after birth. This environmental, or passive, exposure may also affect the children's development.

Effects on Activity, Attention, and Impulsivity

Researchers have also reported associations between prenatal tobacco exposure and increased activity, inattention, and impulsivity. Kristjansson and colleagues found that prenatal tobacco exposure predicted impulsivity and increased overall activity among 4- to 7-year-olds after controlling for prenatal exposure to other drugs and postnatal exposure to second-hand smoke. In addition, Fried and colleagues reported a significant relationship between prenatal tobacco exposure and impulsivity among 6-year-olds in the same cohort.

Milberger and colleagues found a positive relationship between maternal smoking during pregnancy and an increased risk of attention deficit hyperactivity disorder (AD/HD) in exposed children between the ages of 6 and 17, although the study did not control for current maternal smoking or prenatal exposure to other substances. In the MHPCD study of adult mothers, prenatal tobacco exposure significantly predicted increased errors of commission on the Continuous Performance Test among 6-year-olds. However, the mothers' current tobacco use correlated so highly with the prenatal exposure levels that these exposures could not be separated. Eskenazi and Trupin did not find a relationship between prenatal tobacco use and activity.

When the children of the adult mothers in the MHPCD study were assessed at age 10, prenatal tobacco exposure predicted deficits on neuropsychological tests that measured planning ability and fine motor coordination.

Effects on Cognitive Function

Laboratory research with animals has shown that nicotine affects the Central Nervous System (CNS) at exposure levels below those at which growth changes are evident. For example, animal studies have shown associations between fetal nicotine exposure and increased locomotor activity in male rat pups.

In the literature on humans, prenatal tobacco exposure has also been linked to CNS effects, including cognitive and neurobehavioral outcomes, although the reports are inconsistent. At birth, prenatal tobacco exposure has been associated with poorer auditory orientation and autonomic regulation and increased tremors and startles. In a recent race-matched study of cocaine-exposed and non-cocaine-exposed infants, neurological exams showed that prenatal tobacco exposure was significantly related to muscle tone abnormalities when controlling for other variables, including prenatal cocaine and ethanol exposure, head circumference, and prenatal care. The authors concluded that maternal cigarette smoking, rather than cocaine exposure, might be the major predictor of tone abnormalities.

Studies have also reported adverse effects of prenatal tobacco exposure on cognitive and behavioral development in older children. In one study, cognitive functioning at age 3 was higher among the children of mothers who quit smoking during pregnancy than among children whose mothers smoked throughout pregnancy. Poor language development and lower cognitive scores have also been reported in 2-, 3-, and 4-year-old children prenatally exposed to tobacco. When those children were 9 to 12 years old, prenatal tobacco exposure was negatively associated with language and reading abilities.

Other researchers have argued that initially significant associations between prenatal tobacco exposure and cognitive development were explained better by differences in social class and the home environment. For example, after controlling for socioeconomic and environmental differences, Eskenazi and Trupin failed to find consistent relationships between prenatal tobacco exposure and performance on the Raven Colored Matrices Test, a measure of nonverbal reasoning, or the Peabody Picture Vocabulary Test (PPVT). However, in the MHPCD study of adult mothers, prenatal tobacco exposure predicted deficits in visual memory and verbal learning scores on the Wide Range Assessment of Memory and Learning test (WRAML), and these associations remained after consideration of other factors, including socioeconomic status, maternal psychological status, home environment, other prenatal substance exposures, and current maternal tobacco and other substance use.

Behavioral and Psychological Effects

Behavioral and psychological problems have also been linked to prenatal tobacco exposure. Orlebeke and colleagues reported a significant effect of prenatal tobacco exposure on externalizing behaviors, including oppositional, aggressive, and overactive behaviors in 3-year-olds. This study did not control for other prenatal substance exposures or the mothers' current smoking habits. Weitzman and colleagues found that women who smoked both during and after pregnancy rated their children as having more behavior problems, but the researchers found no effects on children who were only exposed during pregnancy.

Brook and colleagues found that mothers who smoked during pregnancy were significantly more likely to have toddlers who displayed negativity than did mothers who only smoked after delivery. This relationship was maintained after controlling for a number of psychosocial risk factors, including the mother's distress, socioeconomic status, and perinatal risk factors. In the adult cohort of the MHPCD project, 3-year-olds who were exposed prenatally to tobacco were significantly more likely to display oppositional behavior, immaturity, and aggressive behavior, according to the mothers' reports. These relationships persisted after controlling for socioeconomic status, current home environment, maternal psychological status, current maternal tobacco use, and other prenatal substance exposures.

The behavior problems observed in toddlers prenatally exposed to tobacco persist through the adolescent and adult years. Fergusson and colleagues followed a birth cohort through age 12 and reported that prenatal tobacco exposure was significantly related to childhood behavior problems, whereas current maternal smoking was not. At ages 16 to 18, children in that cohort who were exposed to prenatal smoking had higher rates of conduct disorder, substance use, and depression than did nonexposed children. Wakschlag and colleagues also reported a significant relationship between prenatal tobacco exposure and conduct disorder in a clinical sample; however, this study did not control for current exposure. In addition, maternal smoking during pregnancy predicted persistent criminal outcomes in adult male offspring in a Danish prospective study.

In another prospective study in Finland, maternal smoking during pregnancy was significantly associated with an increase in violent offenses among the adult male offspring. A few studies have evaluated the relationships between prenatal substance exposure and subsequent substance use in the offspring. Animal researchers have noted that changes resulting from prenatal nicotine exposure might affect susceptibility to later tobacco use. In a retrospective study of humans, Kandel and colleagues reported a fourfold increased risk of tobacco use among female offspring who were exposed to tobacco prenatally.

In a later report, Griesler and colleagues showed that maternal smoking during pregnancy was significantly associated with higher levels of child behavior problems and that these behavior problems increased the likelihood of smoking among daughters between the ages of 9 and 17. The association between prenatal tobacco exposure and early tobacco experimentation was also found in the MHPCD prospective study of adult women and their offspring. In this study, 10-year-old children exposed to tobacco at the level of at least one half pack per day during gestation had a 5.5-fold increased risk for early tobacco experimentation, controlling for prenatal exposure to other substances and their mothers' current smoking habits.

Effects on Infant Growth

Maternal smoking during pregnancy has long been considered an important risk factor for low birth weight (LBW). This association was first reported in 1957 and has been proven in numerous subsequent studies. Birth weight decreases in direct proportion to the number of cigarettes smoked, and children of smokers are 150 to 250 grams lighter than are the children of nonsmokers. The reduction in infant weight is not attributable to earlier gestation, because infants of smokers exhibit growth retardation at all gestational ages.

In a recent study of pregnant teenagers, more than one-half of whom were smokers, prenatal tobacco exposure was significantly related to reduced birth weight, birth length, head circumference, and chest circumference. These reductions were even more pronounced than those found in a similar cohort of the children of adult women. For example, in the study of adult mothers and their children, prenatal tobacco use was significantly associated with a reduction in birth weight of 158 grams per pack per day. In the children of teenage mothers, prenatal tobacco exposure was significantly associated with a reduction in birth weight of 202 grams per pack per day. The increased problems associated with young maternal age and poor fetal outcomes, coupled with the high prevalence of smoking among pregnant teenagers, magnify the risks to children of pregnant teenagers who smoke.

Two key ingredients of cigarette smoke that are known to affect fetal growth are carbon monoxide and nicotine. Carbon monoxide causes fetal hypoxia, a reduction in the amount of oxygen available to the fetus, whereas nicotine can lead to a decrease in the flow of oxygen and other nutrients across the placenta by constricting uterine arteries. In addition, nicotine itself can cross the placenta to affect the fetal cardiovascular and central nervous systems (CNS). Other constituents of tobacco smoke (e.g., cadmium and toluene) have also been shown to cause fetal growth retardation.

Summary and Conclusions

Smoking during pregnancy has been associated significantly with a number of adverse effects on the growth, cognitive development, and behavior of the exposed child. However, because women who smoke during pregnancy are also likely to use alcohol or other drugs, researchers must account for these confounding factors in order to identify accurately the specific and unique role of tobacco exposure. In addition, even nonsmoking mothers can expose their children through environmental tobacco exposure. Compared with alcohol and other drug use, tobacco use is less likely to decline during pregnancy, and women who smoke during pregnancy are more likely to continue to smoke after delivery. This means that children who are prenatally exposed to tobacco are at higher risk for continued exposure to environmental tobacco smoke from the mother and from other household smokers.

Drinking Moderately and Pregnancy—Effects on Child Development

Children exposed to moderate levels of alcohol during pregnancy show growth deficits and intellectual and behavioral problems similar to, although less severe than, those found in children with fetal alcohol syndrome. Research has begun to examine the extent to which these problems affect the child's ability to function on a day-to-day basis at school and with peers. Findings indicate that moderate drinking has much more impact on child development when the mother consumes several drinks in a single day than when she drinks the same quantity in doses of one to two drinks per day over several days.

Moderate drinking during pregnancy is associated with developmental problems in childhood that resemble but are less severe than the growth deficiencies and intellectual and behavioral impairment found among children with fetal alcohol syndrome (FAS). Children with FAS grow more slowly than do other children both before and after birth, exhibit intellectual and social problems, and display a distinctive pattern of abnormal facial features. Intellectual and behavioral impairment are the most disabling characteristics of FAS. About one-half of all FAS patients are mentally retarded (i.e., they have an IQ below 70), and virtually all FAS patients exhibit serious attention and behavioral problems.

Several studies have found that children exposed to alcohol during pregnancy at lower levels than FAS children experience moderate intellectual and behavioral deficits that resemble those of FAS children but on a less severe level. Most of the mothers of children in these studies drank an average of 7 to 14 drinks per week, a range generally considered as moderate drinking. Although the deficits associated with full-blown FAS are devastating, the more subtle developmental problems associated with lower levels of prenatal alcohol exposure are far more prevalent among children than FAS.

Behavioral Function

In addition to the intellectual and attention deficits found among non-FAS alcohol-exposed children, researchers also have documented behavior problems that resemble but are less severe than those found among FAS children. The socialization deficits associated with FAS include poor interpersonal skills and an inability to conform to social conventions. Streissguth has described FAS patients as being unaware of the consequences of [their] behavior, especially the social consequences,

39

showing poor judgment in whom to trust, and unable to take a hint [i.e., needing strong clear commands].

Relatively limited information is available regarding behavioral effects in alcohol-exposed non-FAS children. Using the Achenbach Child Behavior Checklist—Teacher's Report Form (TRF), Brown and colleagues found poorer social competence and more aggressive and destructive behavior in children whose mothers drank throughout their pregnancies than in children whose mothers had stopped drinking in mid-pregnancy or abstained during pregnancy, independent of current maternal drinking patterns. In another study, prenatal alcohol exposure was associated with higher teacher ratings in three of the eight TRF problem areas—social, attention, and aggression—and greater inattention and impulsivity on the DuPaul-Barkley Attention Deficit Hyperactivity Disorder (AD/HD) Scale, after controlling for potential confounding factors such as maternal smoking during pregnancy, quality of parenting, and current caregiver drinking. Analyses showed that the social, aggression, and impulsivity problems were not merely by-products of the children's attention deficits, indicating that alcohol directly affects diverse aspects of central nervous system function. A high proportion of children had problems in the borderline or clinical range. For example, 33 percent of the children prenatally exposed to moderate or heavy levels of alcohol exhibited aggressive behavior problems of this magnitude, compared with only 4 to 5 percent of the general population.

One study found that at age 14, children with higher levels of prenatal alcohol exposure were more likely to have negative feelings about themselves; to be aggressive and delinquent; and to use alcohol, tobacco, and other drugs.

Intellectual Function

Unlike children with FAS, who frequently have reduced IQ scores, non-FAS alcohol-exposed children do not necessarily demonstrate IQ deficits. For example, one study failed to find an overall IQ deficit among non-FAS alcohol-exposed children but found that they exhibited poorer arithmetic, reading, and spelling skills than did non-alcohol-exposed children.

Researchers have documented arithmetic and attention deficits both in FAS children and in at least three groups of children with ARND (alcohol-related neurodevelopmental disorder)—(1) a group of predominantly white, middle-class children in Seattle who were prenatally exposed to moderate amounts of alcohol, (2) a group of economically disadvantaged African-American children in Detroit whose mothers drank moderately during pregnancy, and (3) a group of disadvantaged African-American children in Atlanta who were prenatally exposed to moderate-to-heavy amounts of alcohol.

To measure attention deficits, researchers commonly use tests for the four attention components identified by Mirsky and colleagues. Sustained attention refers to the child's ability to maintain focused concentration and alertness over time. Focused attention is a measure of the length of time the child maintains attention in the presence of distractions.

Executive function involves the child's ability to coordinate, plan, and execute appropriate responses and modify his or her behavior in response to feedback. Working memory is a measure of the child's ability to mentally manipulate the information presented and to link this information with other information retrieved from memory. Although research has documented low levels of sustained attention, focused attention, and executive function in ARND children, these children's most consistent deficits are in working memory.

Effects on Children's Day-to-Day Function

The effects of moderate prenatal alcohol exposure on children's intellectual performance and behavior have been established. When examining the results of psychological tests, however, children with ARND often appear to have relatively subtle impairments (i.e., their average test scores are no more than a few points below normal). Although the average effect may be small, researchers have recently begun to examine whether the effects of moderate drinking are severe enough in certain children to affect their ability to manage on a day-to-day basis at school, home, and with peers.

Growth

Although growth deficits are not a hallmark of ARND, consistent evidence indicates modest growth retardation in alcohol-exposed non-FAS infants before birth, and several studies have reported an association between prenatal alcohol exposure and slower-than-normal growth during the first 6 to 8 months after birth. Moreover, deficits in height and head circumference have been documented in alcohol exposed non-FAS children through age 6. This slower growth pattern contrasts with the traditional finding that infants who weigh less at birth because of maternal smoking during pregnancy grow faster and tend to catch up during their first 5 to 6 months.

Conclusions

Several studies have found that moderate prenatal alcohol exposure has statistically significant effects on children's cognitive and behavioral development. Using the IOM (Institute of Medicine)-proposed terminology, many of these children would be diagnosed as having ARND. ARND differs from FAS, however, in that FAS is characterized by reduced IQ scores and more severe socialization problems.

Nevertheless, evaluations of the specific domains in which deficits occur reveal important parallels between FAS and ARND. In the cognitive domain, arithmetic, attention, and working memory are most severely and consistently affected in both disorders. In the behavioral domain, both disorders are marked by increased impulsivity, aggression, and social problems. Researchers are only beginning to address the importance of these deficits for the day-to-day functioning of the ARND child. The aforementioned data suggest that although some non-FAS alcohol exposed children are only minimally affected by prenatal alcohol exposure, other more susceptible children are impaired to a degree likely to interfere with their ability to function normally.

Detailed information about the functional significance of each of the deficits found among ARND children is needed to fully understand the implications of prenatal alcohol exposure for child development. More attention also should be devoted to determining the specific drinking levels and patterns associated with functionally significant developmental impairment. Research has documented functionally significant deficits in infants whose mothers drank, on average, five or more drinks per occasion once or twice per week.

Although considered excessive for a pregnant woman, this level of drinking falls short of the rate usually associated with having a serious drinking problem. Given the marked individual differences in alcohol metabolism and fetal vulnerability, five drinks per occasion may be too high a threshold for many women. Functional deficits may occur in some children who are repeatedly exposed prenatally to only three or four drinks per occasion, especially if the alcohol is consumed on an empty stomach. In evaluating the risk associated with exposure to environmental and food contaminants, a safety margin is usually incorporated to allow for individual differences in sensitivity.

Chapter 4

Gifted Children with Learning Disabilities

Gifted students with learning disabilities and other disabling conditions remain a major group of underserved and understimulated youth (Cline, 1999). The focus on accommodations for their disabilities may preclude the recognition and development of their cognitive abilities. It is not unexpected, then, to find a significant discrepancy between the measured academic potential of these students and their actual performance in the classroom (Whitmore & Maker, 1985). In order for these children to reach their potential, it is imperative that their intellectual strengths be recognized and nurtured, at the same time as their disability is accommodated appropriately.

Assessment

Identification of giftedness in students who are disabled is problematic. The customary identification methods (standardized tests and observational checklists) are inadequate, without major modification. Standard lists of characteristics of gifted students may be inadequate for unmasking hidden potential in children who have disabilities. Children whose hearing is impaired, for example, cannot respond to oral directions, and they may also lack the vocabulary which reflects the complexity of their thoughts. Children whose speech or language is impaired cannot respond to tests requiring verbal responses. Children

"Dual Exceptionalities," by Colleen Willard-Holt, ERIC (Educational Resources Information Center) Clearinghouse on Disabilities and Gifted Education, ERIC Identifier: ED430344, 1999.

whose vision is impaired may be unable to respond to certain performance measures, and although their vocabulary may be quite advanced, they may not understand the full meaning of the words they use. Children with learning disabilities may use high-level vocabulary in speaking but may be unable to express themselves in writing, or vice versa. In addition, limited life experiences due to impaired mobility may artificially lower scores (Whitmore & Maker, 1985). Since the population of gifted/disabled students is difficult to locate, they seldom are included in standardized test norming groups, adding to the problems of comparison. In addition, gifted children with disabilities often use their intelligence to try to circumvent the disability. This may cause both exceptionalities to appear less extreme: the disability may appear less severe because the child is using the intellect to cope, while the efforts expended in that area may hinder other expressions of giftedness.

The following lists are intended to assist parents and teachers in recognizing intellectual giftedness in the presence of a disability.

Characteristics of Gifted Students with Specific Disabilities

- Gifted Students with Learning Disabilities

    high abstract reasoning ability

    good mathematical reasoning ability

    keen visual memory, spatial skills

    advanced vocabulary

    sophisticated sense of humor

    imaginative and creative

    insightful

    exceptional ability in geometry, science, arts, music

    good problem-finding and problem-solving skills

    difficulty with memorization, computation, phonics, and/or spelling

    distractibility and/or disorganization

    supersensitivity

    perfectionism

    grasp of metaphors, analogies, satire

comprehension of complex systems

unreasonable self expectations

often, failure to complete assignments

difficulties with sequential tasks

wide variety of interests

(*Baum, Owen, & Dixon, 1991; Silverman, 1989*)

- Gifted Students with Visual Impairment

    fast rate of learning

    superior memory

    superior verbal communication skills and vocabulary

    advanced problem-solving skills

    creative production or thought that may progress more slowly than sighted students in some academic areas

    ease in learning Braille

    great persistence

    motivation to know

    sometimes slower rate of cognitive development than sighted students

    excellent ability to concentrate

    (*Whitmore & Maker, 1985*)

- Gifted Students with Physical Disabilities

    development of compensatory skills

    creativity in finding alternate ways of communicating and accomplishing tasks

    impressive store of knowledge

    advanced academic skills

    superior memory

    exceptional problem-solving skills

    rapid grasp of ideas

    ability to set and strive for long-term goals

    greater maturity than age mates

    good sense of humor

persistence, patience

motivation to achieve

curiosity, insight

self criticism and perfectionism

cognitive development that may not be based on direct experience

possible difficulty with abstractions

possible limited achievement due to pace of work

(Cline, 1999; Whitmore & Maker, 1985; Willard-Holt, 1994)

- Gifted Students with Hearing Impairments

    development of speech/reading skills without instruction

    early reading ability

    excellent memory

    ability to function in the regular school setting

    rapid grasp of ideas

    high reasoning ability

    superior performance in school

    wide range of interests

    nontraditional ways of getting information

    use of problem-solving skills in everyday situations

    possibly on grade level

    delays in concept attainment

    self starters

    good sense of humor

    enjoyment of manipulating environment

    intuition

    ingenuity in solving problems

    symbolic language abilities (different symbol system)

    (Cline, 1999; Whitmore & Maker, 1985)

Research indicates that in many cases, a child is diagnosed with ADHD when in fact the child is gifted and reacting to an inappropriate curriculum (Webb & Latimer, 1993). The key to distinguishing between the two is the pervasiveness of the acting out behaviors. If the acting out is specific to certain situations, the child's behavior is more likely related to giftedness; whereas, if the behavior is consistent across all situations, the child's behavior is more likely related to ADHD. It is also possible for a child to be both gifted and ADHD. The following list highlights the similarities between giftedness and ADHD.

- Characteristics of Gifted Students Who Are Bored

   Poor attention and daydreaming when bored

   Low tolerance for persistence on tasks that seem irrelevant

   Begin many projects, see few to completion

   Development of judgment lags behind intellectual growth

   Intensity may lead to power struggles with authorities

   High activity level; may need less sleep

   Difficulty restraining desire to talk; may be disruptive

   Question rules, customs, and traditions

   Lose work, forget homework, are disorganized

   May appear careless

   Highly sensitive to criticism

   Do not exhibit problem behaviors in all situations

   More consistent levels of performance at a fairly consistent pace

   (Cline, 1999; Webb & Latimer, 1993)

- Characteristics of Students with ADHD

   Poorly sustained attention

   Diminished persistence on tasks not having immediate consequences

   Often shift from one uncompleted activity to another

   Impulsivity, poor delay of gratification

   Impaired adherence to commands to regulate or inhibit behavior in social contexts

   More active, restless than other children

   Often talk excessively

Often interrupt or intrude on others (e.g., butt into games)

Difficulty adhering to rules and regulations

Often lose things necessary for tasks or activities at home or school

May appear inattentive to details

Highly sensitive to criticism

Problem behaviors exist in all settings, but in some are more severe

Variability in task performance and time used to accomplish tasks

(Barkley, 1990; Cline, 1999; Webb & Latimer, 1993)

Questions to Ask in Differentiating between Giftedness and ADHD

- Could the behaviors be responses to inappropriate placement, insufficient challenge, or lack of intellectual peers?

- Is the child able to concentrate when interested in the activity?

- Have any curricular modifications been made in an attempt to change inappropriate behaviors?

- Has the child been interviewed? What are his/her feelings about the behaviors?

- Does the child feel out of control? Do the parents perceive the child as being out of control?

- Do the behaviors occur at certain times of the day, during certain activities, with certain teachers or in certain environments?

Implications for Students with Dual Exceptionalities

Commitment to identifying and nurturing the gifts of students with disabilities implies specific changes in the way educators approach identification, instruction, and classroom dynamics.

Identification: Include students with disabilities in initial screening phase. Be willing to accept nonconventional indicators of intellectual talent. Look beyond test scores. When applying cutoffs, bear in mind the depression of scores that may occur due to the disability. Do not aggregate subtest scores into a composite score. Compare with others who have similar disabilities. Weigh more heavily character-istics that enable the child to effectively compensate for the disability. Weigh more heavily areas of performance unaffected by the disabil-ity. Allow the child to participate in gifted programs on a trial basis.

Instruction: Be aware of the powerful role of language; reduce communication limitations and develop alternative modes for thinking and communicating. Emphasize high-level abstract thinking, creativ-ity, and a problem-solving approach. Have great expectations—these children often become successful as adults in fields requiring advanced education. Provide for individual pacing in areas of giftedness and disability. Provide challenging activities at an advanced level. Promote active inquiry, experimentation, and discussion. Promote self-direction. Offer options that enable students to use strengths and preferred ways of learning. Use intellectual strengths to develop coping strategies. Assist in strengthening the student's self concept.

Classroom Dynamics: Discuss disabilities/capabilities and their implications with the class. Expect participation in all activities—strive for normal peer interactions. Facilitate acceptance—model and demand respect for all. Candidly answer peers' questions. Treat a child with a disability the same way a child without a disability is treated. Model celebration of individual differences.

Gifted students with disabilities must be provided with appropri-ate challenges. The personal and societal costs of not developing their potential cannot be overstated.

References

Barkley, R. A. (1990). *Attention Deficit Hyperactivity Disorder: A Hand-book for Diagnosis and Treatment.* New York: Guilford Press.

Baum, S. M., Owen, S. V., & Dixon, J. (1991). To Be Gifted & Learning Disabled. Mansfield Center, CT: Creative Learning Press.

Cline, S. & Schwartz, D. (1999). Diverse Populations of Gifted Chil-dren. NJ: Merrill.

Silverman, L. K. (1989). Invisible Gifts, Invisible Handicaps. *Roeper Review*, 12(1), 37-42.

Thurlow, M. L., Elliott, J. L. & Ysseldyke, J. E. (1998). Testing Stu-dents with Disabilities. Thousand Oaks, CA: Corwin Press.

Webb, J. T. & Latimer, D. (1993). ADHD and Children Who Are Gifted. *ERIC Digest* #522.

Whitmore, J. R. & Maker, C. J. (1985). Intellectual Giftedness in Disabled Persons. Rockville, MD: Aspen.

Willard-Holt, C. (1994). Recognizing Talent: Cross-Case Study of Two High Potential Students with Cerebral Palsy. Storrs, CT: National Research Center on the Gifted/Talented.

Chapter 5

Women with Learning Disabilities

Imagine having important needs and ideas to communicate but being unable to express them. Imagine feeling bombarded by sights and sounds, but being unable to focus or sit still. Imagine trying to read or add, but struggling to make sense of the letters or numbers.

These difficulties make up the common daily experiences of millions of women with learning disabilities. Mothers of children with learning disabilities, and women who are special educators, counselors, and health care professionals also are closely involved with the challenges of learning disabilities. Speech or language impairments alone cause disability in an estimated 6 to 8 million Americans. Despite the challenges imposed by these impairments, almost everyone with these disabilities can live a happy, productive life.

The exact criteria and characteristics for diagnosing learning disabilities vary according to the source, whether the legal system, the federal government, advocacy groups, or individual states. According to the American Psychiatric Association's *Diagnostic and Statistical Manual of Mental Disorders*, however, learning disabilities can be divided into three broad categories:

- developmental speech and language disorders

"Women with DisAbilities: Learning Disabilities," and "Women with DisAbilities: Speech-Language Impairments," undated documents produced by the National Women's Health Information Center (NWHIC), available online at http://www.4woman.gov/wwd/wwd.cfm?page=59, and http://www.4woman.gov/wwd/wwd.cfm?page=81, cited August 2002.

- academic skills disorders (reading, writing and arithmetic disorders) and
- other, which includes coordination, spelling, and memory disorders

The cause of learning disabilities is still unknown. However, possible contributors may be:

- heredity
- complications in pregnancy or at birth
- chemical imbalance
- toxins
- a lag in nervous system development

Adults, for example, can acquire disorders of language due to stroke, head injury, dementia, or brain tumors. Language disorders are also found in adults who failed to develop normal language because of childhood autism, hearing impairments, or other congenital or acquired disorders of brain development. Speech disorders may accompany mental retardation, emotional or psychiatric disorders, and a number of other developmental disorders.

Speech-Language Impairments

Language is the expression of human communication through which knowledge, belief, and behavior can be experienced, explained, and shared. Speech is the vocalization of language, and is an important vehicle for communicating thoughts. Some form of speech-language impairment affects an estimated 6-8 million Americans.

Speech disorders refer to difficulties producing speech sounds or problems with voice quality. There may be problems with the way sounds are formed, or there may be problems with the pitch, volume or quality of the voice. There also may be a combination of several problems. People with voice disorders may have trouble with the way their voices sound. A language disorder is an impairment in the ability to understand and/or use words in context, both verbally and nonverbally. This may include improper use of words and their meanings, inability to express ideas, inappropriate grammatical patterns, reduced vocabulary and inability to follow directions. Some common speech-language impairments include stuttering, aphasia, and vocal cord paralysis.

Men and women are affected in similar ways by speech and language impairments. While the cause of many speech-language impairments is not known, numerous experts believe that they are caused by conditions that affect brain development either before, during, or after birth, such as muscular disorders, hearing problems or developmental delays. Many adults later acquire these disorders from stroke, head injury, dementia, or brain tumors. Language disorders also are found in adults who have had childhood autism, hearing impairments, or other congenital or acquired disorders of brain development. These disorders also can accompany mental retardation, psychiatric disorders, and developmental disorders.

Women living with speech-language impairments can be greatly helped by speech therapy and technology like electronic communication systems, which allow nonspeaking persons with severe physical disabilities to engage in the give and take of shared thought.

To contact the National Women's Health Information Center (NWHIC) call 1-800-994-WOMAN. NWHIC is a service of the Office on Women's Health in the Department of Health and Human Services.

Chapter 6

Adults with Learning Disabilities

In the 1990s, more attention has been focused on adults with learning disabilities (LD) as a result of increased advocacy and research, several major federal laws, and heightened awareness of the changing demands of the workplace. Until now, most programs, research, and funding had been directed toward children, although it is clear that most people do not outgrow learning disabilities (Gerber and Reiff, 1994). This chapter looks at current definitions of learning disabilities, the experiences of adults with LD, factors influencing their successful adjustment to adult life, and strategies for adult educators and counselors.

Definitions of Learning Disability

The field has not quite reached consensus on definitions of LD, and there are professionals as well as members of the public who do not understand them or believe they exist. For example, in a Roper (1995) survey of 1,200 adults, 85% associated LD with mental retardation, 66% with deafness, and 60% with blindness. In Rocco's (1997) research, faculty "questioned the existence of certain conditions or if they existed, the appropriateness of classifying the condition as a disability" (p. 158). However, most definitions describe learning disabilities as a group of disorders that affect the ability to acquire and use listening,

"Adults with Learning Disabilities," by Sandra Kerka, from Education Resources Information Center (ERIC) Clearinghouse on Adult Career and Vocational Education, *ERIC Digest* Number 189, ERIC Identifier: ED414434, 1998.

speaking, reading, writing, reasoning, or math skills (Gerber and Reiff, 1994; National Adult Literacy and Learning Disabilities Center, 1995a; National Center for Learning Disabilities, 1997). These difficulties vary in severity, may persist across the lifespan, and may affect one or more areas of a person's life, including learning, work, and social and emotional functioning.

Federal regulations for implementing the Rehabilitation Act and the Americans with Disabilities Act use the term "specific learning disabilities"—disorders in one or more central nervous system processes involved in perceiving, understanding, and using verbal or nonverbal information (Gerber and Reiff, 1994). Specific indicates that the disability affects only certain learning processes. Although adults with LD consistently describe themselves as being labeled stupid or slow learners (Brown, Druck, and Corcoran in Gerber and Reiff, 1994), they usually have average or above average intelligence.

People with learning disabilities are the largest segment of the disability population, and growing numbers of college students identify themselves as having LD (Gerber and Reiff, 1994). Estimates of the numbers of people affected by LD range from 5-20% of the population (Gadbow and DuBois, 1998; Gerber and Reiff, 1994), meaning that as many as 5 million, 11 million, or 30 million adults have LD. One reason for the variance is misidentification. African-Americans and Hispanics are often inappropriately diagnosed with LD, such as speakers of African-American English whose language may be considered substandard or deficient by assessors (Gregg et al., 1996). There is also the "unresolved question yet persistent belief that one half" of all adults with low literacy skills in fact have learning disabilities (Gerber and Reiff, 1994, p. 121).

Successful Adjustment for Adults with LD

Adults with LD may face challenges in several areas of life, including education, employment, daily routines, and social interactions. However, many are able to make successful life adjustments. Research has recently been directed toward learning what factors help these adults succeed. Most of these studies used such measures of success as educational attainment, income, job level, and job and life satisfaction. Success was influenced by educational experiences and personal characteristics/background. Educational factors included the following: high school completion; quality of elementary-secondary education; quality of postsecondary education, training, and services; and a shift from a remedial to a compensatory approach in special education (Gerber and Reiff, 1994). Successful college students with LD (Telander, 1994) had previous college experience (i.e., they had tried college more than once), took a lighter course load, had more high school English courses, and sought help with study skills.

Personal and background factors were also important for successful adjustment. Most successful adults had relatively moderate LD and higher than average IQ, came from above average socioeconomic backgrounds, and had social and psychological support systems (Gerber and Reiff, 1994; Greenbaum et al., 1996). They were knowledgeable about their disability and creative in compensatory strategies, took control of their lives, were goal oriented and persistent, and chose environments that suited their abilities and disabilities (Reiff et al., 1995; Telander, 1994).

In Gerber, Reiff, and Ginsberg's research (Gerber and Reiff, 1994; Gerber et al., 1996; Reiff et al., 1995), the most important factor was reframing. Reframing means reinterpreting a situation in a productive, positive way. For adults with LD, the stages of reframing are recognizing the disability, accepting it, understanding it and its implications, and taking action. Highly successful adults used reframing, moderately successful ones did not progress through all four stages to the same extent as the highly successful, and the marginally adjusted group did it unsuccessfully or not at all (Gerber et al., 1996). The researchers concluded that success entailed a continuous process of confronting one's strengths and weaknesses and making adjustments.

Strategies and Supports for Adults with Learning Disabilities

Adults with LD need a range of skills and abilities to manage their disabilities in education, training, and employment situations. Appropriate assessment is the starting point for all other strategies and techniques. Teachers who suspect learners may have a disability can be trained in screening methods that will help them recognize when more formal diagnosis is necessary (NALLD, 1995b). Teachers may observe that (1) adult learners have average/above average ability but demonstrate unexpected underachievement; (2) what appear to be problems with vision or hearing are not the result of physical impairments; or (3) behavioral or psychological manifestations (attention, concentration, organization) interfere with learning. Error patterns in reading, writing, speaking, and math may help differentiate between possible LD and other causes of low achievement. If screening results suggest LD, educators should refer adults to professionals trained in formal assessment. Assessments should be appropriate for adults as well as culturally sensitive. The most significant problem for minority persons with LD is cultural bias in assessment, according to Gregg et al. (1996).

Once a learning disability is identified, three categories of assistance are psychosocial, technological and educational. In the psychosocial area, an individual's self-esteem can suffer from years of internalizing labels of stupidity and incompetence and experiencing dependence, fear, anxiety, or helplessness. Four ways to strengthen self-esteem (NALLD, 1994) are awareness (knowing about and documenting the disability), assessment (understanding the disability and one's strengths and weaknesses), accommodation (knowing what compensatory strategies and techniques help), and advocacy (knowing their legal rights and services for which they qualify).

Schools and workplaces offer some accommodations to help with academic and vocational adjustment. However, less attention is paid to social and emotional functioning (Telander, 1994). Social competence—dealing with pressure, change, or criticism; holding conversations; using receptive and expressive language and appropriate humor; being able to make inferences; and being sensitive to others' feelings and moods—is sometimes impaired by cognitive processing difficulties. These social skills impairments may be reinforced by isolation and negative experiences. Adults with LD may also experience frustration, anger, and other emotions arising from academic and social failures, rejection, and the attitudes of others. Laws and accommodations "will only partially redress discrimination of persons with learning disabilities if social/emotional function" is not addressed (Gerber and Reiff, 1994, p. 80).

Assistive technology, "any technology that enables an adult with learning disabilities to compensate for specific deficits" (Gerber and Reiff, 1994, p. 152), has great potential. Many software developments that were not specifically designed for persons with disabilities are proving to be of great assistance in increasing, maintaining, or improving functioning. Assistive technology ranges from low to high tech, the choice depending on the individual, the function to be performed, and the context (Riviere, 1996). Examples include the following (Gerber and Reiff, 1994; Riviere, 1996): (1) for organization, memory, time management problems—highlighters, beepers, digital watches, tape recorders, personal management software; (2) for auditory processing—FM amplification devices, electronic notebooks, computer-aided real-time translation, voice synthesizers, videotapes with closed captioning, variable speech control tape recorders; (3) for visual processing—software display controls, books on disk; (4) for reading—scanners with speech synthesizers that read back text, books on tape and disk, CD-ROMs; and (5) for writing—word processing tools such as spelling and grammar checkers, abbreviation expanders, brainstorming/outlining software. Distance learning networks and the World Wide Web are beginning to be explored for their potential in compensating for disabilities.

As for educational strategies, adult educators should foster an inclusive learning environment that includes sensitivity, attitudes, awareness, accommodations. Other techniques are described by Gadbow and DuBois (1998): providing notetakers, using activities that represent a variety of learning styles, permitting technological devices, providing alternative testing arrangements, extending time allowed for assignments, minimizing distractions, asking learners what accommodations they need. Rocco (1997) suggests that discussion of disability issues be encouraged in adult education, that disability be included in examining the characteristics that bestow or deny power, and that educators reflect critically on innovative ways to assist learners who learn differently, whether or not they are classified as having a learning disability.

References

Gadbow, N. F., and DuBois, D. A. *Adult Learners with Special Needs*. Malabar, FL: Krieger Publishing, 1998.

Gerber, P. J., and Reiff, H., eds. *Learning Disabilities in Adulthood: Persisting Problems and Evolving Issues*. Stoneham, MA: Butterworth-Heinemann, 1994.

Gerber, P. J.; Reiff, H. B.; and Ginsberg, R. "Reframing the Learning Disabilities Experience." *Journal of Learning Disabilities 29*, Number 1 (January 1996): 98-101. (EJ 517 933)

Greenbaum, B.; Graham, S.; and Scales, W. "Adults with Learning Disabilities: Occupational and Social Status after College." *Journal of Learning Disabilities 29*, Number 2 (March 1996): 167-173. (EJ 519 897)

Gregg, N.; Curtis, R. S.; and Schmidt, S. F., eds. *African American Adolescents and Adults with Learning Disabilities: An Overview of Assessment Issues*. Athens: Learning Disabilities Research and Training Center, University of Georgia, 1996. http://www.coe.uga.edu/ldcenter/resources/afro.html

National Adult Literacy and Learning Disabilities Center. *Self-Esteem: Issues for the Adult Learner*. Washington, DC: NALLD, 1994. (ED 374 343)

National Adult Literacy and Learning Disabilities Center. *Adults with Learning Disabilities: Definitions and Issues*. Washington, DC: NALLD, 1995a. (ED 387 989)

National Adult Literacy and Learning Disabilities Center. *Screening for Adults with Learning Disabilities*. Washington, DC: NALLD, 1995b. (ED 387 988)

Reiff, H. B.; Ginsberg, R.; and Gerber, P. J. "New Perspectives on Teaching from Successful Adults with Learning Disabilities." *Remedial and Special Education 16*, Number 1 (January 1995): 29-37. (EJ 497 555)

Riviere, A. *Assistive Technology: Meeting the Needs of Adults with Learning Disabilities*. Washington, DC: NALLD, 1996. (ED 401 686)

Rocco, T. S. "Hesitating to Disclose." In *Proceedings of the 16th Annual Midwest Research-to-Practice Conference in Adult, Continuing, and Community Education*, edited by S. J. Levine, pp. 157-163. East Lansing: Michigan State University, October 1997.

Roper Starch Worldwide, Inc. *Learning Disabilities and the American Public*. Roper Starch Worldwide, Inc., 1995. (ED 389 101)

Telander, J. E. "The Adjustment of Learning Disabled Adults." Ph.D. dissertation, Biola University, 1994. (ED 372 586)

Part Two

Language, Speech, and Processing Disabilities

Chapter 7

Speech and Language Developmental Milestones

What Are Speech and Language?

Speech and language are tools that humans use to communicate or share thoughts, ideas, and emotions. Language is the set of rules, shared by the individuals who are communicating, that allows them to exchange those thoughts, ideas, or emotions. Speech is talking, one way that a language can be expressed. Language may also be expressed through writing, signing, or even gestures in the case of people who have neurological disorders and may depend upon eye blinks or mouth movements to communicate.

While there are many languages in the world, each includes its own set of rules for phonology (phonemes or speech sounds or, in the case of signed language, handshapes), morphology (word formation), syntax (sentence formation), semantics (word and sentence meaning), prosody (intonation and rhythm of speech), and pragmatics (effective use of language).

How Do Speech and Language Normally Develop?

The most intensive period of speech and language development for humans is during the first three years of life, a period when the brain is developing and maturing. These skills appear to develop best in a

National Institute on Deafness and Other Communication Disorders (NIDCD), NIH Publication Number 00-4781, updated April 2001.

world that is rich with sounds, sights, and consistent exposure to the speech and language of others.

There is increasing evidence suggesting that there are critical periods for speech and language development in infants and young children. This means that the developing brain is best able to absorb a language, any language, during this period. The ability to learn a language will be more difficult, and perhaps less efficient or effective, if these critical periods are allowed to pass without early exposure to a language. The beginning signs of communication occur during the first few days of life when an infant learns that a cry will bring food, comfort, and companionship. The newborn also begins to recognize important sounds in his or her environment. The sound of a parent or voice can be one important sound. As they grow, infants begin to sort out the speech sounds (phonemes) or building blocks that compose the words of their language. Research has shown that by six months of age, most children recognize the basic sounds of their native language.

As the speech mechanism (jaw, lips, and tongue) and voice mature, an infant is able to make controlled sound. This begins in the first few months of life with cooing, a quiet, pleasant, repetitive vocalization. By six months of age, an infant usually babbles or produces repetitive syllables such as "ba, ba, ba" or "da, da, da." Babbling soon turns into a type of nonsense speech (jargon) that often has the tone and cadence of human speech but does not contain real words. By the end of their first year, most children have mastered the ability to say a few simple words. Children are most likely unaware of the meaning of their first words, but soon learn the power of those words as others respond to them.

By eighteen months of age, most children can say eight to ten words. By age two, most are putting words together in crude sentences such as "more milk." During this period, children rapidly learn that words symbolize or represent objects, actions, and thoughts. At this age they also engage in representational or pretend play. At ages three, four, and five, a child's vocabulary rapidly increases, and he or she begins to master the rules of language.

What Are Speech and Language Developmental Milestones?

Children vary in their development of speech and language. There is, however, a natural progression or timetable for mastery of these skills for each language. The milestones are identifiable skills that can serve as a guide to normal development. Typically, simple skills need to be reached before the more complex skills can be learned. There is a general age and time when most children pass through these periods. These milestones help doctors and other health professionals determine when a child may need extra help to learn to speak or to use language.

How Do I Know If My Child Is Reaching the Milestones?

Table 7.1 is a checklist that you can follow to determine if your child's speech and language skills are developing on schedule. You should talk to your child's doctor about anything that is answered as "no."

Table 7.1. Speech and Language Developmental Milestones (*continued on p. 66–67*)

Birth to 5 months

Reacts to loud sounds.

Turns head toward a sound source.

Watches your face when you speak.

Vocalizes pleasure and displeasure sounds (laughs, giggles, cries, or fusses).

Makes noise when talked to.

6 - 11 months

Understands "no-no."

Babbles (says "ba-ba-ba" or "ma-ma-ma").

Tries to communicate by actions or gestures.

Tries to repeat your sounds.

12 - 17 months

Attends to a book or toy for about two minutes.

Follows simple directions accompanied by gestures.

Answers simple questions nonverbally.

Points to objects, pictures, and family members.

Says two to three words to label a person or object (pronunciation may not be clear).

Tries to imitate simple words.

Table 7.1. Speech and Language Developmental Milestones *(continued from page 65)*

18 - 23 months

Enjoys being read to.

Follows simple commands without gestures.

Points to simple body parts such as "nose."

Understands simple verbs such as "eat," "sleep."

Correctly pronounces most vowels and n, m, p, h, especially in the beginning of syllables and short words. Also begins to use other speech sounds.

Says 8 to 10 words (pronunciation may still be unclear).

Asks for common foods by name.

Makes animal sounds such as "moo."

Starting to combine words such as "more milk."

Begins to use pronouns such as "mine."

2 - 3 years

Knows about 50 words at 24 months.

Knows some spatial concepts such as "in," "on."

Knows pronouns such as "you," "me," "her."

Knows descriptive words such as "big," "happy."

Says around 40 words at 24 months.

Speech is becoming more accurate but may still leave off ending sounds. Strangers may not be able to understand much of what is said.

Answers simple questions.

Begins to use more pronouns such as "you," "I."

Speaks in two to three word phrases.

Uses question inflection to ask for something (e.g., "My ball?").

Begins to use plurals such as "shoes" or "socks" and regular past tense verbs such as "jumped."

3 - 4 years

Groups objects such as foods, clothes, etc.

Identifies colors.

Uses most speech sounds but may distort some of the more difficult sounds such as l, r, s, sh, ch, y, v, z, th. These sounds may not be fully mastered until age 7 or 8.

Uses consonants in the beginning, middle, and ends of words. Some of the more difficult consonants may be distorted, but attempts to say them.

Table 7.1. Speech and Language Developmental Milestones *(continued)*

3 - 4 years (continued)

Strangers are able to understand much of what is said.

Able to describe the use of objects such as "fork," "car," etc.

Has fun with language. Enjoys poems and recognizes language absurdities such as, "Is that an elephant on your head?"

Expresses ideas and feelings rather than just talking about the world around him or her.

Uses verbs that end in "ing," such as "walking," "talking."

Answers simple questions such as "What do you do when you are hungry?"

Repeats sentences.

4 - 5 years

Understands spatial concepts such as "behind," "next to."

Understands complex questions.

Speech is understandable but makes mistakes pronouncing long, difficult, or complex words such as "hippopotamus."

Says about 200 - 300 different words.

Uses some irregular past tense verbs such as "ran," "fell."

Describes how to do things such as painting a picture.

Defines words.

Lists items that belong in a category such as animals, vehicles, etc.

Answers "why" questions.

5 years

Understands more than 2,000 words.

Understands time sequences (what happened first, second, third, etc.).

Carries out a series of three directions.

Understands rhyming.

Engages in conversation.

Sentences can be 8 or more words in length.

Uses compound and complex sentences.

Describes objects.

Uses imagination to create stories.

What Should I Do If My Child's Speech or Language Appears to Be Delayed?

You should talk to your family doctor if you have any concerns about your child's speech or language development. Table 7.1 should help you talk about your concerns. Your doctor may decide to refer you to a speech-language pathologist, a health professional trained to evaluate and treat people who have speech, language, voice or swallowing disorders (including hearing impairment) that affect their ability to communicate. The speech-language pathologist will talk to you about your child's communication and general development. He or she will also evaluate your child with special speech and language tests. A hearing test is often included in the evaluation because a hearing problem can affect speech and language development.

Depending upon the test results, the speech-language pathologist may suggest activities for home to stimulate speech and language development. These activities may include reading to your child regularly; speaking in short sentences using simple words so that your child can successfully imitate you; or repeating what your child says, using correct grammar or pronunciation. For example, if your child says, "Ball baybo" you can respond with, "Yes, the ball is under the table." This allows you to demonstrate more accurate speech and language without actually "correcting" your child which can eventually make speaking unpleasant for him or her.

The speech-language pathologist may also recommend group or individual therapy or suggest further evaluation by other health professionals such as an audiologist, a health care professional who is trained to identify and measure hearing loss, or a developmental psychologist.

What Research Is Being Conducted on Developmental Speech and Language Problems?

Scientists are examining a variety of issues related to speech and language development. Brain imaging studies are defining the relationship between exposure to speech and language, brain development, and communication skills. Genetic studies are investigating the likelihood that at least some speech and language problems may be inherited or passed down from parents to their children. Additional studies are characterizing inherited communication disorders. The effect of frequent ear infections on the development of speech and language is also an area of investigation.

Other scientists are distinguishing types of speech and language errors to determine which ones may be overcome by maturation alone and which will need some type of intervention or therapy. Another area of study is the effect of speech and language development on later school performance. Further research is characterizing dialects that belong to certain ethnic or regional groups. This knowledge will help professionals distinguish a language difference or dialect (which should be preserved to help an individual identify with a group) from a language disorder, which may require treatment.

Where Can I Get Additional Information?

The American Academy of Pediatrics

141 Northwest Point Boulevard
Elk Grove Village, IL 60007-1098
Tel: 847-4344-4000
Fax: 847-434-8000
Internet: http://www.aap.org
E-Mail: Kidsdoca@aap.org

American Speech-Language-Hearing Association

10801 Rockville Pike
Rockville, MD 20852
Toll Free: 800-638-8255
Tel/TTY: 301-987-5700
Fax: 301-571-0457
Internet: http://www.asha.org
E-Mail: actioncenter@ash.org

Boys Town National Research Hospital

555 N. 30th Street
Omaha, NE 68131
Tel: 402-498-6511
Toll Free: 800-448-3000
Tel/TTY: 402-498-6749
Fax: 402-498-6755
Internet: http://www.boystown.org
E-Mail: bthospital@boystown.org

Easter Seals

230 West Monroe Street
Suite 1800
Chicago, IL 60606

Easter Seals (continued)
Toll Free: 800-221-6827
Tel: 312-726-6200
TTY: 312-726-4258
Fax: 312-726-1494
Internet: http://www.easter-seals.org
E-Mail: info@easter-seals.org

National Black Association for Speech-Language and Hearing (NBASLH)
P.O. Box 50605
Washington, DC 20091-0605
Tel: 202-274-6162
Fax: 202-274-6350
Internet: http://www.nbaslh.org
E-Mail: NBASLH@aol.com

Chapter 8

Language-Based Learning Disabilities

Language-based learning disabilities interfere with age-appropriate reading, spelling, and/or writing. This disorder does not impair intelligence; in fact, most people diagnosed with learning disabilities possess average to superior intelligence. Learning disabilities are caused by a difference in brain structure that is present at birth, is often hereditary, and often related to specific language problems.

The term dyslexia has been used to refer to the specific learning problem of reading. Because of the increased recognition of the relationship between spoken and written language, and the frequent presence of spoken language problems in children with reading problems, the term language-based learning disabilities, or just learning disabilities, is more accurate.

Who Is at Risk

Children at risk for dyslexia and other learning disabilities may have several of the following characteristics:

- A family history of delayed speech-language development or literacy problems

- Difficulty processing sounds in words

Reprinted with permission from "Language-Based Learning Disabilities." ©1997-2002 American Speech-Language-Hearing Association. Retrieved August 2002.

- Difficulty finding the words needed to express basic thoughts/ideas and more complex explanations/descriptions

- Difficulty with the comprehension of spoken and/or written language, including, for older children, classroom handouts and textbooks

- Delayed vocabulary development

- Problems with the understanding and use of grammar in sentences

- Difficulty remembering numbers and letters in sequence, questions, and directions

- Difficulty with organization and planning, including, for older students, the drafting of school papers and longer-term school projects

Other Language Problems

The child with dyslexia has trouble almost exclusively with the written (or printed) word. The child who has dyslexia as part of a larger language learning disability has trouble with both the spoken and the written word. These problems may include:

- Expressing ideas coherently, as if the words needed are on the tip of the tongue but won't come out. Consequently, utterances can be vague and difficult to understand (e.g., using unspecific vocabulary, such as "thing" or "stuff" to replace words that cannot be remembered). Filler words like "um" may be used to take up time while a word is being retrieved from memory.

- Learning new vocabulary that the child hears (e.g., taught in lectures/lessons) and/or sees (e.g., in books)

- Understanding questions and following directions that are heard and/or read

- Recalling numbers in sequence, e.g., telephone numbers and addresses

- Understanding and retaining the details of a story's plot or a classroom lecture

- Slow reading and reduced comprehension of the material

- Learning words to songs and rhymes

- Telling left from right, making it hard to read and write since both skills require this directionality

- Letters and numbers

- Learning the alphabet

- Identifying the sounds that correspond to letters, making learning to read a formidable task

- While writing, mixing up the order of letters in words

- Mixing up the order of numbers that are a part of math calculations

- Poor spelling

- Memorizing the times tables

- Telling time

Other Possible Problem Areas

- Inattention and distractibility (Irrelevant thoughts, ambient noise, and/or excessive visual stimulation get in the way of paying attention to incoming information)

- Organizational skills (These children lose track of possessions, and have trouble completing tasks efficiently and thoroughly. Planning and organizing for writing letters and papers is also affected, resulting in a lack a focus or an unorganized sequence of ideas/thoughts)

- Motor coordination (Some children are delayed in learning how to tie their shoes or may appear clumsy on the playground.)

Speech-Language Pathologist

As part of a collaborative team consisting of the parents and educational professionals (i.e., teacher(s), special educators, psychologist), the speech-language pathologist has several responsibilities. He or she:

- informs teachers and other school professionals as to how to identify children who are at risk for developing problems before they experience failure in the classroom.

- works with professionals to help prevent problems before they occur by promoting opportunities for success with spoken and written language at home and school.

- performs assessments of spoken (speaking and listening) and written (reading and writing) language for children who have been identified by their teachers and parents as having difficulty.

- provides treatment for those children who have language problems contributing to difficulties with reading and writing.

Prevention

The speech-language pathologist consults with both educators and parents to teach and model language activities that promote success. He or she may:

- explain the importance of joint book reading and provides demonstration lessons. For example, the speech-language pathologist may illustrate how to improve students vocabulary skills by having children name items in story pictures and describe the action(s) in these pictures.

- model how to sharpen comprehension skills by asking questions related to a story plot and having the child predict what may happen next in the story.

- have the child retell a story in their own words or act out the story.

- teach how to increase the child's awareness of print in their environment (e.g., recognition of frequently encountered signs and logos) and the conventions of print (e.g., how to hold a book or that reading and writing are done from left to right).

- demonstrate strategies to teach letters and their corresponding sounds.

- show ways that teachers and parents can model literacy activities (e.g., by reading newspapers and magazines, by writing notes and letters, by making writing materials available for everybody' s use).

Speech and Language Assessment

The clinician begins by interviewing the parents and teacher(s) regarding academic concerns and the child's performance in the classroom. For preschool students, the speech-language pathologist gathers information about literacy experiences in the home. For example, are there books and other types of reading material around the home? How frequently does the child see family members writing letters, notes, lists, etc.? How often do family members read stories to the child?

The speech-language pathologist observes the child during classroom activities. He or she evaluates the child's ability to understand verbal and written directions and to attend to written information on the blackboard, daily plans, etc.

When evaluating a preschool child, the speech-language pathologist looks for awareness of print. Can the child recognize familiar signs and logos, hold a book correctly and turn the pages, recognize and/or write his or her name, demonstrate pretend writing (writing that resembles letters and numbers), and recognize and/or write letters. For the older child, the clinician observes whether he or she can read and understand information on handouts and in textbooks.

The speech-language pathologist assesses the student's phonological awareness skills (ability to hear and play with the sounds in words. When evaluating a preschool student, the speech-language pathologist may have the child tap or clap out the different syllables in words. He or she may have the child state whether or not two words rhyme or give a list of words that rhyme with a specified word.

When evaluating an older student, the speech-language pathologist may have him or her put together syllables and sounds to make a word. He or she may have the child break up a word into its syllables and/or sounds (e.g., cat has one syllable but three sounds c-a-t). The speech-language pathologist assesses the older child's phonological memory by having him or her repeat strings of words, numbers, letters, and sounds of increasing length.

Spelling, writing, and reading are assessed with older students. In some settings, the speech-language pathologist completes these assessments as part of a team while in other settings he or she helps the educational team interpret the results of reading and writing assessments completed by other evaluators. The reading evaluation focuses on the student's ability to decode (sound out) words, read irregular spelling patterns, read fluently, comprehend texts that differ in length and complexity, and comprehend different types of material (e.g., stories versus non-fiction texts).

The writing evaluation focuses on the student's ability to spell and write longer texts. Does spelling show that the child understands the sounds that different letters make? Does he or she correctly use irregular spelling patterns? Do writing samples show evidence of planning? Are they organized, sequential, and coherent? Are correct grammar and vocabulary used?

The speech-language pathologist completes a formal evaluation of speech and language skills. Speech articulation (pronunciation and clarity of speech) is assessed. Understanding and use of grammar (syntax), understanding and use of vocabulary (semantics), and the client's ability to provide an extended narrative (language sample) are evaluated. Can the child explain something or retell a story, centering on a topic and chaining a sequence of events together? Does the narrative make sense or is it difficult to follow? Can the child describe the plot in an action picture?

Executive functioning is evaluated. The speech-language pathologist assesses the child's ability to plan, organize, and attend to details (e.g., Does he or she plan/organize his or her writing? Is he or she able to keep track of assignments and school materials?). The speech-language pathologist may read an incomplete story and ask the child to provide a logical beginning, middle, or conclusion. The child is also asked to provide solutions to problems (reasoning and problem solving). For example, what would you do if you locked your keys in your car? How can this problem be avoided in the future?).

Treatment

The goals of speech and language treatment for the child with a reading problem target the specific aspects of reading and writing that the student is missing. For example, if the student is able to decode text but is unable to understand the details of what has been read, comprehension is addressed. If a younger student has difficulty distinguishing the different sounds that make up words, treatment will focus on activities that support growth in this skill area (rhyming, tapping out syllables, etc.).

Individualized programs always relate to the curriculum. Therefore, materials for treatment are taken from or are directly related to curricular content (e.g., textbooks for reading activities, assigned papers for writing activities, practice of oral reports for English class). The student is taught to apply newly learned language strategies to classroom activities and assignments. To assist the child best, the speech-language pathologist may work side-by-side with the child in his or her classroom(s).

Intervention with spoken language (speaking and listening) can also be designed to support the development of written language. For example, after listening to a story, the student may be asked to state and write answers to questions. He or she may be asked to give a verbal and then a written summary of the story.

Articulation (pronunciation) needs are also treated in a way that supports written language. For example, if the child is practicing saying words to improve pronunciation of a certain sound, he or she may be asked to read these words from a printed list.

The speech-language pathologist consults and collaborates with teachers to develop the use of strategies and techniques in the classroom. For example, he or she may help the teacher modify how new material is presented in lessons to accommodate the child's comprehension needs. He or she may also demonstrate what planning strategies the student uses to organize and focus written assignments.

Learning problems should be addressed as early as possible. Many children with learning disabilities that are treated later, when language demands are greater, experience lowered self-esteem due to their previous academic frustrations and failures. Learning problems that go untreated can lead to a significant decrease in confidence, school phobia (e.g., not wanting to go to school, not wanting to do homework), and depression.

Chapter 9

Phonological Disorders

Introduction

What is speech?

Speech is the spoken medium of language. The other two mediums or forms of language are writing and gestures. Gestures range from simple iconic movements, like pretending to drink, through to complex finger spelling and sign systems.

What is phonology?

Phonology is a branch of linguistics. It is concerned with the study of the sound systems of languages. The aims of phonology are to demonstrate the patterns of distinctive sound contrasts in a language, and to explain the ways speech sounds are organized and represented in the mind. The term phonology is used clinically as a referent to an individual's speech sound system-for example, her phonology might refer to her phonological system, or her phonological development.

The information in this chapter is from the September 2002 html version of "Children's Speech and Sound Disorders: Questions and Answers," by Caroline Bowen, PhD. Dr. Bowen is an Australian speech-language pathologist who has an informational website for consumers, students and professionals at www.slpsite.com © 1998-2002. Reprinted with permission.

79

What is phonological development?

The gradual process of acquiring adult speech patterns is called phonological development. Putting it another way, the emergence in children of a properly organized speech sound system is called phonological development. According to Ingram (1989) phonological development involves three aspects:

- the way the sound is stored in the child's mind
- the way the sound is actually said by the child
- the rules or processes that map between the two above

How easy should it be to understand young children's speech?

Table 9.1 provides a rough rule of thumb for how clearly your child should be speaking. Bear in mind that there is considerable individual variation between children. If you are in doubt about your own child's speech sound development an assessment by a speech-language pathologist will quickly tell you if your child is on track and making the right combination of correct sounds and errors for their age.

Table 9.1. A rough guide to how well children's words can be understood by their own parents.

By 18 months a child's speech is normally 25% intelligible

By 24 months a child's speech is normally 50-75% intelligible

By 36 months a child's speech is normally 75-100% intelligible

What are the characteristics of young children's speech?

All children make predictable pronunciation errors (not really errors at all, when you stop to think about it) when they are learning to talk like adults. These errors are called phonological processes, or phonological deviations. Table 9.2 displays the common phonological processes found in children's speech while they are learning the adult sound system of English.

Table 9.2. Phonological Processes in Normal Speech Development (*continued on next page*)

Phonological Process (Phonological Deviation)	Example	Description
Context Sensitive Voicing	"pig" is pronounced as "big", "car" is pronounced as "gar"	A voiceless sound is replaced by a voiced sound. In the examples given, /p/ is replaced by /b/, and /k/ is replaced by /g/. Other examples might include /t/ being replaced by /d/, or /f/ being replaced by /v/.
Word-Final Devoicing	"red" is pronounced as "ret", "bag" is pronounced as "bak"	A final voiced consonant in a word is replaced by a voiceless consonant. Here, /d/ has been replaced by /t/ and /g/ has been replaced by /k/.
Final Consonant Deletion	"home" is pronounced as "hoe", "calf" is pronounced as "car"	The final consonant in the word is omitted. In these examples, /m/ is omitted (or deleted) from "home" and /f/ is omitted from "calf".
Velar Fronting	"kiss" is pronounced as "tiss", "give" is pronounced as "div", "wing" is pronounced as "win"	A velar consonant, that is a sound that is normally made with the middle of the tongue in contact with the palate towards the back of the mouth, is replaced with consonant produced at the front of the mouth. Hence /k/ is replaced by /t/, /g/ is replaced by /d/, and "ng" is replaced by /n/.
Palatal Fronting	"ship" is pronounced as "sip", "measure" is pronounced as "mezza"	The fricative consonants "sh" and "zh" are replaced by fricatives that are made further forward on the palate, towards the front teeth. "sh" is replaced by /s/, and "zh" is replaced by /z/.
Consonant Harmony	"cupboard" is pronounced as "pubbed", "dog" is pronounced as "gog"	The pronunciation of the whole word is influenced by the presence of a particular sound in the word. In these examples: (1) the /b/ in "cupboard" causes the /k/ to be replaced /p/, which is the voiceless cognate of /b/, and (2) the /g/ in "dog" causes /d/ to be replaced by /g/.
Weak Syllable Deletion	"telephone" is pronounced as "teffone", "tidying" is pronounced as "tying"	Syllables are either stressed or unstressed. In "telephone" and "tidying" the second syllable is weak or unstressed. In this phonological process, weak syllables are omitted when the child says the word.

Table 9.2. Phonological Processes in Normal Speech Development (*continued from previous page*)

Phonological Process (Phonological Deviation)	Example	Description
Cluster Reduction	"spider" is pronounced as "pider", "ant" is pronounced as "at"	Consonant clusters occur when two or three consonants occur in a sequence in a word. In cluster reduction part of the cluster is omitted. In these examples /s/ has been deleted form "spider" and /n/ from "ant".
Gliding of Liquids	"real" is pronounced as "weal", "leg" is pronounced as "yeg"	The liquid consonants /l/ and /r/ are replaced by /w/ or /y/. In these examples, /r/ in "real" is replaced by /w/, and /l/ in "leg" is replaced by /y/.
Stopping	"funny" is pronounced as "punny", "jump" is pronounced as "dump"	A fricative consonant (/f/ /v/ /s/ /z/, "sh", "zh", "th" or /h/), or an affricate consonant ("ch" or /j/) is replaced by a stop consonant (/p/ /b/ /t/ /d/ /k/ or /g/). In these examples, /f/ in "funny" is replaced by /p/, and /j/ in "jump" is replaced by /d/.

All children make predictable pronunciation errors (not really errors at all, when you stop to think about it) when they are learning to talk like adults. These errors are called phonological processes, or phonological deviations. This table shows common phonological processes found in children's speech while they are learning the adult sound-system of English.

By what ages are phonological processes typically eliminated?

Phonological processes have usually gone by the time a child is five years of age, though there is individual variation between children. Table 9.3 lists the ages by which each of the processes are is normally eliminated (Grunwell, 1997).

What is articulation?

Articulation is a general term used in phonetics to denote the physiological movements involved in modifying the airflow, in the vocal tract above the larynx, to produce the various speech sounds. Sounds are classified according to their place and manner of articulation in the vocal mechanism (Crystal, 1991).

Table 9.3. Ages at which Phonological Processes Are Normally Gone

Phonological Process	Example	Gone by Approximately
Context sensitive voicing	pig = big	3
Word-final de-voicing	pig = pick	3
Final consonant deletion	comb = coe	3.3
Fronting	car = tar, ship = sip	3.6
Consonant harmony	mine = mime, kittycat = tittytat	3.9
Weak syllable deletion	elephant = efant, potato = tato, television = tevision, banana = nana	4
Cluster reduction	spoon = poon, train = chain, clean = keen	4
Gliding of liquids	run = one, leg = weg, leg = yeg	5
Stopping /f/	fish = tish	3
Stopping /s/	soap = dope	3
Stopping /v/	very = berry	3.6
Stopping /z/	zoo = doo	3.6
Stopping "sh"	shop = dop	4.6
Stopping /j/	jump = dump	4.6
Stopping "ch"	chair = tare	4.6
Stopping voiceless "th"	thing = ting	5
Stopping voiced "th"	them = dem	5

What are articulation development and phonetic development?

The terms articulation development and phonetic development both refer to children's gradual acquisition of the ability to produce individual speech sounds. In Table 9.4 is an outline the ages by which

83

Table 9.4. Normal Phonetic Development

Average age by which the speech sound listed is 75% correct during a child's speech	Speech Sounds	The manner in which the speech sounds are produced
3 years	h as in he	Voiceless fricative
	zh as in measure	Voiceless fricative
	y as in yes	Voiced glide
	w as in we	Voiced glide
	ng as in sing	Voiced nasal
	m as in me	Voiced nasal
	n as in no	Voiced nasal
	p as in up	Voiceless stop
	k as in car	Voiceless stop
	t as in to	Voiceless stop
	b as in be	Voiced stop
	g as in go	Voiced stop
	d as in do	Voiced stop
3 years 6 months	f as in if	Voiceless fricative
4 years	l as in lay	Voiced liquid
	sh as in she	Voiceless fricative
	ch as in chew	Voiceless affricate
4 years 6 months	j as in jaw	Voiced affricate
	s as in so	Voiceless fricative
	z as in is	Voiced fricative
5 years	r as in red	Voiced liquid
6 years	v as in Vegemite	Voiced fricative
8 years	th as in this	Voiced fricative
8 years 6 months	th as in thing	Voiceless fricative

These norms were established for a population of Australian children by Kilminster and Laird (1978). In column 3, the term voiced refers to the vibration of the vocal cords while the sound is being made. The term voiceless is applied to sounds that are made without vocal cord vibration. The terms fricative, glide, stop, nasal, liquid and affricate refer to the way the sounds are made, or the manner of articulation.

children use individual consonants with 75% accuracy during conversation (Kilminster and Laird, 1978).

How are phonological and phonetic development related?

There is a complex relationship between phonological and phonetic development. Normal speech development involves learning both phonetic and phonological features. The bulk of recent research into children's speech development has dealt with phonology: exploring and attempting to explain the process of the elaboration of speech output into a system of contrastive sound units. In recent years, there has also been a considerable body of research into the acquisition of motor speech control, bringing with it a renewed interest in the nexus between phonological development and phonetic development.

Phonological development and phonetic mastery do not synchronize precisely. A common example of this asynchrony, referred to by Smith (1973) as the puzzle phenomenon, is provided by children who realize /s/ and /z/ as "th" sounds, while producing "th-words" with /f/ in place of voiceless "th".

Developmental Phonological Disorders

What are developmental phonological disorders?

Developmental phonological disorders are a group of language disorders, whose cause is unclear, that affect children's ability to develop easily understood speech patterns by the time they are four years old. Developmental phonological disorders can also affect children's ability to learn to read and spell (Bowen, 1998).

Are there other names for developmental phonological disorders?

Developmental phonological disorders are known by many names including phonological disability and developmental phonological learning disorder.

There are two terms that are not included in the list of synonyms. They are phonological processing disorder and phonological processes disorder. Despite their wide usage, these incorrect (and misleading) terms are not synonyms for developmental phonological disorder. Neither are they names for closely related speech sound disorders. They are made up terms that have somehow crept into listservs and discussions. Even SLPs [speech-language pathologists] sometimes use them.

Are developmental phonological disorders something new?

No. In the past, a phonological disorder was termed a functional articulation disorder, and the relationship between it and learning basic school work (like reading and spelling) was not well recognized. Children were just thought to have difficulty in articulating the sounds of speech. Traditional articulation therapy was used to rectify the problem.

Is developmental phonological disorder a functional articulation disorder under a different name?

Developmental phonological disorder is not simply a new name for an old problem. The term reflects the influence of psycholinguistic theory on the way speech-language pathologists now understand phonological disorders. Nowadays, the traditional diagnostic classification of functional articulation disorder is falling into disuse.

Children with phonological disability phonological disorders are usually able to use, or can be quickly taught to use, all the sounds needed for clear speech thus demonstrating that they do not have a problem with articulation as such. In other words, we now know that the problem is not a motor speech disorder. Just to complicate matters, however, some children with developmental phonological disorders also have difficulties with fine motor control and/or motor planning for speech.

What is traditional articulation therapy?

There is no single definition of traditional articulation therapy. It is a term that is applied to a number of therapy approaches that focus on the motor aspects of speech production, with or without auditory discrimination training. In essence, traditional articulation therapy involves behavioral techniques, focused on teaching children new sounds in place of error sounds or omitted sounds, one at a time, and then gradually introducing them (new sounds that is) into longer and longer utterances, and eventually into normal conversational speech.

Is traditional therapy still an acceptable form of treatment?

Traditional therapy techniques, using the format previously outlined, have withstood the test of time, and can still be very suitable for children with functional speech disorders.

What is a functional speech disorder?

A functional speech disorder is a difficulty learning to make specific speech sounds. Children with just a few speech/sound difficulties such as lisping (saying "th" in place of /s/ and /z/), or problems saying /r/, /l/ or "th" are usually described as having functional speech disorders. But, you guessed it! There are synonyms for this too. Functional speech disorders are often referred to as mild articulation disorders or functional articulation disorders. Examples include:

- The word super pronounced as thooper.
- The word zebra pronounced as thebra.
- The word rivers pronounced as wivvers.
- The word leave pronounced as weave.
- The word thing pronounced as fing.
- The word those pronounced as vose.

Note: Some of these sound changes are acceptable in a number of English dialects.

Is traditional articulation therapy an appropriate approach to treating developmental phonological disorders?

The traditional approach is unsuitable for children with developmental phonological disorders. SLP's who include phonological principles in their theory of intervention believe that a phonological approach should be used with children with phonological disorders. Phonological approaches to intervention, of which there are several, are called phonological therapy.

What is phonological therapy?

Phonological therapy refers to the application of phonological principles to the treatment of children with phonological disability disorders (Grunwell, 1995). Phonological therapy:

1. Is based on the systematic nature of phonology.

2. Is characterized by conceptual, rather than motoric, activities.

3. Aims to facilitate age-appropriate phonological patterns through activities that encourage and nurture the development

of the appropriate cognitive organization of the child's under-lying phonological system.

4. Has generalization as its ultimate goal.

Where does the problem (of phonological disorder) lie?

In essence, the child with a developmental phonological disorder has a language difficulty affecting their ability to learn and organize their speech sounds into a system of sound patterns or sound contrasts. The problem is at a linguistic level, and there is no impairment to the child's larynx, lips, tongue, palate or jaw.

Does that mean there is no such thing as an articulation disorder?

Unfortunately, no. Children with dyspraxia or dysarthria have articulation disorders (or motor speech disorders). Children with anatomical (structural) differences such as cleft lip and palate, or tongue-tie or other craniofacial anomalies may also have articulation disorders.

Developmental Apraxia of Speech

What is dyspraxia?

Let's start with a reminder about what it is not. Developmental apraxia of speech is a childhood speech disorder. It is not the same as apraxia or dyspraxia in adults who have had strokes or head injuries.

Children with dyspraxia (or apraxia—both terms are as correct as any of the others) have the capacity to say speech sounds but have a problem with motor planning. They have difficulty making the movements needed for speech, voluntarily.

Dyspraxia can be mild, moderate or severe. It can apparently resolve with appropriate therapy, in that the person's speech sounds acceptable (though the underlying deficit probably remains forever). Alternatively, it can persist for a lifetime, in the form of very little speech and/or very difficult to understand speech, despite a great deal of appropriate therapy.

Is dyspraxia in children called by different names?

Dyspraxia in children is known by various names:

*   apraxia

- apraxia of speech
- developmental apraxia of speech (DAS)
- developmental verbal dyspraxia (DVD)
- developmental articulatory dyspraxia (DAD)
- childhood apraxia of speech (CAS)

Why is dyspraxia in children called by different names?

All the dyspraxia names seem to mean the same thing when it comes to looking at the actual symptoms or features of the child's speech production, mouth movements and slow progress acquiring speech. The most commonly used names for it are probably: developmental apraxia of speech (DAS), developmental articulatory dyspraxia (DAD), and developmental verbal dyspraxia (DVD).

In general each of these terms refer to children who have the capacity (the neuro-muscular wherewithal) to say speech sounds but who have a problem with motor planning. Messages from the brain, intended to tell the speech mechanism (larynx, lips, tongue, palate and jaw) what movements to make to produce speech, do not occur easily for children with dyspraxia. This difficulty comprises both a motor planning problem and a difficulty retrieving speech sounds and patterns when they are required (Ozanne, 1995).

The characteristic speech of such children includes differences in the rhythm and timing (prosody or melody) of speech and inconsistent speech sound errors. The distinguishing characteristic of apraxia of speech is that it is a problem with motor speech planning and programming, with no weakness, paralysis or poor co-ordination of the speech mechanism. It is probably safe to say that whether researchers or clinicians call the disorder DAS, DAD or DVD, they would all agree that the features previously discussed are characteristic of the speech problem they are studying, assessing or treating.

It is also probably true to say that whatever term is being used to name the problem, experienced clinicians at the grass roots level will be drawing on a very similar range of therapy techniques and activities.

All of which begs the question: so why call the problem by different names? There are at least five main theories that attempt to explain the basis of developmental apraxia.

1. It is due to an auditory processing problem

2. It is a very specific 'specific language impairment' affecting language acquisition at the sound-syllable-prosody level

3. It is due to an organizational problem with sequencing the movements required for speech

4. It is due to a difficulty with making volitional (pre-planned) movements for speech production

5. It is due to various combinations of these factors

Importantly, these are theories that are currently being formulated and tested by speech scientists. The fact is, we do not yet have a watertight explanation for dyspraxia.

Many clinicians and researchers actually working with children in the apraxia population who use the terms DAS and DAD tend to be those who veer towards the motor based explanation. Those who use the term DVD tend towards a language based explanation. Some clinicians use the terms DAS and DVD interchangeably. Some, who embrace the probability that the problem might be linguistic and motor in origin use DVD/DAS.

Then again, there are clinicians who use terms such as these because they have dropped into their clinical vernacular, in which case the term used does not reflect a particular theoretical orientation.

What are the characteristics of DVD/DAS?

To recapitulate, the distinguishing characteristic of apraxia of speech is that it is a problem with motor speech planning and programming, with no weakness, paralysis or poor co-ordination of the speech mechanism.

Some authorities believe that the primary difficulty children with dyspraxia have is with volitional (voluntary) movements of the speech production mechanism. Children with DVD/DAS, if they are able to talk, usually make very variable articulation errors, their speech is slow, it seems very effortful to an onlooker, and there is a lot of trial and error involved in trying to make particular sounds. The rhythm of speech usually seems wrong to the listener, and the child seems to put the emphasis in all the wrong spots (that is, there is something obviously unusual about their prosody).

The key features that alert a speech-language pathologist to the possibility of a dyspraxia diagnosis are these:

- The child may have no words, very few words, or up to 100 to 200 words in their vocabulary. They are unlikely to be attempting to make more than a handful of 2-word combinations. Some give the impression of struggling to talk, exhibiting trial and error attempts to say words, accompanied by great frustration. Many use self-taught signs and gestures to augment communication, which may include a lot of ingenious body language and facial expression. Some use a repertoire of sound effects (car noises, and the like) to good effect. Their speech has these characteristics:

Words, in general, are not clearly spoken, though there may be remarkable exceptions such as a very clear (and useful) no. Examples of this lack of clarity might include ball being pronounced as "or" and knee being pronounced as "dee".

Speech errors affect vowels as well as consonants. For instance, milk might be pronounced "mih", "muh", or "meh".

Inconsistency is evident, with the same word being pronounced in several different ways (e.g., me pronounced as "ee", "dee", "bee", "nee", or "mee").

Sounds that are used in some words are omitted from other words. I knew a child who could say p twice in the word poppi (her grandfather) but who pronounced both happy and puppy as "huh-ee".

When asked to imitate speech sounds, sound effects (e.g., car noises: "brm-brm" etc.) or words, the child does not seem to know where to start.

Many of these children can understand language at a more advanced level than their limited speech would suggest. They use a lot of mime and gesture to communicate. And they cannot easily copy mouth movements (i.e., non-speech movements).

Why is it referred to as a controversial diagnosis?

Having said that DAS is a motor speech disorder, it is important to note that it is a somewhat controversial diagnosis, with some authorities seeing it as a purely motor speech disorder with no language (linguistic) component; others seeing it as a linguistically based disorder; others seeing it as a combination of these two; with yet another group doubting its very existence as a diagnostic entity.

What do you think?

My own position is that developmental dyspraxia does exist, as a complex disorder and that no two children with it will be precisely the same. It can range from mild to severe.

Some children with DAS appear to have a motor planning/programming problem with little or no accompanying language component. In my clinical experience this is a rarity. Most appear to have a motor planning/programming difficulty combined with associated linguistic difficulties, particularly phonological problems and difficulties with expressive grammar and syntax. I do not see these language difficulties as part of the DAS, but as difficulties that commonly occur alongside the DAS.

While the idea of a purely linguistic basis (that is, no motor planning component) for DVD is intriguing, to date there is no convincing research data to support such a view.

When can a developmental dyspraxia diagnosis be made?

There is no actual age at which DAS can be diagnosed for sure. It is more to do with stage than age. SLP's often have DAS on their short-list of probable diagnoses for children who are late talkers with difficult-to-understand-speech (especially if they have feeding difficulties and sensory integration issues too) but we cannot be really sure until the child has plenty to say, or, at the very least, is making many speech attempts.

Ideally, the SLP has to be in a position to do a detailed speech and language assessment that includes analyzing speech movements, speech sounds, speech patterns and speech rhythms. To be able to do this the child has to be attempting to say lots of words.

SLP colleagues and I have made diagnoses of DAS in children who had vocabularies of between 100 and 200 words, and who ranged in age from 2-3 to 4-6. We also know of several children for whom a clear diagnosis of DAS was not possible until after the age of 7.

The Dysarthrias

What is dysarthria?

The question should really be what are the dysarthrias—as dysarthrias have many causes and characteristics. Children with the various types of dysarthria have a neuromuscular impairment. That is, the speech mechanism (larynx, lips, tongue, palate and jaw) may be paralyzed, weak or poorly coordinated.

Dysarthrias can affect all motor speech processes: breathing, producing sounds in the larynx, articulation, resonance, and the prosody or rhythm of speech.

Can phonological disorders, dyspraxia and the dysarthrias co-occur?

The three disorders can occur, in varying degrees, in the same individual. For example, a child might have a severe developmental phonological disorder with mild dyspraxic features. Another child might have dyspraxia with mild dysarthria.

Can speech sound disorders occur with other communication disorders?

Specific language impairment (SLI), semantic pragmatic language disorder (SPLD), stuttering, voice disorders, and other communication disorders can occur in the same child, alongside phonological disorders, dyspraxia and dysarthria.

Links (Developmental Apraxia of Speech)

There is a lot of information on the Internet relating to DAS. Some of it, for example the material on the Apraxia-Kids site with its well-moderated Listserv, is helpful, authoritative and factual. Unfortunately, the same cannot be said about some of the other sites that are out there. Be selective in what you take the time to read or print out, and ask your child's speech-language pathologist (or a SLP colleague if you are a professional seeking information) which sites they recommend. When you visit a site, check for yourself that the author has reliable credentials. For instance, you will be able to trust the information on SLP professional association sites (e.g., ASHA), many university sites, and articles by respected researchers in the field or experienced SLP clinicians some of whom also engage in clinical research.

If this is all new to you, above all, if you are the parent of a child who is in the process of diagnosis, or who has recently been diagnosed with DAS, get on with the therapy and try not to jump ahead in time, worrying about symptoms and situations that may never arise for your child. And please be guided by the SLP who knows your child as he or she is the person who is most likely to be able to provide you with really relevant (even if sometimes uncomfortable) answers.

References

Bowen, C. (1998a). Developmental phonological disorders: A practical guide for families and teachers. Melbourne: The Australian Council for Educational Research Ltd.

Crystal, D. (1991). *A Dictionary of Linguistics and Phonetics*. Oxford: Basil Blackwell Ltd.

Grunwell, P. (1995). Changing phonological patterns. *Child Language Teaching and Therapy*, 11, 61-78.

Grunwell, P. (1997). Natural phonology. In M. Ball & R. Kent (Eds.), *The New Phonologies: Developments in Clinical Linguistics*. San Deigo: Singular Publishing Group, Inc.

Ingram, D. (1989). *Phonological Disability in Children.(2nd ed.)*. London: Cole & Whurr, Ltd.

Kilminster, M.G.E., & Laird, E.M. (1978). Articulation development in children aged three to nine years. *Australian Journal of Human Communication Disorders*, 6, 23-30.

Smith, N.V. (1973). *The Acquisition of Phonology: A Case Study*. Cambridge: Cambridge University Press.

Ozanne, A. (1995). The Search for Developmental Verbal Dyspraxia. In B. Dodd (Ed.), *Differential Diagnosis & Treatment of Children with Speech Disorder*. (pp. 91-109). London: Whurr Publishers.

Chapter 10

Motor-Speech Disorder

Many issues surround the decision as to how to treat a child with a motor speech disorder. Perhaps first and foremost is how the clinician views that disorder. My particular point of view is that the term apraxia of speech is a misnomer. My experience and research has indicated that there may in fact be two or three forms of motor speech disorders in children that clinicians historically have lumped under the label of apraxia of speech. In my work, I have called these congenital dysarthria, planning apraxia of speech, and executive apraxia of speech. These terms are intended to show a continuum of clinical impairment ranging from those dominated by motor deficits to those that are more language based. All have a motor planning component to them. This continuum between motor to language processes influences much of my thinking on how to evaluate and treat children with developmental motor speech disorders. With that in mind let me address one treatment program that has worked well for a number of children over the years.

The program is sometimes called the multi-focal program. This is because it addresses three aspects of motor speech disorders that I have seen repeatedly over the years: 1) oral motor deficits and motor deficits in speech production, 2) disorganization in the phonologic

This material is reprinted with permission from, "Treating Children with Motor Speech Disorders," by Michael Crary, PhD., FASHA, and is part of the Apraxia-Kids Internet. Resources at www.apraxia-kids.org. © 1998. For more information, contact the Childhood Apraxia of Speech Association of North America, 123 Eisele Road, Cheswick, PA 15024, 412-767-6589.

system, 3) disorganization in the expressive language system. The multi-focal program incorporates each of these into every therapy session. The balance across the three components is determined by the imbalance in capabilities demonstrated by the child. For example, if a child has significant motoric impairments there may be greater emphasis on the initial component. From a different perspective, a child with significant phonologic deficits with minimal oral motor problems may receive a greater emphasis on the second component and so on and so forth.

The first component, motor speech, utilizes a bite block to stabilize the mandible combined with vowel or consonant-vowel syllables to facilitate lip and tongue movement independent of mandibular support. We have found this to be helpful in both child and adult patients with motor speech disorders. For example, once a bite block is placed the child may be asked to imitate the cardinal vowels of i, a, and u. This forces the tongue to move without mandibular support to the high-front, high-back and low-mid position in the oral cavity we then may add the consonants t, k or d and g introducing the co-articulatory effect of a front and back consonant. These CV units (consonant-vowel) are then strung together and converted to CVC (consonant-vowel-consonant) syllables to vary syllable shape during the early component of the treatment session. We have learned over the years that younger children tend to not tolerate bite blocks as well as older children and therefore these are often used for a shorter duration of time with the younger child.

The second component, phonological reorganization, address the overt characters of sound omissions substitutions etc. One philosophy is that the child develops disorganized production phonology as a result of impaired motor learning processes. From this perspective we have tried to use a therapy technique that reorganizes the phonological system. One of my favorite techniques has been phonemic contrasting. In phonemic contrasting, the child learns a very important lesson about speaking. The child learns that in order for words to have different meanings to the listener they must be produced differently. For example, if the child is deleting final consonants and says the word "boo" when he means to say the word "boot," we have not only a phonologic change, (final consonant omission) but also a semantic change (obvious change in word meaning). In phonemic contrasting, words are paired based on the contrast that you are trying to teach the child. In this system, the focus on individual sounds is minimized and it is the contrast between meaningful word pairs that is emphasized. In the example given the contrast would be final consonant production.

Therefore, if the child said "bood" he or she would be considered to have produced a correct response because a final consonant was produced; even though an incorrect final consonant. What we have found with this technique is: 1) Clinicians can work on many different sound categories in the same treatment sessions focusing on a single contrast, and 2) Though children may not produce the initial correct sounds in these targets, they soon reorganize the phonologic system and correct sounds emerge.

The third component, syntactic reorganization, is used for two purposes. The first is to give the child some carry over practice in a more complex linguistic framework than single words. The second is to give the clinician an opportunity to stimulate more advanced grammar in expressive language. A variety of techniques can be used. One that I have used repeatedly is a modification of the Fokes Sentence Builder. In this technique, sentences are constructed by physically aligning 3x5 cards in the right order. The target words from the second component of therapy (Phonemic Contrasting) can be used as part of the sentence construction. Once simple sentence frames are constructed clinicians can then turn the cards over or reorganize them if memory or sequencing activities are indicated in the treatment plan. Subsequently, we give the child all the cards and ask them to tell a story to terminate the treatment session.

These treatment sessions can be conducted in as little as thirty to forty-five minutes. We have found them to be effective in children with motor speech disorders of varying types. A brief comment on changing from one stimulus to the other; we have found that it is advantages to use a stair stepping model for introducing new stimuli. That means that we never change the motor target, phonologic target, and the grammatic target in the same session. Only one new target is introduced in any given session. Once the child masters that target it is then introduced in a new context such as a more advanced grammatical structure or a more difficult sentence type. In this regard only, the information that you want the child to focus on is changed in any give session.

Context is very important in developing effective therapy program for children with developmental speech disorders. My view is that apraxia is a disorder of motor organization/motor execution that is influenced by motoric and/or linguistic context. Clinicians who can master the ability to identify the context contributing to either success or non-success in speech production for these children can subsequently structure therapy using appropriate context to facilitate improved responses.

97

About the Author

Michael Crary is author of *Developmental Motor Speech Disorders* and numerous other publications.

Chapter 11

Aphasia Can Sometimes Impact Learning

Aphasia is a language disorder that results from damage to portions of the brain that are responsible for language. For most people, these are parts of the left side (hemisphere) of the brain. Aphasia usually occurs suddenly, often as the result of a stroke or head injury, but it may also develop slowly, as in the case of a brain tumor. The disorder impairs the expression and understanding of language as well as reading and writing. Aphasia may co-occur with speech disorders such as dysarthria or apraxia of speech, which also result from brain damage.

Who Has Aphasia?

Anyone can acquire aphasia, but most people who have aphasia are in their middle to late years. Men and women are equally affected. It is estimated that approximately 80,000 individuals acquire aphasia each year. About one million persons in the United States currently have aphasia.

What Causes Aphasia?

Aphasia is caused by damage to one or more of the language areas of the brain. Many times, the cause of the brain injury is a stroke.

"Aphasia," from National Institute on Deafness and Other Communication Disorders (NIDCD), NIH Publication Number 97-4257, reviewed in September 2002 by Dr. David A. Cooke, MD, Diplomate, American Board of Internal Medicine; and excerpts from "Aphasia: Recent Research," National Institute on Deafness and Other Communication Disorders (NIDCD), NIH Publication Number 01-4257, June 2001.

A stroke occurs when, for some reason, blood is unable to reach a part of the brain. Brain cells die when they do not receive their normal supply of blood, which carries oxygen and important nutrients. Other causes of brain injury are severe blows to the head, brain tumors, brain infections, and other conditions of the brain.

Individuals with Broca's aphasia have damage to the frontal lobe of the brain. These individuals frequently speak in short, meaningful phrases that are produced with great effort. Broca's aphasia is thus characterized as a nonfluent aphasia. Affected people often omit small words such as "is," "and," and "the." For example, a person with Broca's aphasia may say, "Walk dog" meaning, "I will take the dog for a walk." The same sentence could also mean, "You take the dog for a walk," or "The dog walked out of the yard," depending on the circumstances. Individuals with Broca's aphasia are able to understand the speech of others to varying degrees. Because of this, they are often aware of their difficulties and can become easily frustrated by their speaking problems. Individuals with Broca's aphasia often have right-sided weakness or paralysis of the arm and leg because the frontal lobe is also important for body movement.

In contrast to Broca's aphasia, damage to the temporal lobe may result in a fluent aphasia that is called Wernicke's aphasia. Individuals with Wernicke's aphasia may speak in long sentences that have no meaning, add unnecessary words, and even create new words. For example, someone with Wernicke's aphasia may say, "You know that smoodle pinkered and that I want to get him round and take care of him like you want before," meaning "The dog needs to go out so I will take him for a walk." Individuals with Wernicke's aphasia usually have great difficulty understanding speech and are therefore often unaware of their mistakes. These individuals usually have no body weakness because their brain injury is not near the parts of the brain that control movement.

A third type of aphasia, global aphasia, results from damage to extensive portions of the language areas of the brain. Individuals with global aphasia have severe communication difficulties and may be extremely limited in their ability to speak or comprehend language.

How Is Aphasia Diagnosed?

Aphasia is usually first recognized by the physician who treats the individual for his or her brain injury. Frequently this is a neurologist. The physician typically performs tests that require the individual to follow commands, answer questions, name objects, and converse. If the physician suspects aphasia, the individual is often referred to a speech-language pathologist, who performs a comprehensive examination of the person's ability to understand, speak, read, and write.

How Is Aphasia Treated?

In some instances an individual will completely recover from aphasia without treatment. This type of spontaneous recovery usually occurs following a transient ischemic attack (TIA), a kind of stroke in which the blood flow to the brain is temporarily interrupted but quickly restored. In these circumstances, language abilities may return in a few hours or a few days. For most cases of aphasia, however, language recovery is not as quick or as complete. While many individuals with aphasia also experience a period of partial spontaneous recovery (in which some language abilities return over a period of a few days to a month after the brain injury), some amount of aphasia typically remains. In these instances, speech-language therapy is often helpful. Recovery usually continues over a 2-year period. Most people believe that the most effective treatment begins early in the recovery process. Some of the factors that influence the amount of improvement include the cause of the brain damage, the area of the brain that was damaged, the extent of the brain injury, and the age and health of the individual. Additional factors include motivation, handedness, and educational level.

Aphasia therapy strives to improve an individual's ability to communicate by helping the person to use remaining abilities, to restore language abilities as much as possible, to compensate for language problems, and to learn other methods of communicating. Treatment may be offered in individual or group settings. Individual therapy focuses on the specific needs of the person. Group therapy offers the opportunity to use new communication skills in a comfortable setting. Stroke clubs, which are regional support groups formed by individuals who have had a stroke, are available in most major cities. These clubs also offer the opportunity for individuals with aphasia to try new communication skills. In addition, stroke clubs can help the individual and his or her family adjust to the life changes that accompany stroke and aphasia. Family involvement is often a crucial component of aphasia treatment so that family members can learn the best way to communicate with their loved one. Family members are encouraged to:

- Simplify language by using short, uncomplicated sentences.

- Repeat the content words or write down key words to clarify meaning as needed.

- Maintain a natural conversational manner appropriate for an adult.

- Minimize distractions, such as a blaring radio, whenever possible.

- Include the person with aphasia in conversations.

- Ask for and value the opinion of the person with aphasia, especially regarding family matters.

- Encourage any type of communication, whether it is speech, gesture, pointing, or drawing.

- Avoid correcting the individual's speech.

- Allow the individual plenty of time to talk.

- Help the individual become involved outside the home. Seek out support groups such as stroke clubs.

Aphasia: Recent Research

The National Institute on Deafness and Other Communication Disorders (NIDCD) is one of the Institutes of the National Institutes of Health. The NIDCD supports and conducts biomedical and behavioral research and research training on normal and disordered processes of hearing, balance, smell, taste, voice, speech, and language. Currently supported aphasia research focuses on evaluating, characterizing, and treating the disorder, as well as on improving the understanding of the relationship between the language disorder and the brain.

New Approaches to Evaluation

Scientists are attempting to reveal the underlying problems that cause specific aphasia symptoms. The goal is to understand how injury to a particular brain structure impairs specific portions of a person's language process. The results could be useful in treating many types of aphasia, since the underlying cause can vary.

Other research is attempting to develop a model of sentence comprehension and production that can help provide a functional explanation for aphasia symptoms. These studies look at how difficulties in word representations and processes contribute to problems with sentence production and comprehension so that specific symptoms can be traced back to identifiable processing deficits. This would help focus treatment on the responsible word processes or representations.

New Approaches to Characterization

Since the same types of aphasia look different from one language to another, some scientists are attempting to distinguish between universal symptoms of the disorder and those that are language specific. Others are examining how people with aphasia maintain their knowledge of a language, but seem to have difficulty accessing that knowledge. Scientists are also comparing aspects of language that are at risk or are protected within and across language types and assessing the effect of stress on language expression in people without aphasia. These studies may help with the development of tests tailored to specific characteristics of individual languages and in clinical services to bilingual communities.

New Therapeutic Approaches

Pharmacotherapy is a new, experimental approach to treating aphasia. Some studies are testing how drugs can be used in combination with speech therapy to improve recovery of various language functions by increasing the task-related flow of activation in the left hemisphere of the brain. These studies indicate that drugs may help improve aphasia in acute stroke and as an adjuvant to language therapy in post acute and chronic aphasia.

Other treatment approaches use computers to improve the language abilities of people with aphasia. Studies have shown that computer-assisted therapy can help people with aphasia retrieve and produce verbs. People who have auditory problems perceiving the difference between phonemes can benefit from computers, which can be used for speech-therapeutic auditory discrimination exercises.

Researchers are also looking at how treatment of other cognitive deficits involving attention and memory can improve communication deficits.

A Closer Look at the Brain

To understand recovery processes in the brain, some researchers are attempting to use functional MRI (magnetic resonance imaging) to uncover the anatomical organization of the human brain regions involved in comprehending words and sentences. This type of research may improve understanding of how these areas reorganize after focal brain injury. The results could have implications for both the basic understanding of brain function and the diagnosis and treatment of neurological diseases.

Chapter 12

Information Processing Disorders

Understanding Information Processing

Our senses (sight, smell, hearing, taste, and touch) are constantly providing us with information. Even more information is stored in our short and long-term memory. For each of the hundreds of things you and your child do each day—get dressed, catch the school bus, feed the dog—you need to decide rapidly which bits of information you need to use to complete the task at hand.

Managing all of the information you store and receive and using it effectively is called information processing. There are several kinds of information processing skills: visual discrimination, visual figure-ground discrimination, visual memory, visual motor processing, visual closure, understanding spatial relationships, auditory discrimination, auditory figure-ground discrimination and auditory memory.

Information Processing Disorders and Learning Disabilities

If you have been told that your child has an information processing disorder, he or she may have difficulty with one or more of the information processing skills listed in the previous paragraph. Many

"Information Processing Disorders (Visual and Auditory Processing Disorders)," © 2001 National Center for Learning Disabilities. Reprinted with permission. For more information from the National Center for Learning Disabilities, visit their website at http://www.ncld.org.

children with learning disabilities have difficulty with these skills. Children with information processing disorders do not use information efficiently to learn, solve problems or complete tasks. The inability to process information efficiently frequently results in frustration and learning failure.

Information Processing Skills and Associated Difficulties

Visual Discrimination

The skill: The ability to use the sense of sight to notice and compare the features of different items to distinguish one item from another. Children with problems in this area may find it difficult to:

- Notice the small differences between some letters and numbers. They may confuse the printed letters b, p, g, and q (or the numbers 6 and 9) because these printed characters have many features in common.

- Notice the difference between certain colors or between similar shapes and patterns.

Visual Figure-Ground Discrimination

The skill: The ability to separate a shape or printed character from its background. Children with problems in this area may find it difficult to:

- Find the specific bit of information they need from a printed page (or computer screen) filled with words and numbers. (Examples: find a friend's phone number on a page in a telephone book, scan a newspaper page for a specific phrase, locate a specific destination on a map.)

Visual Memory

The skill: There are two kinds of visual memory. Long-term visual memory is the ability to recall something seen a long time ago. Short-term visual memory is the ability to remember something seen very recently. Visual memory often depends upon the nature of the information being processed. For example, most people find it easier to remember what an object looked like four weeks ago if the object is associated with a special event. (People with visual memory problems may have trouble even then.) Children with problems in this area may find it difficult to:

- Describe a place they have visited.

- Remember the spelling of a familiar but irregularly spelled word.

- Dial a telephone number without looking carefully at each of the numbers and letters on the telephone.

- Use a calculator, typewriter or computer keyboard with speed and accuracy.

Visual Motor Processing

The skill: Visual motor processing is the kind of thinking needed to use feedback from the eyes to coordinate the movement of other parts of your body. For example, your eyes and hands need to work together to write with a pen or pencil. Children with problems in this area may find it difficult to:

- Write neatly or stay within the margins or on the lines of a page.

- Use scissors or sew.

- Move around without bumping into things.

- Place objects on surfaces so that they are not in danger of falling off.

- Participate in sports that require well-timed and precise movements in space.

Visual Closure

The skill: The ability to know what an object is when only parts of it are visible. Children with problems in this area may find it difficult to:

- Recognize a picture of a familiar object that is missing some parts (a truck without its wheels).

- Identify a word when a letter is missing.

Spatial Relationships

The skill: Spatial relationships describe how objects are positioned in the space around us. We use our ability to recognize and understand spatial relationships as we interact with our surroundings and also when we look at objects (characters or pictures) printed on paper. The ability to recognize and understand spatial relationships helps us know whether objects are near to us or far away, on our left or right, or over or under other objects. Children must have this skill in order to learn to read, write, count, and think about numbers. Children with problems in this area may find it difficult to:

- Find their way from one place to another, even in familiar surroundings.

- Write intelligibly. They may place letters, words and numbers too close together or too far apart.

Auditory Discrimination

The skill: The ability to notice, compare and distinguish the distinct and separate sounds in words. In order to read efficiently, we have to be able to isolate sounds (distinguish one sound from another), especially those sounds that match letters in the alphabet. Most of us make mistakes from time to time because we fail to isolate sounds correctly. For example, "turn left down the hall" may be mistakenly heard as "turn left at the wall." Children with problems in this area may find it difficult to:

- Understand spoken language, follow directions, and remember details.

- Learn to read.

Auditory Figure-Ground Discrimination

The skill: Auditory figure-ground discrimination is the ability to pick out important sounds from a noisy background. Some disorders of attention are associated with auditory figure-ground discrimination difficulties. Children with problems in this area may find it difficult to:

- Separate meaningful sounds from background noise. For example, a child may not be able to easily pick out the words spoken by a teacher standing at the front of the classroom from the sounds made by children playing in the next room or the traffic outside.

- Stay focused on the auditory information that is needed to successfully complete the task at hand.

Auditory Memory

The skill: Like visual memory, there are two kinds of auditory memory. Long-term auditory memory is the ability to recall something heard long ago. Short-term auditory memory is the ability to remember something heard very recently. Children with problems in this area may find it difficult to:

- Remember people's names
- Memorize and recall telephone numbers
- Follow multi-step spoken directions
- Recall stories they have been told or remember lines from songs

Suggestions for Encouraging and Supporting Your Child's Success

Make it easier for your child to process information. Simplify directions you give to your child. Maintain eye contact with your child while speaking to him or her. Speak slowly, especially when providing new information. Ask your child to repeat what he or she heard or read after you have provided information.

Identify your child's strengths. People with learning disabilities often have strong preferences for one type of information processing over another. These preferences are sometimes referred to as learning or working styles. Simple accommodations, such as giving instructions both orally and in writing, can be of enormous help to some individuals with learning disabilities. Try to encourage other family members and your child's teachers to modify the way they interact with your child to make use of your child's strengths.

Take notes. When you first notice that your child is behaving in ways that cause concern, begin to keep an ongoing written account or log that describes the behavior and related events or conversations. Your notes will help you provide the necessary information to your child's teacher, pediatrician, or other professional when you decide to ask for help. Save samples of schoolwork that contain good examples of your child's areas of strength as well as any areas of difficulty.

Ask for help. Contact organizations that specialize in helping people with learning disabilities. There are many organizations that

109

can help children and their families when a disability is discovered. These organizations can often provide the critical resources and support that makes it possible for you to receive the help you need.

Speak to your child's teacher and other school professionals. It is important to establish and maintain ongoing productive, positive relationships with the people who are helping you to educate your child. Tell your child's teacher, counselor or principal about the difficulties your child is facing. Ask them what help is available inside and outside of the classroom.

Arrange for an evaluation. Your discussions with school professionals may result in the need for a formal evaluation. Evaluations can be done through the public schools or through private practitioners. An evaluation should help identify your child's strengths and weaknesses. The evaluator should be able to recommend specific accommodations and strategies to best facilitate your child's learning.

Chapter 13

Auditory Processing Disorder

What Is Auditory Processing?

Auditory processing is the term used to describe what happens when your brain recognizes and interprets the sounds around you. Humans hear when energy that we recognize as sound travels through the ear and is changed into electrical information that can be interpreted by the brain. The disorder part of auditory processing disorder (APD) means that something is adversely affecting the processing or interpretation of information.

Children with APD often do not recognize subtle differences between sounds in words, even though the sounds themselves are loud and clear. For example, the request "Tell me how a chair and a couch are alike" may sound to a child with APD like "Tell me how a couch and a chair are alike." It can even be understood by the child as "Tell me how a cow and a hair are alike." These kinds of problems are more likely to occur when a person with APD is in a noisy environment or when he or she is listening to complex information.

APD goes by many other names. Sometimes it is referred to as central auditory processing disorder (CAPD). Other common names are auditory perception problem, auditory comprehension deficit, central auditory dysfunction, central deafness, and so-called word deafness.

National Institute on Deafness and Other Communication Disorders (NIDCD), NIH Publication Number 01-4949. March 2001. Resources verified August 2002.

111

What Causes Auditory Processing Difficulty?

We are not sure. Human communication relies on taking in complicated perceptual information from the outside world through the senses, such as hearing, and interpreting that information in a meaningful way. Human communication also requires certain mental abilities, such as attention and memory. Scientists still do not understand exactly how all of these processes work and interact or how they malfunction in cases of communication disorders. Even though your child seems to hear normally, he or she may have difficulty using those sounds for speech and language.

The cause of APD is often unknown. In children, auditory processing difficulty may be associated with conditions such as dyslexia, attention deficit disorder, autism, autism spectrum disorder, specific language impairment, pervasive development disorder, or developmental delay. Sometimes this term has been misapplied to children who have no hearing or language disorder but have challenges learning.

What Are the Symptoms?

Children with auditory processing difficulty typically have normal hearing and intelligence. However, they have also been observed to:

- Have trouble paying attention to and remembering information presented orally
- Have problems carrying out multistep directions
- Have poor listening skills
- Need more time to process information
- Have low academic performance
- Have behavior problems
- Have language difficulty (e.g., they confuse syllable sequences and have problems developing vocabulary and understanding language)
- Have difficulty with reading, comprehension, spelling, and vocabulary

How Is It Diagnosed?

A teacher, or a day care provider may be the first person to notice symptoms of auditory processing difficulty in your child. So talking to your child's teacher about school or preschool performance is a good idea. Many health professionals can also diagnose APD in your child. There may need to be ongoing observation with the professionals involved.

Much of what will be done by these professionals will be to rule out other problems. A pediatrician or family doctor can help rule out possible diseases that can cause some of these same symptoms. He or she will also measure growth and development. If there is a disease or disorder related to hearing, you may be referred to an otolaryngologist, a physician who specializes in diseases and disorders of the head and neck.

To determine whether your child has a hearing function problem, an audiologic evaluation is necessary. An audiologist will give tests that can determine the softest sounds and words a person can hear and other tests to see how well people can recognize sounds in words and sentences. For example, for one task, the audiologist might have your child listen to different numbers or words in the right and the left ear at the same time. Another common audiologic task involves giving the child two sentences, one louder than the other, at the same time. The audiologist is trying to identify processing problems.

A speech-language pathologist can find out how well a person understands and uses language. A mental health professional can give you information about cognitive and behavioral challenges that may contribute to problems in some cases, or he or she may have suggestions that will be helpful. Because the audiologist can help with the functional problems of hearing and processing and the speech-language pathologist is focused on language, they may work as a team with your child. All of these professionals seek to provide the best outcome for each child.

What Treatments Are Available?

Several strategies are available to help children with auditory processing difficulty.

Auditory trainers are electronic devices that allow a person to focus attention on a speaker and reduce the interference of background noise. They are often used in classrooms, where the teacher wears a microphone to transmit sound and the child wears a headset to receive the sound. Children who wear hearing aids can use them in addition to the auditory trainer.

Environmental modifications such as classroom acoustics, placement, and seating may help. An audiologist may suggest ways to improve the listening environment, and he or she will be able to monitor any changes in hearing status.

Language-building exercises can increase the ability to learn new words and increase a child's language base.

Auditory memory enhancement, a procedure that reduces detailed information to a more basic representation, may help. Also, informal auditory training techniques can be used by teachers and therapists to address specific difficulties.

Auditory integration training is sometimes promoted by practitioners as a way to retrain the auditory system and decrease hearing distortion.

It is important to know that much research is still needed to understand auditory processing problems, related disorders, and the best interventions for each child or adult. All the strategies undertaken will need to be suited to the needs of the individual child, and their effectiveness will need to be continually evaluated.

Current Research

In recent years, scientists have developed new ways to study the human brain through imaging. Imaging is a powerful tool that allows the monitoring of brain activity without any surgery. Imaging studies are already giving scientists new insights into auditory processing. Some of these studies are directed at understanding auditory processing disorders. One of the values of imaging is that it provides an objective, measurable view of a process. Many of the symptoms described as related to APD are described differently by different people. Imaging will help identify the source of these symptoms. Other scientists are studying the central auditory nervous system. Cognitive neuroscientists are helping to describe how the processes that mediate sound recognition and comprehension work in both normal and disordered systems. Research into the rehabilitation of child language disorders continues. In the future, both basic and clinical research will help us better understand the nature of auditory processing disorders.

Where Can I Learn More?

Contact the following group for information related to audiology and audiology professionals and services.

American Academy of Audiology
8300 Greensboro Drive, Suite 750
McLean, VA 22102
Toll-free: 800-AAA-2336
Tel: 703-790-8466
TTY: 703-790-8466
Internet: http://www.audiology.org

Or, for information related to audiology and speech-language pathology professionals and services, contact:

American Speech-Language-Hearing Association
10801 Rockville Pike
Rockville, MD 20852
Toll-free: 800-638-8255
Tel: 301-897-3279
TTY: 301-897-0157
Fax: 301-897-7355
E-Mail: actioncenter@asha.org
Internet: http://www.asha.org

Part Three

Academic Skills Disorders

Chapter 14

Dyscalculia: Developmental Arithmetic Disorder

What Is Dyscalculia?

Dyscalculia is a learning disability involving math skills. According to the *Journal of Pediatrics*, dyscalculia, which is a lifelong condition, affects about 2% - 6.5% of elementary school age children in the United States. Some of the symptoms of dyscalculia are:

- Normal or advanced language and other skills, often good visual memory for the printed word.

- Poor mental math ability, often with difficulty in common use of money, such as balancing a checkbook, making change, and tipping. Often there is a fear of money and its transactions.

- Difficulty with math processes (e.g., addition, subtraction, multiplication) and concepts (e.g., sequencing of numbers). There is sometimes poor retention and retrieval of concepts, or an inability to maintain a consistency in grasping math rules.

- Poor sense of direction, easily disoriented, as well as trouble reading maps, telling time, and grappling with mechanical processes.

- Difficulty with abstract concepts of time and direction, schedules, keeping track of time, and the sequence of past and future events.

"Dyscalculia," © 2001 National Center for Learning Disabilities. Reprinted with permission. For more information from the National Center for Learning Disabilities, visit their website at http://www.ncld.org.

- Common mistakes in working with numbers include number substitutions, reversals, and omissions.

- May have difficulty learning musical concepts, following directions in sports that demand sequencing or rules, and keeping track of scores and players during games such as cards and board games.

Dyscalculia can be quantitative, which is a deficit in counting and calculating; qualitative, which is a difficulty in the conceptualizing of math processes; and intermediate, which is the inability to work with numbers or symbols.

Dyscalculia is identified by specialists in learning disabilities who use a battery of tests.

What Strategies Can Help?

Individuals with dyscalculia need help in organizing and processing information related to numbers and mathematical concepts. Since math is essentially a form of language using numbers instead of words as symbols, communicate frequently and clearly with a child as to what is needed to do a mathematical problem.

Give a child real-life exposure to how math is a part of everyday life. Have a child help with counting how many papers need to be passed out in a classroom, what ingredients are needed in baking a cake, or how to make change after purchasing something.

Parents and teachers should work together to determine if there are strategies that will help a child, such as using graph paper to help with alignment on a page or a calculator to check work. Teachers may also be able to suggest other textbooks, workbooks, or computer programs that may give students more opportunities to practice skills.

Get a tutor or a learning center to provide additional enrichment opportunities. Take full use of school-sponsored resources.

Praise an individual's accomplishments and pay attention to his or her strengths.

Chapter 15

Adapting Instruction for Students with Mathematic Disabilities

Students with learning disabilities (LD) are increasingly receiving most of their mathematics instruction in general education classrooms. Studies show that these students benefit from general education mathematics instruction if it is adapted and modified to meet the individual needs of the learners (Salend, 1994). Adaptations and modifications come in many forms. They can be as simple as using graph paper to help student with mathematics disabilities keep columnar addition straight or as complex as solving calculus equations with calculators. To ensure effective instruction, adaptations and modifications for instruction are necessary in the areas of lesson planning, teaching techniques, formatting content, adapting media for instruction, and adapting evaluation (Wood, 1992).

In general education classrooms, adaptations and modifications in mathematics instruction are appropriate for all students, not just students with LD. Teachers of mathematics will find that simple changes to the presentation of mathematical concepts enable students to gain a clearer understanding of the process rather than a merely mechanically correct response. Additionally, adapting and modifying instruction for students creates a more positive atmosphere that encourages

The information in this chapter is reprinted from "Adapting Mathematics Instruction in the General Education Classroom for Students with Mathematics Disabilities," by Robin H. Lock, *LD Forum,* 21(2), 19-23 (1996). © 1996 Council for Learning Disabilities. Despite the older date of this article it will be helpful to those seeking information about math instruction for the learning disabled.

students to take risks in problem solving, which strengthens student understanding of the concept (McCoy & Prehm, 1987).

For many teachers with limited or no preparation for working with students with LD, inclusion of students with mathematics disabilities may create concern. This chapter provides information on how to adapt and modify mathematics instruction to promote success and understanding in the areas of mathematical readiness, computation, and problem solving for students with math disabilities. It also presents techniques that promote effective mathematics instruction for these students.

How Can General Education Teachers Facilitate the Learning of Mathematical Skills?

Ariel (1992) stresses the need for all students to develop skill in readiness, computation, and problem solving skills. Following are illustrations of adaptations and modifications that can be implemented to help students succeed in all three areas.

Readiness

According to Ariel (1992), students with LD must acquire (a) general developmental readiness, and (b) conceptual number readiness. General developmental readiness includes ability in the areas of classification, one-to-one correspondence, seriation, conservation, flexibility, and reversibility. Knowledge of the student's level of general readiness allows the teacher to determine how adaptations and modifications must be enacted to allow for the student to progress. For some students, mathematics readiness instruction may need to include the development of language number concepts such as big and small and smallest to largest; and attributes such as color, size, or shape. Instruction, review, and practice of these concepts must be provided for longer time periods for students with mathematics disabilities than for other students.

Conceptual number readiness is essential for the development of addition and subtraction skills (Ariel, 1992). Practice and review with board games or instructional software are effective ways to develop conceptual number readiness for students with mathematics disabilities. Manipulatives, such as Cuisenaire rods and Unifix math materials (e.g., 100 block trays) allow students with math disabilities to visualize numerical concepts and engage in age-appropriate readiness skills.

122

Computational Skills

Adaptations and modifications in the instruction of computational skills are numerous and can be divided into two areas: memorizing basic facts and solving algorithms or problems.

Basic Facts. Two methods for adapting instruction to facilitate recall of basic facts for students with math disabilities include (a) using games for continued practice, and (b) sequencing basic facts memorization to make the task easier. Beattie and Algozzine (cited in McCoy & Prehm, 1987) recommend the use of dice rolls, spinners, and playing cards to give students extra practice with fact memorization and to promote interest in the task by presenting a more game-like orientation. Further, McCoy and Prehm (1987) suggest that teachers display charts or graphs that visually represent the students' progress toward memorization of the basic facts. Sequencing fact memorization may be an alternative that facilitates instruction for students with LD. For example, in teaching the multiplication facts, Bolduc (cited in McCoy & Prehm, 1987) suggests starting with the x0 and x1 facts to learn 36 of the 100 multiplication facts. The x2 and x5 facts are next, adding 28 to the set of memorized facts. The x9s are introduced next, followed by doubles such as 6 x 6. The remaining 20 facts include 10 that are already known if the student is aware of the commutative property (e.g., 4 x 7 = 7 x 4). New facts should be presented a few at time with frequent repetition of previously memorized facts for students with LD.

Solving Algorithms. Computation involves not only memorization of basic facts, but also utilization of these facts to complete computational algorithms. An algorithm is a routine, step-by-step procedure used in computation (Driscoll, 1980 cited in McCoy & Prehm, 1987). In the addition process, McCoy and Prehm (1987) present three alternatives to the standard renaming method for solving problems, including expanded notation (see Table 15.1) partial sums (see Table 15.2), and Hutchings' low-stress algorithm (see Table 15.3). Subtraction for students with mathematics disabilities is made easier through the use of Hutchings' low-stress subtraction method (McCoy & Prehm, 1987) (see Table 15.4) where all renaming is done first. Multiplication and division (McCoy & Prehm, 1987) can be illustrated through the use of partial products (see Table 15.5). Further, arrays that use graph paper to allow students to plot numbers visually on the graph and then count the squares included within the rectangle they produce.

Table 15.1. Expanded Notation

$$29 = \text{2 tens and 9 ones}$$
$$+43 = \text{4 tens and 3 ones}$$

Step one: Add the ones and tens.   6 tens and 12 ones

Step two: Regroup the ones, if necceassary.   6 tens and (1 ten 2 ones)

Step three: Put the tens together.   (6 tens and 1 ten) and 2 ones

Step four: Write the tens in a simpler way.   7 tens and 2 ones

Step five: Write the answer in number form.   72

Table 15.2. Partial Sums

$$39$$
$$+65$$

(sum of the ones)   14
(sum of the tens)   90
                    104

Table 15.3. Hitchings' Low-Stress Algorithm

Problem: 45 + 77 + 56 + 83 + 27 + 39 =

45
77   1) Add 5 + 7 and record 12, put the "1" above the tens.
56   2) Add 2 + 6 and record 8, no tens to carry.
83   3) Add 8 +3 and record 11, put the "1" above the tens.
27   4) Add 1 +7 and record 8, no tens to carry.
39   5) Add 8 + 9 and record 17, put the "1" above the tens.
      6) Add 3 + 4 and record 7, no tens to carry.
      7) Add 7 + 7 and record 14, put the "1" in the hundreds
      8) Add 4 + 5 and record 9, no hundreds to carry.
      9) Add 9 + 8 and record 17, put the "1" in the hundreds.
      10) Add 7 + 2 and record 9, no hundreds to carry.
      11) Add 9 + 3 and record 12, put the "1" in the hundreds.
      12) Add the hundreds place.

Table 15.4. *Hutchings' Low-Stress Subtraction Algorithm*

3247	3247	3247	3 247	3 247
-1736	47	1247	21247	21247
	-1736	-1 736	-1 736	-1 736
				1 511

1) Rewrite the tens and ones places.

2) Determine if renaming is necessary.

3) Rewrite the hundreds, tens and ones places.

4) Determine if renaming is necessary.

5) Renaming is necessary to complete subtraction in the hundreds place. Rewrite the number in the hundreds place.

6) Complete subtraction with renaming already accomplished.

Table 15.5. *Partial Products*

23 x 12

1) $2 \times 3 = 6$

2) $2 \times 20 = 40$

3) $10 \times 3 = 30$

4) $10 \times 20 = 200 / 276$

Table 15.6. *Tips for Modifying Mathematics Computational Assignments*

1. Reduce the number of problems on worksheets for independent practice.

2. Increase the amount of time students have to complete the assignment.

3. Provide adequate space for students to write out solutions.

4. Follow a standard format for developing worksheets.

5. Cut the worksheet in halves or fourths, requiring students to complete one section at a time.

6. Assign only odd or even problems.

7. Highlight the operation to be performed.

8. Move gradually to increasing the number of problems (not more than 20 problems) and decreasing the amount of time to complete the assignment.

Arrays can be used in combination with partial products to modify the multiplication process, thereby enabling students with math disabilities to gain further insight into the multiplication process.

Providing adaptations is often very effective for helping students with mathematics disabilities successfully use facts to solve computational problems. Salend (1994) lists suggestions for modifying mathematics assignments in computation. These suggestions are shown in Table 15.6.

Further adaptations and modifications in computational instruction include color coding of the desired function for the computation problem (Ariel, 1992), either ahead of time by the teacher or during independent practice by the student. This process serves as a reminder to the student to complete the desired function and also may be used as an evaluation device by the teacher to determine the student's knowledge of the mathematical symbols and processes they represent.

Matrix paper allows students a physical guide for keeping the numbers in alignment (Ariel, 1992), thus decreasing the complexity of the task and allowing the teacher and student to concentrate on the mathematical process. In simplifying the task, the teacher then can identify problems in the student's understanding of the process rather than in the performance of the task.

Finally, modeling is another effective strategy for helping students solve computational problems. For example, Rivera and Deutsch-Smith (cited in Salend, 1994) recommend the use of the demonstration plus permanent model strategy, which includes the following three steps designed to increase skill in comprehending the computation process:

(a) the teacher demonstrates how to solve a problem while verbalizing the key words associated with each step in solving the computation problem.

(b) the student performs the steps while verbalizing the key words and looking at the teacher's model.

(c) the student completes additional problems with the teacher's model still available.

Other modeling examples provided by Salend (1994) include the use of charts that provide definitions, correct examples, and step-by-step instructions for each computational process.

Problem solving: Problem solving can be adapted and modified for students with mathematics disabilities in several different ways.

Polloway and Patton (1993) note that students with math disabilities improve their problem solving skills through teacher-directed activities that include:

(a) having students read or listen to the problem carefully

(b) engaging students in focusing on relevant information and/ or significant words needed to obtain the correct answer while discarding the irrelevant by writing a few words about the answer needed (e.g., number of apples), by identifying aloud or circling the significant words in the problem, and by highlighting the relevant numbers.

(c) involving students in verbalizing a solution for the problem using a diagram or sketch when appropriate.

(d) developing strategies for working through the story problem by writing an appropriate mathematical sentence.

(e) performing the necessary calculations, evaluating the answer for reasonableness, and writing the answer in appropriate terms.

Lack of critical thinking skills compounds problem solving difficulties. Several cognitive and meta-cognitive strategies can be used effectively. Using six problem solving strategies that students can monitor on an implementation sheet is recommended. Students verbalize the steps while completing the problem and note their completion of the steps on the monitoring sheet. The six steps are:

1. Read and understand the problem.

2. Look for the key questions and recognize important words.

3. Select the appropriate operation.

4. Write the number sentence (equation) and solve it.

5. Check your answer.

6. Correct your errors.

Further, Mercer (1992) identifies the components necessary for students to engage in successful problem solving. According to Merger, the problem solving process involves 10 steps, which can be expanded into learning strategies to enable students with math disabilities to be more effective in solving word problem. The 10 steps are:

1. Recognize the problem.

2. Plan a procedural strategy (i.e., identify the specific steps to follow).

3. Examine the math relationships in the problem.

4. Determine the math knowledge needed to solve the problem.

5. Represent the problem graphically.

6. Generate the equation.

7. Sequence the computation steps.

8. Check the answer for reasonableness.

9. Self-monitor the entire process.

10. Explore alternative ways to solve the problem.

Hammill and Bartel (in Polloway & Patton,1993) offer many suggestions for modifying mathematics instruction for students with LD. They encourage teachers to think about how to alter instruction while maintaining the primary purpose of mathematics instruction—competence in manipulating numbers in the real world. Their suggestions include:

1. Altering the type or amount of information presented to a student such as giving the student the answers to a story problem and allowing the student to explain how the answers were obtained.

2. Using a variety of teacher-input and modeling strategies such as using manipulatives during the instructional phase with oral presentations.

Techniques to Enhance Mathematics Instruction

For students with math disabilities, effective mathematics instruction is the difference between mathematics as a paper and pencil/right answer type of task and an important real life skill that continues to be used throughout their lifetime. The information following, examines effective instructional techniques that the general educator can incorporate into the classroom for all learners, and especially for students with math disabilities.

Increasing Instructional Time

Providing enough time for instruction is crucial. Too often math time, according to Usnick and McCoy (cited in McCoy & Prehm, 1987) includes a long stretch of independent practice where students complete large numbers of math problems without feedback from the teacher prior to completion. Instructional time is brief, often consisting of a short modeling of the skill without a period of guided practice. By contrast, small group practice where students with math disabilities complete problems and then check within the group for the correct answer, use self-checking computer software programs, and receive intermittent teacher interaction are positive modifications for increasing time for mathematics instruction. Additionally, time must be provided for students to engage in problem solving and other math thinking activities beyond the simple practice of computation, even before students have shown mastery of the computational skills. Hammil and Bartel (cited in Polloway & Patton, 1993) suggest slowing down the rate of instruction by using split mathematics instructional periods and reducing the number of problems required in independent practice.

Using Effective Instruction

Polloway and Patton (1993) suggest that the components of effective instruction play an important role in the success of students with disabilities in general education mathematics instruction. One suggested schedule for the class period includes a period of review of previously covered materials, teacher-directed instruction on the concept for the day, guided practice with direct teacher interaction, and independent practice with corrective feedback. During the guided and independent practice periods, teachers should ensure that students are allowed opportunities to manipulate concrete objects to aid in their conceptual understanding of the mathematical process, identify the overall process involved in the lesson (i.e., have students talk about the fact that addition is combining sets, when practicing addition problems rather than silent practice with numerals on a worksheet), and write down numerical symbols or mathematical phrases such as addition or subtraction signs.

Teaching key math terms as a specific skill rather than an outcome of basic math practice is essential for students with LD (Salend, 1994). The math terms might include words such as sum, difference, quotient, and proper fraction, and should be listed and displayed in the classroom to help jog students' memories during independent assignments.

Varying Group Size

Varying the size of the group for instruction is another type of modification that can be used to create an effective environment for students with math disabilities. Large group instruction, according to McCoy and Prehm (1987), may be useful for brainstorming and problem solving activities. Small group instruction, on the other hand, is beneficial for students by allowing for personal attention from the teacher and collaboration with peers who are working at comparable levels and skills. This arrangement allows students of similar levels to be grouped and progress through skills at a comfortable rate. When using grouping as a modification, however, the teacher must allow for flexibility in the groups so that students with math disabilities have the opportunity to interact and learn with all members of the class.

Using Real Life Examples

Salend (1994) recommended that new math concepts be introduced through everyday situations as opposed to worksheets. With everyday situations as motivators, students are more likely to recognize the importance and relevance of a concept. Real life demonstration enables students to understand more readily the mathematical process being demonstrated. Further, everyday examples involve students personally in the instruction and encourage them to learn mathematics for use in their lives. Changing the instructional delivery system by using peer tutors; computer-based instruction; or more reality-based assignments such as a store for practice with money recognition and making change also provide real life math experiences (Hammill & Bartel cited in Polloway & Patton, 1993).

Varying Reinforcement Styles

Adaptations and modifications of reinforcement styles or acknowledgment of student progress begin with teachers being aware of different reinforcement patterns. Beyond the traditional mathematical reinforcement style, which concentrates on obtaining the right answer, students with mathematics disabilities may benefit from alternative reinforcement patterns that provide positive recognition for completing the correct steps in a problem regardless of the outcome (McCoy & Prehm, 1987). By concentrating on the process of mathematics rather than on the product, students may begin to feel some control over the activity. In addition, teachers can isolate the source of difficulty and provide for specific accommodations in that area. For example, if the student has developed the ability to replicate the steps in a long division problem but has difficulty remembering the correct multiplication facts, the teacher should reward the appropriate steps and provide a calculator or multiplication chart to increase the student's ability to obtain the solution to the problem.

Summary

The mathematical ability of many students with LD can be developed successfully in the general education classroom with proper accommodations and special education instructional support. To this end, teachers should be aware of the necessity for adapting and modifying the environment to facilitate appropriate, engaging instruction for these students. Use of manipulatives is encouraged to provide realistic and obvious illustrations of the underlying mathematical concepts being introduced. Reliance on problem solving strategies to improve students' memories and provide a more structured environment for retention of information also is appropriate. Finally, teachers must evaluate the amount of time spent in instruction, the use of effective instructional practices, student progress, and the use of real life activities that encourage active, purposeful learning in the mathematics classroom.

References

Ariel, A. (1992). *Education of Children and Adolescents with Learning Disabilities.* NY: Merrill.

McCoy, E. M. and Prehm, H. J. (1987). *Teaching Mainstreamed Students: Methods and Techniques.* Denver, CO: Love Publishing Company.

Mercer, C. D. (1992). *Students with Learning Disabilities (4th ed.).* NY: Merrill.

Polloway, E. A. and Patton, J. R. (1993). *Strategies for Teaching Learners with Special Needs (5th ed.).* NY: Merrill.

Salend, S. J. (1994). *Effective Mainstreaming: Creating Inclusive Classrooms (2nd ed.).* NY: MacMillian.

Wood, J. W. (1992). *Adapting Instruction for Mainstreamed and at Risk Student (2nd ed.).* NY: Merrill.

Chapter 16

Dysgraphia: Developmental Writing Disorder

The term dysgraphia has customarily been used to refer to a disorder of written language expression in childhood as opposed to a disorder of written language acquired in adulthood. Written language disorders have also been referred to as developmental output failures. Difficulties in writing have an adverse impact on academic achievement in school and subsequently on business and industry. It is currently estimated that dysgraphia costs American industry and business $30 billion per year.

Written language is the graphomotor execution of sequential symbols to convey thoughts and information. Since writing represents the last and most complex skill to develop, it is the most vulnerable to insult, injury and adverse genetic influences (Deuel, 1994).

Multiple Brain Mechanisms

Writing represents a highly complex neurodevelopmental process, which involves multiple brain mechanisms. It requires the simultaneous and sequential integration of attention, multiple information sources, memory, motor skill, language, and higher cognition.

Reprinted with permission from "Diagnosis and Intervention Strategies for Disorders of Written Language," by Margaret J. Kay, Ed.D., a nationally certified school psychologist and licensed psychologist in private practice in Lancaster, Pennsylvania. © 1995 Margaret J. Kay. For additional information about Dr. Kay, visit http://www.margaretkay.com. Despite the older date of this document, it will be helpful to those seeking information about written language disorders.

Gross and fine-motor coordination, motor memory, and kinetic melody—a term coined by Luria—requires balancing, flexing, and contracting movements as well as simultaneously stimulating some muscle groups while inhibiting other muscle groups.

In order to self-monitor writing output, visual, proprio-kinesthetic, automatic motor memory, and revisualization feedback mechanisms must be engaged. Visual feedback mechanisms include eye-hand coordination and visual-fine motor integration. Proprio-kinesthetic feedback mechanisms include awareness of the movement and location of the fingers in space, internal monitoring of rhythm and rate, and pencil grip. Motor memory feedback mechanisms include motor plans or engrams, visual-fine motor coordination to produce symbols, sequentialization, speed, and accuracy. Revisualization feedback mechanisms include visual memory for symbols, whole word memory, visual attention to detail and spelling. All of these skills require developmental readiness and can be improved with practice.

Requirements for Written Language

The primary requirements for written language include an intact central nervous system, intact cognitive ability, intact language skills (both receptive and expressive), motivation, skill development, practice, and emotional stability. Secondary written language requirements include concepts of organization and flow, writing skill, spelling skill, syntax and grammar knowledge, mechanics, productivity, accuracy, visual and spatial organization, simultaneous processing, revisualization, and automatization.

Dysgraphia Classification Systems

Dysgraphia is often classified as either specific or non-specific (Deuel, 1994). Specific dysgraphia results from spelling disabilities, motor coordination problems, and language disabilities such as aphasia. The components of motor dysgraphia are sometimes related to anatomical problems, executive dysfunction, motor planning deficits, and visual-spatial perception problems.

Non-specific dysgraphia may result from mental retardation, psychosocial deprivation, or poor school attendance. Some children do not develop adequate handwriting skills because they have not received enough instruction in written language.

Deuel (1994) has divided dysgraphia into three subtypes:

- dyslexic dysgraphia

- dysgraphia due to motor clumsiness, and

- dysgraphia due to a defect in the understanding of space

In dyslexic dysgraphia, spontaneously written text is poorly legible and spelling is severely abnormal. Copying of written text is relatively preserved, however, and finger tapping speed on a neuropsychological battery is generally normal.

Dysgraphia due to motor clumsiness is associated with poorly legible spontaneously written text, preserved spelling, and poorly legible copying of written text. Finger tapping in such cases is generally abnormal. Dysgraphia due to a defect in understanding of space is associated with poorly legible spontaneously written text, preserved spelling, poorly legible copying of written text, and normal finger tapping speed.

Assessment Issues

There are a variety of assessment issues which must be addressed in evaluating disorders of written language. These include the various characteristics of the dysgraphic writer, such as fine-motor/writing speed, attention and concentration, writing organization, spelling, knowledge and use of vocabulary, language expression, and perception of details.

Assessment instruments which may be useful in diagnosing written language disorders include the Processing Speed Index scores from the *WISC-III*, the Developmental Test of Visual-Motor Integration, the Bender-Gestalt, the Jordan Left-Right Reversal Test, and a variety of written language achievement measures including the Test of Written Language, the Woodcock-Johnson Psycho-Educational Battery (Revised) and the Diagnostic Achievement Battery (Second Edition).

In addition to characteristics of the writer, the school psychologist must access the type of instruction that has been provided to the learner and the student's response to the writing curriculum. Various characteristics of instruction which should be incorporated into the background knowledge and included in the history taking of the student include: penmanship instruction, instruction on how to organize and arrange thoughts, and instruction on written language rules including capitalization, punctuation, grammar, spelling and sentence structure. The psychologist should determine whether direct instruction has been provided and whether note-taking methods have been taught and practiced.

Traditionally, in many classrooms currently, relatively little time is allocated to the cognitively complex business of writing (Graves, 1983). It may well be the case that many of the difficulties so many students experience with writing are due to the inopportune combination of difficult content to be learned and very little time allocated to learning it (Stein, Dixon & Isaacson, 1994).

Some current writing mechanics trends advocate teaching mechanics only as the student's interests dictate in the course of a planned composition instruction (DuCharme, Earl & Poplin, 1989). Advocates of such trends suggest that mechanical writing skills, such as spelling, should not be taught formally. Rather, students should be encouraged to invent spellings. Others are wary of this type of approach for several reasons.

First, descriptive research (Graham, 1990) indicates that spelling and handwriting difficulties experienced by many students with learning disabilities hamper their effective participation in composition instruction. Second, such an approach virtually preempts the possibility that many diverse learners will learn mechanics in such a way that their knowledge will transfer. Knowledge transference depends upon the careful selection of instruction examples (Gick & Holyoak, 1987). Third, a concerned shift away from teaching writing mechanics represents a swing in the educational pendulum that can produce deficits in knowledge of these important components of writing (Stein, et. al., 1994). Finally, there is little research support for the notion that writing mechanics will take care of themselves more or less automatically in the course of well-designed composition instruction (Isaacson, 1989; Stein, et. al., 1994). Good writers have knowledge of all aspects of writing mechanics and composition alike.

Intervention for Written Language Disorders

Intervention for written language disorders depends upon an accurate localization and assessment of the student's specific deficiencies. When difficulties are related to the child's age or grade, age-specific remediation of deficit skills is recommended. When specific deficiencies are present, bypass strategies may be useful. When dysgraphia is the result of multiple deficiencies, remediation and bypass of the problem become more difficult.

Remediation strategies for early elementary age children with written language problems include writing readiness exercises, instruction and practice using appropriate pencil grip, formation of symbol skills, practice to increase fluency, and direct instruction to improve writing organization.

Writing studies indicate that students with learning disabilities benefit most from instruction that emphasizes writing as a process (Graham & Harris, 1989; Morrocco & Newman, 1986). This instructional model emphasizes the communicative purpose of writing by creating a social context in which students write for real audiences with real purposes. Secondly, it's based on the view of composing a problem solving process involving planning, drafting, revision, and editing.

At the upper elementary level it is often important to begin introducing bypass strategies for the dysgraphic student. Examples include shortening assignments, increasing performance time, grading first on the content of the work and then on the quality, avoiding negative reinforcement, using oral exams and allowing oral presentations from the student, and giving tests in untimed conditions.

Bypass strategies utilizing computers and other assistive devices are also helpful for students with written language disorders. Prior to teaching the use of word processing software, keyboarding skills should be mastered. Keyboarding can be taught by any teacher who can type (Majsterk, 1990). An excellent program to teach keyboarding skills is *Keyboarding Skills for All the Grades* (1987) by Diana Hanbury-King. Keyboarding skills are best taught on a manual typewriter which requires force to push down on the keys. This helps to lock in muscle memory for the position of the keys.

Summary

Written language is the ultimate, most complex method of expression. It involves infinitely complex multiple brain mechanisms, highly synchronized processing and has multiple sources and locations for the disruption of activity. There is a need for accurate diagnosis of written language problems, realistic remedial strategies and realistic expectations for the learner. A combination of accurate diagnosis, remediation using direct instruction techniques, and the use of bypass strategies and assistive technology can be useful in supporting the needs of the learner with written language deficits.

References

Deuel, R.K. (1994). Developmental dysgraphia and motor skill disorders. *Journal of Child Neurology*, 10 (1), 6-8.

DuCharme, C.; Earl, J.; and Poplin, M.S. (1989). The author model: The constructivist view of the writing process. *Learning Disability Quarterly*, 12, 237-242.

Gick, M.L. and Holyoke, K.J. (1987). The cognitive basis of knowledge transfer. In S.M. Cormier and J.D. Hagman (Eds.), *Transfer of Learning: Contemporary Research and Applications* (pp. 9-46). CA: Academic Press.

Graham, S. (1990). The role of production factors in learning disabled students' compositions. *Journal of Educational Psychology*, 80, 356-361.

Graham, S. and Harris, K.R. (1989). Improving learning disabled students' skills at composing essays: Self-instructional strategy training. *Exceptional Children*, 56, 201-214.

Graves, D. (1983). *Writing: Teachers and Children at Work.* NH: Heinemann.

Hanbury-King, D. (1987). *Keyboarding Skills for All the Grades.* MA: Educators Publishing.

Isaacson, S. (1989). Role of secretary vs. author: Resolving the conflict in writing instruction. *Learning Disability Quarterly*, 12, 209-217.

Majsterek, D.J. (1990). Writing disabilities: Is word processing the answer? *Intervention in School and Clinic*, 26 (2), 93-97.

Morrocco, C.C. and Newman, S.B. (1986). Learning disabled students' difficulties in learning to use a work processor: Implications for instruction and software evaluation. *Journal of Learning Disabilities*, 19, 248-253.

Stein, M.; Dixon, R.C.; and Isaacson, S. (1994). Effective writing instruction for diverse learners. *School Psychology Review*, 23 (3), 392-405.

Chapter 17

Strategies for Dealing with Dysgraphia

A common teaching technique is to have the students write information to reinforce the material. For example, spelling programs often encourage students to write each spelling word five times or 20 times. For many students, the kinesthetic process of writing reinforces what is to be learned. However, for a small group of students, rather than reinforcing and consolidating information, the process of writing actually interferes with learning. These students struggle to write and consequently spend much more time than their peers on a writing assignment. Even so, they remember less: the act of writing greatly interferes with learning. Cognitively, so much of their energy is spent on the process that they often do not learn or some times even process the content of what they are working on. Some students with severe dysgraphia may actually complete a writing assignment and then have to reread it to determine what they wrote, especially in a copying task or if they are focusing on neatness.

Educators expect students to learn from the process of writing, yet these students find that the process of writing actually interferes with learning. How, then, can they adequately learn to use the process of writing to express their ideas?

Why does this occur? Dysgraphia is a problem with the writing process. For these students, there is an underlying reason that their

Reprinted with permission from "Strategies for Dealing with Dysgraphia," by Regina G. Richards, M.A., educational therapist and director of the Richards Educational Therapy Center in Riverside, California. © 1999 RET Center Press. Complete information about Ms. Richards is included at the end of this chapter.

papers are messy or that their speed is excessively fast or extremely slow. It is unfair to label them as poorly motivated, careless, lazy, or impulsive. While these interpretations may be true on the surface, they are not the root of what is happening. The root for dysgraphia is actually found within the processing system involved with sequencing, especially the motor movements which should be sequential and very automatic.

Students with dysgraphia need to develop both compensations and remediation strategies. Compensations are techniques to bypass the problem and reduce the negative impact on learning. This is accomplished by avoiding the difficulty, changing the assignment expectations, or using strategies to aid a particular aspect of the task. Compensations can also be termed bypass strategies or accommodations, the latter term used more frequently in legal situations. Remediation provides additional structured practice or re-teaching of the skill or concept using specialized techniques to match the student's processing style and need.

The astute teacher or parent must first determine the point at which the student becomes confused or begins to struggle. Does it begin as soon as the student starts to write? Is it halfway through the paragraph? Is it when the student tries to think about more complex ideas rather than just write a sentence or perform a copying task? When these determinations are made, it is important to identify which components of the task cause the confusions and/or struggles. Is it the use of manuscript, or the use of cursive? Is it the process of dealing with mechanics while writing? Is it the process of trying to think and plan while writing?

Remedial Strategies

It is critical that students do not totally avoid the process of writing, no matter how severe their dysgraphia. Writing is an important life skill necessary for signing documents, filling out forms, writing checks, taking telephone messages or writing a grocery list. Therefore, students need to be able to write, even if they cannot maintain writing for long periods of time.

Young students should receive remediation in letter form, automaticity, and fluency. They need specific multisensory techniques that encourage them to verbalize the motor sequences of the form of letters (for example, b is big stick down, circle away from my body). Students should also use large air writing to develop a more efficient motor memory for the sequence of steps necessary in making each letter. This is because air writing causes students to use many more muscles than they use when writing with a pencil. Multisensory techniques should be utilized for teaching both manuscript and cursive writing. The techniques need to be practiced substantially so that the letters are fairly automatic before the student is asked to use these skills to communicate ideas.

Some students may be able to copy and write single sentences with a fair degree of ease, but they struggle tremendously with paragraph writing. These students will need to be taught techniques that enable them to perform each subpart prior to pulling together all the parts. Substantial modeling will be necessary at each stage for the student to be successful. For example, when writing a paragraph, students can be taught the following eight steps:

1. Think about your ideas and elaborate on each part of the ideas.

2. Organize the ideas you want to express. This type of organization is easily performed using visual graphic organizers. For example, you can create a mind map so that the main idea is placed in a circle in the center of the page and supporting facts are written on lines coming out of the main circle, similar to the arms of a spider or spokes on a wheel. Many visual organizer formats can be used, with different formats appropriate for different situations.

3. Analyze your graphic organizer to determine if you included all of your ideas. If you have difficulty with spelling, make a list of the more difficult or important words you may want to include in your writing. Having this reference list will help your writing flow more because you will not have to stop to think of how to spell the big words.

4. Now, write a draft of your paragraph (or paper), focusing on the content or ideas. If you have a computer, it is best if you type your draft directly on the keyboard. This will make it much easier to proofread and revise.

5. Proof and editing: you will need specific techniques and strategies to proofread your paper, checking for appropriate use of punctuation, capitalization, and grammar. Then use a spell checker to fix your spelling.

6. Revise your paragraph, incorporating the corrections you determined above.

7. Proofread your paragraph again, editing and revising if necessary.

8. Develop a final product, either in typed or written form.

An easy way to remember these steps is to think of the word POWER.

P—plan your paper (step 1)
O—organize your thoughts and ideas (steps 2 and 3)
W—write your draft (step 4)
E—edit your work (steps 5, 6, and 7)
R—revise your work, producing a final draft (step 8)

The student may need substantial modeling at each stage to be successful.

Some dysgraphic students have great difficulty with spelling, especially if sequencing is a major issue for them. Additionally, many dysgraphic students experience dyslexia, a sequential processing problem that affects reading and spelling. These students need very specific remedial assistance in learning to spell phonetically. It is critical that they are able to represent unknown words using good phonetic equivalences. If they are able to spell logically and phonetically, they will be able to use a phonetically-based spell checker, such as a spell checker in one of the Franklin resource products. These handheld devices recognize words using phonetic logic rather than relying on the orthographic sequence, as do most spell checkers on a computer word processing program. The sidebar below presents a poem this author found on the Internet, which exemplifies why a computer spell checker may not be sufficient for some students with spelling struggles.

A Little Poem Regarding

Computer Spell Checkers . .(Author unknown; obtained from Internet)

Eye halve a spelling chequer
It came with my pea sea
It plainly marques four my revue
Miss steaks eye kin knot sea.

Eye strike a key and type a word
And weight four it two say
Weather eye am wrong oar write
It shows me strait a weigh.

As soon as a mist ache is maid
It nose bee fore two long
And eye can put the error rite
Its rare lea ever wrong.

Eye have run this poem threw it
I am shore your pleased two no
Its letter perfect awl the weigh
My chequer tolled me sew.

Another vital aspect of remedial assistance that is especially important for young children involves the student's pencil grip. Students
should be helped and encouraged to use a consistent and efficient
pencil grip right from the beginning of their writing experience. The
distance from the student's finger to the pencil point should consistently be between ¾ inch-1 inch. Pressure on the pencil should be
moderate, not too heavy and not too light. The angle of the pencil
should be approximately 45% with the page and slanted toward the
student's writing arm. The long edge of the student's paper and his
writing arm should be parallel, like railroad tracks. With some young
students, pencil habits can be changed to a more appropriate form by
using a plastic pencil grip (many of which are on the market in a variety of shapes and formats), It is much easier and more efficient to
encourage students at the very beginning of their writing experience
to develop these appropriate habits through frequent modeling and
positive feedback. Older students who have developed firm habits,
even if the habits are not efficient, find that it is very time consuming to
make changes. Therefore, when making a decision on adapting a
student's habits, it is extremely important to consider the time/energy
ratio. Is it worth the amount of time necessary to make the change to
help the student be more efficient? If not, it is critical to make sure
the student has efficient and automatic compensatory strategies.

Many students with dysgraphia are extremely slow in their writing performances. When this is the case, it is critical to determine what
is causing the slowness. Is it the formulation of ideas? Or the organization of ideas? If so, more work needs to be done on pre-organization strategies and this student's language formulation skills need to
be thoroughly assessed by a speech and language pathologist. Is the
student's slowness a result of slowness in actually making the letters?
If this is the case, the student needs much more remedial practice in
forming letters independently, without having to think about content.
This should be done using multisensory techniques, including saying
the letter and/or the sequence of movements while writing the letter;

using large air writing techniques (writing the letter in the air using two fingers, with wrist and elbow fairly straight, though not rigid); writing letters in texture, such as on fine sandpaper or in pudding; and writing large letters using a squirt bottle of colored water against an outside wall.

Some students struggle with writing and become readily fatigued with the process of writing because of their inefficient pencil grip and poor motor sequencing. Many times an occupational therapist, especially one using a sensory integration philosophy, can help in the remedial process with such students. There are also temporary remedial techniques a teacher or parent can use as warm ups or as a writing break. Some suggestions for helping relieve stress and relaxing the writing hand follow. Students can perform any of these for about 10 seconds before writing or in the middle of writing.

- Shake hands fast, but not violently.

- Rub hands together and focus on the feeling of warmth.

- Rub hands on the carpet in circles (or, if wearing clothing with some mild texture, rub hands on thighs, close to knees).

- Use the thumb of the dominant hand to click the top of a ballpoint pen while holding it in that hand. Repeat using the index finger.

- Perform sitting pushups by placing each palm on the chair with fingers facing forward. Students push down on their hands, lifting their body slightly off the chair.

Compensatory Strategies

The overall goal of compensations is to help the student perform more automatically and still participate in and benefit from the writing task. The goal is to allow the student to go around the problem so that she can then focus more completely on the content. Some example strategies include:

Understanding—Understand the student's inconsistencies and performance variabilities.

Print or cursive—Allow the student to use either form. Many dysgraphic students are more comfortable with manuscript printing.

If getting started is a problem, encourage pre-organization strategies, such as use of graphic organizers.

Computer—Encourage student to become comfortable using a word processor on a computer. Students can be taught as early as 1st grade to type sentences directly on the keyboard. In doing so, do not eliminate handwriting for the child: handwriting is still important but computer skills will be invaluable for longer and important tasks.

For older students, encourage use of a speech recognition program combined with the word processor so the student can dictate his papers rather than type them. This increases speed and efficiency and allows the student to focus more completely on complex thoughts and ideas.

Encourage consistent use of spell checker to decrease the overall demands of the writing task and encourage students to wait until the end to worry about spelling.

Encourage use of an electronic resource such as the spell check component in a Franklin Language Master® to further decrease the demands. If student has concurrent reading problems, a Language Master® with a speaking component is most helpful because it will read/say the words. This author prefers the Language Master 6000 because of its large font size and speech clarity.

Do not count off for poor spelling on first drafts, in-class assignments, or on tests. However, depending on age, student may be held responsible for spelling in final drafts completed at home.

Have student proofread papers after a delay, using a checklist of the points to check. If students proofread immediately after writing, they may read what they intended rather than what was actually written. If necessary, shorten writing assignments. Allow extra time for writing activities.

Note taking—Provide student with copy of completed notes (perhaps through a note taking buddy who can use carbon paper) to fill in missing parts of his own notes. Provide a partially completed outline so the student can fill in the details under major headings. As a variety, provide the details and have student fill in headings while listening. Allow student to tape record important assignments and/or take oral tests.

Staging—have students complete tasks in logical steps or increments instead of all at once.

Prioritization—stress or de-emphasize certain task components during a complex activity. For example, students can focus on using descriptive words in one assignment, and in another, focus on using compound sentences. Also, design assignments to be evaluated on specific parts of the writing process (prioritization). Remove neatness as grading criteria, except on computer-generated papers. Reduce copying aspects of tasks, such as providing a math worksheet rather than requiring student to copy problems from the book. A copying buddy can be helpful in copying the problems using carbon paper.

Have younger students use large graph paper for math calculation to keep columns and rows straight. Older student may use loose leaf paper turned sideways to help maintain straight columns. Allow and encourage use of abbreviations for in-class writing assignments (such as b/4 for before or b/c for because). Have the student keep a list of appropriate abbreviations in his notebook and taped to his desk for easy reference. Begin with only a few and increase as the first few become automatic. Reinforce the positive aspects of student's efforts. Be patient. Encourage student to be patient with himself.

A Note on Creativity

Dysgraphia does not have to limit creativity, as identified by the following sample composed on a computer by a 12-year-old dyslexic and dysgraphic student.

a) First draft of creative story as typed by 12-year-old student:

the way I describe a bumby ride is like wothgan mowtsarts mowsek. eshe bumby rowd is like a song. Eshe bumb is the a note eche uncon at the sam time ste is. that was the mewstere to mowts mowsuk it was vare metereus and unperdekdable.So the next time you drive down a bumby theak of mowtsart.

b) Same story. Student read to teacher using his draft:

"The way I describe a bumpy ride is like Wolfgang Mozart's music. Each bumpy road is like a song. Each bump in the road is a note. Each bump is uncontrolled at the same time it still is controlled. That was the magic to Mozart's music. It was very mysterious and unpredictable. So the next time you drive down a bumpy road think of Mozart."

A Note Regarding Development of Word Processing Skills

Many dysgraphic students have difficulty with correct fingering in keyboarding skills. However, it is important to expose students to the correct fingering to develop quick visual locating skills for letters on the keyboard, ideally without having to look each time. One important strategy is to have the student practice keyboarding skills approximately 10 minutes a day (this can be part of a homework assignment). The student should use a variety of child-oriented typing tutor programs and work to develop appropriate skills to the best of her ability. At the same time, whenever the student types for ideas or content, whether a word, a sentence or a whole paragraph, she should be allowed to use whatever fingering she wants. Eventually, the goal is for the student to automatically incorporate at least some correct keyboard fingering when typing content. This author has seen dysgraphic students use a combination of correct keyboard fingering with their own style and reach typing speeds of 60 wpm. With this degree of speed and efficiency, it is unnecessary to force a student to use standard keyboarding techniques. However, many students do begin to use the correct techniques, as this is often much more efficient. However, if practice with correct fingering is avoided or not used frequently enough, the student will never have the opportunity to incorporate the correct skills.

References

Acosta, Simone and Richards, Regina G. "Cursive Writing: A Multisensory Approach," in 1999 *So. California Consortium Resource Directory*, International Dyslexia Association, www.retctrpress.com

Franklin Electronic Publishers, 800/BOOKMAN

Levine, Melvin D. *Developmental Variation and Learning Disorders*, 2nd ed., www.epsbooks.com

Levine, Melvin D. *Educational Care: A System for Understanding and Helping Children with Learning Problems at Home and in School*, www.epsbooks.com

Levine, Melvin D. *Keeping A Head in School*, www.epsbooks.com

Richards, Regina G. *When Writing's a Problem*, Riverside, CA: RET Center Press, www.retctrpress.com, rev. 1999.

Richards, Regina G. The Writing Dilemma: Understanding Dysgraphia [out of print], Riverside, CA: RET Center Press, www.retctrpress.com, 1998.

Richards, Regina G., *The Source® for Dyslexia and Dysgraphia,* LinguiSystems Inc., www.linguisystems.com, 1999.

Related Articles

Many appropriate related articles can be found in the Spring 1998 issue of *Perspectives*, the magazine of the International Dyslexia Association (www.interdys.org). This issue focused on the theme of technology and learning disabilities and includes the following articles which relate to dysgraphia:

Jerome Elkind (The Lexia Institute, Los Altos, CA) "Computer Reading Machines for Poor Readers."

Charles A. MacArthur, Ph.D. (University of Delaware) "Assistive Technology for Writing."

Marshall H. Raskind, Ph.D. (The Frostig Center, Pasadena, CA) "Assistive Technology for Individuals with Learning Disabilities: How Far Have We Come?"

Thomas G. West (Visualization Research, Washington, D.C.) "Words to Images: Technological Change Redefines Educational Goals."

Marshall H. Raskind, Ph.D. and Toby Shaw, M.A. (The Frostig Center, Pasadena, CA) "Assistive Technology for Persons with Learning Disabilities: Product Resource List."

Diagnosis of Dyslexia and Dysgraphia

Green, Jane Fell and Moats, Louisa Cook. "Testing: Critical Components in the Clinical Identification of Dyslexia," in *The Emeritus Series*, International Dyslexia Association.

Richards, Regina G. "The RET Assessment for Dyslexia," in The Source for Dyslexia and Dysgraphia. Linguisystems, Inc., 3100 4th Avenue, East Moline, IL 61244-9700, Ph. 1-800-PRO IDEA.

Richards, Regina G. The Writing Dilemma: Understanding Dysgraphia [out of print], Riverside, CA: RET Center Press, 1998.

About the Author

Regina G. Richards, M.A., began her work in bilingual education, working on curriculum development and test design. She has authored books on language development, reading strategies, and classroom visual development, including *LEARN: Playful Strategies for All Students* (RET Center Press, 2nd ed. 2001) and *Eli, The Boy Who Hated to Write* (RET Center Press 2000). As an educational therapist, she has presented a wide range of workshops at conferences across the country. Since 1970, she has been an instructor at the University of California Extension Programs at both the Riverside and San Diego campuses. She is director of the Richards Educational Therapy Center and was director of Big Springs School for 27 years, agencies that both serve primarily dyslexic and dysgraphic students.

Chapter 18

Dyslexia: Developmental Reading Disorder

Dyslexia is a brain-based type of learning disability that specifically impairs a person's ability to read. These individuals typically read at levels significantly lower than expected despite having normal intelligence. Although the disorder varies from person to person, common characteristics among people with dyslexia are difficulty with phonological processing (the manipulation of sounds) and/or rapid visual-verbal responding.

The main focus of treatment should be on the specific learning problems of affected individuals. The usual course is to modify teaching methods and the educational environment to meet the specific needs of the individual with dyslexia.

For those with dyslexia, the prognosis is mixed. The disability affects such a wide range of people, producing different symptoms and varying degrees of severity, that predictions are hard to make. The prognosis is generally good, however, for individuals whose dyslexia is identified early, who have supportive family and friends and a strong self-image, and who are involved in a proper remediation program.

The NINDS and other institutes of the National Institutes of Health, including the National Institute of Child Health and Human Development and the National Institute of Mental Health, conduct

"Dyslexia Information Page," Reviewed 10-12-2001, National Institute of Neurological Disorders and Stroke (NINDS), available online at http://www.ninds.nih.gov/health_and_medical/disorders/dyslexia_doc.htm; and from "Testing for Dyslexia," a fact sheet published by the International Dyslexia Association. © 2000 International Dyslexia Association. Reprinted with permission.

151

research on dyslexia. Current research avenues focus on developing techniques to diagnose and treat dyslexia and other learning disabilities, increasing the understanding of the biological basis of learning disabilities, and exploring the relationship between neurophysiological processes and cognitive functions with regard to reading ability.

Testing for Dyslexia

Dyslexia is often referred to as a language based learning disability. It is the most common form of learning disability. Approximately 15-20% of the population has a learning disability and The National Institutes of Health report that 60% to 80% of those with learning disabilities have problems with reading and language skills. Individuals with dyslexia usually have difficulty with either receptive oral language skills, expressive oral language skills, reading, spelling, or written expression.

Dyslexia varies in degrees of severity. The prognosis depends on the severity of the disability, specific patterns of strengths and weaknesses with the individual, and the appropriateness of the intervention. It is not a result of lack of motivation, sensory impairment, inadequate instruction, environmental opportunities, low intelligence, or other limiting conditions. It is a condition which is neurologically based and often appears in families. Individuals with dyslexia respond successfully to timely and appropriate intervention.

Why Is an Evaluation Important?

If you suspect dyslexia, it is important to have an evaluation to better understand the problem. Test results determine eligibility for special education services in various states, and they also determine eligibility for programs in colleges and universities. They provide a basis for making educational recommendations and determine the baseline from which remediation programs will be evaluated.

At What Age Should an Individual Be Tested for Dyslexia?

Individuals may be tested for dyslexia at any age. Tests which are selected will vary according to the age of the individual. Young children may be tested for phonological processing, receptive and expressive language abilities, and the ability to make sound/symbol associations. When problems are found in these areas remediation can begin immediately. A diagnosis of dyslexia need not be made in order to offer early intervention in reading instruction.

Who Is Qualified to Make the Diagnosis of Dyslexia?

Professionals who possess expertise in several disciplines are best qualified to make a diagnosis of dyslexia. The testing may be done by a single individual or by a team of specialists. A knowledge and background in psychology, reading, language and education is necessary. The tester must have knowledge of how individuals learn to read and why some people have trouble learning to read, and must also understand how to measure appropriate reading interventions is necessary to make recommendations.

What Test Is Used to Identify Dyslexia?

There is no one single test which can be used to test for dyslexia. A battery of tests must be administered. Tests should be chosen on the basis of their measurement properties and their potential to address referral issues. Various tests may be used but the components of a good assessment should remain constant. Tests which measure expressive oral language, expressive written language, receptive oral language, receptive written language, intellectual functioning, cognitive processing, and educational achievement must be administered.

What Should an Evaluation Include?

The expert evaluator will conduct a comprehensive assessment to determine whether the person's learning problems may be related to other disorders. Attention deficit hyperactivity disorder (ADHD), affective disorders (anxiety, depression), central auditory processing dysfunction, pervasive developmental disorders, and physical or sensory impairments are among the other causes of learning problems that a competent evaluator will consider in making the diagnosis of dyslexia.

The following elements should be included in an assessment for dyslexia:

1. a developmental, medical, behavioral, academic and family history

2. a measure of general intellectual functioning

3. information on cognitive processing (language, memory, auditory processing, visual processing, visual motor integration, reasoning abilities, and executive functioning)

4. tests of specific oral language skills related to reading and writing success to include tests of phonological processing

5. educational tests to determine level of functioning in basic skill areas of reading, spelling, written language, and math— testing in reading/writing should include the following measures:

    single word decoding of both real and nonsense words

    oral and silent reading in context (evaluate rate, fluency, comprehension and accuracy)

    reading comprehension

    dictated spelling test

    written expression: sentence writing as well as story or essay writing

    handwriting

6. a classroom observation, and a review of the language arts curriculum for the school-aged child to assess remediation programs which have been tried

What Happens after the Evaluation?

Discuss the test results with the individual who did the testing. You should receive a written report consisting of both the test scores as well as an explanation of the results of the testing. Administered tests should be specified. The strengths and weaknesses of the individual should be explained and specific recommendations should be made.

In the case of school-aged students, a team meeting should take place when the evaluation is completed. This meeting should include the student's teachers, parents, and individuals who did the testing. When there is a reading problem, the report should suggest recommendations for specific intervention techniques. This instruction should be provided by skilled teachers, specifically trained in structured language and multisensory programs.

Dyslexic adults should receive specific suggestions for coping strategies and remediation. Additional help to implement these strategies and recommendations can also be considered. If the testing was done in connection with a current professional problem, the report should include specific suggestions for modifications and accommodations related to job performance.

How Long Does Testing Take?

An average test battery will take approximately three hours. Sometimes it will be necessary to conduct the testing in more than one session, particularly in the case of a young child whose attention span is very short. The extent of the evaluation is based on clinical judgment.

Results of Testing

Individuals with Disabilities Education Act (IDEA) provides for free testing and special education for children attending public school. Section 504 of the Rehabilitation Act of 1973 and the Americans with Disabilities Act (ADA) provide protection against discrimination in federally funded programs for individuals who meet the criteria for qualification. This includes individuals diagnosed with dyslexia.

Chapter 19

Dyslexia and Mathematics

Not all individuals with dyslexia have problems with mathematics, but many do. There are those who have a good memory for sequences and can execute procedures in a recipe style, i.e., step-by-step. They are able to remember formulas, but may not understand why the formula makes sense. They prefer to do paper and pencil tasks and are attentive to the details, but do not see the big picture. Then, there are those who see the big picture and have insight into the patterns of mathematics, but are poor at computation and have problems with remembering step-by-step procedures. They also understand mathematical concepts and like to solve problems mentally and quickly, yet their answers may be inaccurate. These individuals may have difficulty in verbalizing and explaining their answers.

Too frequently and too readily, individuals with dyslexia who have difficulty with mathematics are misdiagnosed as having dyscalculia—literally trouble with calculating, a neurologically based disability. True dyscalculia is rare (Steeves, 1983).[1] We know that for individuals with dyslexia, learning mathematical concepts and vocabulary and the ability to use mathematical symbols can be impeded by problems similar to those that interfered with their acquisition of the written language (Ansara, 1973).[2] Additionally, we know that the learning of mathematical concepts, more than any other content area, is tied

From "Mathematics and Dyslexia." This article originally appeared in the Fall 1998 issue of *Perspectives,* the newsletter of the International Dyslexia Association. © 1998 International Dyslexia Association. Reprinted with permission.

closely to the teacher's or academic therapist's knowledge of mathematics and to the manner in which these concepts are taught (Lyon, 1996).[3] Therefore, there are individuals with dyslexia who will exhibit problems in mathematics, not because of their dyslexia or dyscalculia, but because their instructors are inadequately prepared in mathematical principles and/or in how to teach them.

In addition, we know that individuals with dyslexia may have problems with the language of mathematics and the concepts associated with it. These include spatial and quantitative references such as before, after, between, one more than, and one less than. Mathematical terms such as numerator and denominator, prime numbers and prime factors, and carrying and borrowing may also be problematic. These individuals may be confused by implicit, multiple meanings of words, e.g., two as the name of a unit in a series and also as the name of a set of two objects. Difficulties may also occur around the concept of place value and the function of zero. Solving word problems may be especially challenging because of difficulties with decoding, comprehension, sequencing, and understanding mathematical concepts. In understanding the complex nature of dyslexia, Ansara (1973)[4] made three general assumptions about learning, in particular, for individuals with dyslexia. These assumptions affect the way one needs to provide instruction. They are:

- learning involves the recognition of patterns which become bits of knowledge that are then organized into larger and more meaningful units

- learning for some children is more difficult than for others because of deficits that interfere with the ready recognition of patterns

- some children have difficulty with the organization of parts into wholes, due to a disability in the handling of spatial and temporal relationships or to unique problems with integration, sequencing, or memory

Therefore, teachers and academic therapists who provide remedial instruction in mathematics to these individuals must have an understanding of the nature of dyslexia and how it affects learning, not only in written language, but also in mathematics. Additionally, the instructor needs to have an understanding of the mathematics curriculum; the ability to use a variety of instructional techniques that are simultaneously multisensory and which provide for explicit instruction that is systematic, cumulative, diagnostic, and both synthetic and analytical — as well as a knowledge of current research in mathematical instruction.

Simply just being good at mathematics is not enough. The teacher and academic therapist need to understand that mathematics is problem-solving which involves reasoning and the ability to read, write, discuss and convey ideas using mathematical signs, symbols and terms. This requires an understanding of mathematical knowledge, both conceptual (relationships constructed internally and connected to already existing ideas) and procedural (knowledge of symbols used to represent mathematics, and the rules and procedures that are used to carry out mathematical tasks). Both are important and need to be understood. For procedural knowledge, the most important connection is to the conceptual knowledge that supports it; otherwise, procedural knowledge will be learned rigidly and used narrowly. Usually, when there is a connection to a conceptual basis, the procedure is not only understood, but the learner will have access to other ideas associated with the concept (Van de Walle, 1994).[5] For individuals with dyslexia, this linkage is critical and language plays an important role.

To assist individuals with dyslexia in making this linkage, it is essential that teachers and academic therapists provide instruction that allows the learner to work through the following cognitive developmental stages when teaching mathematical concepts at all grade levels: concrete, pictorial, symbolic, and abstract. Individuals with dyslexia will learn best when provided with concrete manipulatives with which they can work or experiment. These help build memory as well as allowing for revisualization when memory fails. The next stage, pictorial, is one which may be brief, but is essential for beginning the transition away from the concrete. This is where individuals recognize or draw pictures to represent concrete materials without the materials themselves. Symbols, i.e., numerals, plus signs, etc., are introduced when individuals understand the basic concept, thereby making the connection to procedural knowledge. Finally, the abstract stage is where individuals are able to think about concepts and solve problems without the presence of manipulatives, pictures, and symbols. (Steeves & Tomey, 1998a).[6]

According to Steeves and Tomey (1998a),[7] it is important that the four developmental stages are linked through language for these individuals. There are three kinds of language which allow one to fully integrate mathematical learning. First, is the individual's own language. No matter how imperfect this language is, it is important that the individual discusses, questions, and states what she/he has learned. Second, is the language of the instructor, or standard English, which clarifies the learner's own language, and links to the third language, the language of mathematics. The language of mathematics is not just the vocabulary but the use of sign, symbols, and terms to express mathematical ideas, such as $2 + 4 = 6$. Also, language allows the instructor to determine if the learner understands the concept and is not just following steps demonstrated by the instructor to complete a process, even at the concrete stage.

For these reasons, teachers and academic therapists who, in mathematics, work with individuals with dyslexia, must be well-trained in multisensory structured techniques both in language and mathematics instruction and remediation. They must not only demonstrate competencies in knowledge and skills in teaching language to these individuals, but also demonstrate the following competencies in mathematics (Steeves and Tomey, 1998b).[8]

- Understanding of the mathematics and the use of appropriate methodology, technology, and manipulatives within the following content:

    Number systems, their structure, basic operations and properties

    Elementary number theory, ratio, proportion and percent

    Algebra

    Measurement systems—U.S. and metric

    Geometry: geometric figures, their properties and relationships

    Probability

    Discrete mathematics: symbolic logic, sets, permutations and combinations

    Computer science: terminology, simple programming, and software applications

- Understanding of the sequential nature of mathematics, and the mathematical structures inherent in the content strands.

- Understanding of the connections among mathematical concepts and procedures and their practical applications.

- Understanding of and the ability to use the four processes— becoming mathematical problem-solvers, reasoning mathematically, communicating mathematically, and making mathematical connections at different levels of complexity.

- Understanding the role of technology, and the ability to use graphing utilities and computers to teach mathematics.

- Understanding of and ability to select, adapt, evaluate, and use instructional materials and resources, including technology.

- Understanding of and the ability to use strategies for managing, assessing, and monitoring student learning, including diagnosing student errors.

- Understanding of and the ability to use strategies to teach mathematics to diverse learners.

References

1. Steeves, K.J. (1983). Memory as a factor in the computational efficiency of dyslexic children with high abstract reasoning ability. *Annals of Dyslexia*, 33,141-152. Baltimore: International Dyslexia Association.

2. Ansara A. (1973). The language therapist as a basic mathematics tutor for adolescents. *Bulletin of the Orton Society*, 23, 119-138.

3. Lyon, G.R. (1996). State of Research. In Cramer, S. & Ellis, W. (Eds.), *Learning Disabilities: Lifelong Issues* (pp. 3-61). Baltimore: Brooks Publishing.

4. Ansara A. (1973). The language therapist as a basic mathematics tutor for adolescents. *Bulletin of the Orton Society*, 23, 119-138.

5. Van de Walle, J. A. (1994). *Elementary School Mathematics: Teaching Developmentally (2nd ed.)*. White Plains, NY. Longman.

6. Steeves, K. J., and Tomey, H.A. (1998a). Mathematics and dyslexia: The individual who learns differently may still be successful in math. Manuscript in preparation.

7. Steeves, K. J., and Tomey, H.A. (1998a). Mathematics and dyslexia: The individual who learns differently may still be successful in math. Manuscript in preparation.

8. Steeves, K. J., and Tomey, H.A. (1998b). Personal written communications to the editors.

Chapter 20

Social and Emotional Problems Related to Dyslexia

When researchers first began to study specific developmental dyslexia, they noticed that social and emotional difficulties often accompanied this disorder.[1] Subsequently, however, these difficulties were neglected, and for some years, only the academic and cognitive aspects of dyslexia were studied.

Fortunately, during the 1980s, researchers and clinicians began to focus on the social and emotional problems of dyslexia. Margaret Bruck, in her review of the research, offers two possible explanations for these problems:

- First, the social and emotional difficulties of dyslexia, "are part or a manifestation of the same disorder as is responsible for academic failure."[2]

- Second, Bruck suggests that because dyslexia puts the child at odds with his environment, he experiences great stress, which in turn creates many problems in social and emotional adjustment.

I believe that both hypotheses are correct. Some of the dyslexic's problems have biological causes, while others are reactions to the disability

From "Social and Emotional Problems Related to Dyslexia," by Michael Ryan, Ph.D. This article originally appeared in the Spring 1994 issue of *Perspectives,* the newsletter of the International Dyslexia Association. © 1994 International Dyslexia Association. Reprinted with permission. Despite the older date of this document, it will be helpful to readers seeking information about the social and emotional problems related to dyslexia.

itself. This chapter will focus on the problems that are secondary to specific developmental dyslexia.

First, after discussing the factors that make dyslexia such a problem for children and adults, I will present a summary of the social and emotional reactions that can result from this disability. Finally, the chapter will offer some concrete suggestions to help dyslexics and their families.

Neurologist Samuel Orton was one of the first to describe the emotional aspects of dyslexia. According to his research, the majority of dyslexic preschoolers are happy and well adjusted. Their emotional problems begin to develop when early reading instruction does not match their learning style. Over the years, the frustration mounts as classmates surpass the dyslexic student in reading skills.

Dyslexics' frustration often centers on their inability to meet expectations. Their parents and teachers see a bright, enthusiastic child who is not learning to read and write. Time and again, dyslexics and their parents hear, "He's such a bright child; if only he would try harder." Ironically, no one knows exactly how hard the dyslexic is trying.

The pain of failing to meet other people's expectations is surpassed only by dyslexics' inability to achieve their goals. This is particularly true of those who develop perfectionistic expectations in order to deal with their anxiety. They grow up believing that it is terrible to make a mistake. However, their learning disability, almost by definition, means that these children will make many careless or stupid mistakes. This is extremely frustrating to them, as it makes them feel chronically inadequate.

The dyslexic frequently has problems with social relationships. These can be traced to several causes:

- Dyslexic children may be physically and socially immature in comparison to their peers. This can lead to a poor self-image and less peer acceptance.

- Dyslexics' social immaturity may make them awkward in social situations.

- Many dyslexics have difficulty reading social cues. They may be oblivious to the amount of personal distance necessary in social interactions or insensitive to other people's body language.

- Dyslexia often affects oral language functioning. Affected persons may have trouble finding the right words, may stammer, or may pause before answering direct questions. This puts them at a disadvantage as they enter adolescence, when language becomes more central to their relationships with peers.

My clinical observations lead me to believe that, just as dyslexics have difficulty remembering the sequence of letters or words, they may also have difficulty remembering the order of events. For example, let us look at a normal playground interaction between two children. A dyslexic child takes a toy that belongs to another child, who calls the dyslexic a name. The dyslexic then hits the other child. In relating the experience, the dyslexic child may reverse the sequence of events. He may remember that the other child called him a name, and he then took the toy and hit the other child.

This presents two major difficulties for the dyslexic child. First, it takes him longer to learn from his mistakes. Second, if an adult witnessed the events, and asks the dyslexic child what happened, the child seems to be lying.

Unfortunately, most interactions between children involve not three events, but 15 to 20. With his sequencing and memory problems, the dyslexic may relate a different sequence of events each time he tells the tale. Teachers, parents, and psychologists conclude that he is either psychotic or a pathological liar.

The inconsistencies of dyslexia produce great havoc in a child's life. There is a tremendous variability in the student's individual abilities. Although everyone has strengths and weaknesses, the dyslexic's are greatly exaggerated. Furthermore, the dyslexic's strengths and weaknesses may be closely related.

I once worked with a young adult who received a perfect score on the Graduate Record Exam in mathematics. He could do anything with numbers except remember them. The graduate students he tutored in advanced statistics or calculus had great difficulty believing that he could not remember their telephone numbers.

These great variations produce a roller coaster effect for dyslexics. At times, they can accomplish tasks far beyond the abilities of their peers. At the next moment, they may be confronted with a task that they cannot accomplish. Many dyslexics call this walking into black holes. To deal with these kinds of problems, dyslexics need a thorough understanding of their learning disability. This will help them predict both success and failure.

Dyslexics also perform erratically within tasks. That is, their errors are inconsistent. For example, I once asked a dyslexic adult to write a hundred-word essay on television violence. As one might expect, he misspelled the word television five times. However, he misspelled it a different way each time. This type of variation makes remediation more difficult.

Finally, dyslexics' performance varies from day to day. On some days, reading may come fairly easily. However, another day, they may be barely able to write their own name. This inconsistency is extremely confusing not only to the dyslexic, but also to others in his environment.

Few other handicapping conditions are intermittent in nature. A child in a wheelchair remains there; in fact, if on some days the child can walk, most professionals would consider it a hysterical condition. However, for the dyslexic, performance fluctuates. This makes it extremely difficult for the individual to learn to compensate, because he or she cannot predict the intensity of the symptoms on a given day.

Anxiety is the most frequent emotional symptom reported by dyslexic adults. Dyslexics become fearful because of their constant frustration and confusion in school. These feelings are exacerbated by the inconsistencies of dyslexia. Because they cannot anticipate failure, entering new situations becomes extremely anxiety provoking.

Anxiety causes human beings to avoid whatever frightens them. The dyslexic is no exception. However, many teachers and parents misinterpret this avoidance behavior as laziness. In fact, the dyslexic's hesitancy to participate in school activities such as homework is related more to anxiety and confusion than to apathy.

Many of the problems caused by dyslexia occur out of frustration with school or social situations. Social scientists have frequently observed that frustration produces anger. This can be clearly seen in many dyslexics.

The obvious target of the dyslexic's anger would be schools and teachers. However, it is also common for the dyslexic to vent his anger on his parents. Mothers are particularly likely to feel the dyslexic's wrath. Often, the child sits on his anger during school to the point of being extremely passive. However, once he is in the safe environment of home, these very powerful feelings erupt and are often directed toward the mother. Ironically, it is the child's trust of the mother that allows him to vent his anger. However, this becomes very frustrating and confusing to the parent who is desperately trying to help her child.

This anger is particularly evident in adolescents. By its very nature, dyslexia causes children to become more dependent on the adults in their environment. They need extra tutoring and help with their homework.

As youngsters reach adolescence, society expects them to become independent. The tension between the expectation of independence and the child's learned dependence causes great internal conflicts. The adolescent dyslexic uses his anger to break away from those people on which he feels so dependent.

Because of these factors, it may be difficult for parents to help their teenage dyslexic. Instead, peer tutoring or a concerned young adult may be better able to intervene and help the child.

The dyslexic's self-esteem appears to be extremely vulnerable to frustration and anxiety. According to Erik Erickson, during the first years of school, every child must resolve the conflicts between a positive self-image and feelings of inferiority. If children succeed in school, they will develop positive feelings about themselves and believe that they can succeed in life.

If children meet failure and frustration, they learn that they are inferior to others, and that their efforts make very little difference. Instead of feeling powerful and productive, they learn that their environment acts upon them. They feel powerless and incompetent.

Researchers have learned that when typical learners succeed, they credit their own efforts for their success. When they fail, they tell themselves to try harder. However, when the dyslexic succeeds, he is likely to attribute his success to luck. When he fails, he simply sees himself as stupid.

Research also suggests that these feelings of inferiority develop by the age of ten. After this age, it becomes extremely difficult to help the child develop a positive self-image. This is a powerful argument for early intervention.

Depression

Depression is also a frequent complication in dyslexia. Although most dyslexics are not depressed, children with this kind of learning disability are at higher risk for intense feelings of sorrow and pain. Perhaps because of their low self-esteem, dyslexics are afraid to turn their anger toward their environment and instead turn it toward themselves.

However, depressed children and adolescents often have different symptoms than do depressed adults. The depressed child is unlikely to be lethargic or to talk about feeling sad. Instead, he or she may become more active or misbehave to cover up the painful feelings. In the case of masked depression, the child may not seem obviously unhappy. However, both children and adults who are depressed tend to have three similar characteristics:

- First, they tend to have negative thoughts about themselves, i.e., a negative self-image.

167

- Second, they tend to view the world negatively. They are less likely to enjoy the positive experiences in their life. This makes it difficult for them to have fun.

- Finally, most depressed youngsters have great trouble imagining anything positive about the future. The depressed dyslexic not only experiences great pain in his present experiences, but also foresees a life of continuing failure.

Like any handicapping condition, dyslexia has a tremendous impact on the child's family. However, because dyslexia is an invisible handicap, these effects are often overlooked. Dyslexia affects the family in a variety of ways. One of the most obvious is sibling rivalry. Non-dyslexic children often feel jealous of the dyslexic child, who gets the majority of the parents' attention, time, and money. Ironically, the dyslexic child does not want this attention. This increases the chances that he or she will act negatively against the achieving children in the family.

Specific developmental dyslexia runs in families. This means that one or both of the child's parents may have had similar school problems. When faced with a child who is having school problems, dyslexic parents can react in one of two ways. They may deny the existence of dyslexia and believe if the child would just buckle down, he or she could succeed. Or, the parents may relive their failures and frustrations through their child's school experience. This brings back powerful and terrifying emotions, which can interfere with the adult's parenting skills.

During the past 18 years, I have interviewed many dyslexic adults. Some have learned to deal successfully with their learning problems, while others have not. My experiences suggest that in addition to factors such as intelligence and socio-economic status, other things affect the dyslexic's chances for success.

First, early in the child's life, someone has been extremely supportive and encouraging. Second, the young dyslexic found an area in which he or she could succeed. Finally, successful dyslexics appear to have developed a commitment to helping others. Both teachers and parents need to offer consistent, ongoing encouragement and support. However, one rarely hears about this very important way to help youngsters.

I believe encouragement involves as least four elements. First, listening to children's feelings. Anxiety, anger, and depression are daily companions for dyslexics. However, their language problems often make it difficult for them to express their feelings. Therefore, adults must help them learn to talk about their feelings.

Teachers and parents must reward effort, not just the product. For the dyslexic, grades should be less important than progress.

When confronting unacceptable behavior, adults must not inadvertently discourage the dyslexic child. Words such as "lazy" or "incorrigible" can seriously damage the child's self-image. Finally, it is important to help students set realistic goals for themselves. Most dyslexic students set perfectionistic and unattainable goals. By helping the child set an attainable goal, teachers can change the cycle of failure.

Even more important, the child needs to recognize and rejoice in his or her successes. To do so, he or she needs to achieve success in some area of life. In some cases, the dyslexic's strengths are obvious, and many dyslexics' self-esteem has been salvaged by prowess in athletics, art, or mechanics. However, the dyslexic's strengths are often more subtle and obtuse. Parents and teachers need to find ways to relate the child's interests to the demands of real life.

Finally, many successful dyslexic adults deal with their own pain by reaching out to others. They may do volunteer work for charities or churches, or choose vocations that require empathy and a social conscience. These experiences help dyslexics feel more positive about themselves and deal more effectively with their pain and frustration.

Many opportunities exist in our schools, homes, and churches for dyslexics to help others. One important area is peer tutoring. If dyslexic students do well in math or science, they can be asked to tutor a classmate who is struggling. Perhaps that student can reciprocate as a reader for the dyslexic student. Tutoring younger children, especially other dyslexics, can be a positive experience for everyone involved. Helping dyslexics feel better about themselves and deal effectively with their feelings is a complex task.

First, teachers must understand the cognitive and affective problems caused by dyslexia. Then they must design strategies that will help the dyslexic, like every other child, to find joy and success in academics and personal relationships.

About the Author

Dr. Michael Ryan is a psychologist with a private practice in Kalamazoo, MI. He specializes in working with learning-disabled persons. A dyslexic himself, Dr. Ryan is a past president of the Michigan

Branch of The International Dyslexia Association and a former national vice president of IDA.

References

1. Orton, S. 1937. *Reading, Writing, and Speech Problems in Children*. New York: W.W. Norton and Company, p. 133.

2. Bruck, M. 1986. Social and Emotional Adjustment of Learning Disabled Children: A Review of the Issues, *Handbook of Cognitive, Social, and Neuropsychological Aspects of Learning Disabilities*, S. Ceci, ed., Hillsdale, NJ: Lawrence Erlbaum Associates, p. 362.

Chapter 21

Learning to Read with a Learning Disability

Introduction

The National Information Center for Children and Youth with Disabilities (NICHCY) is pleased to provide you with information about the problems many children, youth, and adults experience with learning—in particular, with learning to read.

Having difficulty with reading is by no means unusual. Millions of people in the United States have trouble reading. Some may not be able to read at all, while others have basic reading skills but might be considered slow readers. It is useful to know that problems with reading are often accompanied by problems with writing, listening, or speaking. Each person having trouble in any or all of these areas should know that help is available.

There are many reasons why a person might have difficulty in developing reading skills. One of the most common reasons is that the person has what is known as a learning disability. Dyslexia is one such learning disability. There are also many other types of learning disabilities that can cause problems with learning to read or learning in general.

Not all troubles with reading are caused by learning disabilities. It is important to determine what is causing the problem. Some causes other than learning disabilities are poor vision or hearing, emotional

Excerpted from "Reading and Learning Disabilities," from the National Information Center for Children and Youth with Disabilities (NICHCY), Briefing paper FS17, 3rd Edition, February 2000.

disturbance, or mental retardation. A person having trouble with reading should talk with specialists in the reading field and receive a thorough assessment. Through tests and other evaluation techniques, the nature of the reading problem can be determined. Then action can be taken to help the person overcome or learn to compensate for his or her specific problem.

Helping Your Child Learn: Some Suggestions for Parents

If you suspect that your child is having trouble learning to read, or trouble with learning in general, there is help available. For parents of school-age children, the first source of help should be the public school serving your area. Contact your child's school principal, express your concerns, and ask to have your child evaluated to see if he or she has a disability. If the school thinks your child may have a disability and may need special education and related services, it must evaluate your child before providing your child with these services. This evaluation is at no cost to you.

The results of the evaluation will show whether or not your child has a problem with reading or learning and, if so, the nature of the problem. You may be told that your child has dyslexia or another type of learning disability. If the evaluation shows that your child does have a learning disability and, because of that disability, needs special education, the school is required by federal and state law to provide special education for your child—also at no cost to you or your family.

Suppose, however, that the results of the evaluation show that your child does not have a disability. In this case, there are a number of actions you can take. If you think that the school's evaluation of your child was not appropriate—for example, only one test was given or the evaluation was based solely upon observation of your child—you can ask the school system to pay for what is known as an Independent Educational Evaluation (IEE). There are usually guidelines for obtaining an IEE at the school's expense. Ask the school or your state's Parent Training and Information (PTI) center about the process you will need to follow to request an IEE. (Contact information for your PTI is available from NICHCY.)

Of course, you can always have your child evaluated independently and pay for the evaluation yourself. Whether the school pays for the IEE or whether you do, the results of this second evaluation must be taken into account in determining whether or not your child has a disability and needs special education.

If evaluation results still indicate that your child's problems in learning to read are not caused by a disability, your child will not be eligible for special education services through the public school. However, most schools have services available for students who are having trouble reading. Your child may be enrolled in a remedial reading program or work with a reading resource teacher to improve his or her skills. You may also wish to contact some of the organizations dealing with literacy.

Suppose, however, that the evaluation results show that your child does have a learning disability and is eligible to receive special education services. You and school personnel then meet to discuss the results of the evaluation and to develop what is known as an Individualized Education Program (IEP). Among other things, the IEP will describe the level at which your child is currently performing, as well as identify the specific services or instruction your child will receive to address his or her specific needs. Classroom accommodations are also possible and can help a student compensate for his or her learning disability. Accommodations can include:

- Taped textbooks available through Recording for the Blind and Dyslexic

- Extended time to take tests

- Tutoring

- Use of a notetaker, for students who have trouble listening in class and taking notes

- Use of a scribe during test taking, for students who have trouble writing but who can express their answers verbally to the scribe, who writes down the responses

- Use of a reader during test taking, for students who have trouble reading test questions

- Tape recording of class lectures

- Testing in a quiet place, for students who are easily distracted

The suggestions presented in the remainder of this chapter focus upon what parents can do to help a child with a learning disability learn and function within the home.

Learn more about learning disabilities. Information on learning disabilities (LD) can help you understand that your child does not learn in the same way as other people do. Find out as much as you can about the problems your child has with learning, what types of learning tasks will be hard for your child, what sources of help are available, and what you can do to make life and learning easier for your child.

Become an unobtrusive detective. Look for clues that can tell you how your child learns best. Does he or she learn best through looking, listening, or touching? What is your child's weakest approach to learning? Also pay attention to your child's interests, talents, and skills. All this information can be of great help in motivating and fostering your child's learning.

Teach through your child's areas of strength. For example, he or she may have great difficulty reading information but readily understand when listening. Take advantage of that strength. Rather than force reading, which will present your child with a failure situation, let your child learn new information by listening to a book on tape or watching a video.

Respect and challenge your child's natural intelligence. He or she may have trouble reading or writing, but that doesn't mean learning can't take place in many other ways. Most children with learning disabilities have average or above average intelligence that can be engaged and challenged through using a multi-sensory approach. Taste, touch, seeing, hearing, and moving are valuable ways of gathering information.

Remember that mistakes don't equal failure. Your child may have the tendency to see his or her mistakes as huge failures. You can model, through good-humored acceptance of your own mistakes, that mistakes can be useful. They can lead to new solutions. They are not the end of the world. When your child sees you taking this approach to mistakes—your own and the mistakes of others—he or she can learn to view his or her mistakes in the same light.

Recognize that there may be some things your child won't be able to do or will have lifelong trouble doing. Help your child to understand that this doesn't mean he or she is a failure. After all, everyone has something they can't do. Capitalize on the things your child can do.

Be aware that struggling with your child over reading, writing, and homework can draw you into an adversarial position with your child.

The two of you will end up angry and frustrated with each other, which sends the message to your child that, yet again, he or she has failed. You can contribute positively to your child's schooling by participating actively in the development of your child's Individualized Education Program (IEP) and by sharing with the school the special insights about your child that only you as a parent have.

Use television creatively. Television, or videos, can be a good medium for learning. If the child is helped to use it properly, it is not a waste of time. For example, your child can learn to focus, sustain attention, listen carefully, increase vocabulary, and see how the parts fit together to make a whole. You can augment learning by asking questions about what was seen. What happened first? Then what happened? How did the story end? Such questions encourage learning of sequence, an area that causes trouble for many children with learning disabilities. Be patient, though. Because your child does not see or interpret the world in the same way you do, progress may be slow.

Make sure books are at your child's reading level. Most children with learning disabilities will be reading below grade level. To experience success at reading, then, it's important that they have books to read that are on their reading level (rather than their age level). Foster reading by finding books on topics of interest to your child or by reading to him. Also let your child choose his or her own books to read.

Encourage your child to develop his or her special talent. What is your child good at? What does he or she especially enjoy? Encouraging your child to pursue areas of talent lets him or her experience success and discover a place to shine.

Adults with Reading or Learning Problems

Adults who have trouble reading or learning usually have had these problems since they were children. Their problems may stem from having a learning disability that went undetected or untreated as a child. If an adult has a learning disability, he or she will experience many of the difficulties described in Dr. Larry Silver's article about learning disabilities in children. The difference for adults who have learning problems is that they no longer spend their day in school and cannot turn to the public school system for evaluation and special instruction. They may not know why they have trouble learning, and don't know where to go to find out.

Help is available. It's important, however, to know what is causing the adult's problem with reading or learning. Knowing the reason makes it possible for the individual to get the kind of help he or she needs. The problem may arise because the person has a learning disability. If so, then the person needs to work with instructors who know about learning disabilities. He or she needs to receive instruction designed for individuals with learning disabilities. But not all reading or learning problems are caused by learning disabilities. Perhaps as a child the person did not get enough basic instruction to build the foundation that leads to skilled reading and learning. Becoming involved in a literacy program might meet this person's needs.

The first step, then, is to find out if the learning problems are caused by the presence of a learning disability. A thorough assessment can give clues as to whether or not a learning disability exists and can pinpoint areas of strength and difficulty.

Resources for Families

Anderson, W.; Chitwood, S.; and Hayden, D. (1997). *Negotiating the Special Education Maze: A Guide for Parents and Teachers (3rd ed.).* Bethesda, MD: Woodbine House. (Available from Woodbine House at 1-800-843-7323.)

Armstrong, T. (1998). *In Their Own Way: Discovering and Encouraging Your Child's Personal Learning Style.* Los Angeles: Jeremy P. Tarcher, Inc. (Available from Putnam Publishing at 1-800-631-8571.)

Cronin, E.M. (1997). *Helping Your Dyslexic Child: A Guide to Improving Your Child's Reading, Writing, Spelling, Comprehension, and Self-Esteem.* Rocklin, CA: Prima. (Available from Prima Publishing at 916-632-4400.)

Directory of Facilities and Services for the Learning Disabled (17th Ed.). (1998). Novato, CA: *Academic Therapy*. (Available from *Academic Therapy* at 1-800-422-7249.)

Fisher, G. and Cummings, R. (1993). *The Survival Guide for Teenagers with LD (Learning Differences).* Minneapolis, MN: Free Spirit. (Available from Free Spirit Publishing at 1-800-735-7323.)

Fowler, M.C. (1994, October). Attention deficit/hyperactivity disorder. NICHCY Briefing Paper, 1-16. (Available from NICHCY at 1-800-695-0285. Also available on-line.)

Gehret, J. (1996). *The Don't-Give-Up Kid and Learning Differences (3rd Ed.).* Fairport, NY: Verbal Images Press. (Available from Verbal Images Press at 1-800-888-4741.)

Lab School of Washington. (1993). Issues of parenting children with learning disabilities (audiotape series of 12 lectures). Washington, DC: Author. (Available from the Lab School at 202-965-6600.)

Mackenzie, L. (1997). *The Complete Learning Disabilities Directory.* Lakeville, CT: Grey House. (Available from Grey House Publishing at 860-435-0868.)

Silver, L. (1998). *The Misunderstood Child: Understanding and Coping with Your Child's Learning Disabilities (3rd Ed.).* New York, NY: Times Books. (Available from Random Books at 1-800-733-3000.)

Smith, C. and Strick, L.W. (1999). *Learning Disabilities from A to Z.* New York, NY: Simon & Schuster. (Available from Simon & Schuster at 1-800-223-2336.)

Smith, S. (1995). *No Easy Answers (Rev. ed.).* New York, NY: Bantam. (Available from Bantam Doubleday Dell at 1-800-323-9872.)

Resources for Adults

American Council on Education. (1998). GED test accommodations for candidates with specific learning disabilities. Washington, DC: Author. (Available from GED Testing Fulfillment Service at 301-604-9073.)

Cordoni, B. (1991). *Living with a Learning Disability (Rev. ed.).* Carbondale, IL: Southern Illinois University Press. (Available from So. Illinois University Press at 618-453-2281.)

Cramer, S. and Ellis, W. (1996). *Learning Disabilities: Lifelong Issues.* Baltimore, MD: Paul H. Brookes. (Available from Paul H. Brookes at 1-800-638-3775.)

Guyer, B.P. and Shaywitz, S.E. (1997). *The Pretenders: Gifted People Who Have Difficulty Learning.* Homewood, IL: High Tide Press. (May be ordered on-line through amazon.com.)

Hayes, M.L. (1993). You don't outgrow it: Living with learning disabilities. Novato, CA: *Academic Therapy.* (Available from Academic Therapy at 1-800-422-7249.)

HEATH Resource Center and the National Adult Literacy and Learning Disabilities Center. (1994). National resources for adults with learning disabilities. Washington, DC: Authors. (Available from HEATH.)

Latham, P.H.; Latham, P.S.; and Ratey, N. (1996). *Tales from the Workplace: A Book of Stories Illustrating How to Succeed in the Workplace with Attention Deficit Disorder or Learning Disabilities*. Washington, DC: JKL. (Available from JKL Communications at 202-223-5097.)

Latham, P.S. and Latham, P.H. (1994). *Attention Deficit Disorder and Learning Disabilities in the Workplace: A Guide for Success*. Washington, DC: JKL. (Available from JKL Communications at 202-223-5097.)

Murphy, S.T. (1992). On being LD: Perspectives and strategies of young adults. Port Chester, NY: National Professional Resources. (Available from National Professional Resources at 1-800-453-7461.)

Nosek, K. (1997). *Dyslexia in Adults: Taking Charge of Your Life*. Dallas, TX: Taylor. (Available from Taylor Publishing at 1-800-677-2800.)

Reiff, H.B.; Ginsberg, G.; and Gerber, P.J. (1997). *Exceeding Expectations: Successful Adults with Learning Disabilities*. Austin, TX: Pro-Ed. (Available from Pro-Ed at 1-800-897-3202.)

Tuttle, C.G. and Tuttle, G.A. (1996). *Challenging Voices: Writings By, for, and about Individuals with Learning Disabilities*. Los Angeles, CA: Lowell House. (Available from Lowell House at 1-800-323-4900.)

Resources for Educators

Carvey, D.W. (1993). *Dysgraphia: Why Johnny can't write (a handbook for teachers and parents)* (2nd ed.). Austin, TX: Pro-Ed. (Available from Pro-Ed at 1-800-897-3202.)

Harris, K.R. and Graham, S. (1996). *Making the Writing Process Work: Strategies for Composition and Self-Regulation*. Cambridge, MA: Brookline. (Available from Brookline Books at 1-800-666-2665.)

Küpper, L. (Ed.). (1996). Educating students with learning disabilities. NICHCY Bibliography, 12, 1-16. (Available from NICHCY at 1-800-695-0285 or on-line.)

Küpper, L. (Ed.). (1996). Learning strategies for students with learning disabilities. NICHCY Bibliography, 14, 1-16. (Available from NICHCY at 1-800-695-0285 or on-line.)

Mercer, C.D. and Mercer, A.R. (1997). *Teaching Students with Learning Problems (5ᵗʰ Ed.)*. New York: Prentice Hall College Division. (Available from Prentice Hall at 1-800-947-7700.)

National Adult Literacy and Learning Disabilities Center. (1999). Bridges to practice: A research-based guide for literacy practitioners serving adults with learning disabilities [Training package with five guidebooks and a video]. Washington, DC: Author. (Available from the Academy for Educational Development at 202-884-8185.)

Strichart, S.S.; Iannuzi, P.; and Magrum II, C.T. (1998). *Teaching Study Skills and Strategies to Students with Learning Disabilities, Attention Deficit Disorders, or Special Needs (2ⁿᵈ Ed.)*. Upper Saddle River, NJ: Prentice Hall Trade. (Available from Prentice Hall at 1-800-947-7700.)

Winebrenner, S. and Espeland, P. (Eds.). (1996). *Teaching Kids with Learning Difficulties in the Regular Classroom: Strategies and Techniques Every Teacher Can Use to Challenge and Motivate Struggling Students*. Minneapolis, MN: Free Spirit Press. (Available from Free Spirit Publishing at 1-800-735-7323.)

Part Four

Other Conditions
That Impede Learning

Chapter 22

Asperger Syndrome

Rosalyn Lord is a parent of a child with Asperger syndrome, living in the U.K. Though she is not a professional, her understanding of Asperger syndrome and some of the strategies that are successful with our children are right on target. This chapter, which she authored has been widely circulated, and gives some accurate and useful insights for parents and professionals.

Asperger syndrome is a developmental disorder falling within the autistic spectrum affecting two-way social interaction, verbal and nonverbal communication and a reluctance to accept change, inflexibility of thought and to have all absorbing narrow areas of interest.

Individuals are usually extremely good on rote memory skills (facts, figures, dates, times etc.) Many excel in math and science. There is a range of severity of symptoms within the syndrome, the very mildly affected child often goes undiagnosed and may just appear odd or eccentric.

While Asperger syndrome is much more common than autism it is still a rare condition and few people, including professionals, will know about it much less have experience of it. It seems to affect more boys than girls. In general terms they find making friends difficult, not understanding the subtle clues needed to do so. They often use language in a slightly odd way and take literal meanings from what is read or heard. They are happiest with routines and a structured

The information in this chapter is reprinted from "Asperger Syndrome," by Rosalyn Lord. © 2000 Rosalyn Lord. Available online at http://aspennj.org/lord.htm. Reprinted with permission.

environment, finding it difficult to decide what to do they fall back on to their preferred activities. They love praise, winning and being first, but find losing, imperfection and criticism very difficult to take. Bad behavior often stems from an inability to communicate their frustrations and anxieties. They need love, tenderness, care, patience and understanding. Within this framework they seem to flourish.

Children with Asperger syndrome are for the most part bright, happy and loving children. If we can help break through to their own little world we can help them to cope a little better in society. They have a need to finish tasks they have started. Strategies can be developed to reduce the stress they experience at such times. Warnings that an activity is to finish in x minutes can help with older children. With younger children attempts to save the task help—videoing a program, mark in a book etc.

As the children mature some problems will get easier, but like all other children new problems will emerge. Some teenagers can feel the lack of friendships difficult to cope with as they try hard to make friends in their own way but find it hard to keep them. This is not always the case; many have friends who act as buddies for long periods of time. Social skills will have to be taught in an effort for them to find a place in the world—so take all opportunities to explain situations time and time again—and one day it may work.

Please bear in mind that some information on Asperger syndrome tends to detail all the problems which can be found within a syndrome but that does not mean every child will have all of them. Each child will also have different levels of achievements and difficulties. They are after all just as the others—individuals.

Is Asperger Syndrome the Same As Autism?

The debate on this question still continues, some experts say that Asperger syndrome should be classified separately, others argue that the core difficulties are the same, only the degree to which they are seen in the children actually makes the difference. One expert, Uta Frith, has referred to Asperger children as "Having a dash of autism."

Autism is often interpreted as a withdrawal from normal life—to live in the persons own fantasy world. This is no longer the real meaning of autism. The severity of the impairments is much greater than in Asperger syndrome, and often the child will have little or no language. Learning problems are more common in classic autism. In Asperger syndrome speech is usual and intelligence (cognitive ability) is usually average or even above average.

For the moment it is taken that the similarities are enough for both autism and Asperger syndrome to be considered within the same spectrum of developmental disorders. While a clear diagnosis is essential, it can change through life. The autistic traits seen in young children can often seem less severe as the child matures and learns strategies to cope with his/her difficulties.

Key Features

The main areas affected by Asperger syndrome are:

- Social interaction
- Communication
- Narrow interests/preoccupations
- Repetitive routines/rituals, inflexibility

Social Interaction

Children with Asperger syndrome have poor social skills. They cannot read the social cues and, therefore, they don't give the right social and emotional responses. They can lack the desire to share information and experiences with others. These problems are less noticeable with parents and adults, but it leads to an inability to make age appropriate friends. This in turn can lead to frustration and subsequent behavior problems. They find the world a confusing place. They are often alone; some are happy like this, others are not. They are more noticeably different among peer groups in unstructured settings i.e. playgrounds. Their naiveté can cause them to be bullied and teased unless care is taken by assistants or buddies to integrate and help protect them. They can often focus on small details and fail to see the overall picture of what is happening in any situation.

Communication

Both verbal and non-verbal communications pose problems. Spoken language is often not entirely understood, so it should be kept simple, to a level they can understand. Take care to be precise. Metaphors (non-literal expressions—"food for thought") and similes (figures of speech—"as fit as a fiddle") have to be explained as children with Asperger syndrome tend to make literal and concrete interpretations. Language acquisition—learning to speak—in some cases can be delayed. They make much use of phrases they have memorized, although they may not be used in the right context. A certain amount of translation may be needed in order to understand what they are trying to say.

Spoken language can sometimes be odd; perhaps they don't have the local accent or they are too loud for a situation or overly formal or speak in a monotonous tone. If the child with Asperger syndrome has a good level of spoken language you must not assume their understanding is at the same level. Some talk incessantly (hyperverbal) often on a topic of interest only to themselves without knowing the boredom of the listener.

Difficulties in using the right words or forming conversations is part of semantic-pragmatic difficulties. They appear often to talk at, rather than to you, giving information rather that holding proper conversations. Body language and facial expressions of a child with Asperger syndrome can appear odd (stiff eye gaze rather than eye contact) and find reading these things in others gives rise to further difficulties. Reading at an early age is known as hyperlexia. Some children have remarkable reading abilities although you should check to see if they also understand the text.

Narrow Interests/Preoccupations

One of the hallmarks of Asperger syndrome is the child's preoccupation (or obsession) with certain topics, often on themes of transport—trains in particular—or computers, dinosaurs, maps etc. These preoccupations, usually in intellectual areas, change over time but not in intensity, and maybe pursued to the exclusion of other activities.

Repetitive Routines, Rituals, Inflexibility

Children often impose rigid routine on themselves and those around them, from how they want things done, to what they will eat etc. It can be very frustrating for all concerned. Routines will change from time to time; as they mature they are perhaps a little easier to reason with. This inflexibility shows itself in other ways too, giving rise to difficulties with imaginative and creative thinking. The child tends to like the same old thing done in the same old way over and over again. They often can't see the point of a story or the connection between starting a task and what will be the result. They usually excel at rote memory—learning information without understanding, but it can still be an asset. Attempts should always be made to explain everything in a way they can understand. Don't assume because they parrot information back that they know what they are talking about.

Education

If the child with Asperger syndrome is to be educated in a mainstream school it is important that the correct amount of support is made available. In order to get the correct support a statement of special educational needs should be drawn up from the various advice supplied by you and the specialists. This procedure, when it begins, can take 6 months and be a very stressful and confusing time—don't be afraid to contact people who can help; this need not be a professional it may just be someone who has done it all before.

It is beneficial if the school of your choice is willing to learn about the difficulties that they and the child will face, some schools are better than other on this score. Looking at several schools will give a better picture of exactly what is available. The support currently offered in mainstream schools is by Special Support Assistants (SSA) for a certain number of hours each week based on the child's needs in order to help the child access the curriculum and develop in a social setting. A support teacher with specialist knowledge of autism should support the child, SSA, teacher and school in understanding and teaching the child. Other professional input may also be required such as speech and language therapy to help develop skills.

The home/school link is vital, a diary can prove invaluable giving two way communication on achievements and problems on a regular basis.

Helpful Strategies

There are many things you can do to help your child better understand the world and in doing so make everyone's lives a little easier. The following ideas are only suggestions which you may or may not find helpful.

- Keep all your speech simple—to a level they understand.
- Keep instructions simple—for complicated jobs use lists or pictures.
- Try to get confirmation that they understand what you are talking about/or asking—don't rely on a stock yes or no.
- Explain why they should look at you when you speak to them. Encourage them and give lots of praise for any achievement—especially when they use a social skill without prompting.
- In some young children who appear not to listen, the act of singing your words can have a beneficial effect.

- Limit any choices to two or three items.

- Limit their special interest time to set amounts of time each day if you can.

- Use turn taking activities as much as possible, not only in games but at home too.

- Pre-warn them of any changes, and give warning prompts if you want them to finish a task—"when you have colored that in we are going shopping."

- Try to build in some flexibility in their routine, if they learn early that things do change and often without warning it can help.

- Don't always expect them to act their age. They are usually immature and you should make some allowances for this.

- Try to identify stress triggers. Avoid them if possible. Be ready to distract with some alternative—"come and see this," etc.

- Find a way of coping with behavior problems. Perhaps trying to ignore it if it's not too bad or hugging sometimes can help.

- Promises and threats you make will have to be kept so try not to make them too lightly.

- Teach them some strategies for coping—telling people who are teasing perhaps to go away or to breathe deeply and count to 20 if they feel the urge to cry in public.

- Begin early to teach the difference between private and public places and actions, so that they can develop ways of coping with more complex social rules later in life.

- Let them know that you love them just as they are, and that you are proud of them. It can be very easy with a child who rarely speaks not to tell them all the things you feel inside.

Remember, they are children just like the rest, they have their own personalities, abilities, likes and dislikes. They just need extra support, patience and understanding from everyone around them.

Chapter 23

Attention Deficit/Hyperactivity Disorder (AD/HD)

What Is Attention Deficit Hyperactivity Disorder (AD/HD)?

AD/HD refers to a family of related chronic neurobiological disorders that interfere with an individual's capacity to regulate activity level (hyperactivity), inhibit behavior (impulsivity), and attend to tasks (inattention) in developmentally appropriate ways. The core symptoms of AD/HD include an inability to sustain attention and concentration, developmentally inappropriate levels of activity, distractibility, and impulsivity. Children with AD/HD have functional impairment across multiple settings including home, school, and peer relationships. AD/HD has also been shown to have long-term adverse effects on academic performance, vocational success, and social-emotional development. Children with AD/HD experience an inability to sit still and pay attention in class regardless of the negative consequences of such behavior. They experience peer rejection and engage in a broad array of disruptive behaviors. Their academic and social difficulties have far-reaching and long-term consequences. These children have higher injury rates. As they grow older, children with untreated AD/HD, in combination with conduct disorders, experience drug abuse, antisocial behavior, and injuries of all sorts. For many individuals, the impact of AD/HD continues into adulthood.

Excerpted from "Attention Deficit Hyperactivity Disorder (AD/HD)—Questions and Answers," National Institute of Mental Health (NIMH), 2000.

What Are the Symptoms of AD/HD?

Inattention. People who are inattentive have a hard time keeping their mind on one thing and may get bored with a task after only a few minutes. Focusing conscious, deliberate attention to organizing and completing routine tasks may be difficult.

Hyperactivity. People who are hyperactive always seem to be in motion. They can't sit still; they may dash around or talk incessantly. Sitting still through a lesson can be an impossible task. They may roam around the room, squirm in their seats, wiggle their feet, touch everything, or noisily tap a pencil. They may also feel intensely restless.

Impulsivity. People who are overly impulsive, seem unable to curb their immediate reactions or think before they act. As a result, they may blurt out answers to questions or inappropriate comments, or run into the street without looking. Their impulsivity may make it hard for them to wait for things they want or to take their turn in games. They may grab a toy from another child or hit when they are upset.

How Is AD/HD Diagnosed?

The diagnosis of AD/HD can be made reliably using well-tested diagnostic interview methods. Diagnosis is based on history and observable behaviors in the child's usual settings. Ideally, a health care practitioner making a diagnosis should include input from parents and teachers. The key elements include a thorough history covering the presenting symptoms, differential diagnosis, possible coexisting conditions, as well as medical, developmental, school, psychosocial, and family histories. It is helpful to determine what precipitated the request for evaluation and what approaches had been used in the past. As of yet, there is no independent test for AD/HD. This is not unique to AD/HD, but applies as well to most psychiatric disorders, including other disabling disorders such as schizophrenia and autism.

How Many Children Are Diagnosed with AD/HD?

AD/HD is the most commonly diagnosed disorder of childhood, estimated to affect 3 to 5 percent of school-age children, and occurring three times more often in boys than in girls. On average, about one child in every classroom in the United States needs help for this disorder.

Aren't There Various Types of AD/HD?

According to *DSM-IV*, the fourth and most recent edition of the *DSM* (short for the *Diagnostic and Statistical Manual of Mental Disorders*), while most individuals have symptoms of both inattention and hyperactivity-impulsivity, there are some individuals in whom one or another pattern is predominant (for at least the past 6 months).

How Are Schools Involved in Diagnosing, Assessing, and Treating AD/HD?

Physicians and parents should be aware that schools are federally mandated to perform an appropriate evaluation if a child is suspected of having a disability that impairs academic functioning. This policy was recently strengthened by regulations implementing the 1997 reauthorization of the Individuals with Disabilities Act (IDEA), which guarantees appropriate services and a public education to children with disabilities from ages 3 to 21. For the first time, IDEA specifically lists AD/HD as a qualifying condition for special education services. If the assessment performed by the school is inadequate or inappropriate, parents may request that an independent evaluation be conducted at the school's expense. Furthermore, some children with AD/HD qualify for special education services within the public schools, under the category of Other Health Impaired. In these cases, the special education teacher, school psychologist, school administrators, classroom teachers, along with parents, must assess the child's strengths and weaknesses and design an Individualized Education Program (IEP). These special education services for children with AD/HD are available though IDEA.

Is AD/HD Inherited?

Research shows that AD/HD tends to run in families, so there are likely to be genetic influences. Children who have AD/HD usually have at least one close relative who also has AD/HD. And at least one-third of all fathers who had AD/HD in their youth have children with AD/HD. Even more convincing of a possible genetic link is that when one twin of an identical twin pair has the disorder, the other is likely to have it too.

Is AD/HD on the Increase? If So, Why?

No one knows for sure whether the prevalence of AD/HD per se has risen, but it is very clear that the number of children identified with the disorder who obtain treatment has risen over the past decade. Some of this increased identification and increased treatment seeking is due in part to greater media interest, heightened consumer awareness, and the availability of effective treatments. A similar pattern is now being observed in other countries. Whether the frequency of the disorder itself has risen remains unknown, and needs to be studied.

Can AD/HD Be Seen in Brain Scans of Children with the Disorder?

Neuroimaging research has shown that the brains of children with AD/HD differ fairly consistently from those of children without the disorder in that several brain regions and structures (pre-frontal cortex, striatum, basal ganglia, and cerebellum) tend to be smaller. Overall brain size is generally 5% smaller in affected children than children without AD/HD. While this average difference is observed consistently, it is too small to be useful in making the diagnosis of AD/HD in a particular individual. In addition, there appears to be a link between a person's ability to pay continued attention and measures that reflect brain activity. In people with AD/HD, the brain areas that control attention appear to be less active, suggesting that a lower level of activity in some parts of the brain may be related to difficulties sustaining attention.

Can a Preschool Child Be Diagnosed with AD/HD?

The diagnosis of AD/HD in the preschool child is possible, but can be difficult and should be made cautiously by experts well trained in childhood neurobehavioral disorders. Developmental problems, especially language delays, and adjustment problems can sometimes imitate AD/HD. Treatment should focus on placement in a structured preschool with parent training and support. Stimulants can reduce oppositional behavior and improve mother-child interactions, but they are usually reserved for severe cases or when a child is unresponsive to environmental or behavioral interventions.

What Is the Impact of AD/HD on Children and Their Families?

Life can be hard for children with AD/HD. They're the ones who are so often in trouble at school, can't finish a game, and have trouble making friends. They may spend agonizing hours each night struggling to keep their mind on their homework, then forget to bring it to school. It is not easy coping with these frustrations day after day for children or their families. Family conflict can increase. In addition, problems with peers and friendships are often present in children with AD/HD. In adolescence, these children are at increased risk for motor vehicle accidents, tobacco use, early pregnancy, and lower educational attainment. When a child receives a diagnosis of AD/HD, parents need to think carefully about treatment choices. And when they pursue treatment for their children, families face high out-of-pocket expenses because treatment for AD/HD and other mental illnesses is often not covered by insurance policies. School programs to help children with problems often connected to AD/HD (social skills and behavior training) are not available in many schools. In addition, not all children with AD/HD qualify for special education services. All of this leads to children who do not receive proper and adequate treatment. To overcome these barriers, parents may want to look for school-based programs that have a team approach involving parents, teachers, school psychologists, other mental health specialists, and physicians.

Aren't There Nutritional Treatments for AD/HD?

Many parents have exhausted nutritional approaches, such as eliminating sugar from the diet, before they seek medical attention. However, there are no well-established nutritional interventions that have been consistently demonstrated to be efficacious for assisting the great majority of children with AD/HD. A small body of research has suggested that some children may benefit from these interventions, but delaying the implementation of well-established, effective interventions while engaged in the search for unknown, generally unproven allergens, is likely to be harmful for many children.

What Are Behavioral Treatments?

There are various forms of behavioral interventions used for children with AD/HD, including psychotherapy, cognitive-behavioral therapy, social skills training, support groups, and parent and educator skills training. An example of very intensive behavior therapy was used in the NIMH Multimodal Treatment Study of Children with AD/HD (MTA), which involved the child's teacher, the family, and participation in an all-day, 8-week summer camp. The consulting therapist worked with teachers to develop behavior management strategies that address behavioral problems interfering with classroom behavior and academic performance. A trained classroom aide worked with the child for 12 weeks in his or her classroom, to provide support and reinforcement for appropriate, on-task behavior. Parents met with the therapist alone and in small groups to learn approaches for handling problems at home and school. The summer day camp was aimed at improving social behavior, academic work, and sports skills.

How Often Are Stimulant Prescriptions Used?

Data from 1995 show that physicians treating children and adolescents wrote six million prescriptions for stimulant medications—methylphenidate (Ritalin) and dextroamphetamine (Dexedrine). Of all the drugs used to treat psychiatric disorders in children, stimulant medications are the most thoroughly studied.

Isn't Stimulant Use on the Increase?

Stimulant use in the United States has increased substantially over the last 25 years. A recent study saw a 2.5-fold increase in methylphenidate between 1990 and 1995. This increase appears to be largely related to an increased duration of treatment, and more girls, adolescents, adults, and inattentive individuals (in addition to those individuals with both hyperactivity and inattentiveness/attention deficit) receiving treatment.

Are There Differences in Stimulant Use Across Racial and Ethnic Groups?

There are significant differences in access to mental health services between children of different racial groups; and, consequently, there are differences in medication use. In particular, African American children are much less likely than Caucasian children to receive psychotropic medications, including stimulants, for treatment of mental disorders.

Why Are Stimulants Used When the Problem Is Overactivity?

The answer to this question is not well established, but one theory suggests that AD/HD is related to difficulties in inhibiting responses to internal and external stimuli. Evidence to date suggests that those areas of the brain thought to be involved in planning, foresight, weighing of alternative responses, and inhibiting actions when alternative solutions might be considered, are underaroused in persons with AD/HD. Stimulant medication may work on these same areas of the brain, increasing neural activity to more normal levels. More research is needed, however, to firmly establish the mechanisms of action of the stimulants.

Wasn't There a Large Conference Held at NIH on AD/HD Recently?

In 1998, the NIH held a two-day Consensus Conference on AD/HD, bringing together national and international experts, as well as representatives from the public. The Consensus statement is now available at http://odp.od.nih.gov/consensus/cons/110/110_statement.htm.

What Are the Future Research Directions for AD/HD?

Continued research on AD/HD is needed from many perspectives. The societal impact of AD/HD needs to be determined. Studies in this regard include (1) strategies for implementing effective medication management or combination therapies in different schools and pediatric healthcare systems; (2) the nature and severity of the impact on adults with AD/HD beyond the age of 20, as well as their families; and (3) determination of the use of mental health services related to diagnosis and care of persons with AD/HD. Additional studies are needed to improve communication across educational and health care settings to ensure more systematized treatment strategies. Basic research is also needed to better define the behavioral and cognitive components that underpin AD/HD, not just in children with AD/HD, but also in unaffected individuals. This research should include (1) studies on cognitive development, cognitive and attentional processing, impulse control, and attention/inattention; (2) studies of prevention/early intervention strategies that target known risk factors that may lead to later AD/HD; and (3) brain imaging studies before the initiation of medication and following the individual through young adulthood and middle age. Finally, further research should be conducted on the comorbid (coexisting) conditions present in both childhood and adult AD/HD, and treatment implications.

Chapter 24

Autism

What Is Autism?

The brain disorder autism begins in early childhood and persists throughout adulthood affecting three crucial areas of development: verbal and nonverbal communication, social interaction, and creative or imaginative play.

Autism is the most common of a group of conditions called pervasive developmental disorders (PDDs). PDDs involve delays in many areas of childhood development. The first signs of autism are usually noticed by the age of three. Many individuals who are autistic also develop epilepsy, a brain disorder that causes convulsive seizures, as they approach adulthood. Other characteristics may include repetitive and ritualistic behaviors, hand flapping, spinning or running in circles, excessive fears, self-injury such as head banging or biting, aggression, insensitivity to pain, temper tantrums, and sleeping and eating disturbances. Autistic individuals live a normal life span, but most require lifelong care and supervision.

Leo Kanner first identified autism in 1943 when he described 11 self-absorbed children who had "autistic disturbances of affect contact." At first, autism was thought to be an attachment disorder resulting from poor parenting. This has been proved to be a myth. While the cause remains a mystery, most specialists now view autism as a

"Communication in Autism," from the National Institute on Deafness and Other Communication Disorders (NIDCD), NIH Publication Number 99-4315, October 1998.

brain disorder that makes it difficult for the person to process and respond to the world. Autism has been observed in several members of the same families. Therefore, many scientists believe that, at least in some individuals, autism may be genetic. Scientists have identified some genes as playing a possible role in the development of autism.

Who Is Affected by Autism?

Autism is one of the most common developmental disabilities. Individuals are of all races and ethnic and socioeconomic backgrounds. Current estimates suggest that approximately 400,000 individuals in the United States have autism. Autism is three to four times more likely to affect boys than girls. Autism occurs in individuals of all levels of intelligence. Approximately 75 percent are of low intelligence while 10 percent may demonstrate high intelligence in specific areas such as math.

How Do Speech and Language Normally Develop?

The most intensive period of speech and language development is during the first three years of life, a period when the brain is developing and maturing. These skills appear to develop best in a world that is rich with sounds, sights, and consistent exposure to the speech and language of others. At the root of this development is the desire to communicate or interact with the world.

The beginning signs of communication occur in the first few days of life when an infant learns that a cry will bring food, comfort, and companionship. Newborns also begin to recognize important sounds such as the sound of their mother's voice. They begin to sort out the speech sounds (phonemes) or building blocks that compose the words of their language. Research has shown that by 6 months of age, most children recognize the basic sounds of their native language.

As the speech mechanism (jaw, lips, tongue, and throat) and voice mature, an infant is able to make controlled sounds. This begins in the first few months of life with cooing, a quiet, pleasant, repetitive vocalization. Usually by 6 months of age an infant babbles or produces repetitive syllables such as "ba, ba, ba" or "da, da, da." Babbling soon turns into a type of nonsense speech called jargon that often has the tone and cadence of human speech but does not contain real words. By the end of their first year, most children have mastered the ability to say a few simple words. Children are most likely unaware of the meaning of their first words, but soon learn the power of those words as others respond to them.

By 18 months of age most children can say 8 to 10 words and, by age 2, are putting words together in crude sentences such as "more milk." During this period children rapidly learn that words symbolize or represent objects, actions, and thoughts. At this age they also engage in representational or pretend play. At ages three, four, and five a child's vocabulary rapidly increases, and he or she begins to master the rules of language. These rules include the rules of phonology (speech sounds), morphology (word formation), syntax (sentence formation), semantics (word and sentence meaning), prosody (intonation and rhythm of speech), and pragmatics (effective use of language).

What Causes Speech and Language Problems in Autism?

Although the cause of speech and language problems in autism is unknown, many experts believe that the difficulties are caused by a variety of conditions that occur either before, during, or after birth affecting brain development. This interferes with an individual's ability to interpret and interact with the world. Some scientists tie the communication problems to a theory of mind or impaired ability to think about thoughts or imagine another individual's state of mind. Along with this is an impaired ability to symbolize, both when trying to communicate and in play.

What Are the Communication Problems of Autism?

The communication problems of autism vary, depending upon the intellectual and social development of the individual. Some may be unable to speak, whereas others may have rich vocabularies and are able to talk about topics of interest in great depth. Despite this variation, the majority of autistic individuals have little or no problem with pronunciation. Most have difficulty effectively using language. Many also have problems with word and sentence meaning, intonation, and rhythm.

Those who can speak often say things that have no content or information. For example, an autistic individual may repeatedly count from one to five. Others use echolalia, a repetition of something previously heard. One form, immediate echolalia, may occur when the individual repeats the question, "Do you want something to drink?"

instead of replying with a "yes" or "no." In another form called delayed echolalia, an individual may say, "Do you want something to drink?" whenever he or she is asking for a drink.

Others may use stock phrases such as, "My name is Tom," to start a conversation, even when speaking with friends or family. Still others may repeat learned scripts such as those heard during television commercials. Some individuals with higher intelligence may be able to speak in depth about topics they are interested in such as dinosaurs or railroads but are unable to engage in an interactive conversation on those topics.

Most autistic individuals do not make eye contact and have poor attention duration. They are often unable to use gestures either as a primary means of communication, as in sign language, or to assist verbal communication, such as pointing to an object they want. Some autistic individuals speak in a high-pitched voice or use robot-like speech. They are often unresponsive to the speech of others and may not respond to their own names. As a result, some are mistakenly thought to have a hearing problem. The correct use of pronouns is also a problem for autistic individuals. For example, if asked, "Are you wearing a red shirt today?" the individual may respond with, "You are wearing a red shirt today," instead of "Yes, I am wearing a red shirt today."

For many, speech and language develop, to some degree, but not to a normal ability level. This development is usually uneven. For example, vocabulary development in areas of interest may be accelerated. Many have good memories for information just heard or seen. Some may be able to read words well before the age of five but may not be able to demonstrate understanding of what is read. Others have musical talents or advanced ability to count and perform mathematical calculations. Approximately 10 percent show savant skills or detailed abilities in specific areas such as calendar calculation, musical ability, or math.

How Are the Speech and Language Problems of Autism Treated?

If autism or some other developmental disability is suspected, the child's physician will usually refer the child to a variety of specialists, including a speech-language pathologist, who performs a comprehensive evaluation of his or her ability to communicate and designs and administers treatment.

No one treatment method has been found to successfully improve communication in all individuals who have autism. The best treatment begins early, during the preschool years, is individually tailored, targets both behavior and communication, and involves parents or primary caregivers. The goal of therapy should be to improve useful communication. For some, verbal communication is a realistic goal. For others, the goal may be gestured communication. Still others may have the goal of communicating by means of a symbol system such as picture boards.

Treatment should include periodic in-depth evaluations provided by an individual with special training in the evaluation and treatment of speech and language disorders, such as a speech-language pathologist. Occupational and physical therapists may also work with the individual to reduce unwanted behaviors that may interfere with the development of communication skills.

Some individuals respond well to highly structured behavior modification programs; others respond better to in-home therapy that uses real situations as the basis for training. Other approaches such as music therapy and sensory integration therapy, which strives to improve the child's ability to respond to information from the senses, appear to have helped some autistic children, although research on the efficacy of these approaches is largely lacking.

Medications may improve an individual's attention span or reduce unwanted behaviors such as hand-flapping, but long-term use of these kinds of medications is often difficult or undesirable because of their side effects. No medications have been found to specifically help communication in autistic individuals. Mineral and vitamin supplements, special diets, and psychotherapy have also been used, but research has not documented their effectiveness.

What Research Is Being Conducted to Improve the Communication of Individuals with Autism?

In addition to ongoing research on other aspects of autism across the National Institutes of Health (NIH), researchers at the National Institute on Deafness and Other Communication Disorders (NIDCD) are also investigating the communication difficulties or differences of people who have autism. At the heart of the research effort is a five-year collaborative NIH effort between the NIDCD and the National Institute of Child Health and Human Development (NICHD), which was launched in May 1997. The effort involves more than 65 scientists at 24 universities from around the world, including the United States, Canada, Britain, France, and Germany, who are examining how autism develops. In addition, scientists are also exploring the speech and language features in autism, evaluating current treatment practices, and designing new treatments. Additional studies include investigations of brain development and functioning in autism and the use and effects of certain drugs on communication behavior.

Chapter 25

Brain Injury

Traumatic Brain Injury: Cognitive and Communication Disorders

What Is Traumatic Brain Injury?

Traumatic brain injury is sudden physical damage to the brain. The damage may be caused by the head forcefully hitting an object such as the dashboard of a car (closed head injury) or by something passing through the skull and piercing the brain, as in a gunshot wound (penetrating head injury). The major causes of head trauma are motor vehicle accidents. Other causes include falls, sports injuries, violent crimes, and child abuse.

Text in this chapter is from the following sources: Text under the heading "Traumatic Brain Injury: Cognitive and Communication Disorders," is from the National Institute on Deafness and Other Communication Disorders (NIDCD), 1998, available online at http://www.nidcd.nih.gov/health/pubs_vsl/ tbrain.html. Text under the heading "The Student with a Brain Injury: Achieving Goals for a Higher Education," is excerpted and reprinted with permission from *The Student with a Brain Injury: Achieving Goals for Higher Education* (2001), published by the HEATH Resource Center of the George Washington University School of Education and Human Development, the national clearinghouse on postsecondary education for individuals with disabilities. This publication was prepared under Cooperative Agreement No. H326H98002, awarded to the American Council on Education by the U.S. Department of Education. For additional information about the HEATH Resource Center, visit http://www.heath.gwu.edu.

The physical, behavioral, or mental changes that may result from head trauma depend on the areas of the brain that are injured. Most injuries cause focal brain damage, damage confined to a small area of the brain. The focal damage is most often at the point where the head hits an object or where an object, such as a bullet, enters the brain.

In addition to focal damage, closed head injuries frequently cause diffuse brain injuries or damage to several other areas of the brain. The diffuse damage occurs when the impact of the injury causes the brain to move back and forth against the inside of the bony skull. The frontal and temporal lobes of the brain, the major speech and language areas, often receive the most damage in this way because they sit in pockets of the skull that allow more room for the brain to shift and sustain injury. Because these major speech and language areas often receive damage, communication difficulties frequently occur following closed head injuries. Other problems may include voice, swallowing, walking, balance, and coordination difficulties, as well as changes in the ability to smell and in memory and cognitive (or thinking) skills.

Who Suffers from Head Trauma?

Head trauma can affect anyone at any age. Males who are between 15 and 24 years of age have been more vulnerable because of their high-risk lifestyles. Young children and individuals over 75 years of age are also more susceptible to head injury. Falls around the home are the leading cause of injury for infants, toddlers, and elderly people. Violent shaking of an infant or toddler is another significant cause. The leading causes for adolescents and adults are automobile and motorcycle accidents, but injuries that occur during violent crimes are also a major source.

Approximately 200,000 Americans die each year from their injuries. An additional half million or more are hospitalized. About 10 percent of the surviving individuals have mild to moderate problems that threaten their ability to live independently. Another 200,000 have serious problems that may require institutionalization or some other form of close supervision.

What Are the Cognitive and Communication Problems That Result from Traumatic Brain Injury?

Cognitive and communication problems that result from traumatic brain injury vary from person to person. These problems depend on many factors which include an individual's personality, preinjury abilities, and the severity of the brain damage.

The effects of the brain damage are generally greatest immediately following the injury. However, some effects from traumatic brain injury may be misleading. The newly injured brain often suffers temporary damage from swelling and a form of bruising called contusions. These types of damage are usually not permanent and the functions of those areas of the brain return once the swelling or bruising goes away. Therefore, it is difficult to predict accurately the extent of long-term problems in the first weeks following traumatic brain injury.

Focal damage, however, may result in long-term, permanent difficulties. Improvements can occur as other areas of the brain learn to take over the function of the damaged areas. Children's brains are much more capable of this flexibility than are the brains of adults. For this reason, children who suffer brain trauma might progress better than adults with similar damage.

In moderate to severe injuries, the swelling may cause pressure on a lower part of the brain called the brainstem, which controls consciousness or wakefulness. Many individuals who suffer these types of injuries are in an unconscious state called a coma. A person in a coma may be completely unresponsive to any type of stimulation such as loud noises, pain, or smells. Others may move, make noise, or respond to pain but be unaware of their surroundings. These people are unable to communicate. Some people recover from a coma, becoming alert and able to communicate.

In conscious individuals, cognitive impairments often include having problems concentrating for varying periods of time, having trouble organizing thoughts, and becoming easily confused or forgetful. Some individuals will experience difficulty learning new information. Still others will be unable to interpret the actions of others and therefore have great problems in social situations. For these individuals, what they say or what they do is often inappropriate for the situation. Many will experience difficulty solving problems, making decisions, and planning. Judgment is often affected.

Language problems also vary. Problems often include word-finding difficulty, poor sentence formation, and lengthy and often faulty descriptions or explanations. These are to cover for a lack of understanding or inability to think of a word. For example, when asking for help finding a belt while dressing, an individual may ask for "the circular cow thing that I used yesterday and before."

Many have difficulty understanding multiple meanings in jokes, sarcasm, and adages or figurative expressions such as, "A rolling stone gathers no moss," or "Take a flying leap." Individuals with traumatic brain injuries are often unaware of their errors and can become frustrated or angry and place the blame for communication difficulties on the person to whom they are speaking. Reading and writing abilities are often worse than those for speaking and understanding spoken words. Simple and complex mathematical abilities are often affected.

The speech produced by a person who has traumatic brain injury may be slow, slurred, and difficult or impossible to understand if the areas of the brain that control the muscles of the speech mechanism are damaged. This type of speech problem is called dysarthria. These individuals may also experience problems swallowing. This is called dysphagia. Others may have what is called apraxia of speech, a condition in which strength and coordination of the speech muscles are unimpaired but the individual experiences difficulty saying words correctly in a consistent way. For example, someone may repeatedly stumble on the word "tomorrow" when asked to repeat it, but then be able to say it in a statement such as, "I'll try to say it again tomorrow."

How Are the Cognitive and Communication Problems Assessed?

The assessment of cognitive and communication problems is a continual, ongoing process that involves a number of professionals. Immediately following the injury, a neurologist (a physician who specializes in nervous system disorders) or another physician may conduct an informal, bedside evaluation of attention, memory, and the ability to understand and speak. Once the person's physical condition has stabilized, a speech-language pathologist may evaluate cognitive and communication skills, and a neuropsychologist may evaluate other cognitive and behavioral abilities. Occupational therapists also assess cognitive skills related to the individual's ability to perform activities of daily living (ADL) such as dressing or preparing meals. An audiologist should assess hearing. All assessments continue at frequent intervals during the rehabilitative process so that progress can be documented and treatment plans updated. The rehabilitative process may last for several months to a year.

How Are the Cognitive and Communication Problems Treated?

The cognitive and communication problems of traumatic brain injury are best treated early, often beginning while the individual is still in the hospital. This early therapy will frequently center on increasing skills of alertness and attention. They will focus on improving orientation to person, place, time, and situation, and stimulating speech understanding. The therapist will provide oral-motor exercises in cases where the individual has speech and swallowing problems.

Longer term rehabilitation may be performed individually, in groups, or both, depending upon the needs of the individual. This therapy often occurs in a rehabilitation facility designed specifically for the treatment of individuals with traumatic brain injury. This type of setting allows for intensive therapy by speech-language pathologists, physical therapists, occupational therapists, and neuropsychologists at a time when the individual can best benefit from such intensive therapy. Other individuals may receive therapy at home by visiting therapists or on an outpatient basis at a hospital, medical center, or rehabilitation facility.

The goal of rehabilitation is to help the individual progress to the most independent level of functioning possible. For some, ability to express needs verbally in simple terms may be a goal. For others, the goal may be to express needs by pointing to pictures. For still others, the goal of therapy may be to improve the ability to define words or describe consequences of actions or events.

Therapy will focus on regaining lost skills as well as learning ways to compensate for abilities that have been permanently changed because of the brain injury. Most individuals respond best to programs tailored to their backgrounds and interests. The most effective therapy programs involve family members who can best provide this information. Computer-assisted programs have been successful with some individuals.

What Research Is Being Done for the Cognitive and Communication Problems Caused by Traumatic Brain Injury?

Researchers are studying many issues related to the special cognitive and communication problems experienced by individuals who have traumatic brain injuries. Scientists are designing new evaluation tools to assess the special problems that children who have suffered traumatic brain injuries encounter. Because the brain of a child is vastly different from the brain of an adult, scientists are also examining the effects of various treatment methods that have been developed specifically for children. These new strategies include the use of computer programs. In addition, research is examining the effects of some medications on the recovery of speech, language, and cognitive abilities following traumatic brain injury.

The Student with a Brain Injury: Achieving Goals for Higher Education

Cognitive Impairments

Cognitive impairments resulting from a brain injury are the most significant and often the hardest to recognize—a fact that can confound a student's adjustment to postsecondary life and learning. A student with a brain injury may experience some or all of the following cognitive impairments:

- Impaired memory or retrieval of information.
- Impaired comprehension.
- Gaps in prior learning.
- Slow thought processing.
- Reduced attention span.
- Geographic or temporal disorientation.
- Apraxia (total or partial memory loss of how to perform complex muscular movements).
- Difficulty understanding cause and effect.
- Lack of awareness of impairments and needs.
- Inability to prioritize thoughts or determine the main idea.
- Difficulty following a sequence or schedule.
- Misunderstandings or misperceptions of subtle, abstract, conceptual, or complex information.

Cognitive impairments also may lead individuals to exhibit identifiable behavioral problems such as impulsive decision making, missed classes or appointments, misunderstanding of course material or assignments, anger or depression that appears unwarranted or exaggerated, difficulty managing others' frustrations with them (particularly when no visible disabilities are present), and social inappropriateness.

Recovery from brain injury is a long journey. While some impairments gradually may improve over time, they are just as likely to fluctuate from day to day with fatigue, stress, or overstimulation. Constant change in severity and types of impairment are facts of life for the student with a brain injury; but however anticipated they may be, these fluctuations will challenge and occasionally frustrate the student's family, friends, instructors, and advisors.

Physical and Sensory Impairments

Students with brain injuries may experience a host of physical or sensory disabilities, including neurological disabilities resulting directly from injury to the brain and other disabilities only indirectly related. The following physical and sensory problems frequently occur with brain injuries:

- Fatigue or decreased stamina.
- Broken or paralyzed limbs.
- Blindness or visual impairments.
- Hearing loss.
- Cranial-facial injuries.
- Quadriplegia and other mobility impairments.
- Impaired motor skills (delayed reaction times, tremors, and apraxia).
- Chronic pain.
- Slurred speech and other speech impairments.
- Seizures.
- Hormonal changes (for example, temporary or permanent interruption of menstruation).
- Metabolic disturbances.

Whatever the cause and whatever the combination of cognitive, physical, and sensory impairments, cognitive impairments complicate the ability to accommodate physical and sensory impairments. For example, a student learning to wear hearing aids after a TBI (to offset a hearing loss that occurred with the TBI) may experience memory deficits and difficulty learning new concepts, and may therefore be unable to operate and maintain the hearing aids or to develop new speech reading skills.

Psychosocial Impairments

Higher education offers significant opportunities for cognitive stimulation and age-appropriate socializing opportunities that enable a person with a brain injury to reconnect with the world, rediscover abilities, understand new limitations while developing compensatory strategies, and regain confidence and self esteem. Yet, the combined academic and social demands of higher education may prove psychologically stressful for students with brain injuries. In fact, these students commonly experience some or all of the following feelings when adjusting to the challenges of higher education:

- Loneliness.
- Isolation.
- Depression.
- Loss of self-esteem and confidence.
- An inability to control emotions.
- A sense of disconnection from peers.
- A sense of having lost their old selves and not liking the new people they have become.
- Frustration adjusting to and balancing the multiple demands of postsecondary study and independence.
- Inability to manage stress.
- Embarrassment about forgetting important things such as assignments, schedules, dates, and names of faculty and other students.

Impact on the Learning Process

Erratic academic performance should not be interpreted as failure or a sign that the student with a brain injury cannot learn or lacks intelligence. Rather, difficulty performing a particular task gives the student with brain injury important information about his new capabilities and learning style, thus informing future choices about what and how to study. Through repeated trial and error, the student can devise the optimal combination of class schedule, supports, accommodations, and perhaps medical interventions for success.

Essential to achieving that balance is understanding how brain injury affects learning. After injury, once routine ways of thinking become difficult and tiring, and once-easy tasks now may be impossible. Some individuals with brain injuries have extreme difficulty processing and remembering complex information. Academic tasks, such as the precise sequencing of steps required in a chemistry experiment or applying theoretical math formulas to solve word problems, can prove very challenging. The student may require special accommodations, such as access to lecture content in easy-to-read written format prior to class or a note taker to highlight main ideas discussed during class, to execute key learning objectives.

After experiencing a brain injury, the person may lose prior learning of important concepts. For example, a student may continue to earn good grades in high school after brain injury, yet she may not remember the basic math or history facts learned in earlier grades. A brain injury may also impair the student's ability to retrieve information when needed, even though the student otherwise remembers the information. Many students with brain injuries frequently experience difficulty conveying thoughts in writing or speech, as well. In fact, brain injury can alter a person's entire cognitive process. Relearning to think following a brain injury is comparable to transitioning to a manual shift car following a lifetime of driving an automatic: tasks once deemed easy become tiring and frustrating.

A student's learning habits prior to injury can either positively or negatively influence future learning. Those with good study skills, who completed work legibly and on time and who communicated well with teachers prior to their injury, will be well served by these habits afterwards. Those who learned easily with minimal studying may have difficulty accepting, understanding, or even remembering that learning now is slower or that they need help accomplishing tasks once managed independently. Students who were average or even exceptional before their injury may have difficulty succeeding when applying their prior level of effort.

Like most students, those with brain injuries best learn whatever is most meaningful to them—a student interested in history before the injury may find it to be her easiest subject afterwards. (Students with more severe brain injuries may need help remembering their prior interests when considering their higher education goals.) Yet, the impact on cognition resulting from a brain injury may force a student to adjust learning goals despite aptitude or interest in a given subject before injury. For example, an exceptional math student, prior to injury, may no longer be able to perform abstract reasoning or remember formulas. While certain accommodations may help, the student may have to pursue another major.

Financial Impact

The financial impact of a brain injury can be substantial. Hospitalization and rehabilitation expenses can ravage a family budget, making the associated costs of higher education—such as tuition, books, and room and board—unaffordable. And, in many instances, families of people with brain injuries often are new to the world of disability and, therefore, unfamiliar with available resources and financial aid or with the various government agencies that serve people with disabilities.

Requirements for scholarship money, such as a high grade-point average, inadvertently may exclude students with brain injuries. Federal financial aid programs that require students to maintain full course loads may extend beyond the reach of even high-achieving students with brain injuries, as fatigue or other impairments prevent them from carrying the required number of credit hours. Complex paperwork and myriad deadlines also are common obstacles to the student with a brain injury who has financial need; such students will require one-on-one guidance and assistance with the financial aid application process.

While the authors of this chapter do not know of any nationally awarded grants or scholarships specifically intended for students with brain injuries, the HEATH resource paper, *Creating Options: A Resource on Financial Aid for Students with Disabilities*, contains current information about federal and state aid programs and describes other disability-related scholarships. The paper also provides helpful links to web-based scholarship search engines. (Contact HEATH to receive a free print copy of the paper, or download it directly from the HEATH web site at http://www.heath-resource-center.org.)

Comparisons with Other Disability Categories

Although federal civil rights laws require all higher education programs to provide support services for students with documented disabilities, many programs have limited experience accommodating students with brain injuries. As colleges and universities become accustomed to serving students with learning disabilities (LD)—a growing population on many campuses—the danger is that institutions will give students with brain injuries standard LD accommodations, without regard for the unique and unpredictable nature of their injuries.

Each brain injury is unique. Teaching approaches that work for specific LDs may or may not work for the student with a brain injury. While the two groups share some similarities in learning needs and styles, students with brain injuries have markedly different needs from those with LDs, including their adjustment to the disability, types of memory or other cognitive difficulties, medical complications, presence of physical impairments, and the day-to-day fluctuation of impairments commonly experienced during recovery from brain injury.

Students with brain injuries frequently must relearn concepts, skills, and information not retained after the injury, or perhaps not yet regained during recovery. Any physical, sensory, or communication disabilities they have in addition to cognitive difficulties also must be addressed. Students with brain injuries have different needs than students with LD or other types of disabilities, and therefore frequently require different support services.

But students with brain injuries and those with LDs do share some similarities in how they learn. Both frequently demonstrate uneven cognitive profiles—some cognitive skills are strong, others are considerably weaker. And both types of students frequently experience problems with one or more of the following cognitive processes that affect learning: attention, impulse control, problem solving, reading comprehension, understanding abstract associations and relationships, noticing subtleties or absurdities in social situations, and visual or auditory processing. Classroom and testing accommodations that institutions may effectively use with both groups of students include preferential seating, extra time on tests, and individualized instructions for tests and assignments.

Certain behaviors of students with brain injuries may mirror those of students with emotional disabilities or substance abuse problems. For example, a student with emotional/psychiatric problems may be withdrawn, may overreact emotionally to misunderstandings about class expectations or academic criticism, or may act inappropriately around peers. Such behaviors exhibited by a student with a brain injury may result from a neurological inability to control emotions, memory deficits (such as forgetting important aspects of an assignment), or social isolation caused by fatigue or uncertainty about relating to peers.

Cognitive impairments from a brain injury are the result of neurological trauma; the injured person has no voluntary control over them. Brain injuries may slow cognitive processes, such as verbal and physical responses to questions or demands. While students with mental health needs may react, or not react, due to passive/aggressive natures, those with brain injuries may require more time for a response. Because of these differences, some medications, behavior modification programs, and counseling approaches commonly used for mental health problems may not be effective for the student who has sustained a brain injury.

213

Education and Related Services for Students with Brain Injuries

Serving students with brain injuries still is relatively new for elementary and secondary education systems and may be enormously challenging for all involved. Many students with traumatic brain injuries have, in fact, received special education and related services under placement categories other than TBI. (Prior to the passage of IDEA in 1990, a special education disability category did not exist specifically for brain injury.) Studies indicate that only about half of all students with brain injuries receive any special education services; instead, many receive primarily homebound instruction and others simply receive a 504 Plan.

A 504 Plan is a written agreement between the school and the student with a disability, and his or her family, to provide accommodations for the student regardless of special education placement; this plan is provided under Section 504 of the Rehabilitation Act of 1973. For example, a student who requires only monitoring and administering of medication related to a disability (such as seizures) could receive that accommodation but would not be served under a special education reporting category. A student with a brain injury may be appropriately served with simple schedule modifications, or classroom and instructional accommodations such as in-class note taking assistance, taped lectures, reduced environmental distractions, or individualized instructions for assignments.

In other instances, students who should have received special education services may not have been identified due to a lack of knowledge about the impact of brain injury on the part of educators, family members, and even medical or rehabilitation professionals. These students frequently complete secondary schooling without accommodations or assistance for their disability; therefore, they may not know of strategies or tools that can help them to succeed in postsecondary education.

Miscommunication among school, medical, and rehabilitation personnel, and between students and their families, is common during the transition from medical or rehabilitation facilities to school. Such miscommunication can delay assessment and placement or can result in the assignment of inappropriate services. Students with brain injuries and their families often have no experience advocating for and receiving accommodations, and many newly injured students do not yet understand their disability-related needs. Depending on the length of time since the injury, the injury's severity, and the individual's needs and experiences, these problems may persist throughout the student's higher education career.

Suggestions for Students

Higher education can prove to be enormously beneficial to your recovery from a brain injury. In the right situation and with the right supports, further education and increased independence will challenge and expand the limits of your potential while helping you to recover abilities and develop a renewed sense of identity. Regular practice at performing myriad daily tasks, such as preparing assignments, maintaining a calendar, establishing and sustaining friendships, and living independently, can accelerate and maximize rehabilitation.

You can choose from many higher education options, and any one of them may best match your present needs, interests, and recovery. You may wish to begin by taking vocational training classes in disciplines such as auto mechanics, computing, child care, or skilled trades. Such classes may provide the foundation for satisfying and challenging employment or lead you into a two- or four-year degree program.

Whatever path you choose, you will find resources and professionals to guide you toward and through your university, college, community college, or technical school endeavors and to help answer questions and resolve challenges as they arise. The following list will help you consider your options for postsecondary study. Allow yourself plenty of time to reflect on and periodically reconsider these fundamental questions:

- What are your goals for higher education? Do you want to earn a degree or a certificate?

- How might higher education aid in reaching your goals for rehabilitation?

- What do you want to study? You may need help remembering subjects or activities that you most enjoyed before your injury. Ask friends and family to discuss these areas of study.

- Where do you want to go to school? Do you want to stay close to home at first or are you ready to live farther away?

- What do you need to do to get accepted to the school(s) of your choice (for example, applications, transcripts, high school diploma, or equivalent)?

- What are your new strengths and weaknesses in learning, managing a schedule, balancing activities, and remembering details?

Choosing the right postsecondary program is challenging for any student, but especially for students with special needs resulting from disabilities. Many higher education institutions maintain a separate office through which they administer to the special needs of students with disabilities. These offices usually operate under the name of Office of Special Services (OSS), Office of Disability Support Services (DSS), or other similar titles. It is imperative that you speak directly with DSS administrators, faculty, and students at any program that you are seriously considering. If possible, you should arrange to visit a campus or facility before enrolling, to gauge the feel and culture and to assess campus accessibility. Ask the following important questions when searching for the best possible postsecondary program for you:

- Does the campus have a DSS office and at least one staff member who is familiar with the effects of brain injury?

- Is there a support group for students with brain injuries on campus or nearby?

- If needed, are all buildings accessible to students with physical disabilities? Is the campus navigable for students with mobility impairments?

- Does the institution offer priority registration (for example, registering early and individually) or at least a strong program of assistance with registration and scheduling of classes?

- Does the institution offer tutoring services? How are such services obtained? Who pays?

- Is institution-sponsored financial aid adequate? Is assistance available for filling out forms or answering questions?

- Are medical and rehabilitation services for people with brain injuries available nearby?

- Can students receive the syllabus for each class prior to the first meeting?

- Does the institution provide note takers and assistance obtaining a note taker?

- Is the campus manageable in size, layout, complexity, and distractions?

- Can a student take a reduced course load and still receive all associated student benefits, if needed (such as health care and financial aid)?

- Does the institution offer academic advising with a faculty member who understands the needs of students with brain injuries?

- Does the institution offer career guidance?

- Does the institution offer a broad range of accommodations and special services?

- Have other students with brain injuries been successful at this institution?

Once you have been admitted to the programs of your choice, you will likely need to develop a plan for researching and applying for financial assistance. Such a plan will include consulting books and web sites about financial aid, as well as the institution's financial aid office to learn about any campus-based or state-based funding that may be available. Also contact state agencies, such as the Division of Rehabilitative Services, Council for Developmental Disabilities, and your state BIA chapter (see http://www.biausa.org/states.htm for contact information on each state chapter).

In addition to making plans to finance your education, you should consider the following list to help you prepare for this new experience:

- Find out how and with whom you must register (in most cases, it is the DSS office) to become eligible for services as a student with a disability. Reasonable accommodations become available only after you have declared your disability and presented documentation of the disability.

- Seek assistance identifying the specific resources that are available to help you with the areas you find most challenging (for example, math or writing labs on campus, or community based professionals such as physical therapists or speech-language pathologists). Talk to someone within those programs or who administers these services before you enroll.

- Seek advice from a DSS counselor, faculty member, or student advisor about which courses to take and in what combinations and sequence, and how many courses you can comfortably manage at one time.

- Seek assistance resolving your housing or transportation needs well in advance of the beginning of classes.

- Practice the route from your housing to your classrooms, library, and other frequented destinations.

- Ask the DSS office to recommend and coordinate faculty, therapists, and anyone else who can help you achieve success.

- Keep multiple copies of academic plans, schedules, and other important papers in different places (such as your files or bulletin board, your parents' files, a friend's room, and with your DSS counselors) for ready access.

- Experiment with daily and weekly planners and other time-management tools to help you remember class schedules, appointments, and deadlines.

- Identify any assistive devices, such as learning software, that are helpful to you. The campus computer center or library may already have some assistive hardware or software suitable to your particular needs. The Office for Technology-Related Assistance in your home state and in the state where your institution is located can recommend strategies for obtaining and paying for assistive devices. (To locate these offices, contact the Rehabilitation Engineering and Assistive Technology Society of North America, or go to http://www.resna.org/taproject/at/statecontacts. html, where links to each state office are provided.

Remember, don't give up, even if you encounter setbacks or are forced to change direction. The process of discovering your new strengths and weaknesses will take time. Through persistence, you will create your own path to success. Speak regularly with family members, DSS personnel, or other students about your experiences, your successes, and your frustrations. Get in the habit of asking for help whenever you need it. Over time, you may find a favorite professor, respected classmate, or close relative who will be willing to act as your mentor—someone who inspires, supports, and challenges you as you make your way through postsecondary education and on to rewarding work and maximum independence.

Also remember that you should not rely on faculty members, counselors, and administrators to come to you and tell you what you need. Rather, you are responsible for being your own advocate. In order to become eligible for services and accommodations, a student with a brain injury must identify himself to the DSS office as a student with a disability and must present documentation of that disability. Once registered as a student with a disability on your campus, federal disability laws entitle you to request and receive "reasonable accommodations." Such accommodations merely provide equal access and opportunity to the same programs and activities enjoyed by students without disabilities; they are not designed to guarantee your success. Therefore, you must continue to talk with faculty and advisors about your needs and problems.

The following list identifies accommodations that have helped many students with brain injuries to succeed in higher education. Consult with DSS staff or an appropriate administrator to determine if any of these are warranted or available based on your needs. (Some of these strategies may accede the legal standard of "reasonable accommodation;" others may be unfamiliar to faculty. Thus, you may not always receive the particular accommodation that you want. If a disagreement about a requested accommodation arises, be flexible, work with your DSS provider to identify a next-best alternative, and recognize when to pursue a new direction.)

- Using memory aids such as organizational software, note taking aids, hand-held pocket organizers, notepads, or tape recorders.

- Using thought-organizing aids and strategies such as graphic organizers or information diagramming to sort out the most important points of lectures or readings and to prepare written assignments.

- Developing written strategies for taking tests, writing term papers, or managing lab assignments before attempting these tasks.

- Requesting the help of tutors to aid in understanding class material and to keep up with assignments.

- Gaining access to advance copies of clearly written class syllabi, including a description of all class requirements.

- Using index cards to chunk (or group small bits of) information, key concepts, or new vocabulary.

- Taking more frequent tests that cover smaller amounts of material than the rest of the class.

- Receiving extra time to prepare for oral presentations, to take exams, or to complete papers.

- Requesting frequent feedback from the instructor regarding performance expectations, information to be tested, and course learning objectives.

- Taking lengthy exams in intervals with short breaks.

- Scheduling weekly appointments with the campus writing center, if available, to obtain help in organizing and outlining papers and proofreading drafts. Similarly, math labs offer additional instruction and tutorial assistance.

Suggestions for Parents and Other Family Members

Although all postsecondary programs must provide services for students with disabilities, few institutions have extensive experience serving students with brain injuries, or offer special programs or services for brain injury. You should expect a longer pathway to academic goals for the student with a brain injury than for other family members who attended similar postsecondary institutions. The student may need to change programs several times in a trial-and-error manner before finding a good fit. Others may need to change majors several times, or adjust their academic goals by switching from a four-year program to a two-year college or technical school. The following strategies have helped other family members of students with brain injuries throughout their higher education career:

- Stay as informed as possible about brain injury, its effects, and any support that the student may need.

- Assist the student in clarifying her interests and needs by discussing her goals for higher education, as well as her personal preferences for such things as region of the country, climate, proximity to home, navigability of campus, or size of school. These discussions will help the student identify the type of program—whether part of a college or university, community college, or technical school—that fits her needs.

- Assist the student in developing plans that consider financial need, desired academic supports, living arrangements, and transportation.

- Attend meetings, if appropriate, for orientation to the campus or other parent/family activities so that you familiarize yourself with the campus environment and with DSS personnel.

- Assist the student, as much as possible, with keeping accurate and up-to-date academic records, plans, transcripts, course schedules, and syllabi.

- Remain positive and supportive if the student experiences setbacks.

- Support the student's decision to change majors or institutions if such a change seems warranted.

Suggestions for Instructors

There is a growing body of literature on the education and learning of people with brain injuries to inform instructors about the particular challenges confronting these students and how to teach them more effectively. The following list describes some techniques for you as an instructor to consider when teaching students with brain injuries. While many of these techniques are not strictly required, incorporating them into your teaching method might enable easier access of content for all students.

- Provide all accommodations, support, and assistive devices indicated by the student's DSS counselor.

- Present information, training, or experiences that are age appropriate and pertinent at that time (and remember that interests may change during the recovery process).

- Make learning experiences meaningful and present material in a context that helps reinforce the student's memory of that material.

- Reinforce and provide feedback to the student about the process of thinking, rather than targeting rote memorization techniques, to encourage metacognition (or, thinking about thinking). Offer comments that reinforce the importance of the thinking process, such as "that's good thinking" or "that's an interesting thought," and ask questions beginning with "how," "why," or "what if."

- Provide cognitive mediation: In other words, discuss thought organization strategies and provide your own examples that practice this technique, such as how to construct a research paper from the development of key ideas.

- Teach or practice requisite skills for new tasks or tasks that were difficult before injury.

- Teach skills and concepts in small, manageable chunks and review each before moving on to the next skill or concept.

- Provide opportunities for the student to paraphrase what he has learned or give her specific instructions for assigned tasks. This technique helps to avoid misunderstanding and clarifies any potential pitfalls the student may encounter while performing the task.

- Where possible and appropriate, integrate theory with practice and practice with theory.

- Be patient. Offer multiple trials for the student to make errors and help them see the value in learning from their mistakes.

- Use task analysis—the strategy of breaking down a task or activity into small steps—where appropriate.

- Use a diagnostic/prescriptive approach to teaching, by targeting teaching methods to a particular student's strengths and disability-related needs.

Suggestions for Academic Advisors

Studies that address the general learning process of students with brain injuries and their experiences at the elementary and secondary levels suggest that following a brain injury, the learning process is altered and some aspects of normal learning are permanently impaired. The injured brain can heal, however, and make remarkable adaptations and effective use of compensatory strategies. As an advisor to a student with a brain injury, you may wish to consider the following suggestions:

- Familiarize yourself with the effects of a brain injury, especially in the areas of cognition and emotional adjustment.

- Request information from the student and family, if appropriate, about the student's history of recovery from brain injury and about her special needs (for example, partial loss of vision or hearing may accompany the injury but may not be readily apparent).

- Work with the student to assess the educational environment, to identify needed accommodations, and to determine a course load that is not overly demanding.

- Maintain regular communication with the student and monitor the current plan's effectiveness or need of modification.

- Refer the student to support resources on or near campus, if needed, or to a counselor who can determine what type of support the student might need.

- Consider recommending a reduced course load, instructors with whom you feel the student might work most successfully, and courses that match the student's abilities at that time.

- Provide written information in easy-to-remember formats that are not overwhelming to the student, and provide duplicate copies to the parents or DSS personnel, if appropriate. (Remember to be mindful of a student's guaranteed right to confidentiality. By law, you may not disclose information to parents without the student's permission. Visit the web site of *Disability Access Information and Support* at http://www.janejarrow.com for a detailed discussion of confidentiality.)

Suggestions for Disability Support Services Providers and Therapists

In your roles as DSS providers and therapists for students with brain injuries, you may need to be more proactive in identifying required support than you typically are for students with other disabilities. The only thing constant about brain injury is that it changes all the time. The effects of a brain injury often fluctuate from day to day, and in the course of recovery the brain moves through stages in healing and acquiring new coping strategies. As a result, those with brain injuries may become confused about their abilities and limitations. (Service providers and therapists should not simply accept at face value what students with brain injuries report about their progress.)

Students also may be confused about or unaware of the accommodations and supports they need, in which case the service provider may recommend that a neuropsychologist or speech-language pathologist assess the student's needs. Such assessment provides a detailed profile of a student's cognitive strengths and weaknesses. DSS staff can then help the student understand the results of the assessment and use them to plan majors, select courses and schedules, and identify effective compensatory strategies. Assessment results may indicate that the student needs to adopt new approaches.

Some brain injuries also impair a student's ability to initiate action, making it difficult for them to seek help or to be effective self-advocates. Therapists and DSS personnel should encourage students to develop these skills, which are so critical to the postsecondary success of students with all types of disabilities. Furthermore, students with recent injuries may be unfamiliar with available supports; DSS personnel can provide this important information.

DSS professionals help students identify needed accommodations. They also can rehearse with students how to request these accommodations from faculty and other instructors. Role-playing is an effective tool for teaching these skills. For example, the DSS professional assumes the role of instructor while the student practices describing the brain injury and requesting needed accommodations. Service providers also should encourage frequent meetings with students and provide information in a concise, easy-to-remember format.

Students with brain injuries also may need help reacquiring many of the skills necessary for independent daily living, such as doing laundry; maintaining a well-balanced diet; prioritizing tasks; opening bank accounts and balancing checkbooks; keeping track of scheduled work, school, and social activities; record keeping; and using informational sources such as libraries, the Internet, maps, and dictionaries. When working with students with brain injuries, remember that their ambitions remain unchanged despite the injury: They still desire meaningful work, satisfying relationships, good health, and a sense of making a positive contribution to the world.

Chapter 26

Dyspraxia

What Is Dyspraxia?

Dyspraxia is an underdevelopment of the brain resulting in messages not being properly transmitted to the body, producing a number of consequences in physical and cognitive areas. It affects at least 2% of the population in varying degrees and 70% of those affected are male. Dyspraxia can be subtle or more pronounced, and often a person's disability is not readily apparent. The various forms of dyspraxia are:

- **Ideomotor Dyspraxia.** Inability to perform single motor tasks, such as combing hair or waving goodbye.

- **Ideational Dyspraxia.** Difficulty with multi-level tasks, such as taking the proper sequence of steps for brushing teeth.

- **Dressing Dyspraxia.** Difficulty with dressing and putting clothes on in order.

- **Oromotor Dyspraxia.** Difficulty with speech.

- **Constructional Dyspraxia.** Difficulty with spatial relations.

© 2001 National Center for Learning Disabilities (NCLD), available online at http://www.ncld.org/info/indepth/dyspraxia.cfm, reprinted with permission. For more information, visit the National Center for Learning Disabilities website at http://www.ncld.org.

Some of the symptoms of a child with dyspraxia may be:

- Coordination problems, including awkwardness in walk, clumsiness, or trouble with hopping, skipping, throwing and catching a ball, or riding a bike

- Confusion about which hand to use for tasks

- Cannot hold a pen or pencil properly

- Sensitive to touch; may find some clothes feel uncomfortable; there may be an intolerance to having hair or teeth brushed, or nails and hair cut

- Poor short term memory

- Trouble with reading and writing

- Poor sense of direction

- Speech problems, slow to learn to speak or speech may be incoherent

- Phobias or obsessive behavior

- Impatience

While older children may be verbally adept, they may not develop the social skills to get along with their peers. While children with dyspraxia can be of average of above average intelligence, they often have immature behavior. Elements of logic and reason may be difficult to comprehend.

What Strategies Can Help?

There is no cure for dyspraxia but the earlier a child is treated then the greater the chance of improvement. Occupational therapists, physiotherapists, and accommodations at school can all help a child to cope with dyspraxia.

A child with dyspraxia wants to communicate, but often cannot. Putting pressure on a child will only inhibit him or her further. Use verbal activities, especially those that are repetitive, to develop language skills, including songs, poems, nursery rhymes, etc.

If your child is unable to communicate well, the use of sign language or a communication board to supplement speech temporarily not only decreases the frustration but also even seems to help with speech development.

For motor difficulties, practice tasks with a child, allowing him or her to learn the sequence one must follow.

Encourage physical activities to strengthen a child's overall performance and coordination.

Start with simple physical tasks and work up to harder and more complicated tasks involving multiple steps.

Remember that frustration and anxiety will only hamper a child's success. Be patient with the steps a child needs in order to grasp an activity.

Encourage your child to make friends, and expose your child to activities outside the home. In this way a child sees and experiences the broader world and can start to develop appropriate social skills.

Chapter 27

Gerstmann Syndrome

What Is Gerstmann Syndrome?

Gerstmann syndrome is a neurological disorder characterized by four primary symptoms: a writing disability (agraphia or dysgraphia), a lack of understanding of the rules for calculation or arithmetic (acalculia or dyscalculia), an inability to distinguish right from left, and an inability to identify fingers (finger agnosia). The disorder should not be confused with Gerstmann-Sträussler-Scheinker disease, a type of transmissible spongiform encephalopathy.

In adults, the syndrome may occur after a stroke or in association with damage to the parietal lobe. In addition to exhibiting the above symptoms, many adults also experience aphasia, (difficulty in expressing oneself when speaking, in understanding speech, or in reading and writing). There are few reports of the syndrome, sometimes called developmental Gerstmann syndrome, in children. The cause is not known. Most cases are identified when children reach school age, a time when they are challenged with writing and math exercises. Generally, children with the disorder exhibit poor handwriting and spelling skills, and difficulty with math functions, including adding, subtracting, multiplying, and dividing. An inability to differentiate right from left and to discriminate among individual fingers may also be

"NINDS Gerstmann Syndrome Information Page," National Institute of Neurological Disorders and Stroke (NINDS), available online at http://www.ninds.nih.gov/health_and_medical/disorders/gerstmanns.htm; reviewed July 2001.

apparent. In addition to the four primary symptoms, many children also suffer from constructional apraxia, an inability to copy simple drawings. Frequently, there is also an impairment in reading. Children with a high level of intellectual functioning as well as those with brain damage may be affected with the disorder.

Is There Any Treatment?

There is no cure for Gerstmann syndrome. Treatment is symptomatic and supportive. Occupational and speech therapies may help diminish the dysgraphia and apraxia. In addition, calculators and word processors may help school children cope with the symptoms of the disorder.

What Is the Prognosis?

In adults, many of the symptoms diminish over time. Although it has been suggested that in children symptoms may diminish over time, it appears likely that most children probably do not overcome their deficits, but learn to adjust to them.

What Research Is Being Done?

The NINDS supports research on disorders that result from damage to the brain such as dysgraphia. The NINDS and other components of the National Institutes of Health also support research on learning disabilities. Current research avenues focus on developing techniques to diagnose and treat learning disabilities and increase understanding of the biological basis of them.

Chapter 28

Klinefelter Syndrome

What Is Klinefelter Syndrome?

In 1942, Dr. Harry Klinefelter and his coworkers at the Massachusetts General Hospital in Boston published a report about nine men who had enlarged breasts, sparse facial and body hair, small testes, and an inability to produce sperm.

By the late 1950s, researchers discovered that men with Klinefelter syndrome, as this group of symptoms came to be called, had an extra sex chromosome, XXY instead of the usual male arrangement, XY.

In the early 1970s, researchers around the world sought to identify males having the extra chromosome by screening large numbers of newborn babies. One of the largest of these studies, sponsored by the National Institute of Child Health and Human Development (NICHD), checked the chromosomes of more than 40,000 infants.

Based on these studies, the XXY chromosome arrangement appears to be one of the most common genetic abnormalities known, occurring as frequently as 1 in 500 to 1 in 1,000 male births. Although the syndrome's cause, an extra sex chromosome, is widespread, the syndrome itself—the set of symptoms and characteristics that may result from having the extra chromosome—is uncommon. Many men live out their lives without ever even suspecting that they have an additional chromosome.

"A Guide for XXY Males and Their Families," by Robert Bock, National Institute of Child Health and Human Development (NICHD), NIH Publication Number 93-3202, modified June 19, 2001. Resources verified August 2002.

231

"I never refer to newborn babies as having Klinefelter's, because they don't have a syndrome," said Arthur Robinson, M.D., a pediatrician at the University of Colorado Medical School in Denver and the director of the NICHD-sponsored study of XXY males. "Presumably, some of them will grow up to develop the syndrome Dr. Klinefelter described, but a lot of them won't."

For this reason, the term "Klinefelter syndrome" has fallen out of favor with medical researchers. Most prefer to describe men and boys having the extra chromosome as "XXY males." In addition to occasional breast enlargement, lack of facial and body hair, and a rounded body type, XXY males are more likely than other males to be overweight, and tend to be taller than their fathers and brothers.

For the most part, these symptoms are treatable. Surgery, when necessary, can reduce breast size. Regular injections of the male hormone testosterone, beginning at puberty, can promote strength and facial hair growth, as well as bring about a more muscular body type.

A far more serious symptom, however, is one that is not always readily apparent. Although they are not mentally retarded, most XXY males have some degree of language impairment. As children, they often learn to speak much later than do other children and may have difficulty learning to read and write. And while they eventually do learn to speak and converse normally, the majority tend to have some degree of difficulty with language throughout their lives. If untreated, this language impairment can lead to school failure and its attendant loss of self-esteem.

Fortunately, however, this language disability usually can be compensated for. Chances for success are greatest if begun in early childhood.

Chromosomes and Klinefelter Syndrome

Chromosomes, the spaghetti-like strands of hereditary material found in each cell of the body, determine such characteristics as the color of our eyes and hair, our height, and whether we are male or female.

Women usually inherit two X chromosomes—one from each parent. Men tend to inherit an X chromosome from their mothers, and a Y chromosome from their fathers. Most males with the syndrome Dr. Klinefelter described, however, have an additional X chromosomes— a total of two X chromosomes and one Y chromosome.

Causes

No one knows what puts a couple at risk for conceiving an XXY child. Advanced maternal age increases the risk for the XXY chromosome count, but only slightly. Furthermore, recent studies conducted by NICHD grantee Terry Hassold, a geneticist at Case Western Reserve University in Cleveland, OH, show that half the time, the extra chromosome comes from the father.

Dr. Hassold explained that cells destined to become sperm or eggs undergo a process known as meiosis. In this process, the 46 chromosomes in the cell separate, ultimately producing two new cells having 23 chromosomes each. Before meiosis is completed, however, chromosomes pair with their corresponding chromosomes and exchange bits of genetic material. In women, X chromosomes pair; in men, the X and Y chromosome pair. After the exchange, the chromosomes separate, and meiosis continues.

In some cases, the Xs or the X chromosome and Y chromosome fail to pair and fail to exchange genetic material. Occasionally, this results in their moving independently to the same cell, producing either an egg with two Xs, or a sperm having both an X and a Y chromosome. When a sperm having both an X and a Y chromosome fertilizes an egg having a single X chromosome, or a normal Y-bearing sperm fertilizes an egg having two X chromosomes, an XXY male is conceived.

Diagnosis

Because they often don't appear any different from anyone else, many XXY males probably never learn of their extra chromosome. However, if they are to be diagnosed, chances are greatest at one of the following times in life: before or shortly after birth, early childhood, adolescence, and in adulthood (as a result of testing for infertility).

In recent years, many XXY males have been diagnosed before birth, through amniocentesis or *chorionic villus* sampling (CVS). In amniocentesis, a sample of the fluid surrounding the fetus is withdrawn. Fetal cells in the fluid are then examined for chromosomal abnormalities. CVS is similar to amniocentesis, except that the procedure is done in the first trimester, and the fetal cells needed for examination are taken from the placenta. Neither procedure is used routinely, except when there is a family history of genetic defects, the pregnant woman is older than 35, or when other medical indications are present.

"If I were going to say something to parents who have had a prenatal diagnosis, it would be "You are so lucky that you know," said Melissa, the mother of one XXY boy. "Because there are parents who don't know that their sons have this problem. And they will never be able to help them lead a normal life. But you can."

The next most likely opportunity for diagnosis is when the child begins school. A physician may suspect a boy is an XXY male if he is delayed in learning to talk and has difficulty with reading and writing. XXY boys may also be tall and thin and somewhat passive and shy. Again, however, there are no guarantees. Some of the boys who fit this description will have the XXY chromosome count, but many others will not.

A few XXY males are diagnosed at adolescence, when excessive breast development forces them to seek medical attention. Like some chromosomally normal males, many XXY males undergo slight breast enlargement at puberty. Of these, only about a third—10 percent of XXY males in all—will develop breasts large enough to embarrass them.

The final chance for diagnosis is at adulthood, as a result of testing for infertility. At this time, an examining physician may note the undersized testes characteristic of an XXY male. In addition to infertility tests, the physician may order tests to detect increased levels of hormones known as gonadotropins, common in XXY males.

A karyotype is used to confirm the diagnosis. In this procedure, a small blood sample is drawn. White blood cells are then separated from the sample, mixed with tissue culture medium, incubated, and checked for chromosomal abnormalities, such as an extra X chromosome.

What to Tell Families, Friends, and XXY Boys

Expectant parents awaiting the arrival of their XXY baby have difficult choices to make: whom to tell and how much to tell about their son's extra chromosome. Fortunately, however, there are some guidelines that new parents can take into account when making their decisions.

One school of thought holds that the best course is to go on slowly, waiting at least 1 year before telling anyone—grandparents included—about the child's extra chromosome. Many people are frightened by the diagnosis, and their fears will color their perceptions of the child. For example, some people may confuse the term Klinefelter syndrome with Down syndrome, a condition resulting in mild to moderate mental retardation.

Others may prefer to reveal the diagnosis early. Some parents have found that grandparents, aunts, uncles—and even extended family members—are more supportive when given accurate information. Another important decision parents must make is when to tell their son about his diagnosis. Some experts recommend telling the child early. When the truth is withheld, children often suspect that their parents are hiding something and may imagine a condition that is worse than their actual diagnosis.

This school of thought maintains that by the time he is 10 or 11 years old, the child can be told that his cells differ slightly from those of other people. Soon after, he can be filled in on the details: that the cell difference is due to an additional X chromosome, which is responsible for his undersized testes and any reading difficulties he may have. At this time, the child can be reassured that he does not have a disease and will not become sick. The child should also be told that some people may misunderstand this information and that he should exercise discretion in sharing it with others.

By roughly the age of 12, depending on the child's emotional maturity, he can be told that he will most probably be infertile. Parents should stress that neither the X chromosome nor the infertility associated with it mean that he is in any way less masculine than other males his age. The child's parents or his physician can explain that although he may not be able to make a baby, he can consider adopting one. Parents may also need to reassure an XXY boy that his small testes will in no way interfere with his ability to have a normal sex life.

Adherents of this school of thought believe that learning about possible infertility in such a gradual manner will be less of a shock than finding out about it all at once, late in the teen years. Conversely, other experts believe that holding back the information does not appear to do any harm. Instead, telling an XXY boy about his extra chromosome too early may have some unpleasant consequences. An 11 or 12-year-old, for example, may associate infertility with sexual disorders and other concepts he may not yet understand.

Moreover, children, when making friends, tend to share secrets. But childhood friendships may be fleeting, and early confidences are sometimes betrayed. A malicious or thoughtless child may tell all the neighborhood children that his former companion is a freak because he has an extra chromosome.

For this reason, the best time to reveal the information may be mid-to-late adolescence, when an XXY male is old enough to understand his condition and better able to decide with whom he wishes to share this knowledge.

Childhood

According to Dr. Robinson, the director of the NICHD-funded study, XXY babies differ little from other children their age. They tend to start life as what many parents call good babies—quiet, undemanding, and perhaps even a little passive. As toddlers, they may be somewhat shy and reserved. They usually learn to walk later than most other children, and may have similar delays in learning to speak.

In some, the language delays may be more severe, with the child not fully learning to talk until about age 5. Others may learn to speak at a normal rate, and not meet with any problems until they begin school, where they may experience reading difficulties. A few may not have any problems at all in learning to speak or in learning to read.

XXY males usually have difficulty with expressive language the ability to put thoughts, ideas, and emotions into words. In contrast, their faculty for receptive language—understanding what is said—is close to normal.

"It's one of the conflicts they have," said Melissa, the mother of an XXY boy. "My son can understand the conversations of other 10 year olds. But his inability to use the language the way other 10-year olds use it makes him stand out."

In addition to academic help, XXY boys, like other language disabled children, may need help with social skills. Language is essential not only for learning the school curriculum, but also for building social relationships. By talking and listening, children make friends—in the process, sharing information, attitudes, and beliefs. Through language, they also learn how to behave—not just in the schoolroom, but also on the playground. If their sons' language disability seems to prevent them from fitting in socially, the parents of XXY boys may want to ask school officials about a social skills training program.

Throughout childhood—perhaps, even, for the rest of their lives—XXY boys retain the same temperament and disposition they first displayed as infants and toddlers. As a group, they tend to be shy, somewhat passive, and unlikely to take a leadership role. Although they do make friends with other children, they tend to have only a few friends at a time. Researchers also describe them as cooperative and eager to please.

Detecting Language Problems Early

The parents of XXY babies can compensate for their children's language disability by providing special help in language development, beginning at an early age. However, there is no easy formula to meet the language needs of all XXY boys. Like everyone else, XXY males are unique individuals. A few may not have any trouble learning to read and write, while the rest may have language impairments ranging from mild to severe.

If their son's speech seems to be lagging behind that of other children, parents should ask their child's pediatrician for a referral to a speech pathologist for further testing. A speech pathologist specializes in the disorders of voice, speech, and language. (The American Speech, Language and Hearing Association, distributes a free pamphlet on the stages of language development during the first 5 years of life.)

Parents should also pay particular attention to their children's hearing. Like other small children, XXY infants and toddlers may suffer from frequent ear infections. With any child, such infections may impair hearing and delay the acquisition of language. Such a hearing impairment may be a further setback for an XXY child who is already having language difficulties.

Guidelines for Detecting Language Problems

Shortly after the first birthday, children should be able to make their wishes known with simple one word utterances. For example, a child may say "milk" to mean "I want more milk." Gradually, children begin to combine words to produce two-word sentences, such as "More milk." By age three, most children use an average of about four words per sentence. If a child is not communicating effectively with single words by 18 to 24 months, then parents should seek a consultation with a speech and language pathologist.

The XXY Boy in the Classroom

Although there are exceptions, XXY boys are usually well behaved in the classroom. Most are shy, quiet, and eager to please the teacher. But when faced with material they find difficult, they tend to withdraw into quiet daydreaming. Teachers sometimes fail to realize they have a language problem, and dismiss them as lazy, saying they could do the work if they would only try. Many become so quiet that teachers forget they're even in the room. As a result, they fall farther and farther behind, and eventually may be held back a grade.

Help Under the Law

According to Dr. Robinson, XXY boys do best in small, uncrowded classrooms where teachers can give them a lot of individual attention. He suggests that parents who can meet the expense consider sending their sons to a private school offering special educational services.

Parents who cannot afford private schools should become familiar with Public Law 94-142, the Education for All Handicapped Children Act— now called the Individuals with Disabilities Education Act. This law, adopted by Congress in 1975, states that all children with disabilities have a right to a free, appropriate public education. The law cannot ensure that every child who needs special educational services will automatically get them. But the law does allow parents to take action when they suspect their child has a learning disability.

Chances for success are greatest for parents who are well informed and work cooperatively with the schools to plan educational and related service programs for their sons. For in-depth information on Public Law 94-142, parents may contact the National Information Center for Children and Youth with Disabilities (NICHCY).

Parents may also wish to contact their local and state boards of education for information on how the law has been implemented in their area. In addition, local educational groups may be able to provide useful information on working with school systems. Parents should also consider taking a course in educational advocacy. The local public school system, the state board of education, or local parents groups may be able to tell parents where they can enroll in such a course.

Services for Infants, Toddlers and Pre-Schoolers

The chances for reducing the impact of a learning disability are greatest in early childhood. Public Law 99-457 is an amendment to Public Law 94-142 that assists states in providing special educational services for infants, toddlers, and preschoolers. Eligibility requirements and entrance procedures vary from state to state. To learn the agencies to contact in their area, parents may call the Federation for Children with Special Needs. The NICHCY distributes the brochure *A Parent's Guide to Accessing Programs for Infants, Toddlers, and Preschoolers with Handicaps.*

Teaching Tips

XXY males often have decreased immediate auditory recall they have trouble remembering what they have just heard. Parents and teachers can help them remember by approaching memory through visual channels. Illustrating words with pictures may help. Gesturing is another useful technique. For example, a teacher might accompany the word "yes" with a nod of the head. Similarly, shaking the head from side to side is the universal gesture for "no." Other useful gestures include waving goodbye, showing the child an upraised palm to indicate "stop," and holding the arms outstretched to mean "so big."

XXY males frequently have trouble finding the right word to describe an object or a situation. Parents and teachers can help them build vocabulary through a variety of techniques. One way is to provide them with synonyms, such as pointing out that a car is also called an automobile. Another important teaching tool is categorizing—showing the child that an item belongs to a larger class of items. With this technique, a child could be told that cars, buses, trucks, and bicycles are all vehicles, machines that carry people and things from place to place.

Because XXY boys have difficulty expressing themselves, they may do poorly on essay-style test questions. Multiple choice questions will give teachers a better idea of what an XXY child has learned and prove less stressful for him as well. Similarly, rather than asking an open-ended question, parents and teachers may wish to present alternatives. Instead of asking "What would you like to do now?" they may wish to offer a choice: "Would you rather work on your spelling or work on your math?"

Parents and teachers can help XXY boys develop the ability to express themselves through solicited dialogue engaging them in conversation through a series of questions. The same technique can be used to get the child to develop his narrative (storytelling) abilities. For example, a parent might begin by asking a child what he did at recess that day, and by following up with questions that get the child to talk about his activities: "Did you go down the slide? Were you afraid when you climbed all the way to the top of the ladder? And then what? Did you go on the seesaw? Who sat on the other end?"

Parents can also help XXY boys develop their expressive language abilities simply by providing good examples. Through a technique known as modeling, they can help organize their children's thoughts and provide them with examples of how to express oneself. For instance, if a younger child indicated that he wanted a toy fire engine by pointing at it and grunting, the parent could hand it to him while saying "Here you are. This is a fire engine." Similarly, if an older child asked "Are we going to put the stuff in the thing?" the parent might reply "Yes, we're going to put the oranges in the shopping cart."

Research indicates that XXY boys may do poorly in an open classroom situation and seem to prefer a structured, tightly organized environment centered around familiar routines. First, teachers can reduce distraction by placing them in front row seats. Teachers also should present information slowly and repeat key points several times, if necessary. XXY boys should not be given tasks that have many small steps. Rather, each step should be presented individually. On completion, the child may then be asked to work on the next item in the series.

As mentioned, XXY boys may withdraw from material they find difficult and retreat into day dreaming. A teacher or parent should gently regain the child's attention and help him to focus again on the task at hand. Similarly, XXY boys may have difficulty putting one task aside and beginning another one. Again, the parent or teacher should gently shift the child's attention, by saying something like "Drawing time is over. Let's put away the crayons and take out the math book."

Adolescence

In general, XXY boys enter puberty normally, without any delay of physical maturity. But as puberty progresses, they fail to keep pace with other males. In chromosomally normal teenaged boys, the testes gradually increase in size, from an initial volume of about 2 ml, to about 15 ml. In XXY males, while the penis is usually of normal size, the testes remain at 2 ml, and cannot produce sufficient quantities of the male hormone testosterone. As a result, many XXY adolescents, although taller than average, may not be as strong as other teenaged boys, and may lack facial or body hair.

As they enter puberty, many boys will undergo slight breast enlargement. For most teenaged males, this condition, known as gynecomastia, tends to disappear in a short time. About one-third of XXY boys develop enlarged breasts in early adolescence slightly more than do chromosomally normal boys. Furthermore, in XXY boys, this condition may be permanent. However, only about 10 percent of XXY males have breast enlargement great enough to require surgery.

Most XXY adolescents benefit from receiving an injection of testosterone every 2 weeks, beginning at puberty. The hormone increases strength and brings on a more muscular, masculine appearance.

Adolescence and the high school years can be difficult for XXY boys and their families, particularly in neighborhoods and schools where the emphasis is on athletic ability and physical prowess. "They're usually tall, good-looking kids, but they tend to be awkward," Dr. Robinson said of the XXY teenagers he has met through his study. "They don't necessarily make good football players or good basketball players."

Lack of strength and agility, combined with a history of learning disabilities, may damage self-esteem. Unsympathetic peers, too, sometimes may make matters worse, through teasing or ridicule. "Lots of kids have a tough time during adolescence," Dr. Robinson said. "But a higher proportion of XXY boys have a tough time. High school is very competitive, and these kids are not very good competitors, in general."

Dr. Robinson again stressed, however, that while XXY males share many characteristics, they cannot be pigeonholed into rigid categories. Several of his patients have played football, and one, in particular, is an excellent tennis player.

Damage to self esteem may be more severe in XXY teenagers who are diagnosed in early or late adolescence. Teachers—and even parents— may have dismissed their scholastic difficulties as laziness. Lack of athletic prowess and the inability to use language properly in social settings may have helped to isolate them from their peers. Some may react by sliding quietly into depression and withdraw from contact with other people. Others may find acceptance in a dangerous crowd.

For these reasons, XXY males diagnosed as teenagers may need psychological counseling as well as help in overcoming their learning disabilities. Help with learning disabilities is available through public school systems for XXY males high-school age and under. Referrals to qualified mental health specialists may be obtained from family physicians.

Testosterone Treatment

Ideally, XXY males should begin testosterone treatment as they enter puberty. XXY males diagnosed in adulthood are also likely to benefit from the hormone. A regular schedule of testosterone injections will increase strength and muscle size, and promote the growth of facial and body hair.

In addition to these physical changes, testosterone injections often bring on psychological changes as well. As they begin to develop a more masculine appearance, the self-confidence of XXY males tends to increase. Many become more energetic and stop having sudden, angry changes in moods. What is not clear is whether these psychological changes are a direct result of testosterone treatment or are a side benefit of the increased self-confidence that the treatment may bring. As a group, XXY boys tend to suffer from depression, principally because of their scholastic difficulties and problems fitting in with other males their age. Sudden, angry changes in mood are typical of depressed people.

Other benefits of testosterone treatment may include decreased need for sleep, an enhanced ability to concentrate, and improved relations with others. But to obtain these benefits an XXY male must decide, on his own, that he is ready to stick to a regular schedule of injections. Sometimes, younger adolescents, who may be somewhat immature, seem not quite ready to take the shots. It is an inconvenience, and many don't like needles.

Most physicians do not push the young men to take the injections. Instead, they usually recommend informing XXY adolescents and their parents about the benefits of testosterone injections and letting them take as much time as they need to make their decision. Individuals may respond to testosterone treatment in different ways.

Although the majority of XXY males ultimately will benefit from testosterone, a few will not. To ensure that the injections will provide the maximum benefit, XXY males who are ready to begin testosterone injections should consult a qualified endocrinologist (a specialist in hormonal interactions) who has experience treating XXY males.

Side effects of the injections are few. Some individuals may develop a minor allergic reaction at the injection site, resulting in an itchy welt resembling a mosquito bite. Applying a non-prescription hydrocortisone cream to the area will reduce swelling and itching.

In addition, testosterone injections may result in a condition known as benign prostatic hyperplasia (BPH). This condition is common in chromosomally normal males as well, affecting more than 50 percent of men in their sixties, and as many as 90 percent in their seventies and eighties. In XXY males receiving testosterone injections, this condition may begin sometime after age 40.

The prostate is a small gland about the size of a walnut, which helps to manufacture semen. The gland is located just beneath the bladder and surrounds the urethra, the tube through which urine passes out of the body. In BPH, the prostate increases in size, sometimes squeezing the bladder and urethra and causing difficulty urinating, dribbling after urination, and the need to urinate frequently.

XXY males receiving testosterone injections should consult their physicians about a regular schedule of prostate examinations. BPH can often be detected early by a rectal exam. If the prostate greatly interferes with the flow of urine, excess prostate tissue can be trimmed away by a surgical instrument that is inserted in the penis, through the urethra.

Chromosomal Variations

Occasionally, variations of the XXY chromosome count may occur, the most common being the XY/XXY mosaic. In this variation, some of the cells in the male's body have an additional X chromosome, and the rest have the normal XY chromosome count. The percentage of cells containing the extra chromosome varies from case to case. In some instances, XY/XXY mosaics may have enough normally functioning cells in the testes to allow them to father children.

A few instances of males having two or even three additional X chromosomes have also been reported in the medical literature. In these individuals, the classic features of Klinefelter syndrome may be exaggerated, with low I.Q. or moderate to severe mental retardation also occurring.

In rare instances, an individual may possess both an additional X and an additional Y chromosome. The medical literature describes XXYY males as having slight to moderate mental retardation. They may sometimes be aggressive or even violent. Although they may have a rounded body type and decreased sex drive, experts disagree whether testosterone injections are appropriate for all of them.

One group of researchers reported that after receiving testosterone injections, an XXYY male stopped having violent sexual fantasies and ceased his assaults on teenaged girls. In contrast, Dr. Robinson found that testosterone injections seemed to make an XXYY boy he had been treating more aggressive.

Scientists admit, however, that because these cases are so rare, not much is known about them. Most of the XXYY males who have been studied were referred to treatment because they were violent and got into trouble with the law. It is not known whether XXYY males are inherently aggressive by nature, or whether only a few extreme individuals come to the attention of researchers precisely because they are aggressive.

Sexuality

The parents of XXY boys are sometimes concerned that their sons may grow up to be homosexual. This concern is unfounded, however, as there is no evidence that XXY males are any more inclined toward homosexuality than are other men. In fact, the only significant sexual difference between XXY men and teenagers and other males their age is that the XXY males may have less interest in sex. However, regular injections of the male sex hormone testosterone can bring sex drive up to normal levels.

In some cases, testosterone injections lead to a false sense of security. After receiving the hormone for a time, XXY males may conclude they've derived as much benefit from it as possible and discontinue the injections. But when they do, their interest in sex almost invariably diminishes until they resume the injections.

Infertility

The vast majority of XXY males do not produce enough sperm to allow them to become fathers. If these men and their wives wish to become parents, they should seek counseling from their family physician regarding adoption and infertility. However, no XXY male should automatically assume he is infertile without further testing. In a very small number of cases, XXY males have been able to father children.

In addition, a few individuals who believe themselves to be XXY males may actually be XY/XXY mosaics. Along with having cells with the XXY chromosome count, these males may also have cells with the normal XY chromosome count. If the number of XY cells in the testes is great enough, the individual should be able to father children.

Karyotyping, the method traditionally used to identify an individual's chromosome count, may sometimes fail to identify XY/XXY mosaics. For this reason, a karyotype should never be used to predict whether an individual will be infertile or not.

Health Considerations

Compared with other males, XXY males have a slightly increased risk of autoimmune disorders. In this group of diseases, the immune system, for unknown reasons, attacks the body's organs or tissues. The most well known of these diseases are type 1 (insulin dependent) diabetes, autoimmune thyroiditis, and lupus erythematosus. Most of these conditions can be treated with medication.

XXY males with enlarged breasts have the same risk of breast cancer as do women—roughly 50 times the risk XY males have. For this reason, these XXY adolescents and men need to practice regular breast self examination. The free booklet *Breast Exams: What You Should Know* is available from the National Cancer Institute. Although the booklet was written primarily for women, the breast self examination technique also can be used by XXY males. XXY males may also wish to consult their physicians about the need for more thorough breast examinations by medical professionals.

In addition, XXY males who do not receive testosterone injections may have an increased risk of developing osteoporosis in later life. In this condition, which usually afflicts women after the age of menopause, the bones lose calcium, becoming brittle and more likely to break.

Adulthood

Unfortunately, comparatively little is known about XXY adults. Studies in the United States have focused largely on XXY males identified in infancy from large random samples. Only a few of these individuals have reached adulthood; most are still in adolescence. At this time, researchers simply do not know what kind of adults they will become.

"Some of them have really struggled through adolescence," said Dr. Bruce Bender, the psychologist for the NICHD-sponsored study of XXY males. "But we don't know whether they'll have serious problems in adulthood, or, like many troubled teenagers, overcome their problems and lead productive lives."

Comparatively few studies of XXY males diagnosed in adulthood have been conducted. By and large, the men who took part in these studies were not selected at random but identified by a particular characteristic, such as height. For this reason, it is not known whether these individuals are truly representative of XXY men as a whole or represent a particular extreme. One study found a group of XXY males diagnosed between the ages of 27 and 37 to have suffered a number of setbacks, in comparison to a similar group of XY males. The XXY men were more likely to have had histories of scholastic failure, depression and other psychological problems, and to lack energy and enthusiasm.

But by the time the XXY men had reached their forties, most had surmounted their problems. The majority said that their energy and activity levels had increased, that they were more productive on the job, and that their relationships with other people had improved. In fact, the only difference between the XY males and the XXY males was that the latter were less likely to have been married.

That these men eventually overcame their troubled pasts is encouraging for all XXY males and particularly encouraging for those diagnosed in childhood. Had they received counseling, support, and testosterone treatments beginning in childhood, these men might have avoided the difficulties of their twenties and thirties. Although a supportive environment through childhood and adolescence appears to offer the greatest chance for a well-adjusted adulthood, it is not too late for XXY men diagnosed as adults to seek help.

Research has shown that testosterone injections, begun in adulthood, can be beneficial. Psychological counseling also offers the best hope of overcoming depression and other psychological problems. For referrals to endocrinologists qualified to administer testosterone or to mental health specialists, XXY men should consult their physicians.

Resources

The American Speech Language and Hearing Association
10801 Rockville Pike
Rockville, MD 20852
Toll Free: 800-638-8255
Tel: 301-897-8682
Internet: http://www.asha.org
E-Mail: actioncenter@asha.org

Distributes a pamphlet parents may consult to determine if their children's communication abilities are developing at a normal rate.

Federation for Children with Special Needs
1135 Tremont Street, Suite 420
Boston, MA 02120
Toll Free: 800-331-0688
Tel: 617-236-7210
Fax: 617-572-2094
Internet: http://www.fcsn.org
E-Mail: fcsninfo@fcsn.org

Maintains a listing of local and state agencies providing special educational services for infants, toddlers, and preschoolers under Public Law 99-457.

Learning Disabilities Association of America
4156 Library Road
Pittsburgh, PA 15234-1349
Tel: 412-341-1515
Fax: 412-344-0224
Internet: http://www.ldanatl.org
E-Mail: info@ldaamerica.org

Provides information on dyslexia and other learning disabilities. Has local chapters throughout the country.

The National Cancer Institute
6116 Executive Boulevard
MSC8322
Bethesda, MD 20892-8322
Toll Free: 800-422-6237
Internet: http://www.nci.nih.gov

Offers the free booklet *Breast Exams: What You Should Know*. The last page of the booklet is a pull-out chart listing the instructions for breast self examination. Although the booklet was written primarily for women, the breast self examination technique also can be used by XXY males.

The National Information Center for Children and Youth with Disabilities (NICHCY)

P.O. Box 1492
Washington, DC 20013
Toll Free: 800-695-0285 (Voice/TTD)
Tel: 202-884-8200 (Voice/TTD)
Fax: 202-884-8441
Internet: http://www.nichcy.org
E-Mail: nichcy@aed.org

Distributes information on Public Law 94-142, the Individuals with Disabilities Education Act.

Chapter 29

Hearing Impairments

When a child has a hearing loss during the developmental years, all areas of development can be affected significantly. A hearing loss limits ease of acquisition of a communication system, which further influences development of interactions with others, the ability to make sense out of the world, and ease of acquiring academic skills. Early identification of a hearing loss is critical to a child's academic and emotional adjustment. What is a hearing loss, and how is it caused?

There are three major types of hearing losses. The first is called a conductive loss. This occurs when something goes wrong with the outer or middle ear, impeding sound waves from being conducted or carried to the inner ear. The second type of loss is called a sensorineural loss and occurs when damage to the inner ear or the auditory nerve impedes the sound message from being sent to the brain. The third type is referred to as a central auditory processing disorder because, although there is no specific damage to the ear itself, the neural system involved in understanding what is heard is impaired. Children with central auditory processing disorder may have normal hearing as measured by an audiometer (device used to test hearing levels), but they often have difficulty understanding what they hear. A child may also have a combination of these forms of hearing loss (Easterbrooks & Baker-Hawkins, 1994).

"Educating Children Who Are Deaf or Hard of Hearing: Overview," by Susan Easterbrooks, ERIC Clearinghouse on Disabilities and Gifted Educations, *ERIC Digest* Number E549, ERIC Identifier: ED414667, 1997. Despite the older date of this article, the information remains helpful to those seeking to understand the effects of hearing loss during the developmental years.

Many terms are used to refer to the population of individuals who have difficulty hearing. The word deaf by federal definition means a hearing loss which adversely affects educational performance and which is so severe that the child is impaired in processing linguistic (communication) information through hearing, with or without amplification (hearing aids). The term hard of hearing means a hearing loss, whether permanent or fluctuating, that adversely affects a child's educational performance but which allows the child access to some degree of communication with or without amplification (Individuals with Disabilities Education Act, 1990). The term Deaf used with a capital D refers to those individuals with hearing losses who identify themselves with the Deaf Culture. These individuals view themselves as a population united by a common heritage, a shared experience, a multi-generational history, and a language, American Sign Language (ASL) (Padden & Humphries, 1988).

The term hearing-impaired is used inconsistently around the country today. Some use it to mean all degrees of hearing loss while others use it to refer to the hard-of-hearing population. The terms deaf mute and deaf and dumb are antiquated. Not only are they seen as outdated, they are also viewed as offensive.

How Many People Have Hearing Losses?

The National Center for Health Statistics (Adams & Benson, 1992) estimated that more than 22.5 million Americans have some degree of hearing loss. Of these individuals, 1,053,000 were under 18 years of age. This means that one of every six children has diminished hearing to some degree at any given point in time (Berg, 1986). Schildroth and Hotto (1994) reported results of demographic information on 48,300 children identified as having hearing losses. The students in their research represented 60-65% of the number reported by the federal Office of Special Education Programs (OSEP), U.S. Department of Education. The vast number of individuals with hearing losses are hard of hearing or are older adults who have lost their hearing.

What Are the Signs of a Hearing Loss, and How Is It Diagnosed?

In very young children the signs of a hearing loss are lack of attention or inconsistent attention, lack of vocal interactions or reduced vocal interactions, and lack of or reduction in language development, especially related to the quiet word endings such as -ed, -ing, and -s.

250

In school-aged children, the signs of a hearing loss are a high degree of frustration with school and with others, low grades or a noticeable drop in grades, or a change in patterns of paying attention (Davis, 1989). In adults, the signs of a hearing loss are complaints that others are mumbling or playing equipment such as the TV or radio too loudly.

How Do People with Hearing Losses Communicate?

The debate over the best way to teach a child with a hearing loss to communicate has raged since the 1500s (Winefield, 1987). Although this debate continues today, there are a growing number of individuals who recognize that no one system of communication is right for all children. The choice of a communication system must be made on an individual basis, taking into consideration the characteristics of the child, the resources available, and the commitment of an individual family to a communication method. Additional *ERIC Digests* explore each of these options in depth. As an orientation, the following definitions are useful:

The Auditory-Verbal philosophy is a set of guiding principles for early intervention that are used to support the development of residual (remaining) hearing and speech and that focus on a strong development of listening skills.

The Auditory-Oral philosophy is a set of principles that are used to develop spoken language and listening skills at all ages and that may incorporate visual methods of teaching these.

Cued Speech is a sound-based system of hand cues that supplement speech reading.

English-Based Sign Systems are those systems that use signs from ASL plus invented signs along with prefixes and suffixes to represent the English language in signed form.

The Bilingual-Bicultural philosophy stresses the importance of early development of ASL, which has a grammar different from spoken or signed English, as the deaf child's natural language, using ASL as a bridge into English as a second language.

Total Communication refers to a philosophy of using the system most needed by the child at any given time. Total Communication usually involves simultaneous use of speech and sign and is the most commonly used form of instruction (Schildroth & Hotto, 1993).

Other factors complicate the picture of which system should be used to teach children who are deaf and hard of hearing to communicate. Cochlear implants are computerized devices implanted into the cochlea of individuals who are deaf, which influence the ability to develop speech and listening skills. They are supported by the various oral philosophies.

Attendance at a residential school is considered a key component in the success of a child whose family has chosen the Bilingual-Bicultural approach to education. The presence of additional learning disorders may also affect a child's progress in any method or philosophy; therefore, this challenging-to-test population must be assessed adequately.

Where Are Children Who Are Deaf or Hard of Hearing Educated?

According to the annual report of the Center for Assessment and Demographic Studies (CADS) at Gallaudet University (Schildroth & Hotto, 1996), 21% of the students in the study attended residential schools, 8% attended day schools, and 70% attended their local schools. These figures represent about 60-65% of the children reported on the federal child count, and the assumption is often made that the additional students not in the CADS study are being educated in local education agencies that are unaware that they may participate in the CADS process. Whatever the reason, over the past two decades, more and more children who are deaf or hard of hearing are receiving instruction in general education environments.

What Kind of Technology Is Available for People Who Are Deaf or Hard of Hearing?

Today the options for support from technology are exciting. A wide variety of hearing aids can be tailored to individual patterns of loss. Students in classrooms may use a variety of assistive listening devices that help them hear the teacher while filtering out ambient noise.

Telecommunication Devices for the Deaf (TDDs) are available to provide people who are deaf with access to telephones (Compton, 1991). Many states have relay services that work in conjunction with TDDs. Television sets are now produced with built-in closed captioning capabilities, or for older TVs, viewers may purchase captioners. A variety of alerting devices are available which use visual means to alert individuals to doorbells, telephones, a knock at the door, a baby's crying, oven timers, and smoke detectors, among other sounds of daily life. Vibrating devices may be used in place of an alarm clock. In addition, computer technology such as fax machines, programs for teaching speech, real-time graphic display devices for recording lectures, and a myriad of machines and programs are affecting education and daily life to an ever-increasing degree.

References

Adams, P.F. and Benson, V. (1992). Current estimates from the National Health Interview Survey, 1991. *Vital and Health Statistics, Series 10*. National Center for Health Statistics.

Berg, F. (1986). Characteristics of the target population. In F. Berg, J.C. Blair, J.H. Viehweg & A. Wilson-Vlotman (Eds.), *Educational Audiology for the Hard of Hearing Child*. (pp. 157-180). New York: Grune and Stratton.

Compton, C. (1991). Assistive devices: Doorways to independence. Washington, DC: Gallaudet University.

Davis, D. (1989). *Otitis Media: Coping with the Effects in the Classroom*. Stanhope, NJ: Hear You Are, Inc.

Easterbrooks, S. and Baker-Hawkins, S. (1994). Deaf and hard of hearing students educational services guidelines. Alexandria, VA: National Association of State Directors of Special Education. Individuals with Disabilities Education Act, PL 101-476. (1990).

Schildroth, A. and Hotto, S. (1994). Annual survey of hearing impaired children and youth: 1991-92 school year. *American Annals of the Deaf*, 138(2), 163-171.

Schildroth, A. and Hotto, S. (1996). Changes in student program and characteristics, 1984-85 and 1994-95. *American Annals of the Deaf*, 141(2), 68-71.

Padden, C. and Humphries, T. (1988). Deaf in America: Voices from a culture. Cambridge, MA: Harvard University.

Winefield, R. (1987). Never the twain shall meet. Washington, DC: *Gallaudet University Press*.

Chapter 30

Landau-Kleffner Syndrome

What Is Landau-Kleffner Syndrome?

Landau-Kleffner syndrome (LKS) is a childhood disorder. A major feature of LKS is the gradual or sudden loss of the ability to understand and use spoken language. All children with LKS have abnormal electrical brain waves that can be documented by an electroencephalogram (EEG), a recording of the electric activity of the brain. Approximately 80 percent of the children with LKS have one or more epileptic seizures that usually occur at night. Behavioral disorders such as hyperactivity, aggressiveness and depression can also accompany this disorder. LKS may also be called infantile acquired aphasia, acquired epileptic aphasia or aphasia with convulsive disorder. This syndrome was first described in 1957 by Dr. William M. Landau and Dr. Frank R. Kleffner, who identified six children with the disorder.

What Are the Signs of Landau-Kleffner Syndrome?

LKS occurs most frequently in normally developing children who are between 3 and 7 years of age. For no apparent reason, these children begin having trouble understanding what is said to them. Doctors often refer to this problem as auditory agnosia or word deafness. The auditory agnosia may occur slowly or very quickly. Parents often

National Institute on Deafness and Other Communication Disorders (NIDCD), 1997, updated 1999, available online at http://www.nidcd.nih.gov/ health/pubs_vhl/landklfs.htm.

think that the child is developing a hearing problem or has become suddenly deaf. Hearing tests, however, show normal hearing. Children may also appear to be autistic or developmentally delayed.

The inability to understand language eventually affects the child's spoken language which may progress to a complete loss of the ability to speak (mutism). Children who have learned to read and write before the onset of auditory agnosia can often continue communicating through written language. Some children develop a type of gestural communication or sign-like language. The communication problems may lead to behavioral or psychological problems. Intelligence usually appears to be unaffected.

The loss of language may be preceded by an epileptic seizure that usually occurs at night. At some time, 80 percent of children with LKS have one or more seizures. The seizures usually stop by the time the child becomes a teenager. All LKS children have abnormal electrical brain activity on both the right and left sides of their brains.

How Common Is Landau-Kleffner Syndrome?

More than 160 cases have been reported from 1957 through 1990.

What Causes Landau-Kleffner Syndrome?

The cause of LKS is unknown. Some experts think there is more than one cause for this disorder. All of the children with LKS appear to be perfectly normal until their first seizure or the start of language problems. There have been no reports of children who have a family history of LKS. Therefore, LKS is not likely to be an inherited disorder.

What Is the Outcome of Landau-Kleffner Syndrome?

There have not been many long-term follow-up studies of children with LKS. This lack of evidence, along with the wide range of differences among affected children, makes it impossible to predict the outcome of this disorder. Complete language recovery has been reported; however, language problems usually continue into adulthood. The continued language problems can range from difficulty following simple commands to no verbal communication. If recovery takes place, it can occur within days or years. So far, no relationship has been found between the extent of the language impairment, the presence or absence of seizures and the amount of language recovery. Generally, the earlier the disorder begins, the poorer the language recovery.

Most children outgrow the seizures, and electrical brain activity on the EEG usually returns to normal by age 15.

What Treatments Are Available?

Medication to control the seizures and abnormal brain wave activity (anticonvulsants) usually has very little effect on language ability. Corticosteroid therapy has improved the language ability of some children. Sign language instruction has benefited others.

Chapter 31

Multiple Chemical Sensitivity/Environmental Illness (MCS-EI)

According to reports from campuses and recent conferences, disability support service providers and institutional administrators have seen an increase in requests for accommodations for students with a diagnosis of Multiple Chemical Sensitivity/Environmental Illness, or MCS/EI.

Accommodating students in this disability category on college and university campuses illustrates how disability support specialists are often required to show creative sensitivity paired with sophisticated insight into social issues, public laws, and human needs.

The Americans with Disabilities Act of 1990 (ADA) defines a person with a disability as anyone with a physical or mental impairment that substantially limits one or more major life activity. If a student's functional ability is severely limited by the symptoms of MCS/EI, he or she would be considered a person with a disability under the ADA, and campus support staff must provide reasonable accommodations so that there will be access to the program.

Accommodating the student who has been diagnosed with MCS/EI can be a challenge. It requires willingness and an ability to assess the

Reprinted with permission from *Students with Multiple Chemical Sensitivity/Environmental Illness: An Accommodation Challenge* (1996), published by the HEATH Resource Center of the George Washington University School of Education and Human Development, the national clearinghouse on postsecondary education for individuals with disabilities. This factsheet was prepared under Cooperative Agreement No. H326H98002, awarded to the American council on Education by the U.S. Department of Education. For additional information about the HEATH Resource Center, visit www.heath.gwu.edu. Despite the older date of this document, the reader will find the information useful.

needs of the student—that is, to weigh the evidence of disability and identify appropriate accommodations. Since this condition has such a highly individualized profile, each situation presents a unique set of conditions and requires a highly individualized response.

Symptoms

Some of the symptoms attributed to MCS/EI include headaches, asthma and other breathing problems, vision problems, increased sensitivity to odors, bloating and other intestinal problems, short- and long-term memory loss, flu-like symptoms, dizziness, mental confusion, fatigue, depression, and chronic exhaustion. Symptoms may occur in more than one organ system in the body—for example, both the nervous and the respiratory systems.

Exposure to the offending substances may be via the air, food, water, or skin contact.

Persons with MCS/EI often have symptoms from exposure to chemicals at concentrations far below the levels tolerable by most people. Although floor waxes, cleaners, pesticides, and perfumes can cause discomfort to people who are not chemically sensitive, such discomfort is usually of short duration and does not present a serious threat to that person's health. However, a person with MCS/EI can be physically distressed for days or weeks as a result of exposure to even a small amount of the same substance.

Accommodations

Frequently, an accommodation for a student with MCS/EI involves finding a way for that student to avoid exposure to the offending substances—usually chemicals or microscopic organisms. Thus, accommodations might include notification prior to painting, pesticide application, or renovations; changing the class meeting site; or scheduling classes in areas and at times when the surroundings are least problematic. Encouraging other students not to apply scented deodorant, hair spray, or perfume may also help the person with MCS/EI. In addition, rescheduling classes in buildings with windows that open and in spaces that are well ventilated and free of tobacco smoke, pesticides, cleaning products, deodorizers, and exhaust fumes may help ward off problems for students with MCS/EI.

Distance learning accommodations may provide part of the answer. Yet this cannot be viewed as the entire solution to accommodating the student with MCS/EI, because over-reliance on distance learning could further limit a student's access to the full college experience. A student with MCS/EI who depends solely on off-campus instruction runs the risk of social isolation, which may intensify his or her problems.

Controversy

Multiple Chemical Sensitivity/Environmental Illness is one of medicine's most controversial disorders. MCS/EI is an invisible disability that manifests itself in widely different ways. Invisible disabilities are often the least understood by peers, administrators, and helping professionals. The numerous theories on the causes of MCS/EI compound the controversy. Some clinical ecologists theorize that MCS/EI is caused by an initial high-level exposure to chemicals, while others believe that it is due to chronic low-level exposure that causes the immune system in some people to overreact to subsequent exposures or to lose some of its ability to protect the body against harmful substances.

According to the National Institute of Environmental Health Sciences (an institute of the National Institutes of Health), Multiple Chemical Sensitivity/Environmental Illness is an acquired syndrome of chemical intolerance that causes severe disability in affected individuals, although the mechanism that produces symptoms and the nature of the organic pathology are unknown.

Under some circumstances, MCS/EI has been considered a disabling condition under ADA. The Department of Housing and Urban Development established disability status for MCS in 1992. People with MCS/EI have won workers' compensation cases. Yet, the medical community remains divided over whether MCS/EI should be considered a disease. Many allergists even reject an MCS/EI diagnosis as unconventional and unproved. Therefore, MCS/EI is not currently recognized by the Centers for Disease Control and has no diagnostic criteria or tests—nor is a case definition expected soon.

Absence of a case definition results in two obstacles to resolution of the controversy: Physicians have no guidelines with which to make a diagnosis, and funding for scientific study is difficult to obtain.

In an effort to open a dialogue, the Agency for Toxic Substances and Disease Registry is putting together an interagency working group made up of various government agencies to study the disorder.

Physicians who recognize MCS/EI include some occupational and environmental health specialists and those physicians who specialize in the new field of clinical ecology. Conventional medical intervention offers little or no relief, sometimes masking the problem or causing a whole new set of symptoms.

Despite medical controversy and theoretical debate, many people are qualified to receive accommodations as a result of having one or more major life activities impaired by MCS/EI, and many of these are students who request and are entitled to disability accommodations from the postsecondary institution they attend.

Chapter 32

Non-Verbal
Learning Disorder Syndrome

What Is Nonverbal Learning Disorder Syndrome?

It is not uncommon for children with hydrocephalus to have learning disabilities. Nonverbal Learning Disorder Syndrome (NVLD) is a specific type of learning disability that affects children's academic progress as well as their social and emotional development. This specific type of learning disability has been identified in some children with hydrocephalus.

NVLD encompasses a combination of learning, academic, social and emotional issues. Most children with learning disabilities do not have significant problems with normal social and emotional development. Some children may have the academic difficulties associated with NVLD but do quite well socially and emotionally. A valid diagnosis of NVLD includes a combination of learning, academic, social and emotional issues as described in this chapter. Additionally, because the pattern of academic strengths and weaknesses may not show up early in life, and difficulties with social relations are not always apparent

From "What Is Non-Verbal Learning Disorder Syndrome?" by Emily S. Fudge, Executive Director of the Hydrocephalus Association, San Francisco, CA. This article originally appeared in the *Hydrocephalus Association Newsletter* (Spring 1997). The information contained in this article is adapted from a paper by Rochelle Harris, Ph.D., David H. Bennett, Ph.D., Brian Belden, Ph.D., Lynne Covitz, Ph.D., and Vicki Little, Ph.D., of the Section of Developmental Medicine and Psychology, Children's Mercy Hospital, Kansas City, MO. © 1997. Reprinted with permission. Despite the older date of this article, it contains helpful information about nonverbal learning disorder syndrome.

in the very young, it is often difficult to make a diagnosis of NVLD until a child is in middle-to-late elementary school.

Academic Characteristics

Children with NVLD have difficulty with mechanical arithmetic, particularly more complex math involving many columns (such as long division). They have problems keeping columns straight, often mixing up which column to put a number in when they carry over in addition. They can have difficulty with word problems or math reasoning, being unable to read a math problem and know what operation to perform. Higher math skills that rely on spatial abilities or seeing the relation between concepts (such as in geometry or algebra) are especially difficult for them to acquire.

Children with NVLD often do quite well with word recognition, oral reading and spelling. While they might be slower in learning to recognize their letters, once they master early reading skills they show good phonetic skills (word pronunciation). However, reading comprehension is weak, especially for more abstract or novel subject matter. The child with NVLD may be able to read a paragraph quite fluently but then be unable to extract the main point or answer conceptual questions about what has just been read.

Language abilities are also unique in children with NVLD. Some may show an initial delay in early expressive speech but then rapidly show gains, progressing to become very talkative or even excessively verbal. This speech pattern (verbosity) has been termed cocktail party speech because although a great deal may be said, the content may have little substance or value. Compared to their peers, children with NVLD tend to rely more heavily on language to engage and relate to people, to gather information and to relieve anxiety. For instance, when young, instead of picking up and manipulating an object that is new to them, they may instead question an adult about what it is, how it works, etc.

Children with NVLD may develop a great deal of skill in talking their way out of challenging tasks or facing novel situations that provoke anxiety. Their rote verbal capacities and rote verbal memory skills may be a personal strength but they show poor language pragmatics or the functional use of language.

Nonverbal tasks may be quite difficult for children with NVLD. On tasks that require fine motor coordination these children often show early delay. Early paper/pencil tasks can be extremely frustrating for them and later handwriting may show poor quality. On formal tasks

264

of cognitive functioning they do much better on verbal than nonverbal tasks. Tasks that require interpreting or pulling together visual information can be hard, especially if it is not possible to explain the task verbally with step-by-step instruction. Additionally, verbal tasks that entail more complex problem solving or the integration of information from various sources are quite hard for children with NVLD. Children struggle with common academic tasks such as answering questions at the end of a chapter or performing on tests where the questions are worded differently from the study material.

Humor or sarcasm can be hard for children with the NVLD to appreciate. They often cannot understand jokes, or they interpret them in such a concrete way that the humor is lost. Sarcasm, expressed by the mismatch between a spoken message and the facial expression or tone of voice, requires integration of information from different sensory modalities. Children with NVLD may interpret the message quite literally, missing altogether the information needed to recognize that it is sarcasm.

Social or Adaptive Characteristics

Novel situations can be particularly troublesome as they require generating responses that cannot be anticipated or practiced beforehand. Children with NVLD often rely on rote or practiced behaviors that may not be appropriate for the context. For example, if they learn the right way to introduce themselves to an unfamiliar adult (by shaking hands and saying "pleased to meet you") they may attempt the same response in a group of children where it might be viewed as odd or nerdy. When peers do give them subtle feedback, such as raised eyebrows, they miss the information completely and therefore cannot modify their behavior next time. Peers may pull away or nonverbally signal the end of a conversation and children with NVLD may pursue the interaction, talking even as the peer turns his back. Children with NVLD want friends, just like everyone else, and they may intensify their efforts to reach out, despite repeated rejection. The recognition that they are being rejected may not come until they are older; their hurt and confusion grows because they are unable to understand the increasingly complex social rules of adolescence.

Causes of Nonverbal Learning Disorder Syndrome

Although no cause for this disorder has been definitely identified, it is known that deficits in the functioning of the right hemisphere of the brain play a significant role. The brain is divided into two hemi-spheres, the right and left, which typically complement each other in functioning but are suited for different types of processing. The right hemisphere can integrate information from several sensory modalities at once (can interpret visual and spoken information at once, thereby clarifying how a facial expression can change the meaning of a verbal message) and is best for processing novel information. The left hemisphere processes information presented in a step-by-step fashion and is best at using information once it is well practiced or rote. Spoken language is processed by the left hemisphere, visual or nonverbal information is processed by the right hemisphere, and the right hemisphere also becomes involved in understanding anything novel or contradictory between the verbal and nonverbal messages.

Deficits in the functioning of the right hemisphere, observed in children with NVLD, could emerge through various avenues. If there is any early interruption in the development of the central nervous system, the right hemisphere is more likely to be compromised than the left. Direct damage to the right hemisphere through trauma, tumors and/or seizures can cause compromise in right hemisphere functioning. Sometimes there is no known reason for observed weakness in right hemisphere functioning.

Interventions

Children with NVLD do best with instruction that is verbal and descriptive in nature. Instead of showing them how to perform a math operation, for instance, they should be verbally instructed in a step-by-step manner.

Assess reading comprehension carefully because good oral reading can hide the extent of weak comprehension. Teach strategies to aide comprehension such as learning to identify the topic sentence and highlighting important information for later study or review. Tell them what specific facts they will need to know for a test rather than asking them to determine, on their own, what important information within a text or lecture they should focus on.

Because language concepts can be weak, children with NVLD need to understand terms such as same versus different, part-to-whole relationships, how to classify or categorize objects and the difference between cause and effect. In expressive language instruction they should focus on staying on the topic, listening without interruption, and recognizing when someone has signaled the end of a conversation.

Spatial concepts are difficult for children with NVLD so they may need to learn verbal self-instruction for analyzing and reproducing designs. Certain tasks such as map reading or learning the location of all the capital cities should be avoided altogether. If telling time on a clock face is very challenging, teach telling time with a digital clock instead.

Written work can be extremely frustrating due to the combination of mechanical problems related to fine motor delays and poor visual spatial skills. Decrease the quantity of writing expected and instead allow verbal expression of information. Also, teach early keyboard skills.

Involve the school counselor or social worker to foster social development at school. Friendship groups that involve a small number of selected peers are one intervention. Teachers can help identify which classmates would be most responsive and supportive of your child. Specific, concrete instruction such as teaching the child how and when to initiate peer interactions, how to wait one's turn or the appropriate moment to speak, how to make consistent eye contact and pleasant facial expressions can be very beneficial.

Create a supportive home environment in which your child feels secure and successful. Minimize demands that highlight your child's weaknesses by being very clear and specific about what you expect. Observe your child carefully in novel or complex situations to gain an appreciation of strengths and weaknesses and set your expectations accordingly.

Remember that watching you do something is not the best way for your child to learn. Instead, instruct them in a step-by-step manner. Reminder lists of even basic tasks such as daily hygiene and simple chores are very helpful. It is all right to point out to them what they may not yet have recognized about themselves, i.e., "You do much better when you know what's going to happen than when you get unexpected surprises." Constructive suggestions rather than criticism work best.

And, as you've heard countless times before, you are the best advocate for your child. Collaborate with your child's school about proper interventions and work hard to develop and maintain a positive relationship with school personnel so that you can share what has worked for your child in the past and brainstorm with them about other interventions that might be helpful.

Nonverbal Learning Disorder Syndrome is not a widely recognized diagnosis and school personnel may be genuinely unsure about how best to serve your child. A comprehensive and thorough neuropsychological assessment by an experienced clinician, with regular follow-ups, is critical to insure that appropriate strategies are put in place to assist your child in realizing his or her potential.

Chapter 33

Tourette Syndrome

Tourette Syndrome (TS) is a neurological disorder characterized by repeated, involuntary body movements (tics) such as blinking, twitching, shoulder shrugging, or leg jerking and vocal sounds such as throat clearing or sniffing. Symptoms typically appear before the age of 18 and the condition occurs in all ethnic groups with males affected 3 to 4 times more often than females.

Associated conditions can include obsessivity, attentional problems, and impulsiveness. Since many people with TS have yet to be diagnosed, there are no absolute figures, but the official estimate by the National Institutes of Health is that 100,000 Americans have full-blown TS. Symptoms include:

- Multiple motor and one or more vocal tics at some time during the illness, although not necessarily simultaneously

- The occurrence of tics many times a day (usually in bouts) nearly every day or intermittently throughout a span of more than one year

- Periodic changes in the number, frequency, type, location, and severity of the tics; for example, symptoms may disappear for weeks or months at a time

- Onset before the age of 18

"Teaching Children with Tourette Syndrome," by Bernadette Knoblauch, from *ERIC Digest* E570, ERIC Identifier: ED429397, ERIC Clearinghouse on Disabilities and Gifted Education, 1998.

Associated Behaviors

Additional problems may include:

• Obsessions, which consist of repetitive unwanted or bothersome thoughts.

• Compulsions and ritualistic behaviors. Examples include touching an object with one hand after touching it with the other hand to even things up, repeatedly checking to see that the flame on the stove is turned off, or repeating a sentence many times until it sounds right.

• Attention Deficit Disorder (ADD) with or without Hyperactivity (or ADHD). Indications of ADHD may include: difficulty with concentration; failing to finish what is started; not listening; being easily distracted; often acting before thinking; shifting constantly from one activity to another; needing a great deal of supervision; and general fidgeting. ADD without hyperactivity includes all of the above symptoms except for the high level of activity.

• Learning disabilities, including reading and writing difficulties, arithmetic disorders, and perceptual problems.

• Difficulties with impulse control, which may occasionally result in overly aggressive behaviors or socially inappropriate acts. Defiant and angry behaviors can also occur.

In many cases, medication can help control the symptoms, but there may be side effects, some of which interfere with cognitive processes. Stimulants such as Ritalin, Cylert, and Dexedrine that are prescribed for ADHD may increase tics, and their use is controversial. Other types of therapy may also be helpful, including psychotherapy, behavior modification therapy that can teach the substitution of one tic for another that is more acceptable, and the use of relaxation techniques, biofeedback, and exercise to reduce the stress that often exacerbates tics.

Establishing the Proper Learning Environment

While school children with TS as a group have the same IQ range as the general population, many may have some kind of learning problem. That condition, combined with attention deficits and the problems of dealing with frequent tics, often call for special educational assistance. The use of tape recorders, typewriters, or computers for reading and writing problems, untimed exams (in a private room if vocal tics are a problem), and permission to leave the classroom when tics become overwhelming are often helpful.

The following are tips for dealing effectively with TS symptoms in the classroom setting:

- Some movements and noises can be annoying or disruptive to the class. Please remember that they are occurring involuntarily, and do not react with anger or annoyance. This requires patience but reprimanding a student with TS is like disciplining a student with cerebral palsy for being clumsy. If the teacher is not tolerant, others in the class may feel free to ridicule the child with TS. If some aspect of the child's tics affect the privacy or safety of others (e.g., touching others), it is important to find ways to work around the problem, but acceptance of the child is critical even when the behaviors are unacceptable.

- Provide opportunities for short breaks out of the classroom. Time in a private place to relax and release the tics can often reduce symptoms in class. Private time may also enhance the student's ability to focus on schoolwork, because energy will not be used to suppress the tics.

- Allow the student to take tests in a private room, so energy will not be expended on suppressing tics during a quiet time in the classroom.

- If tics are particularly disruptive, consider eliminating recitation in front of the class for a while. Oral reports might be tape recorded, so those skills can be judged without the added stress of standing before the class.

- Work with other students to help them understand the tics and reduce ridicule and teasing. School counselors, psychologists, and representatives from the local Tourette Syndrome Association chapter can provide information and appropriate audiovisual materials for students and staff.

Accommodations for Writing Problems

Many children with TS also have visual-motor integration problems. Therefore, tasks that require seeing material, processing it, then writing it down are often difficult and time consuming. This problem also affects copying from the board or from a book, completing long assignments, neatness of written work, and prescribed times for completion of written work. Even very bright children with TS who have no trouble grasping concepts may be unable to finish written work because of visual-motor impairments. Sometimes it appears as though the student is lazy or avoiding work, but in reality the effort to record the work on paper may be overwhelming. A number of accommodations can be made to help children with writing difficulties succeed in the classroom.

- Modify written assignments by: having the child copy down and complete every other math problem; allowing the child to present a taped report rather than a written one; allowing a parent to record work or act as secretary so the child can dictate his ideas to facilitate concept formation. It helps to focus on what the child has mastered rather than the quantity of written work produced.

- Since the student with visual-motor problems may not be able to write quickly enough to get important information on paper, assign a reliable note-taking buddy or homework partner who can use carbon paper to make copies of notes and assignments. Be sure to work this out discreetly, so the child with TS does not feel different in yet another way.

- On tests with computer scoring sheets, allow the student to write on the test booklet. This helps avoid poor grades caused by the visual confusion that can occur when using the grid answer sheet. When possible, allow as much time as needed for taking tests.

- Students with visual-motor problems may be poor spellers. Rather than penalizing for spelling errors, encourage proofreading and using a word processor with a spell checker.

- Students with TS seem to have special problems with written math. Encourage the use of manipulatives in teaching math and the use of a calculator to perform rote calculations. Using grid paper with large boxes or turning regular lined paper sideways to form columns can also help the child maintain straight columns when calculating.

Accommodations for Language Problems

- Provide visual input as well as auditory whenever possible. The student could receive written directions as well as oral ones, or have a copy of a lecture outline to follow while listening to instructions. Pictures and graphs that illustrate the text are usually quite effective.

- Give directions one or two steps at a time. Ask the student to repeat the instructions. Then have the student complete one or two items and check with you to see that they have been done properly.

- If you notice a student mumbling while working, suggest a seat where he will not disturb others. Sometimes quietly reauditorizing instructions or information to himself can help a student grasp and remember the assignment.

Children with TS may repeat their own words or those of someone else. This may sound like stuttering but it actually involves the utterance or words or whole phrases. Other students may exploit this problem by whispering inappropriate things so that the child with TS will involuntarily repeat them and get into trouble. Be alert to this provocation.

This urge to repeat can be seen in reading and writing activities. Students may be unable to complete work because they get stuck rereading or rewriting words or phrases over and over. This is called looping. The following can be helpful.

- Have the student take a break or switch to other work.

- When reading, give the child a note card with a cut out window that displays only one word at a time. The student slides the window along while reading so the previous word is covered and the chances of getting stuck are reduced.

- When writing, have the student use pencil or pen without an eraser or allow the student to complete the work orally. Brief reminders to move on may help.

Accommodations for Attention Problems

- Seat the child in front of the teacher for all instruction and directions to minimize the visual distraction of classmates.

- Seat the child away from windows, doors, or other sources of distraction, i.e., where reading groups meet. Give the student an office, a quiet workplace. This could be in a corner, the hall, or the library. This place should not be used as a punishment, but rather a place the student can choose to go to when focusing becomes more difficult. Have the student work in short intense periods with breaks to run an errand or simply wiggle in the seat. Change tasks frequently. For example, complete five math problems, then do some spelling, etc.

- Contract for work to be done in advance. For example, finish a specific number of problems by a certain reasonable time. Short assignments with frequent checks are more effective than two or three sheets of independent work at one time.

- With younger children, simple gestures, such as a hand on the student's shoulder, can be a helpful reminder to focus during listening periods.

References

A Physician's Guide to the Diagnosis and Treatment of Tourette Syndrome, 3rd edition.

Bronheim, Suzanne. (1994). *An Educator's Guide to Tourette Syndrome,* Tourette Syndrome Association, Inc., Bayside, NY. ED321467.

Wertheim, Judy. (1994). *Coping with Tourette Syndrome in the Classroom, Revised.* Tourette Syndrome Association, Inc., Bayside, NY. ED385075.

Chapter 34

Turner Syndrome

Genetic Features of Turner Syndrome

Turner syndrome is a disorder caused by the loss of genetic material from one of the sex chromosomes. Humans normally have a total of 46 chromosomes (which are tiny, DNA-containing elements) that are present in every cell of the body. DNA encodes genes, which specify all the proteins that make up the body and control its functions.

In humans, there are 23 matched pairs of chromosomes in every cell. Each cell contains 22 pairs of chromosomes called autosomes that are the same in males and females. The remaining pair of chromosomes, the X and Y chromosomes, are not shaped similarly, and thus are not matched in the same way as the autosomes.

The X and Y chromosomes are called sex chromosomes. They are responsible for the difference in development between males and females. A Y chromosome contains genes responsible for testis development; and the presence of an X chromosome paired with a Y chromosome will determine male development. On the other hand, two X chromosomes are required for normal ovarian development in females.

"Genetic Features of Turner Syndrome," and "Clinical Features of Turner Syndrome," undated documents produced by the National Institute of Child Health and Human Development (NICHD), available online at http://turners.nichd.nih.gov, cited August 2002.

X Chromosome Monosomy

During the process in which oocytes (eggs) or sperm are formed, one of the sex chromosomes is sometimes lost. An embryo receiving only a Y chromosome cannot survive, but an embryo receiving only an X chromosome may survive and develop as a female with Turner syndrome. In order to examine the matching pairs of chromosomes for a person, doctors can perform a blood test and look at the chromosomes found in the lymphocytes, a particular type of blood cell. This will determine the karyotype of that individual.

The karyotype of X monosomy is termed 45X, meaning that an individual has 44 autosomes and a single X chromosome. The usual female karyotype is 46, XX.

X Chromosome Mosaicism

A sex chromosome may also be lost during early stages of embryonic development, such that some cells of the growing body receive a single X chromosome. This condition is called mosaicism, and the clinical features of Turner syndrome correlate with the relative percentage of 45X cells within the body.

If only a small percentage of cells have been affected, the phenotypes of Turner syndrome may be relatively mild. In other words, mosaicism may lessen the severity of certain clinical features. An example of the lessened effects due to mosaicism is if a woman with Turner syndrome experiences regular menstrual cycles until her late 20's rather than not having any menstrual cycle at all.

The genetic diagnosis in such cases may require the examination of many, many blood cells, and/or the examination of other cell types such as skin cells. The genotype is usually specified as 45X (10)/46XX (90) to indicate for example, that 10% of cells examined were found to have X monosomy.

X Chromosome Defects

A third cause of Turner syndrome involves X chromosome defects rather than complete loss. For example, one X chromosome may be fragmented, have portions deleted or other structural problems such as ring formation preventing the normal expression of X chromosome genes.

The clinical consequences of having one normal and one structurally defective X chromosome vary widely. A small deletion may result in a single feature such as ovarian failure or short stature and no other effects. Larger deletions or deletions affecting critical areas regulating the whole chromosome may result in a full spectrum of Turner syndrome problems.

Moreover, the presence of small ring X chromosome causes severe consequences, because in addition to absence of some important genes, there may be deleterious expression of X chromosome genes that are normally silenced, or inactivated in the second X chromosome. The diagnosis of abnormal X chromosomes may require specialized, molecular cytogenetic studies to identify small deletions or inversions of X chromosome material.

Is Turner Syndrome Hereditary?

While Turner syndrome is genetic in that it involves the loss or abnormal expression of X chromosome genes, it is not usually hereditary in the conventional sense. That is, it does not typically run in families. The one exception to this observation are families with a X chromosome deletion which is stable enough to be passed down through the generations and which also allows fertility.

Turner syndrome affects all races, nationalities and regions of the world equally, and parents who have produced many unaffected children may still have a child with Turner syndrome. There are no known toxins or environmental hazards that increase the chances of Turner syndrome. A woman with Turner syndrome has a low probability of being fertile, since the ovaries are negatively impacted in this disorder. However, if she does become pregnant and passes on her normal X chromosome to her offspring, no continuation of the syndrome is expected.

Clinical Features of Turner Syndrome

Turner syndrome affects approximately 1 out of every 2,500 female live births worldwide. It embraces a broad spectrum of features, from major heart defects to minor cosmetic issues. Some individuals with Turner syndrome may have only a few features, while others may have many. Almost all people with Turner syndrome have short stature and loss of ovarian function, but the severity of these problems varies considerably amongst individuals.

Cognitive Function/Educational Issues

In general, individuals with Turner syndrome have normal intelligence. This is in contrast to other chromosomal syndromes such as Down's syndrome (Trisomy 21). However, girls and women with Turner syndrome may have difficulty with specific visual-spatial coordination tasks (e.g.

mentally rotating objects in space) and learning math (geometry, arithmetic). This very specific learning problem has been termed the "Turner neurocognitive phenotype" and appears due to loss of X chromosome genes important for selected aspects of nervous system development.

Some girls and women with Turner syndrome experience difficulties with memory and motor coordination. These problems may be related to estrogen deficiency and individuals often improve when given estrogen treatment. The verbal skills of individuals with Turner syndrome are usually normal.

Appearance

Individuals with Turner syndrome may have a short neck with a webbed appearance, a low hairline at the back of the neck, and low-set ears. Hands and feet of affected individuals may be swollen or puffy at birth, and often have soft nails that turn upward at the ends when they are older. All these features appear to be due to obstruction of the lymphatic system during fetal development. Another characteristic cosmetic feature is the presence of multiple pigmented nevi, which are colored spots on the skin.

Short Stature

Almost all individuals with Turner syndrome have short stature. This is partially due to the loss of action SHOX gene on the X chromosome. This particular gene is important for long bone growth. The loss of SHOX may also explain some of the skeletal features found in Turner syndrome, such as short fingers and toes, and irregular rotations of the wrist and elbow joints. Linear growth is attenuated in utero, and statural growth lags during childhood and adolescence, resulting in adult heights of 143-145 cm (approximately 4 feet 8 inches). Final adult height in Turner syndrome can be increased by a few inches if growth hormone (GH) treatment is given relatively early in childhood. However, not all individuals with Turner syndrome get a good growth response to GH.

Puberty/Reproduction

Unknown genes on the X chromosome regulate the development and functions of the ovary. Most individuals with Turner syndrome experience loss of ovarian function early in childhood, and thus do not enter puberty at the normal age. Some teenagers may undergo some breast development and begin menstruating, but cease further development and menses during the later teen years. A few women with Turner syndrome have apparently normal ovarian function with regular menses until the mid-20s before ovarian failure occurs. A few spontaneous pregnancies have been reported.

It is standard medical practice to treat girls with Turner syndrome with estrogen to induce breast development and other features of puberty if menses has not occurred by age 15 years at the latest. Girls and women with Turner syndrome should be maintained on estrogen/progesterone treatment to maintain their secondary sexual development and to protect their bones from osteoporosis until at least the usual age of menopause (50 years).

Most women with Turner syndrome do not have ovaries with healthy oocytes capable of fertilization and embryo formation. Current assisted reproductive technology, however, may allow women to become pregnant with donated oocytes.

Cardiovascular

From 5-10% of children with Turner syndrome are found to have a severe constriction of the major blood vessel coming out from the heart, a condition known as coarctation of the aorta. This defect is thought to be the result of an obstructed lymphatic system compressing the developing aorta during fetal life. This can be surgically corrected as soon as it is diagnosed.

Other major defects in the heart and its major vessels are reported to a much lesser degree. As many as 15% of adults with Turner syndrome are reported to have bicuspid aortic valves, meaning that the major blood vessel from the heart has only two rather than three components to the valve regulating blood flow. This condition has been discovered mainly by medical imaging studies on women without symptoms, and may not be clinically obvious. It requires careful medical monitoring, since bicuspid aortic valves can deteriorate or become infected. In general, it is advised that all persons with Turner syndrome undergo annual cardiac evaluations.

Many women with Turner syndrome have high blood pressure, which may be apparent even in childhood. In some cases this high blood pressure may be due to aortic constriction, or to kidney abnormalities. In a majority of women, however, no specific cause for the high blood pressure has been found.

Kidney

Kidney problems are present in approximately 1/3 of individuals with Turners and may contribute to high blood pressure. Three types of kidney problems have been reported: a single horseshoe-shaped kidney, as opposed to two distinct, bean-shaped structures; an abnormal urine collecting system; or an abnormal artery supply to the kidneys. While these problems may be corrected surgically and the kidneys usually function normally, they may be associated with a tendency towards high blood pressure and infections.

Osteoporosis

There is a high incidence of osteoporosis—meaning thin or weak bones—in women with Turner syndrome. Osteoporosis leads to loss of height, curvature of the spine and increased bone fractures.

The primary cause of osteoporosis in individuals with Turners appears to be inadequate circulating estrogen in the body. Turner women who have low levels of estrogen due to ovarian failure can take estrogen treatments, which will help prevent osteoporosis. It is possible that other factors contribute to the severity of osteoporosis in Turner syndrome. For example, there may be defects in bone structure or strength related to the loss of unknown X chromosome genes. This is an area of major medical significance, which demands further study to help prevent osteoporosis and fractures in women with Turner syndrome.

Diabetes

Type II diabetes, also known as insulin resistant diabetes (glucose intolerance), has a high occurrence rate in individuals with Turner syndrome. Individuals with Turner syndrome have twice the risk of the general population for developing this disease. It appears that the muscles of many persons with Turner syndrome fail to utilize glucose efficiently, and this may contribute to the development of high blood sugar (diabetes).

The reason for the high risk of diabetes amongst individuals with Turner syndrome is unknown. Diabetes type 2 can be controlled through careful monitoring of blood-sugar levels, diet, exercise, regular doctor visits and sometimes medication.

Thyroid

Approximately 1/3 of individuals with Turner syndrome have a thyroid disorder, usually hypothyroidism. Symptoms of this condition include decreased energy, dry skin, cold-intolerance and poor growth.

In most cases, it is caused by an immune system attack on the thyroid gland (also known as Hashimoto's thyroiditis). Although it is not known why thyroid disorders occur with a high frequency in Turner syndrome, the condition is easily treated with thyroid hormone supplements.

Chapter 35

Williams Syndrome

What Is Williams Syndrome?

Williams syndrome is a rare, congenital (present at birth) disorder characterized by physical and developmental problems including an impulsive and outgoing (excessively social) personality, limited spatial skills and motor control, and intellectual disability (i.e., developmental delay, learning disabilities, mental retardation, or attention deficit disorder). Other features include characteristic elfin-like facial features, heart and blood vessel problems, hypercalcemia (elevated blood calcium levels), low birth weight, slow weight gain, feeding problems, irritability during infancy, dental and kidney abnormalities, hyperacusis (sensitive hearing), and musculoskeletal problems. Symptoms vary among patients. Although individuals with Williams syndrome may show competence in areas such as language, music, and interpersonal relations, their IQs are usually below average, and they are considered moderately to mildly retarded. Scientists have learned that most individuals with Williams syndrome have a deletion of genetic material on chromosome 7. This probably causes the physical and developmental problems experienced by patients.

"NINDS Williams Syndrome Information Page," National Institute of Neurological Disorders and Stroke (NINDS), 2001; available online at http://www.ninds.nih.gov/health_and_medical/disorders/Williams.htm.

Is There Any Treatment?

There is neither a cure for Williams syndrome nor a standard course of treatment. Treatment is symptomatic and supportive. Individuals with Williams syndrome need regular monitoring for potential medical problems by a physician familiar with the disorder, as well as specialized services to maximize their potential.

What Is the Prognosis?

The prognosis for individuals with Williams syndrome varies. Some may be able to master self-help skills, complete academic or vocational school, and live in supervised homes or on their own, while others may not progress to this level.

Part Five

Educational Issues

Chapter 36

Diagnosis and Assessment of Learning Disabilities

Introduction

In response to the expressed need for guidance related to the documentation of a learning disability in adolescents and adults, the Association on Higher Education And Disability (AHEAD) has developed the following guidelines. The primary intent of these guidelines is to provide students, professional diagnosticians and service providers with a common understanding and knowledge base of those components of documentation which are necessary to validate a learning disability and the need for accommodation. The information and documentation that establishes a learning disability should be comprehensive in order to make it possible for a student to be served in a postsecondary setting.

The document presents guidelines in four important areas: 1) qualifications of the evaluator, 2) recency of documentation, 3) appropriate clinical documentation to substantiate the learning disability, and 4) evidence to establish a rationale supporting the need for accommodations.

Under the Americans with Disabilities Act (ADA) and Section 504 of the Rehabilitation Act of 1973, individuals with learning disabilities are guaranteed certain protections and rights of equal access to

The information in this chapter is reprinted with permission from *Guidelines for Documentation of Learning Disability in Adolescents and Adults*. © 1997 The Association on Higher Education and Disability (AHEAD), Columbus, OH USA. For additional information, visit http://www.ahead.org.

programs and services; thus the documentation should indicate that the disability substantially limits some major life activity. The following guidelines are provided in the interest of assuring that LD documentation is appropriate to verify eligibility and to support requests for accommodations, academic adjustments and/or auxiliary aids. It is recommended that postsecondary institutions using these guidelines consult with their legal counsel before establishing a policy on documentation relating to individuals with disabilities. In countries not regulated by this legislation further modification may be appropriate.

These guidelines are designed to be a framework for institutions to work from in establishing criteria for eligibility. It is acknowledged that different educational settings with different student populations will need to modify and adapt these guidelines to meet the needs and backgrounds of their student populations.

Documentation Guidelines

Qualifications of the Evaluator

Professionals conducting assessments, rendering diagnoses of learning disabilities, and making recommendations for appropriate accommodations must be qualified to do so. Comprehensive training and direct experience with an adolescent and adult LD population is essential.

The name, title and professional credentials of the evaluator, including information about license or certification (e.g., licensed psychologist) as well as the area of specialization, employment and state/province in which the individual practices should be clearly stated in the documentation. For example, the following professionals would generally be considered qualified to evaluate specific learning disabilities provided that they have additional training and experience in the assessment of learning problems in adolescents and adults: clinical or educational psychologists, school psychologists, neuropsychologists, learning disabilities specialists, medical doctors, and other professionals. Use of diagnostic terminology indicating a learning disability by someone whose training and experience are not in these fields is not acceptable. It is of utmost importance that evaluators are sensitive and respectful of cultural and linguistic differences in adolescents and adults during the assessment process. It is not considered appropriate for professionals to evaluate members of their families. All reports should be on letterhead, typed, dated, signed and otherwise legible.

Documentation

The provision of all reasonable accommodations and services is based upon assessment of the impact of the student's disabilities on his or her academic performance at a given time in the student's life. Therefore, it is in the student's best interest to provide recent and appropriate documentation relevant to the student's learning environment.

Flexibility in accepting documentation is important, especially in settings with significant numbers of non-traditional students. In some instances, documentation may be outdated or inadequate in scope or content. It may not address the student's current level of functioning or need for accommodations because observed changes may have occurred in the student's performance since the previous assessment was conducted. In such cases, it may be appropriate to update the evaluation report. Since the purpose of the update is to determine the student's current need for accommodations, the update, conducted by a qualified professional, should include a rationale for ongoing services and accommodations.

Substantiation of the Learning Disability

Documentation should validate the need for services based on the individual's current level of functioning in the educational setting. A school plan such as an individualized education program (IEP) or a 504 plan is insufficient documentation, but it can be included as part of a more comprehensive assessment battery. A comprehensive assessment battery and the resulting diagnostic report should include a diagnostic interview, assessment of aptitude, academic achievement, information processing and a diagnosis.

Diagnostic Interview

An evaluation report should include the summary of a comprehensive diagnostic interview. Learning disabilities are commonly manifested during childhood, but not always formally diagnosed. Relevant information regarding the student's academic history and learning processes in elementary, secondary and postsecondary education should be investigated. The diagnostician, using professional judgment as to which areas are relevant, should conduct a diagnostic interview which may include: a description of the presenting problem(s); developmental, medical, psychosocial and employment histories; family history (including primary language of the home and the student's current level of English fluency); and a discussion of dual diagnosis where indicated.

287

Assessment

The neuropsychological or psycho-educational evaluation for the diagnosis of a specific learning disability must provide clear and specific evidence that a learning disability does or does not exist. Assessment, and any resulting diagnosis, should consist of and be based on a comprehensive assessment battery which does not rely on any one test or subtest.

Evidence of a substantial limitation to learning or other major life activity must be provided. Minimally, the domains to be addressed must include the following:

1. Aptitude: A complete intellectual assessment with all subtests and standard scores reported.

2. Academic Achievement: A comprehensive academic achievement battery is essential with all subtests and standard scores reported for those subtests administered. The battery should include current levels of academic functioning in relevant areas such as reading (decoding and comprehension), mathematics, and oral and written language.

3. Information Processing: Specific areas of information processing (e.g., short- and long-term memory, sequential memory, auditory and visual perception/processing, processing speed, executive functioning and motor ability) should be assessed.

Other assessment measures such as non-standard measures and informal assessment procedures or observations may be helpful in determining performance across a variety of domains. Other formal assessment measures may be integrated with the above instruments to help determine a learning disability and differentiate it from co-existing neurological and/or psychiatric disorders (i.e., to establish a differential diagnosis). In addition to standardized tests, it is also very useful to include informal observations of the student during the test administration.

Specific Diagnosis

Individual learning styles, learning differences, academic problems and test difficulty or anxiety, in and of themselves, do not constitute a learning disability. It is important to rule out alternative explanations for problems in learning such as emotional, attentional or motivational problems that may be interfering with learning but do not constitute a learning disability. The diagnostician is encouraged to use direct language in the diagnosis and documentation of a learning disability, avoiding the use of terms such as "suggests" or "is indicative of." If the data indicate that a learning disability is not present, the evaluator should state that conclusion in the report.

Test Scores

Standard scores and/or percentiles should be provided for all normed measures. Grade equivalents are not useful unless standard scores and/or percentiles are also included. The data should logically reflect a substantial limitation to learning for which the student is requesting the accommodation. The particular profile of the student's strengths and weaknesses must be shown to relate to functional limitations that may necessitate accommodations. The tests used should be reliable, valid and standardized for use with an adolescent/adult population. The test findings should document both the nature and severity of the learning disability. Informal inventories, surveys and direct observation by a qualified professional may be used in tandem with formal tests in order to further develop a clinical hypothesis.

Clinical Summary

A well-written diagnostic summary based on a comprehensive evaluation process is a necessary component of the report. Assessment instruments and the data they provide do not diagnose; rather, they provide important elements that must be integrated by the evaluator with background information, observations of the client during the testing situation, and the current context. It is essential, therefore, that professional judgment be utilized in the development of a clinical summary. The clinical summary should include:

1. demonstration of the evaluator's having ruled out alternative explanations for academic problems as a result of poor education, poor motivation and/or study skills, emotional problems, attentional problems and cultural/language differences;

2. indication of how patterns in the student's cognitive ability, achievement and information processing reflect the presence of a learning disability;

3. indication of the substantial limitation to learning or other major life activity presented by the learning disability and the

degree to which it impacts the individual in the learning context for which accommodations are being requested; and

4. indication as to why specific accommodations are needed and how the effects of the specific disability are accommodated.

The summary should also include any record of prior accommodation or auxiliary aids, including any information about specific conditions under which the accommodations were used (e.g., standardized testing, final exams, licensing or certification examinations).

Recommendations for Accommodations

It is important to recognize that accommodation needs can change over time and are not always identified through the initial diagnostic process. Conversely, a prior history of accommodation does not, in and of itself, warrant the provision of a similar accommodation.

The diagnostic report should include specific recommendations for accommodations as well as an explanation as to why each accommodation is recommended. The evaluators should describe the impact the diagnosed learning disability has on a specific major life activity as well as the degree of significance of this impact on the individual. The evaluator should support recommendations with specific test results or clinical observations.

If accommodations are not clearly identified in a diagnostic report, the disability service provider should seek clarification and, if necessary, more information. The final determination for providing appropriate and reasonable accommodations rests with the institution. In instances where a request for accommodations is denied in a postsecondary institution, a written grievance or appeal procedure should be in place.

Confidentiality

The receiving institution has a responsibility to maintain confidentiality of the evaluation and may not release any part of the documentation without the student's informed and written consent.

Recommendations for Consumers

For Assistance in Finding a Qualified Professional

- contact the disability services coordinator at the institution you attend or plan to attend to discuss documentation needs; and

- discuss your future plans with the disability services coordinator. If additional documentation is required, seek assistance in identifying a qualified professional.

In Selecting a Qualified Professional

- ask what his or her credentials are;
- ask what experience he or she has had working with adults with learning disabilities; and
- ask if he or she has ever worked with the service provider at your institution or with the agency to which you are sending material.

In Working with the Professional

- take a copy of these guidelines to the professional;
- encourage him or her to clarify questions with the person who provided you with these guidelines;
- be prepared to be forthcoming, thorough and honest with requested information; and
- know that professionals must maintain confidentiality with respect to your records and testing information.

As Follow-Up to the Assessment by the Professional

- request a written copy of the assessment report;
- request the opportunity to discuss the results and recommendations;
- request additional resources if you need them; and
- maintain a personal file of your records and reports.

Tests for Assessing Adolescents and Adults

When selecting a battery of tests, it is critical to consider the technical adequacy of instruments including their reliability, validity and standardization on an appropriate norm group. The professional judgment of an evaluator in choosing tests is important. The following list is provided as a helpful resource, but it is not intended to be definitive or exhaustive.

Aptitude

- Wechsler Adult Intelligence Scale—Revised (WAIS-R)
- Woodcock-Johnson Psychoeducational Battery—Revised: Tests of Cognitive Ability
- Kaufman Adolescent and Adult Intelligence Test
- Stanford-Binet Intelligence Scale (4th ed.)
- The Slosson Intelligence Test—Revised and the Kaufman Brief Intelligence Test are primarily screening devices which are not comprehensive enough to provide the kinds of information necessary to make accommodation decisions.

Academic Achievement

- Scholastic Abilities Test for Adults (SATA)
- Stanford Test of Academic Skills
- Woodcock-Johnson Psychoeducational Battery—Revised: Tests of Achievement
- Wechsler Individual Achievement Test (WIAT)

or specific achievement tests such as:

- Nelson-Denny Reading Skills Test
- Stanford Diagnostic Mathematics Test
- Test of Written Language—3 (TOWL-3)
- Woodcock Reading Mastery Tests – Revised

Specific achievement tests are useful instruments when administered under standardized conditions and interpreted within the context of other diagnostic information. The Wide Range Achievement Test—3 (WRAT-3) is not a comprehensive measure of achievement and therefore is not useful if used as the sole measure of achievement.

Information Processing

Acceptable instruments include the Detroit Tests of Learning Aptitude—3 (DTLA-3), the Detroit Tests of Learning Aptitude—Adult (DTLA-A), information from subtests on WAIS-R, Woodcock-Johnson Psychoeducational Battery—Revised: Tests of Cognitive Ability, as well as other relevant instruments.

Chapter 37

Related Services for Children with Disabilities

Introduction

The Individuals with Disabilities Education Act Amendments of 1997 (IDEA '97) mandates that "...all children with disabilities have available to them a free appropriate public education [FAPE] that emphasizes special education and related services designed to meet their unique needs and prepare them for employment and independent living" [Section 601(d)(1)(A)]. In accordance with the IDEA '97 and other federal laws, more than 5.9 million children with disabilities (ages 3 through 21) across the nation received special education and related services in the 1997-98 school year (U.S. Department of Education, 1999b).

What, precisely, are related services, and why are they an important part of educating children with disabilities? Who is eligible for related services, and how are related services delivered? This chapter briefly examines the answers to these and other questions by looking at:

- the related services listed in the Federal regulations;

- how students become eligible for related services;

- how related services are typically obtained for students;

"Related Services," from the National Information Center for Children and Youth with Disabilities (NICHCY), *News Digest*, ND16 (2nd Edition), September 2001.

293

- additional related services not listed specifically in the Federal regulations (i.e., artistic/cultural programs) but that can assist a student in benefiting from special education;

- how related services are typically delivered, coordinated, and funded; and

- related services under Section 504 of the Rehabilitation Act of 1973.

An Overview of Related Services Under IDEA

Several important federal laws address the educational needs of children and youth with disabilities. One such law, passed in 1975, is the Education for All Handicapped Children Act, otherwise known as EHA or Public Law (P.L.) 94-142. This law mandated that special education and related services be made available to all eligible school-aged children and youth with disabilities. Since the time of EHA's enactment, Federal funds have been provided to help State and local educational agencies provide special education and related services to children with disabilities.

In 1990, as part of its reauthorization by Congress, the EHA was renamed the Individuals with Disabilities Education Act, or IDEA (P.L. 101-476). The law was again amended in June 1997 as P.L. 105-17. The 1997 law is called the Individuals with Disabilities Education Act—referred to hereafter as IDEA '97.

Finding Specific Sections of the Regulations

As you read the following explanations about the law, you will find references to specific sections of the Federal regulations (such as Section 300.24) implementing the IDEA '97. You can use these references to locate the precise sections in the Federal regulations that address the issue being discussed. For example, following the list of related services, you are given the reference Section 300.24(a). This reference tells you that, if you wanted to read the exact words the regulations use, you would look under Section 300.24(a) of the Code of Federal Regulations (CFR) for Title 34 (sometimes referred to as 34 CFR).

What Are Related Services?

In general, the final regulations for IDEA '97 define the term related services as "transportation and such developmental, corrective, and other supportive services as are required to assist a child with a disability to benefit from special education..." [Section 300.24(a)]. The following are included within the definition of related services:

- speech-language pathology and audiology services;
- psychological services;
- physical and occupational therapy;
- recreation, including therapeutic recreation;
- early identification and assessment of disabilities in children;
- counseling services, including rehabilitation counseling;
- orientation and mobility services;
- medical services for diagnostic or evaluation purposes;
- school health services;
- social work services in schools;
- parent counseling and training; and
- transportation. [Section 300.24(a)].

With the exception of "early identification and assessment of disabilities in children," each of these services will be discussed in this chapter. It is important to know that the definition of related services contained within IDEA '97's regulations goes on to define these individual terms more specifically.

Who Is Eligible for Related Services?

Under IDEA '97, a student must need special education to be considered eligible for related services (unless the related service needed by the child is considered special education rather than a related service under State standards) [Section 300.7(a)(2)(ii)]. A child must have a full and individual evaluation to determine:

- if he or she has a disability as defined under IDEA '97, and
- if, because of that disability, he or she needs special education and related services.

For the purposes of this chapter on related services, it is useful to know that the law requires that a child be assessed in all areas related to his or her suspected disability. This includes, if appropriate, evaluating the child's:

- health,
- vision,
- hearing,
- social and emotional status,
- general intelligence,
- academic performance,
- communicative status, and
- motor abilities. [Section 300.532(g)]

A variety of assessment tools and strategies must be used to gather relevant functional and developmental information about the child [Section 300.532(b)]. The evaluation must be sufficiently comprehensive so as to identify all of the child's special education and related services needs, whether or not those needs are commonly linked to the disability category in which he or she has been classified [Section 300.532(h)].

If the evaluation shows that the child does, indeed, have a disability and that, because of that disability, he or she needs special education and related services, then he or she meets the criteria for special education and related services.

How Do People Know What Related Services a Child Needs?

The evaluation process is intended to provide decision makers with the information they need to determine: (a) if the student has a disability and needs special education and related services, and, if so, (b) an appropriate educational program for the student. It also allows them to identify the related services a student will need.

Following the child's evaluation and the determination that he or she is eligible for special education and related services, a team of individuals called the IEP team—which includes the parents and, where appropriate, the student—sits down and writes an Individualized Education Program (IEP) for the student. The IEP team looks carefully at the evaluation results, which show the child's areas of strength and need. The team decides what measurable annual goals (including benchmarks or short-term objectives), among other things, are appropriate for the child. Part of developing the IEP also includes specifying "the special education and related services and supplementary aids and services to be provided to the child, or on behalf of the child, and a statement of the program modifications or supports for school personnel that will be provided" for the child:

- to advance appropriately toward attaining the annual goals,

- to be involved and progress in the general curriculum (that is, the curriculum used by nondisabled students),

- to participate in extracurricular and other nonacademic activities, and

- to be educated and participate with other children with disabilities and nondisabled children. [Section 300.347(a)(3)]

Thus, based on the evaluation results, the IEP team discusses, decides upon, and specifies the related services that a child needs in order to benefit from special education. Making decisions about how often a related service will be provided, and where and by whom is also a function of the IEP team.

It is important to recognize that each child with a disability may not require all of the available types of related services. Moreover, as Attachment 1 accompanying the regulations to IDEA '97 points out, "As under prior law, the list of related services is not exhaustive and may include other developmental, corrective, or supportive services (such as artistic and cultural programs, art, music, and dance therapy) if they are required to assist a child with a disability to benefit from special education in order for the child to receive FAPE" (U.S. Department of Education, 1999a, p. 12548).

As States respond to the requirements of Federal law, many have legislated their own related service requirements, which may include services beyond those specified in IDEA '97. Further, "if it is determined through the [IDEA's] evaluation and IEP requirements that a child with a disability requires a particular supportive service in order to receive FAPE, regardless of whether that service is included in these [Federal] regulations, that service can be considered a related service...and must be provided at no cost to the parents" (p. 12548).

It is useful to note that IDEA '97 does not expressly require that the IEP team include related services personnel. However, if a particular related service is going to be discussed in an IEP meeting, it would be appropriate for such personnel to be included or otherwise involved in developing the IEP. IDEA '97 final regulations state that, at the discretion of the parent or the public agency, "other individuals who have knowledge or special expertise regarding the child, including related services personnel as appropriate" may be part of a child's IEP team [Section 300.344(a)(6)]. Appendix A of the regulations specifically states (at Question 30) that, if a child with a disability has an identified need for related services, the public agency responsible for the child's education should ensure that a qualified provider of that service either:

- attends the IEP meeting, or

- provides a written recommendation concerning the nature, frequency, and amount of service to be provided to the child. (U.S. Department of Education, 1999a, p. 12478)

Once the IEP team has determined which related services are required to assist the student to benefit from his or her special education, these must be listed in the IEP. The IEP also must include a statement of measurable annual goals (including benchmarks or short-term objectives) related to:

- meeting the child's needs that result from his or her disability to enable the child to be involved in and progress in the general curriculum (or for preschool children, as appropriate, to participate in appropriate activities), and

- meeting each of the child's other educational needs that result from the disability. [Section 300.347(a)(2)]

In addition to this key information, the IEP must also specify with respect to each service:

- when the service will begin; and

- the anticipated frequency (how often), location (where), and duration (how long) of the service. [Section 300.347(a)(6)]

The IEP is a written commitment for the delivery of services to meet a student's educational needs. A school district must ensure that all of the related services specified in the IEP, including the amount, are provided to a student.

Changes in the amount of services listed in the IEP cannot be made without holding another IEP meeting. However, if there is no change in the overall amount of service, some adjustments in the scheduling of services may be possible without the necessity of another IEP meeting.

Do the Parents Have to Pay for the Related Services the Child Receives?

No. School districts may not charge parents of eligible students with disabilities for the costs of related services that have been included on the child's IEP. Just as special and regular education must be provided to an eligible student with a disability at no cost to the parent or guardian, so, too, must related services when the IEP team has determined that such services are required in order for the child to receive FAPE and have included them in the student's IEP.

A Closer Look at Specific Related Services

Perhaps the best way to develop an understanding of related services is to look at each in more detail. Because there are quite a few services that can be considered as related services, the information presented about each of the following related services is intended only as an introduction. It is not the intent of this chapter, just as it is not the intent of the law, to exhaustively describe each related service. It may be helpful, however, to read further about the services in order to know what related services are most commonly provided to students with disabilities and, in some situations, their families.

Speech-Language Pathology Services

Speech-language pathology services are provided by speech-language professionals and speech-language assistants in accordance with State regulations, to address the needs of children and youth with communication disabilities. Under the IDEA '97 final regulations, these services include:

- "identification of children with speech or language impairments;

- "diagnosis and appraisal of specific speech or language impairments;

- "referral for medical or other professional attention necessary for the habilitation of speech or language impairments;

- "provision of speech and language services for the habilitation or prevention of communicative impairments; and

- "counseling and guidance of parents, children, and teachers regarding speech and language impairments." [Section 300.24(b)(14)]

Assistive Technology Devices and Services

Assistive technology (AT) refers to various types of devices and services designed to help students with disabilities function within their environments. Many areas are covered under the umbrella of assistive technology, including computers, adaptive toys and games, devices to improve positioning and mobility, devices designed to help individuals with disabilities communicate (called augmentative communication devices), and electronic aids to daily living (RESNA Technical Assistance Project, 1992).

An assistive technology device means "any item, piece of equipment, or product system, whether acquired commercially off the shelf, modified, or customized, that is used to increase, maintain, or improve the functional capabilities of a child with a disability" (Section 300.5). Assistive technology devices may be used for personal care, sensory processing of information, communication, mobility, or leisure. For young children, assistive technology may involve adaptive toys or simple computer software games to stimulate eye-hand coordination (Derer, Polsgrove, & Rieth, 1996). For other children, it may involve adaptive eating utensils, electronic augmentative communication devices, or a voice-activated word processing software program.

An assistive technology service means "...any service that directly assists a child with a disability in the selection, acquisition, or use of an assistive technology device" (Section 300.6). School districts are responsible for helping individuals with disabilities select and acquire appropriate assistive technology devices and train them in their use, if doing so is necessary for them to receive FAPE (Section 300.308). Such services include:

- evaluating a child's needs, including a functional evaluation in the child's customary environment;

- purchasing, leasing, or otherwise providing for the acquisition of assistive technology devices by children with disabilities;

- selecting, designing, fitting, customizing, adapting, applying, maintaining, repairing, or replacing assistive technology devices;

- coordinating and using other therapies, interventions, or services with assistive technology devices (such as those associated with existing education and rehabilitation plans and programs);

- training or technical assistance for a child with a disability or, if appropriate, the child's family; and

- training or technical assistance for professionals (including individuals providing education or rehabilitation services); employers; or other individuals who provide services to, employ, or are substantially involved in the major functions of that child. (Section 300.6)

Rothstein and Everson (1995) suggest several guidelines for decision making regarding assistive technology, including:

- look for simple solutions;

- consider the learning and work style of the student;

- consider the long-range implications of the student's disability and the device;

- look at each device for ease of use and maintenance, timeliness, adaptability, portability, dependability, durability, and technical support needed;

- investigate all options;

- compare similar devices from different manufacturers, and

- purchase devices only after consulting with a professional.

Consideration of a child's need for assistive technology devices and services occurs on a case-by-case basis in connection with the development of a child's IEP. Thus, when an IEP of a student with a disability is being developed, reviewed, or revised (if appropriate), the IEP team must determine his or her need for an assistive technology device or service, determine those devices that will facilitate the student's education, and list them in the IEP. The public agency must then provide them to the student at no cost to the parents.

May a child use a school-purchased AT device in his or her home or other setting? According to the IDEA '97's final regulations, the answer to this question would be determined on a case-by-case basis. Such use in non-school settings would be "required if the child's IEP team determines that the child needs access to those devices in order to receive FAPE" [Section 300.308(b)]—for example, to complete homework. Question 36 of Appendix A of the regulations adds that "the parents cannot be charged for normal use, wear and tear. However, while ownership of the devices in these circumstances would remain with the public agency, State law, rather than Part B [of IDEA], generally would govern whether parents are liable for loss, theft, or damage due to negligence or misuse of publicly owned equipment used at home or in other settings in accordance with a child's IEP" (U.S. Department of Education, 1999a, p. 12479).

Audiology

Audiology includes:

- identifying children with hearing loss;

- determining the range, nature, and degree of hearing loss, including referral for medical or other professional attention for the habilitation of hearing;

- providing habilitative activities, such as language habilitation, auditory training, speech reading (lip-reading), hearing evaluation, and speech conservation;

- creating and administering programs for prevention of hearing loss;

- counseling and guidance of children, parents, and teachers regarding hearing loss; and

- determining children's needs for group and individual amplification, selecting and fitting an appropriate aid, and evaluating the effectiveness of amplification. [Section 300.24(b)(1)]

Some schools have hearing screening programs and staff trained to conduct audiologic screenings of children. Others may participate in regional cooperatives or other arrangements that provide audiological services. Those school districts that do not have diagnostic facilities to evaluate students for hearing loss and related communication problems or central auditory processing disorders may refer students to a clinical setting, such as a hospital or audiology clinic, or make other contractual arrangements (American Speech-Language-Hearing Association, personal communication, August 1, 2000).

Counseling Services

Counseling services, according to the American School Counselor Association (1999), focus on the needs, interests, and issues related to various stages of student growth. School counselors may help students with personal and social concerns such as developing self-knowledge, making effective decisions, learning health choices, and improving responsibility. Counselors may also help students with future planning related to setting and reaching academic goals, developing a positive attitude toward learning, and recognizing and utilizing academic strengths. Other counseling services may include parent counseling and training and rehabilitation counseling (that is, counseling specific to career development and employment preparation) (Maag & Katsiyannis, 1996).

Counseling services are services provided by qualified social workers, psychologists, guidance counselors, or other qualified personnel [Section 300.24(b)(2)]. A school counselor is a certified professional who meets the State's certification standards. In some schools, the counselor may also perform some functions similar to those of the school psychologist as described below under Psychological Services.

Parent Counseling and Training

Parent counseling and training is an important related service that can help parents enhance the vital role they play in the lives of their children. When necessary to help an eligible student with a disability benefit from the educational program, parent counseling and training can include:

- "Assisting parents in understanding the special needs of their child;

- "Providing parents with information about child development; and

- "Helping parents to acquire the necessary skills that will allow them to support the implementation of their child's IEP or IFSP" [Individualized Family Service Plan]. [Section 300.24(b)(7)]

The last aspect—that of helping parents acquire necessary skills to support the implementation of their child's IEP or IFSP—is new in IDEA '97 and was added to:

> recognize the more active role acknowledged for parents [as] very important participants in the education process for their children. Helping them gain the skills that will enable them to help their children meet the goals and objectives of their IEP or IFSP will be a positive change for parents, will assist in furthering the education of their children, and will aid the schools as it will create opportunities to build reinforcing relationships between each child's educational program and out-of-school learning. (U.S. Department of Education, 1999a, p. 12549)

Psychological Services

Psychological services are delivered as a related service when necessary to help eligible students with disabilities benefit from their special education. In some schools, these services are provided by a school psychologist, but some services are also appropriately provided by other trained personnel, including school social workers and counselors. Under IDEA '97 regulations, the term psychological services includes:

- "administering psychological and educational tests and other assessment procedures;

- "interpreting assessment results;

- "obtaining, integrating, and interpreting information about a student's behavior and conditions relating to learning;

- "consulting with other staff members in planning school programs to meet the special needs of children as indicated by psychological tests, interviews, and behavioral evaluations;

- "planning and managing a program of psychological services, including psychological counseling for students and parents; and

- "assisting in developing positive behavioral intervention strategies." [Section 300.24(b)(9)]

IDEA '97 requires that, in the case of a child whose behavior impedes his or her learning or that of others, the IEP team consider, if appropriate, strategies (including positive behavioral interventions, strategies, and supports) to address that behavior [Section 300.346 (a)(2)(i)]. These interventions and strategies may focus not only on the result of an absent, inadequate, inconsistent, or negative behavior blocking learning but also on the curricular and instructional issues that may trigger problems (Dwyer, 1997). Positive behavioral interventions and supports involve a comprehensive set of strategies aimed at providing a student with a disability an improved lifestyle that includes reductions in problem behaviors, changes in social relationships, an expansion of prosocial skills, and an increase in school and community inclusion (Fox, Vaughn, Dunlap, & Bucy, 1997).

Psychologists and school social workers may be involved in assisting in developing these positive behavioral intervention strategies. However, as the U.S. Department of Education (1999a) notes: "There are many other appropriate professionals in a school district who might also play a role. These examples of personnel who may assist in this activity are not intended to imply either that school psychologists and social workers are automatically qualified to perform these duties or to prohibit other qualified personnel from serving in this role, consistent with State requirements" (p. 12550).

Social Work Services in Schools

Issues or problems at home or in the community can adversely affect a student's performance at school, as can a student's attitudes or behaviors in school. Social work services in schools may become necessary in order to help a student benefit from his or her educational program. Social work services in schools includes:

- "preparing a social or developmental history on a child with a disability;

- "group and individual counseling with the child and family;

- "working in partnership with parents and others on those problems in a child's living situation (home, school, and community) that affect the child's adjustment in school;

- "mobilizing school and community resources to enable the child to learn as effectively as possible in his or her educational program; and

- "assisting in developing positive behavioral intervention strategies." [Section 300.24(b)(13)]

Artistic/Cultural Programs

Artistic/cultural programs are specifically mentioned in Attachment 1 of the Federal regulations for IDEA '97 as "other developmental, corrective, or supportive services (such as artistic and cultural programs, art, music, and dance therapy) if they are required to assist a child with a disability to benefit from special education in order for the child to receive FAPE" (U.S. Department of Education, 1999a, p. 12548). Artistic and cultural programs are designed by art therapists, dance therapists, and music therapists to address the individual needs of students with disabilities. These professionals:

- assess the functioning of individual students;

- design programs appropriate to the needs and abilities of students;

- provide services in which music, movement, or art is used in a therapeutic process to further the child's emotional, physical, cognitive, and/or academic development or integration; and

- often act as resource persons for classroom teachers.

Art therapy provides individuals with disabilities with a means of self-expression and opportunities to expand personal creativity and control. By involving students with art and the creative art process, art therapists work to help students address their unique needs, which may include resolving emotional conflicts, developing self-awareness or social skills, managing behavior, solving problems, reducing anxiety, and improving self-esteem (American Art Therapy Association, 2000).

Dance/movement therapy uses movement as a means for promoting personal growth and furthering the emotional, cognitive, and physical integration of an individual (American Dance Therapy Association, 1998). Dance therapy can develop and promote good posture, discipline, concentration, coordination, agility, speed, balance, strength, and endurance.

Music therapy uses music and music-related strategies to assist or motivate a student to reach specific educational goals as well as address his or her physical, psychological, cognitive, behavioral, and social needs (American Music Therapy Association, 2000). Music and music learning are often used to strengthen nonmusical areas such as academic skills, physical coordination, communication, sensory-motor development, expression of emotions, and stress reduction.

Medical Services

Medical services are considered a related service only under specific conditions. By definition, the term "means services provided by a licensed physician to determine a child's medically related disability that results in the child's need for special education and related services" [Section 300.24(b)(4)]. Thus, medical services are provided (a) by a licensed physician, and (b) for diagnostic or evaluation purposes only.

Occupational Therapy

Occupational therapy (OT) services can enhance a student's ability to function in an educational program. These services are "provided by a qualified occupational therapist" and include:

- "improving, developing, or restoring functions impaired or lost through illness, injury, or deprivation;

- "improving [a child's] ability to perform tasks for independent functioning if functions are impaired or lost; and

- "preventing, through early intervention, initial or further impairment or loss of function" [Section 300.24(b)(5)].

Occupational therapy services in schools may include such services as:

- self-help skills or adaptive living (e.g., eating, dressing);

- functional mobility (e.g., moving safely through school);

- positioning (e.g., sitting appropriately in class);

- sensory-motor processing (e.g., using the senses and muscles);

- fine motor (e.g., writing, cutting) and gross motor performance (e.g., walking, athletic skills);

- life skills training/vocational skills; and

- psychosocial adaptation.

Orientation and Mobility Services

According to Hill and Snook-Hill (1996), orientation involves knowing where you are, where you are going, and how to get to a destination by interpreting information in the environment, while mobility involves moving safely through the environment. IDEA '97 added orientation and mobility (O&M) services to the list of related services specified at Section 300.24. O&M services are defined as "services provided to blind or visually impaired students by qualified personnel to enable those students to attain systematic orientation to and safe movement within their environments in school, home, and community" [Section 300.24(b)(6)(i)]. This includes teaching students the following, as appropriate:

- "spatial and environmental concepts and use of information received by the senses (such as sound, temperature, and vibrations) to establish, maintain, or regain orientation and line of travel (e.g., using sound at a traffic light to cross the street);

- "to use the long cane to supplement visual travel skills or as a tool for safely negotiating the environment for students with no available travel vision;

307

- "to understand and use remaining visual and distance low vision aids; and

- "other concepts, techniques, and tools." [Section 300.24(b)(6)(ii)]

Attachment 1 to the regulations discusses why O&M services are not appropriate for students with disabilities other than visual impairments and draws a distinction between O&M services and what is commonly referred to as travel training.

Some children with disabilities other than visual impairments need travel training if they are to safely and effectively move within and outside their school environment, but these students (e.g., children with significant cognitive disabilities) do not need orientation and mobility services as that term is defined in these regulations. Orientation and mobility services is a term of art that is expressly related to children with visual impairments, and includes services that must be provided by qualified personnel who are trained to work with those children. (U.S. Department of Education, 1999a, p. 12549)

Thus, children with disabilities other than those with visual impairments who need assistance in learning how to safely navigate a variety of settings would generally not receive O&M services but, rather, travel training. Travel training is defined in the IDEA '97 final regulations at Section 300.26(b)(4), as part of the definition of special education. The term means "providing instruction, as appropriate, to children with significant cognitive disabilities, and any other children with disabilities who require this instruction, to enable them to:

- (i) Develop an awareness of the environment in which they live; and

- (ii) Learn the skills necessary to move effectively and safely from place to place within that environment (e.g., in school, in the home, at work, and in the community)." [Section 300.26(b)(4)]

Physical Therapy

Physical therapy means "services provided by a qualified physical therapist" [Section 300.24(b)(8)]. These services generally address a child's posture, muscle strength, mobility, and organization of movement in educational environments. Physical therapy may be provided to prevent the onset or progression of impairment, functional limitation, disability, or changes in physical function or health resulting from injury, disease, or other causes. Qualified providers of these services may:

- provide treatment to increase joint function, muscle strength, mobility, and endurance;

- address gross motor skills that rely on the large muscles of the body involved in physical movement and range of motion;

- help improve the student's posture, gait, and body awareness; and

- monitor the function, fit, and proper use of mobility aids and devices.

Recreation

Recreation services generally are intended to help students with disabilities learn how to use their leisure and recreation time constructively. Through these services, students can learn appropriate and functional recreation and leisure skills (Schleien, Green, & Heyne, 1993). According to the IDEA '97 final regulations, recreation as a related service includes:

- assessment of leisure function;

- therapeutic recreation services;

- recreation programs in schools and community agencies; and

- leisure education. [Section 300.24(b)(10)]

Recreational activities generally may fall into one or more of the following classifications: (1) physical, cultural, or social; (2) indoor or outdoor; (3) spectator or participant; (4) formal or informal; (5) independent, cooperative, or competitive; or (6) sports, games, hobbies, or toy play (Moon & Bunker, 1987). Recreational activities may be provided during the school day or in after-school programs in a school or a community environment. Some school districts have made collaborative arrangements with the local parks and recreation programs or local youth development programs to provide recreational services.

As part of providing this related service, persons qualified to provide recreation carry out activities such as:

- assessing a student's leisure interests and preferences, capacities, functions, skills, and needs;

- providing recreation therapeutic services and activities to develop a student's functional skills;

- providing education in the skills, knowledge, and attitudes related to leisure involvement;

- helping a student participate in recreation with assistance and/or adapted recreation equipment;

- providing training to parents and educators about the role of recreation in enhancing educational outcomes;

- identifying recreation resources and facilities in the community; and

- providing recreation programs in schools and community agencies.

Rehabilitation Counseling Services

Rehabilitation counseling services are "services provided by qualified personnel in individual or group sessions that focus specifically on career development, employment preparation, achieving independence, and integration in the workplace and community. The term also includes vocational rehabilitation services provided to a student with disabilities by vocational rehabilitation programs funded under the Rehabilitation Act of 1973, as amended." [Section 300.24(b)(11)] The role of the rehabilitation counselor, according to the Council on Rehabilitation Education (1996), is to provide students with disabilities "assistance to their vocation, social, and personal functioning through the use of professionally recognized interaction skills and other appropriate services" (p. 36). To this end, rehabilitation counseling services generally may include:

- assessment of a student's attitudes, abilities, and needs;

- vocational counseling and guidance;

- vocational training; and

- identifying job placements in individual or group sessions.

School Health Services

School health services under the IDEA '97 final regulations means "services provided by a qualified school nurse or other qualified person" [Section 300.24(b)(12)]. These services may be necessary because some children and youth with disabilities would otherwise be unable to attend a day of school without supportive health care. School health services may include interpretation, interventions, administration of health procedures, the use of an assistive health device to compensate for the reduction or loss of a body function (Rapport, 1996), and case management.

Typically, school health services are provided by a qualified school nurse or other qualified trained person who is supervised by a qualified nurse. In some instances, if a school nurse is not employed by a school district, health services may be provided and/or coordinated by a public health nurse, a pediatric home care nurse, or a hospital- or community-based pediatric nurse practitioner or specialist. States and local school districts often have guidelines that address school health services. State agency guidelines that address school health services for special health care needs may address staffing requirements, infection control, medication administration, nursing procedures, classroom modifications, transportation, and policies (Porter, Haynie, Bierle, Caldwell, & Palfrey, 1997). Possible school health services include:

- special feedings;
- clean intermittent catheterization;
- suctioning;
- the management of a tracheostomy;
- administering and/or dispensing medications;
- planning for the safety of a student in school;
- ensuring that care is given while at school and at school functions to prevent injury (e.g., changing a student's position frequently to prevent pressure sores);
- chronic disease management; and
- conducting and/or promoting education and skills training for all (including the student) who serve as caregivers in the school setting.

Transportation

Transportation as a related service is included in an eligible student's IEP if the IEP team determines that such a service is needed. Transportation includes:

- travel to and from school and between schools;
- travel in and around school buildings; and

311

- specialized equipment (such as special or adapted buses, lifts, and ramps), if required to provide special transportation for a child with a disability [Section 300.24(b)(15)].

Public school districts must provide transportation to students with disabilities in two situations. These are:

- if a district provides transportation to and from school for the general student population, then it must provide transportation for a student with a disability; and

- if a school district does not provide transportation for the general student population, then the issue of transportation for students with disabilities must be decided on a case-by-case basis if the IEP team has determined that transportation is needed by the child and has included it on his or her IEP (Office of Special Education Programs, 1995).

If the IEP team determines that a student with a disability needs transportation to benefit from special education, it must be included in the student's IEP and provided as a related service at no cost to the student and his or her parents (Office of Special Education Programs, 1995). Not all students with disabilities are eligible to receive transportation as a related service. As Attachment 1 of the Federal regulations for IDEA '97 points out: It is assumed that most children with disabilities will receive the same transportation provided to nondisabled children, unless the IEP team determines otherwise. However, for some children with disabilities, integrated transportation may not be achieved unless needed accommodations are provided to address each child's unique needs. If the IEP team determines that a disabled child requires transportation as a related service in order to receive FAPE, or requires accommodations or modifications to participate in integrated transportation with nondisabled children, the child must receive the necessary transportation or accommodations at no cost to the parents. This is so, even if no transportation is provided to nondisabled children. (U.S. Department of Education, 1999a, p. 12551)

A student's need for transportation as a related service and the type of transportation to be provided must be discussed and decided by the IEP team. Whether transportation goals and objectives are required in the IEP depends on the purpose of the transportation. If transportation is being provided solely to and from school, in and around school, and between schools, no goals or objectives are needed. If instruction is provided to a student to increase his or her independence

312

or improve his or her behavior during transportation, then goals and objectives must be included in the student's IEP (Office of Special Education Programs, 1995).

Delivering Related Services

Once a child has been evaluated and found eligible for special education and related services, the IEP team develops an individualized education program (IEP) for the child. This will include specifying the special education and related services that the child will receive as part of his or her free appropriate public education (FAPE). Beyond specifying the related services, however, is the delivery of the services.

Who Provides Related Services?

Providers of related services in the schools typically include (but are not limited to) professionals such as: school counselors, school psychologists, school social workers, school health professionals, speech-language pathologists, and occupational and physical therapists. The training and credentialing of these professionals will vary from State to State.

IDEA requires that related services are provided by qualified personnel. However, neither the law nor the regulations specify the levels of training that an individual needs in order to be considered "qualified." It is the State that establishes what constitutes "suitable qualifications for personnel providing special education and related services" [Section 300.136(a)(1)(ii)]. This includes establishing the "highest entry-level academic degree needed for any State-approved or recognized certification, licensing, registration, or other comparable requirements that apply to a profession or discipline" in which a person is providing special education and related services [Section 300.136(a)(2)].

The IDEA also permits, but does not require, the use of paraprofessionals and assistants who are appropriately trained and supervised to assist in the provision of special education and related services. The use of paraprofessionals and assistants is contingent upon State law, regulations, or written policy giving States the option of determining whether paraprofessionals and assistants can be used to assist in the provision of special education and related services, and, if so, to what extent their use would be permissible (U.S. Department of Education, 1999a, pp. 12561-12562).

Apart from the requirements of the IDEA '97 and standards of training that individual States establish as suitable qualifications for

their various related services providers, a number of professional organizations exist and publish standards as well. These groups can be
a valuable source of information to parents and professionals alike.
While States may consider the recognized standards of professional
organizations in deciding what are appropriate professional requirements in the State, there is nothing in the statute or the regulations
that requires States to do so (U.S. Department of Education, 1999a,
p. 12560; see also Section 300.136(b)(3)].

How Are Related Services Generally Delivered?

A school district must ensure that all of the related services specified in the student's IEP are provided, including the amount specified. The district usually decides how the services listed in the IEP
will be delivered to the student. For example, the district may provide the services through its own personnel resources, or it may contract with another public or private agency, which then provides the
services. Contracted service providers must meet the same standards
for credentialing and training as public agency service providers do.

Generally, there are two basic kinds of related services interventions offered by schools to meet the range of student needs. These are:

1. *Direct Services.* Direct services usually refers to hands-on,
    face-to-face interactions between the related services profes-
    sional and the student. These interactions can take place in a
    variety of settings, such as the classroom, gym, health office,
    resource room, counseling office, or playground. Typically, the
    related service professional analyzes student responses and
    uses specific techniques to develop or improve particular
    skills. The professional should also:

    • monitor the student's performance within the educational
      setting so that adjustments can be made to improve stu-
      dent performance, as needed, and

    • consult with teachers and parents on an ongoing basis, so
      that relevant strategies can be carried out through indi-
      rect means at other times.

2. *Indirect Services.* Indirect services may involve teaching, con-
    sulting with, and/or directly supervising other personnel (in-
    cluding paraprofessionals and parents) so that they can carry
    out therapeutically appropriate activities. For example, a
    school psychologist might train teachers and other educators

314

how to implement a program included in a student's IEP to decrease the child's problem behaviors. Similarly, a physical therapist may serve as a consultant to a teacher and provide expertise to solve problems regarding a student's mobility through school (Dunn, 1991). Good practice is generally thought to include the following aspects:

- The intervention procedure is designed by the related service professional (with IEP team input) for an individual student.

- The related service professional has regular opportunities to interact with the student.

- The related service professional provides ongoing training, monitoring, supervision, procedural evaluation, and support to staff members and parents.

One type of service intervention is not necessarily better than the other (American Occupational Therapy Association, 1999) as long as the safety of the student is not compromised. In most school systems student needs are addressed through a combination of direct and indirect services (Smith, 1990). The type of service provided depends upon the individual needs of the student and his or her educational goals. Decisions about direct or indirect service delivery, therefore, are made on an individual, case-by-case basis.

It is not uncommon for districts to employ certified or trained assistants—such as a Physical Therapy Assistant, a Certified Occupational Therapy Assistant, or a Speech-Language Pathology Assistant—to assist in the delivery of related services. In fact, in recent years there has been an increased emphasis on team members (e.g., teacher, therapist, and family member) delivering services under the supervision of an expert rather than only having an expert deliver direct services to a child (American Occupational Therapy Association, 1999). The final regulations for IDEA '97 make clear that nothing in the statute or regulations prohibits the use of paraprofessionals and assistants who are appropriately trained and supervised to assist in the provision of special education and related services, in accordance with State law, regulations, or written policy [Section 300.136(f)].

Where Are Related Services Provided?

In recent years, there has been a significant shift in where related services are provided. Rather than providing services in a separate room, as was the more common practice in years past, schools are emphasizing providing some services to students in natural activities and environments. Today it is not unusual to find speech-language services integrated into instructional activities in the regular education classroom, or occupational or physical therapy provided during physical education classes in gyms. As an example, asthma medication or glucose monitoring (as a school health service) may be done in the classroom or wherever the student with a disability happens to be. Thus, services may be delivered in a regular education class, a special education class, a gym, a therapy room, or in other locations in the school, home, or community.

Of course, there may be some services that need to be delivered in a separate setting such as a counseling room or office in order to assure confidentiality for the student and family. Such services may include individual and group counseling, parent counseling, and, frequently, consultation with staff and parents about individual students.

It is interesting to note that this shift in location accompanies a lesser focus on the traditional medical model of related services and greater attention given to an educational-results model. The medical model, typically found within a hospital or clinical setting, focuses on identifying and treating the particular illness, trauma, or deficit in a clinical setting. The educational model stresses the importance of the student's attaining IEP goals and objectives as well as addressing the capabilities and challenges presented by the particular disability (Hanft & Striffler, 1995).

How Are Related Services Coordinated?

Depending on the nature and type of related services to be provided, many professionals may be involved with, or on behalf of, the student with a disability. This may include one or more therapists, a special educator, a regular educator, counselor, a school psychologist, social workers, the school nurse or other health services staff, paraprofessionals, or the school principal. Clearly, there must be communication between the IEP team and the related service provider(s) to ensure that services are being delivered as specified in the IEP and that the student is making progress. If the student is not progressing as expected, adjustments in his or her program may be needed. The IEP team would need to make any such decisions. When a student's IEP includes related services, it may be appropriate for related services professionals to be involved in the review of student progress and any decision to modify instruction or reevaluate the student's needs. Furthermore, if adjustments are made in the IEP, each teacher, related service provider, and other service provider who is responsible for implementing the revised IEP must be informed of:

- his or her specific responsibilities related to implementing the child's IEP; and

- the specific accommodations, modifications, and supports that must be provided to the child in accordance with the IEP. [Section 300.342(b)(3)]

The IEP team may determine that it is highly desirable that related services be delivered in educational settings through a team approach. Related services are not isolated from the educational program. Rather, they are related to the educational needs of students and are intended to assist the child in benefiting from the educational program. In order to ensure the integrated delivery of services, some school systems use a case management approach in which a team leader coordinates and oversees services on behalf of the student. In some schools, this person might be the child's special education teacher. In other schools, supervisory school district personnel may assume this responsibility.

How Are Related Services Funded?

State and local educational agencies are responsible for assuming the costs of public education, including the cost of special education and related services. Under IDEA '97, students with disabilities are entitled to a free appropriate public education (FAPE) and are entitled to receive these services at no cost to themselves or their families.

Part of the moneys to finance special education and related services comes to States and local educational agencies (LEAs) through Federal funding of IDEA. What other funding sources are available to States and LEAs, besides the IDEA, to help cover the costs of special education and related services?

Interagency agreements or other arrangements. One of the primary methods for ensuring services, strengthened through IDEA '97, is the establishment and use of interagency agreements between the public agency responsible for the child's education and other noneducational public agencies in the State or locale. States may engage in other mechanisms that result in interagency coordination and timely and appropriate delivery of services [Section 300.142(a)(4)]. Pertinent noneducational public agencies, according to IDEA '97, are those:

> otherwise obligated under Federal or State law, or assigned responsibility under State policy...to provide or pay for any services that are also considered special education or related services...that are necessary for ensuring FAPE to children with disabilities within the State... [Section 300.142(b)(1)]

This includes the State Medicaid agency and other public insurers of children with disabilities. A noneducational public agency, as described above, may not disqualify an eligible service for Medicaid reimbursement because that service is provided in a school context [Section 300.142(b)(1)(ii)].

In order to receive funds under IDEA '97, the State Education Agency must have in effect agreements or other mechanisms with such agencies in order to define the financial responsibility that each agency has for providing services to ensure FAPE to children with disabilities [Section 300.142(a)(1)]. Moreover, the financial responsibility of each noneducational public agency comes before the financial responsibility of the local educational agency (or the State agency responsible for developing the child's IEP) [Section 300.142(a)(1)].

Public insurance. Insurance is another potential source of funding for related services. With certain limitations, "the public agency may use the Medicaid or other public insurance benefits programs in which a child with disabilities participates to provide or pay for services," as permitted by the public insurance program. Limitations include:

- The public agency may not require parents to sign up or enroll in public insurance programs in order for their child to receive FAPE under Part B of IDEA.

- The public agency may not require parents to incur an out-of-pocket expense, such as the payment of a deductible or co-pay amount incurred in filing a claim for services. The public agency, however, may pay the cost that the parent would otherwise be required to pay.

- The public agency may not use a child's benefits under a public insurance program if that use would (a) decrease available lifetime coverage or any other insured benefit; (b) result in the family paying for services that would otherwise be covered by the public insurance program and that are required for the child outside of the time the child is in school; (c) increase premiums or lead to the discontinuation of insurance; or (d) risk loss of eligibility for home and community-based waivers, based on the sum total of health-related expenditures. [Section 300.142(e)]

Private insurance. The IDEA '97 final regulations state that a public agency may access a parent's private insurance proceeds only if the parent provides informed consent [Section 300.142(f)(1)]. Each time the public agency proposes to access the parent's private insurance proceeds, it must obtain the parent's informed consent and inform the parent that his or her refusal to permit such access to private insurance does not relieve the public agency of its responsibility to ensure that all required services are provided at no cost to the parents [Section 300.142(f)(2)].

However, IDEA '97 states that "nothing in this part relieves an insurer or similar third party from an otherwise valid obligation to provide or to pay for services provided to a child with a disability" [Section 300.301(b)]. When parents voluntarily access private insurance to pay for related services, an insurance company cannot refuse payment by claiming that the school district is required under IDEA '97 to provide the services. Moreover, there can be no delay in implementing a child's IEP, because the payment source for providing or paying for special education and related services to the child is being determined [Section 300.301(c)].

Section 504 of the Rehabilitation Act

Under IDEA, a public school student must be receiving special education in order to receive related services. The only exception to this is if the related service needed by the child is considered special education rather than a related service under State standards [Section 300.7(a)(2)(ii)]. However, there is another Federal law, Section 504 of the Rehabilitation Act of 1973, as amended, that applies to IDEA-eligible students and in some cases may provide protections for a student who is ineligible for services under IDEA. A student with a disability who does not need special education but who needs a related services may be eligible for that services under Section 504.

Section 504 of the Rehabilitation Act of 1973, as amended, is a civil rights law that prohibits recipients of Federal funds from discriminating on the basis of disability. This law applies to, among other entities, public elementary and secondary school districts. Under Section

319

504 regulations, a person with a disability (referred to in the regulation as handicapped person) is a person who has a physical or mental impairment which substantially limits one or more major life activities, has a record of such an impairment, or is regarded as having such an impairment [34 CFR Section 104.3(j)(1)].

To ascertain whether a student is protected by Section 504, an evaluation would need to be conducted to determine whether he or she is a handicapped person within the meaning of Section 504. Public elementary and secondary school districts receiving Federal financial assistance are required by Section 504 regulations to provide a free appropriate public education to students with disabilities in their jurisdiction [34 CFR Section 104.33(a)]. A free appropriate public education under Section 504 consists of "regular or special education and related aids and services that...are designed to meet individual educational needs of handicapped persons as adequately as the needs of nonhandicapped persons are met" and are provided in accordance with Section 504 requirements relevant to educational setting, evaluation and placement, and procedural safeguards [34 CFR Section 104.33(b)].

Decisions about what educational and related services are appropriate for a child under Section 504 must be made by a placement group including persons knowledgeable about the child, the meaning of evaluation data, and placement options [34 CFR Section 104.35(c)]. The placement group decides whether the child needs regular or special education and related aids and services (34 CFR Section 104.35). Section 504 also applies to recipients of Federal financial assistance that operate private elementary and secondary education programs. These recipients may not, on the basis of handicap, exclude a qualified handicapped person from such programs, if the person can, with minor adjustments, be provided an appropriate education within the recipient's program [34 CFR Section 104.39(a)].

Section 504 is enforced by the Department of Education's Office for Civil Rights (OCR). Parents and professionals interested in more information about how Section 504 affects the provision of educational and related services to qualified persons with disabilities should contact the OCR enforcement office that serves their state. If you need assistance identifying the regional office nearest you, or would like more information about Section 504 in general, please contact NICHCY.

References

American Art Therapy Association. (2000). Art therapy: Definition of a profession [On-line]. Available: www.arttherapy.org/definitions.htm

American Dance Therapy Association. (1998). Dance/movement therapy: Frequently asked/answered questions (FAQ) [On-line]. Available: www.citi.net/ADTA/adtafaq.htm

American Music Therapy Association. (2000). Frequently asked questions about music therapy [On-line]. Available: www.musictherapy.org/faqs.html

American Occupational Therapy Association (1999). Occupational therapy services for children and youth under the Individuals with Disabilities Education Act (2nd ed.). Bethesda, MD: Author.

American School Counselor Association. (1999). The role of the professional school counselor [On-line]. Available: www.schoolcounselor.org/role.htm

Council on Rehabilitation Education. (1996). Accreditation manual for rehabilitation counselor education programs. Rolling Meadows, IL: Author.

Derer, K.; Polsgrove, L.; and Rieth, H. (1996). A survey of assistive technology applications in schools and recommendations for practice. *Journal of Special Education Technology*, XIII(2), 62-80.

Dunn, W. (1991). Consultation as a process: How, when and why? In C. Royeen (Ed.), *School-Based Practice for Related Services*. Bethesda, MD: American Occupational Therapy Association.

Dwyer, K. (1997, November). School psychology and behavioral interventions. *Communique*, 26(3), 1, 4-5.

Fox, L.; Vaughn, B.; Dunlap, G.; and Bucy, M. (1997). Parent-professional partnership in behavioral support: A qualitative analysis of one family's experience. *Journal of the Association for Persons with Severe Handicaps*, 22(4), 198-207.

Hanft, B.; and Striffler, N. (1995). Incorporating developmental therapy in early childhood programs: Challenges and promising practices. *Young Children*, 8(2), 37-47.

Hill, E.; and Snook-Hill, M. (1996). Orientation and mobility. In M. C. Holbrook (Ed.), *Children with Visual Impairments: A Parent's Guide*. Bethesda, MD: Woodbine House.

Maag, J.; and Katsiyannis, A. (1996). Counseling as a related service for students with emotional or behavioral disorders: Issues and recommendations. *Behavioral Disorders*, 21(4), 293-305.

Moon, M.; and Bunker, L. (1987). Recreation and motor skills programming. In M. Snell (Ed.), *Systematic Instruction of the Moderately and Severely Handicapped* (pp. 214-244). Columbus, OH: Charles E. Merrill.

Office of Special Education Programs, U.S. Department of Education. (1995, July 12). Letter to Smith. Washington, DC: Author.

Porter, S.; Haynie, M.; Bierle, T.; Caldwell, T.; and Palfrey, J. (1997). *Children and Youth Assisted by Medical Technology in Educational Settings: Guidelines for Care*. Baltimore, MD: Paul H. Brookes.

Rapport, M. (1996). Legal guidelines for the delivery of special health care services in schools. *Exceptional Children*, 62(6), 537-549.

RESNA Technical Assistance Project. (1992). Assistive technology and the individualized education program. Arlington, VA: RESNA Press.

Rothstein, R. and Everson, J. (1995). Assistive technology for individuals with sensory impairments. In K. Flippo; K. Inge; and J. Barcus (Eds.), *Assistive Technology: A Resource for School, Work, and Community* (pp. 105-129). Baltimore, MD: Paul H. Brookes.

Schleien, S.; Green, F.; and Heyne, L. (1993). Integrated community recreation. In M. Snell (Ed.), *Instruction of Students with Severe Disabilities (4ᵗʰ Ed.)* (pp. 526-555). New York: Macmillan.

Smith, P. (1990). Integrating related services into programs for students with severe and multiple handicaps. Lexington, KY: Kentucky Systems Change Project, Interdisciplinary Human Development Institute.

U.S. Department of Education. (1999a, March 12). Assistance to states for the education of children with disabilities and the early intervention program for infants and toddlers with disabilities; final regulations. Federal Register, 64(48), 12406-12671.

U.S. Department of Education. (1999b). To assure a free appropriate public education: 21st annual report to Congress on the implementation of the Individuals with Disabilities Education Act. Washington, DC: Author.

Chapter 38

Questions Often Asked by Parents about Special Education Services

This chapter addresses some common questions regarding special education services and assistance in school, to children with disabilities.

I think my child may need special help in school. What do I do?

Begin by finding out more about special services and programs for students in your school system. Also find out more about the Individuals with Disabilities Education Act (IDEA). This law gives eligible children with disabilities the right to receive special services and assistance in school. These services are known as special education and related services. They can be important in helping your child at school.

What is special education?

Special education is instruction that is specially designed to meet the unique needs of children who have disabilities. This is done at no cost to the parents. Special education can include special instruction in the classroom, at home, in hospitals or institutions, or in other settings.

Excerpted from "Questions Often Asked by Parents about Special Education Services," National Information Center for Children and Youth with Disabilities (NICHCY) Briefing Paper, LG1 (4th Edition), September 1999.

Over 5 million children ages 6 through 21 receive special education and related services each year in the United States. Each of these children receives instruction that is specially designed:

- to meet the child's unique needs (that result from having a disability); and

- to help the child learn the information and skills that other children are learning.

This definition of special education comes from the Individuals with Disabilities Education Act (IDEA), Public Law 105-17.

Who is eligible for special education?

Certain children with disabilities are eligible for special education and related services. The IDEA provides a definition of a child with a disability. This law lists 13 different disability categories under which a child may be found eligible for special education and related services. These categories are listed in Table 38.1.

According to the IDEA, the disability must affect the child's educational performance. The question of eligibility, then, comes down to a question of whether the child has a disability that fits in one of IDEA's 13 categories and whether that disability affects how the child does in school. That is, the disability must cause the child to need special education and related services.

Your Child's Evaluation

How do I find out if my child is eligible for special education?

The first step is to find out if your child has a disability. To do this, ask the school to evaluate your child. Call or write the Director of Special Education or the principal of your child's school. Say that you think your child has a disability and needs special education help. Ask the school to evaluate your child as soon as possible.

The public school may also think your child needs special help, because he or she may have a disability. If so, then the school must evaluate your child at no cost to you. However, the school does not have to evaluate your child just because you have asked. The school may not think your child has a disability or needs special education. In this case, the school may refuse to evaluate your child. It must let you know this decision in writing, as well as why it has refused.

If the school refuses to evaluate your child, there are two things you can do immediately:

- Ask the school system for information about its special education policies, as well as parent rights to disagree with decisions made by the school system. These materials should describe the steps parents can take to challenge a school system's decision.

- Get in touch with your state's Parent Training and Information (PTI) center. The PTI is an excellent resource for parents to learn more about special education, their rights and responsibilities, and the law. The PTI can tell you what steps to take next to find help for your child. Call NICHCY to find out how to get in touch with your PTI, or see our State Resource Sheet for your state. The PTI is listed there.

Services to Very Young Children

Infants and toddlers can have disabilities, too. Services to these very young children are also part of the IDEA. These services are called early intervention services (for children birth through two years) and preschool services (for children ages 3-5). These services can be very important in helping the young child develop and learn.

For more information about early intervention and preschool programs, contact NICHCY. Ask for *A Parent's Guide: Accessing Programs for Infants, Toddlers, and Preschoolers with Disabilities*.

What happens during an evaluation?

Evaluating your child means more than the school just giving your child a test or two. The school must evaluate your child in all the areas where your child may be affected by the possible disability. This may include looking at your child's health, vision, hearing, social and emotional well-being, general intelligence, performance in school, and how well your child communicates with others and uses his or her body. The evaluation must be complete enough (full and individual) to identify all of your child's needs for special education and related services.

Evaluating your child appropriately will give you and the school a lot of information about your child. This information will help you and the school decide if your child has a disability; and design instruction for your child. The evaluation process involves several steps.

Reviewing existing information. A group of people, including you, begins by looking at the information the school already has about your child. You may have information about your child you wish to share as well. The group will look at information such as:

- your child's scores on tests given in the classroom or to all students in your child's grade;

- the opinions and observations of your child's teachers and other school staff who know your child; and

- your feelings, concerns, and ideas about how your child is doing in school.

Deciding if more information is still needed. The information collected will help the group decide if your son or daughter has a particular type of disability; how your child is currently doing in school; whether your child needs special education and related services; and what your child's educational needs are.

Group members will look at the information they collected and see if they have enough information to make these decisions. If the group needs more information to make these decisions, the school must collect it.

Collecting more information about your child. If more information about your child is needed, the school will give your child tests or collect the information in other ways. Your informed written permission is required before the school may collect this information. The evaluation group will then have the information it needs to make these decisions.

So the school needs my permission to collect this extra information?

Yes. Before the school can conduct additional assessments of your child to see if he or she has a disability, the school must ask for your informed written permission. It must also describe how it will conduct this evaluation. This includes describing the tests that will be used and the other ways the school will collect information about your child. After you give your informed written permission, the school may evaluate your child.

How does the school collect this information?

The school collects information about your child from many different people and in many different ways. Tests are an important part of an evaluation, but they are only a part. The evaluation should also include:

- the observations and opinions of professionals who have worked with your child;
- your child's medical history, when it relates to his or her performance in school; and
- your ideas about your child's school experiences, abilities, needs, and behavior outside of school, and his or her feelings about school.

The following people will be part of the group evaluating your child:

- you, as parents;
- at least one regular education teacher, if your child is or may be participating in the regular education environment;
- at least one of your child's special education teachers or service providers;
- a school administrator who knows about policies for special education, about children with disabilities, about the general curriculum (the curriculum used by nondisabled students), and about available resources;
- someone who can interpret the evaluation results and talk about what instruction may be necessary for your child;
- individuals (invited by you or the school) who have knowledge or special expertise about your child;
- your child, if appropriate;
- representatives from any other agencies that may be responsible for paying for or providing transition services (if your child is 16 years or, if appropriate, younger and will be planning for life after high school); and
- other qualified professionals.

These other qualified professionals may be responsible for collecting specific kinds of information about your child. They may include:

- a school psychologist;
- an occupational therapist;

- a speech and language pathologist (sometimes called a speech therapist);

- a physical therapist and/or adaptive physical education therapist or teacher;

- a medical specialist; and

- others.

Professionals will observe your child. They may give your child written tests or talk personally with your child. They are trying to get a picture of the whole child. For example, they want to understand:

- how well your child speaks and understands language;

- how your child thinks and behaves;

- how well your child adapts to changes in his or her environment;

- how well your child has done academically;

- what your child's potential or aptitude (intelligence) is;

- how well your child functions in a number of areas, such as moving, thinking, learning, seeing, hearing; and

- what job-related and other post-school interests and abilities your child has.

The IDEA gives clear directions about how schools must conduct evaluations. For example, tests and interviews must be given in your child's native language (for example, Spanish) or in the way he or she typically communicates (for example, sign language). The tests must also be given in a way that does not discriminate against your child, because he or she has a disability or is from a different racial or cultural background.

The IDEA states that schools may not place children into special education programs based on the results of only one procedure such as a test. More than one procedure is needed to see where your child may be having difficulty and to identify his or her strengths.

In some cases, schools will be able to conduct a child's entire evaluation within the school. In other cases, schools may not have the staff to do all of the evaluation needed. These schools will have to hire outside people or agencies to do some or all of the evaluation. If your child is evaluated outside of the school, the school must make the arrangements. The school will say in writing exactly what type of testing is to be done. All of these evaluation procedures are done at no cost to parents.

In some cases, once the evaluation has begun, the outside specialist may want to do more testing. If the specialist asks you if it is okay to do more testing, make sure you tell the specialist to contact the school. If the testing is going beyond what the school originally asked for, the school needs to agree to pay for the extra testing.

Your Child's Eligibility

What does the school do with these evaluation results?

The information gathered from the evaluation will be used to make important decisions about your child's education. All of the information about your child will be used to decide if your child is eligible for special education and related services; and to help you and the school decide what your child needs educationally.

How is a decision made about my child's eligibility for special education?

As was said earlier, the decision about your child's eligibility for services is based on whether your son or daughter has a disability that fits into one of the IDEA's 13 disability categories (see Table 38.1.) and whether that disability affects how your child does in school. This decision will be made when the evaluation has been completed, and the results are in.

In the past, parents were not involved under IDEA in making the decision about their child's eligibility for special education and related services. Now, under the newest changes to IDEA (passed in 1997), parents are included in the group that decides a child's eligibility for special education services. This group will look at all of the information gathered during the evaluation and decide if your child meets the definition of a child with a disability. (This definition will come from the IDEA and from the policies your state or district uses.) If so, your child will be eligible for special education and related services.

Under the IDEA, a child may not be found eligible for services if the determining reason for thinking the child is eligible is that the child has limited English proficiency, or the child has a lack of instruction in math or reading.

If your child is found eligible, you and the school will work together to design an educational program for your child. As parents, you have the right to receive a copy of the evaluation report on your child and the paperwork about your child's eligibility for special education and related services.

What happens if my child is not eligible for services?

If the group decides that your child is not eligible for special education services, the school system must tell you this in writing and explain why your child has been found not eligible. Under the IDEA, you must also be given information about what you can do if you disagree with this decision.

Read the information the school system gives you. Make sure it includes information about how to challenge the school system's decision. If that information is not in the materials the school gives you, ask the school for it. Also get in touch with your state's Parent Training and Information (PTI) center. The PTI can tell you what steps to take next. Your PTI is listed on NICHCY's State Resource Sheet for your state.

Table 38.1. IDEA's Categories of Disability

Autism

Deafness

Deaf-blindness

Hearing impairment

Mental retardation

Multiple disabilities

Orthopedic impairment

Other health impairment

Serious emotional disturbance

Specific learning disability

Speech or language impairment

Traumatic brain injury

Visual impairment, including blindness

To find out more about these disabilities and how IDEA defines them, contact NICHCY and ask for "General Information about Disabilities."

Writing an IEP

So my child has been found eligible for special education. What next?

The next step is to write what is known as an Individualized Education Program—usually called an IEP. After a child is found eligible, a meeting must be held within 30 days to develop to the IEP.

What is an Individualized Education Program?

An Individualized Education Program (IEP) is a written statement of the educational program designed to meet a child's individual needs. Every child who receives special education services must have an IEP.

The IEP has two general purposes: (1) to set reasonable learning goals for your child; and (2) to state the services that the school district will provide for your child.

It is very important that children with disabilities participate in the general curriculum as much as possible. That is, they should learn the same curriculum as nondisabled children, for example, reading, math, science, social studies, and physical education, just as nondisabled children do. In some cases, this curriculum may need to be adapted for your child to learn, but it should not be omitted altogether. Participation in extracurricular activities and other nonacademic activities is also important. Your child's IEP needs to be written with this in mind.

For example, what special education services will help your child participate in the general curriculum—in other words, to study what other students are studying? What special education services or supports will help your child take part in extracurricular activities such as school clubs or sports? When your child's IEP is developed, an important part of the discussion will be how to help your child take part in regular classes and activities in the school.

Re-Evaluation

Will my child be re-evaluated?

Yes. Under the IDEA, your child must be re-evaluated at least every three years. The purpose of this re-evaluation is to find out:

- if your child continues to be a child with a disability, as defined within the law, and

- your child's educational needs.

The re-evaluation is similar to the initial evaluation. It begins by looking at the information already available about your child. More information is collected only if it's needed. If the group decides that additional assessments are needed, you must give your informed written permission before the school system may collect that information. The school system may only go ahead without your informed written permission if they have tried to get your permission and you did not respond.

Although the law requires that children with disabilities be re-evaluated at least every three years, your child may be re-evaluated more often if you or your child's teacher(s) request it.

Other Special Education Issues

Is the school responsible for ensuring that my child reaches the goals in his or her IEP?

No. The IEP sets out the individualized instruction to be provided to your child, but it is not a contract. The school is responsible for providing the instructional services listed in an IEP. School officials must make a good-faith effort to help your child meet his or her goals. However, the school is not responsible if your child does not reach the goals listed in the IEP. If you feel that your child is not making progress toward his or her goals, then you may wish to contact the school and express your concerns. The IEP team may need to meet and revise your child's IEP.

What if I disagree with the school about what is right for my child?

You have the right to disagree with the school's decisions concerning your child. This includes decisions about:

- your child's identification as a child with a disability,
- his or her evaluation,
- his or her educational placement, and
- the special education and related services that the school provides to your child.

In all cases where the family and school disagree, it is important for both sides to first discuss their concerns and try to compromise. The compromise can be temporary. For example, you might agree to try out a particular plan of instruction or classroom placement for a certain period of time. At the end of that period, the school can check your child's progress. You and other members of your child's IEP team can then meet again, talk about how your child is doing, and decide what to do next. The trial period may help you and the school come to a comfortable agreement on how to help your child.

If you still cannot agree with the school, it's useful to know more about the IDEA's protections for parents and children. The law and regulations include ways for parents and schools to resolve disagreements. These include:

- mediation, where you and school personnel sit down with an impartial third person (called a mediator), talk openly about the areas where you disagree, and try to reach agreement;

- due process, where you and the school present evidence before an impartial third person (called a hearing officer), and he or she decides how to resolve the problem; and

- filing a complaint with the State Education Agency (SEA), where you write directly to the SEA and describe what requirement of IDEA the school has violated. The SEA must either resolve your complaint itself, or it can have a system where complaints are filed with the school district and parents can have the district's decision reviewed by the SEA. In most cases, the SEA must resolve your complaint within 60 calendar days.

Your state will have specific ways for parents and schools to resolve their differences. You will need to find out what your state's policies are. Your local department of special education will probably have these guidelines. If not, contact the state department of education and ask for a copy of their special education policies. The telephone number and address of the state department of education are listed on NICHCY's State Resource Sheet for your state.

You may also wish to call the Parent Training and Information (PTI) center in your state. They are an excellent resource for parents to learn more about special education. Your PTI is listed on NICHCY's State Resource Sheet for your state.

Talking to Other Parents Helps

You can learn a lot from talking to parents of children who are already receiving special education services. There are many different local parent groups. Find one, and go to a meeting. If there aren't any groups in your area, contact the nearest group and ask for its newsletter. These can be full of information, too.

How can I get more services for my child?

Suppose your child gets speech therapy two times a week, and you think he or she needs therapy three times a week. What do you do?

First, you can talk with your child's teacher or speech-language pathologist (sometimes called a speech therapist). Ask to see the evaluation of his or her progress. If you are not satisfied with your child's progress, then request an IEP meeting to review your child's progress and increase speech therapy. Discuss your child's needs with the IEP team and talk about changing the IEP. The other team members will either agree with you and change the IEP, or they will disagree with you.

If the rest of the IEP team does not agree that your child needs more services, try to work out a compromise. If you cannot, then parents can take the problem beyond the IEP team. Mediation, due process, and filing a complaint are ways to resolve disagreements. But always remember that you and the school will be making decisions together about your child's education for as long as your child goes to that school and continues to be eligible for special education services. A good working relationship with school staff is important now and in the future. Therefore, when disagreements arise, try to work them out within the IEP team before requesting mediation or due process or before filing a complaint.

How can I support my child's learning?

Some suggestions that can help you support your child's learning and maintain a good working relationship with school professionals are:

- Let your child's teacher(s) know that you want to be involved in your child's educational program. Make time to talk with the teacher(s) and, if possible, visit the classroom.

- Explain any special equipment, medication, or medical problem your child has.

- Let the teacher(s) know about any activities or big events that may influence your child's performance in school.

- Ask that samples of your child's work be sent home. If you have questions, make an appointment with the teacher(s) to talk about new ways to meet your child's goals.

- Ask the teacher(s) how you can build upon your child's school activities at home.

- Give your child chores at home. Encourage behavior that leads to success in school, such as accepting responsibility, behaving, being organized, and being on time.

- Volunteer to help in the classroom or school. This will let you see how things work in the school and how your child interacts with others. It will also help the school.

- Remember that you and the school want success for your child. Working together can make this happen.

What if I still have questions and need more information?

You can contact your state's Parent Training and Information (PTI) center. Your PTI will have a lot of information to share about the special education process in your state.

You can also contact NICHCY again. We have information on all aspects of the IEP process. We also have information on other issues that are important to families who have a child with a disability. NICHCY staff can send you more publications, answer questions, and put you in touch with other organizations who can work with you and your family.

Chapter 39

Basics about Your Child's Evaluation

Laura's Story

When Laura was 8 years old, her teacher, Mrs. Adams, saw that Laura was having a lot of trouble with reading and writing. This surprised Mrs. Adams, because Laura was very good at remembering things she heard. She asked the school to check, or evaluate, Laura to see if she had a disability.

Laura's parents had also been worried about Laura's problems. When the school asked for permission to evaluate Laura, Laura's parents said yes.

The evaluation took about one month. It involved many different things and people. The evaluation group, including Laura's parents, looked at Laura's school records and test scores. The group gave Laura more tests and talked to her. They also talked to her teacher and her parents. They watched how she did her work and learned more about where and when she has problems. In the end, the evaluation showed that Laura has a learning disability. Now the school knows why she has trouble with reading and writing. Laura is now getting special help in school.

The Individuals with Disabilities Education Act (IDEA)

Our country's special education law is called the Individuals with Disabilities Education Act (IDEA). The IDEA is a very important law

"Basics for Parents: Your Child's Evaluation," from *Basics for Parents (BP1)*, September 1999, a publication of the National Information Center for Children and Youth with Disabilities (NICHCY).

for children with disabilities, their families, and schools. The evaluation process described in chapter is based on what this law requires.

If you want to know all the law's requirements, you may wish to request a copy of the law and its regulations. Ask NICHCY how to do this.

The Purpose of Evaluation: Finding Out Why

Many children have trouble in school. Some, like Laura, have trouble learning to read or write. Others have a hard time remembering new information. Still others may have trouble behaving themselves. Children can have all sorts of problems.

It's important to find out why a child is not doing well in school. The child may have a disability. By law, schools must provide special help to eligible children with disabilities. This help is called special education and related services.

You may ask the school to evaluate your child, or the school may ask you for permission to do an evaluation. If the school thinks your child may have a disability and may need special education and related services, they must evaluate your child before providing your child with these services. This evaluation is at no cost to you. The evaluation will tell you and the school if your child has a disability; and what kind of special help your child needs in school.

Step 1: Using What Is Known

A group of people, including you, will evaluate your child. This group will begin by looking at what is already known about your child. The group will look at your child's school file and recent test scores. You and your child's teacher may provide information to be included in this review. The evaluation group needs enough information to decide if your child has a disability. It also needs to know what kind of special help your child needs. Is there enough information about your child to answer these questions? If your child is being evaluated for the first time, maybe not.

Step 2: Collecting More Information

The group of people, including you, involved in your child's evaluation will tell the school what information it still needs about your child, and the school must collect that information. Before the school can conduct additional testing, school personnel must ask you for permission. They must tell you what the evaluation of your child will involve. This includes describing (a) the tests they will use with your child, and (b) the other ways they will collect information about your child. Once you give your informed written permission, the school may evaluate your child to collect the additional information it needs.

The school will collect this information in many different ways and from many different people, including you if you have information you wish to share. Tests are an important part of an evaluation, but they are only a piece. The evaluation should also include:

- the observations and opinions of professionals who have worked with your child;

- your child's medical history, when it is relevant to his or her performance in school; and

- your ideas about your child's experiences, abilities, needs, and behavior in school and outside of school, and his or her feelings about school.

Professionals will observe your child. They may give your child tests. They are trying to get a picture of the whole child. It's important that the school evaluate your child in all areas where he or she might have a disability. For example, they will want to know more about:

- how well your child speaks and understands language;

- how your child thinks and behaves;

- how well your child adapts to change;

- what your child has achieved in school;

- what your child's potential or aptitude (intelligence) is;

- how well your child functions in areas such as movement, thinking, learning, seeing, and hearing; and

- what job-related and other post-school interests and abilities your child has.

Evaluating your child completely will help you and the school decide if your child has a disability. The information will also help you and the school plan instruction for your child.

Who Is Involved in Your Child's Evaluation?

The group involved in your child's evaluation will include these people:

- at least one of your child's regular education teachers (if your child is, or may be, participating in the regular education environment);

- at least one of your child's special education teachers or service providers;

- a school administrator who knows about policies for special education, children with disabilities, the general curriculum (that is, the curriculum used by nondisabled children), and available resources;

- you, as parents or guardians;

- someone who can interpret the evaluation results and talk about what instruction may be necessary for your child;

- individuals (invited by you or the school) with knowledge or special expertise about your child;

- your child, if appropriate;

- representatives from other agencies that may be responsible for paying for or providing transition services (if your child is 16 years or younger, if appropriate); and

- other qualified professionals, as appropriate (such as a school psychologist, occupational therapist, speech therapist, physical therapist, medical specialist(s), or others).

Four Evaluation "Musts"

Using the native language: The evaluation must be conducted in your child's native language (for example, Spanish) or other means of communication (for example, sign language, if your child is deaf), unless it clearly isn't possible to do so.

No discrimination: Tests must be given in a way that does not discriminate against your child because he or she has a disability or is from a different racial or cultural background.

Trained evaluators: The people who test your child must know how to give the tests they decide to use. They must give each test according to the instructions that came with the test.

More than one procedure: Evaluation results will be used to decide if your child is a child with a disability and to determine what kind of educational program your child needs. These decisions cannot be made based on only one procedure such as only one test.

Step 3: Deciding If Your Child Is Eligible for Special Education

The next step is to decide if your child is eligible for special education and related services. This decision will be based on the results of your child's evaluation and the policies in your area about eligibility for these special services.

It's important that your child's evaluation results be explained to you in a way that's easy to understand. In other words, it's not enough to talk about your child's scores on tests. What do the scores mean? Is your child doing as well as other children his or her age? What does your child do well? Where is your child having trouble? What is causing the trouble?

If you don't understand something in your child's evaluation results, be sure to speak up and ask questions. This is your child. You know your child very well. Do the results make sense, considering what you know about your child? Share your special insights. Your knowledge of your child is important.

Based on your child's evaluation results, a group of people will decide if your child is eligible for special education and related services. Under the IDEA, you have the right to be part of any group that decides your child's eligibility for special education and related services. This decision is based in part on IDEA's definition of a child with a disability. You should know that:

- The IDEA lists 13 different disability categories (see Table 39.1) under which a child may be eligible for services.

- The disability must affect the child's educational performance.

- A child may not be identified as having a disability just because he or she speaks a language other than English and does not speak or understand English well. A child may not be identified as having a disability just because he or she has not had enough instruction in math or reading.

As a parent, you have the right to receive a copy of the evaluation report on your child. You also have the right to receive a copy of the paperwork about your child's eligibility for special education and related services.

341

If your child is eligible for special education and related services (such as speech therapy), then you and the school will meet and talk about your child's special educational needs. If your child is not eligible for special education and related services, the school must tell you so in writing. You must also receive information about what to do if you disagree with this decision. If this information is not in the materials the school gives you, ask for it. You have the right to disagree with the eligibility decision and be heard. Also ask how the school will help your child if he or she will not be getting special education services.

Step 4: Developing Your Child's Educational Program

If, however, your child is found eligible for special education and related services, the next step is to write an Individualized Education Program (IEP) for your child. This is a written document that you and school personnel develop together. The IEP will describe your child's educational program, including the special services your child will receive.

Table 39.1. IDEA's Categories of Disability

Autism

Deaf-blindness

Deafness

Hearing impairment

Mental retardation

Multiple disabilities

Orthopedic impairment

Other health impairment (i.e., having limited strength, vitality, or alertness that affects a child's educational performance)

Serious emotional disturbance

Specific learning disability

Speech or language impairment

Traumatic brain injury

Visual impairment, including blindness

In Summary: Four Steps in Evaluation

Your child is having trouble in school. Someone notices, maybe you, maybe a teacher. You both want your child to do well in school. The first step is to evaluate your child to find out what is causing your child to have problems.

Step 1: Using what's already known. The group of people (which must include you) evaluating your child looks at what information is already available about your child. Does the group need more? If so, the school must collect it.

Step 2: Collecting more information. The school asks for your permission to evaluate your child. You give informed written permission. The school then collects more information about your child.

Step 3: Deciding your child's eligibility. Is your child eligible for special education and related services? Based on the evaluation results, the group of school professionals and you, the parents, decide.

Step 4: Developing your child's educational program. If your child is eligible, you and the school will develop an educational program to meet your child's needs.

Chapter 40

Individualized Education Program (IEP): What You Should Know

Introduction

Each public school child who receives special education and related services must have an Individualized Education Program (IEP). Each IEP must be designed for one student and must be a truly individualized document. The IEP creates an opportunity for teachers, parents, school administrators, related services personnel, and students (when appropriate) to work together to improve educational results for children with disabilities. The IEP is the cornerstone of a quality education for each child with a disability.

To create an effective IEP, parents, teachers, other school staff—and often the student—must come together to look closely at the student's unique needs. These individuals pool knowledge, experience and commitment to design an educational program that will help the student be involved in, and progress in, the general curriculum. The IEP guides the delivery of special education supports and services for the student with a disability. Without a doubt, writing—and implementing—an effective IEP requires teamwork.

This chapter explains the IEP process, which we consider to be one of the most critical elements to ensure effective teaching, learning, and better results for all children with disabilities. The chapter is

Excerpted from "A Guide to the Individualized Education Program," from the Office of Special Education and Rehabilitation Services, U.S. Department of Education, July 2000. Available online at http://www.ed.gov/offices/OSERS/OSEP/Products/IEP_Guide.

designed to help teachers, parents and anyone involved in the education of a child with a disability develop and carry out an IEP. The information in this chapter is based on what is required by our nation's special education law—the Individuals with Disabilities Education Act, or IDEA.

The IDEA requires certain information to be included in each child's IEP. It is useful to know, however, that states and local school systems often include additional information in IEPs in order to document that they have met certain aspects of federal or state law. The flexibility that states and school systems have to design their own IEP forms is one reason why IEP forms may look different from school system to school system or state to state. Yet each IEP is critical in the education of a child with a disability.

The Basic Special Education Process Under IDEA

The writing of each student's IEP takes place within the larger picture of the special education process under IDEA. Before taking a detailed look at the IEP, it may be helpful to look briefly at how a student is identified as having a disability and needing special education and related services and, thus, an IEP.

Step 1. Child is identified as possibly needing special education and related services. The state must identify, locate, and evaluate all children with disabilities in the state who need special education and related services. To do so, states conduct "Child Find" activities. A child may be identified by "Child Find," and parents may be asked if the "Child Find" system can evaluate their child. Parents can also call the "Child Find" system and ask that their child be evaluated. Or a referral or request for evaluation may be requested. A school professional may ask that a child be evaluated to see if he or she has a disability. Parents may also contact the child's teacher or other school professional to ask that their child be evaluated. This request may be verbal or in writing. Parental consent is needed before the child may be evaluated. Evaluation needs to be completed within a reasonable time after the parent gives consent.

Step 2. Child is evaluated. The evaluation must assess the child in all areas related to the child's suspected disability. The evaluation results will be used to decide the child's eligibility for special education and related services and to make decisions about an appropriate educational program for the child. If the parents disagree with the evaluation, they have the right to take their child for an Independent Educational Evaluation (IEE). They can ask that the school system pay for this IEE.

Step 3. Eligibility is decided. A group of qualified professionals and the parents look at the child's evaluation results. Together, they decide if the child is a child with a disability, as defined by IDEA. Parents may ask for a hearing to challenge the eligibility decision.

Step 4. Child is found eligible for services. If the child is found to be a child with a disability, as defined by IDEA, he or she is eligible for special education and related services. Within 30 calendar days after a child is determined eligible, the IEP team must meet to write an IEP for the child.

Step 5. IEP meeting is scheduled. The school system schedules and conducts the IEP meeting. School staff must:

- contact the participants, including the parents;
- notify parents early enough to make sure they have an opportunity to attend;
- schedule the meeting at a time and place agreeable to parents and the school;
- tell the parents the purpose, time, and location of the meeting;
- tell the parents who will be attending; and
- tell the parents that they may invite people to the meeting who have knowledge or special expertise about the child.

Step 6. IEP meeting is held and the IEP is written. The IEP team gathers to talk about the child's needs and write the student's IEP. Parents and the student (when appropriate) are part of the team. If the child's placement is decided by a different group, the parents must be part of that group as well.

Before the school system may provide special education and related services to the child for the first time, the parents must give consent. The child begins to receive services as soon as possible after the meeting.

If the parents do not agree with the IEP and placement, they may discuss their concerns with other members of the IEP team and try to work out an agreement. If they still disagree, parents can ask for mediation, or the school may offer mediation. Parents may file a complaint with the state education agency and may request a due process hearing, at which time mediation must be available.

Step 7. Services are provided. The school makes sure that the child's IEP is being carried out as it was written. Parents are given a copy of the IEP. Each of the child's teachers and service providers has access to the IEP and knows his or her specific responsibilities for carrying out the IEP. This includes the accommodations, modifications, and supports that must be provided to the child, in keeping with the IEP.

Step 8. Progress is measured and reported to parents. The child's progress toward the annual goals is measured, as stated in the IEP. His or her parents are regularly informed of their child's progress and whether that progress is enough for the child to achieve the goals by the end of the year. These progress reports must be given to parents at least as often as parents are informed of their nondisabled children's progress.

Step 9. IEP is reviewed. The child's IEP is reviewed by the IEP team at least once a year, or more often if the parents or school ask for a review. If necessary, the IEP is revised. Parents, as team members, must be invited to attend these meetings. Parents can make suggestions for changes, can agree or disagree with the IEP goals, and agree or disagree with the placement.

If parents do not agree with the IEP and placement, they may discuss their concerns with other members of the IEP team and try to work out an agreement. There are several options, including additional testing, an independent evaluation, or asking for mediation (if available) or a due process hearing. They may also file a complaint with the state education agency.

Step 10. Child is reevaluated. At least every three years the child must be reevaluated. This evaluation is often called a "triennial." Its purpose is to find out if the child continues to be a child with a disability as defined by IDEA, and what the child's educational needs are. However, the child must be reevaluated more often if conditions warrant or if the child's parent or teacher asks for a new evaluation.

A Closer Look at the IEP

Clearly, the IEP is a very important document for children with disabilities and for those who are involved in educating them. Done correctly, the IEP should improve teaching, learning and results. Each child's IEP describes, among other things, the educational program that has been designed to meet that child's unique needs.

Contents of the IEP

By law, the IEP must include certain information about the child and the educational program designed to meet his or her unique needs. In a nutshell, this information is as follows.

Current performance. The IEP must state how the child is currently doing in school (known as present levels of educational performance). This information usually comes from the evaluation results such as classroom tests and assignments, individual tests given to decide eligibility for services or during reevaluation, and observations made by parents, teachers, related service providers, and other school staff. The statement about current performance includes how the child's disability affects his or her involvement and progress in the general curriculum.

Annual goals. These are goals that the child can reasonably accomplish in a year. The goals are broken down into short-term objectives or benchmarks. Goals may be academic, address social or behavioral needs, relate to physical needs, or address other educational needs. The goals must be measurable—meaning that it must be possible to measure whether the student has achieved the goals.

Special education and related services. The IEP must list the special education and related services to be provided to the child or on behalf of the child. This includes supplementary aids and services that the child needs. It also includes modifications (changes) to the program or supports for school personnel—such as training or professional development—that will be provided to assist the child.

Participation with nondisabled children. The IEP must explain the extent (if any) to which the child will not participate with nondisabled children in the regular class and other school activities.

Participation in state and district-wide tests. Most states and districts give achievement tests to children in certain grades or age groups. The IEP must state what modifications in the administration of these tests the child will need. If a test is not appropriate for the child, the IEP must state why the test is not appropriate and how the child will be tested instead.

Dates and places. The IEP must state when services will begin, how often they will be provided, where they will be provided, and how long they will last.

Transition service needs. Beginning when the child is age 14 (or younger, if appropriate), the IEP must address (within the applicable parts of the IEP) the courses he or she needs to take to reach his or her post-school goals. A statement of transition services needs must also be included in each of the child's subsequent IEPs.

Needed transition services. Beginning when the child is age 16 (or younger, if appropriate), the IEP must state what transition services are needed to help the child prepare for leaving school.

Age of majority. Beginning at least one year before the child reaches the age of majority, the IEP must include a statement that the student has been told of any rights that will transfer to him or her at the age of majority. (This statement would be needed only in states that transfer rights at the age of majority.)

Measuring progress. The IEP must state how the child's progress will be measured and how parents will be informed of that progress.

Additional State and School-System Content

States and school systems have a great deal of flexibility about the information they require in an IEP. Some states and school systems have chosen to include in the IEP additional information to document their compliance with other state and federal requirements. (Federal law requires that school districts maintain documentation to demonstrate their compliance with federal requirements.) Generally speaking, extra elements in IEPs may be included to document that the state or school district has met certain aspects of federal or state law, such as:

*   holding the meeting to write, review and, if necessary, revise a child's IEP in a timely manner;

*   providing parents with a copy of the procedural safeguards they have under the law;

- placing the child in the least restrictive environment; and

- obtaining the parents' consent.

IEP Forms in Different Places

While the law tells us what information must be included in the IEP, it does not specify what the IEP should look like. No one form or approach or appearance is required or even suggested. Each state may decide what its IEPs will look like. In some states individual school systems design their own IEP forms.

Thus, across the United States, many different IEP forms are used. What is important is that each form be as clear and as useful as possible, so that parents, educators, related service providers, administrators, and others can easily use the form to write and implement effective IEPs for their students with disabilities.

The IEP Team Members

By law, certain individuals must be involved in writing a child's Individualized Education Program. Note that an IEP team member may fill more than one of the team positions if properly qualified and designated. For example, the school system representative may also be the person who can interpret the child's evaluation results.

These people must work together as a team to write the child's IEP. A meeting to write the IEP must be held within 30 calendar days of deciding that the child is eligible for special education and related services.

Each team member brings important information to the IEP meeting. Members share their information and work together to write the child's Individualized Education Program. Each person's information adds to the team's understanding of the child and what services the child needs.

Parents are key members of the IEP team. They know their child very well and can talk about their child's strengths and needs as well as their ideas for enhancing their child's education. They can offer insight into how their child learns, what his or her interests are, and other aspects of the child that only a parent can know. They can listen to what the other team members think their child needs to work on at school and share their suggestions. They can also report on whether the skills the child is learning at school are being used at home.

Teachers are vital participants in the IEP meeting as well. At least one of the child's regular education teachers must be on the IEP team if the child is (or may be) participating in the regular education environment. The regular education teacher has a great deal to share with the team. For example, he or she might talk about:

- the general curriculum in the regular classroom;
- the aids, services or changes to the educational program that would help the child learn and achieve; and
- strategies to help the child with behavior, if behavior is an issue.

The regular education teacher may also discuss with the IEP team the supports for school staff that are needed so that the child can:

- advance toward his or her annual goals;
- be involved and progress in the general curriculum;
- participate in extracurricular and other activities; and
- be educated with other children, both with and without disabilities.

Supports for school staff may include professional development or more training. Professional development and training are important for teachers, administrators, bus drivers, cafeteria workers, and others who provide services for children with disabilities.

The child's special education teacher contributes important information and experience about how to educate children with disabilities. Because of his or her training in special education, this teacher can talk about such issues as:

- how to modify the general curriculum to help the child learn;
- the supplementary aids and services that the child may need to be successful in the regular classroom and elsewhere;
- how to modify testing so that the student can show what he or she has learned; and
- other aspects of individualizing instruction to meet the student's unique needs.

Beyond helping to write the IEP, the special educator has responsibility for working with the student to carry out the IEP. He or she may:

- work with the student in a resource room or special class devoted to students receiving special education services;

- team teach with the regular education teacher; and

- work with other school staff, particularly the regular education teacher, to provide expertise about addressing the child's unique needs.

Another important member of the IEP team is the individual who can interpret what the child's evaluation results mean in terms of designing appropriate instruction. The evaluation results are very useful in determining how the child is currently doing in school and what areas of need the child has. This IEP team member must be able to talk about the instructional implications of the child's evaluation results, which will help the team plan appropriate instruction to address the child's needs.

The individual representing the school system is also a valuable team member. This person knows a great deal about special education services and educating children with disabilities. He or she can talk about the necessary school resources. It is important that this individual have the authority to commit resources and be able to ensure that whatever services are set out in the IEP will actually be provided.

The IEP team may also include additional individuals with knowledge or special expertise about the child. The parent or the school system can invite these individuals to participate on the team. Parents, for example, may invite an advocate who knows the child, a professional with special expertise about the child and his or her disability, or others (such as a vocational educator who has been working with the child) who can talk about the child's strengths and/or needs. The school system may invite one or more individuals who can offer special expertise or knowledge about the child, such as a paraprofessional or related services professional. Because an important part of developing an IEP is considering a child's need for related services, related service professionals are often involved as IEP team members or participants. They share their special expertise about the child's needs and how their own professional services can address those needs. Depending on the child's individual needs, some related service professionals attending the IEP meeting or otherwise helping to develop the IEP might include occupational or physical therapists, adaptive physical education providers, psychologists, or speech-language pathologists.

When an IEP is being developed for a student of transition age, representatives from transition service agencies can be important participants. Whenever a purpose of meeting is to consider needed transition services, the school must invite a representative of any other agency that is likely to be responsible for providing or paying for transition services. This individual can help the team plan any transition services the student needs. He or she can also commit the resources of the agency to pay for or provide needed transition services. If he or she does not attend the meeting, then the school must take alternative steps to obtain the agency's participation in the planning of the student's transition services.

And, last but not least, the student may also be a member of the IEP team. If transition service needs or transition services are going to be discussed at the meeting, the student must be invited to attend. More and more students are participating in and even leading their own IEP meetings. This allows them to have a strong voice in their own education and can teach them a great deal about self-advocacy and self-determination.

The Regular Education Teacher as Part of the IEP Team

Appendix A of the federal regulations for Part B of IDEA answers many questions about the IEP. Question 24 addresses the role of the regular education teacher on the IEP team. Here's an excerpt from the answer:

"...while a regular education teacher must be a member of the IEP team if the child is, or may be, participating in the regular education environment, the teacher need not (depending upon the child's needs and the purpose of the specific IEP team meeting) be required to participate in all decisions made as part of the meeting or to be present throughout the entire meeting or attend every meeting. For example, the regular education teacher who is a member of the IEP team must participate in discussions and decisions about how to modify the general curriculum in the regular classroom to ensure the child's involvement and progress in the general curriculum and participation in the regular education environment.

"Depending upon the specific circumstances, however, it may not be necessary for the regular education teacher to participate in discussions and decisions regarding, for example, the physical therapy needs of the child, if the teacher is not responsible for implementing that portion of the child's IEP.

"In determining the extent of the regular education teacher's participation at IEP meetings, public agencies and parents should discuss and try to reach agreement on whether the child's regular education teacher that is a member of the IEP team should be present at a particular IEP meeting and, if so, for what period of time. The extent to which it would be appropriate for the regular education teacher member of the IEP team to participate in IEP meetings must be decided on a case-by-case basis."

Related Services

A child may require any of the following related services in order to benefit from special education. Related services, as listed under IDEA, include (but are not limited to):

- Audiology services
- Counseling services
- Early identification and assessment of disabilities in children
- Medical services
- Occupational therapy
- Orientation and mobility services
- Parent counseling and training
- Physical therapy
- Psychological services
- Recreation
- Rehabilitation counseling services
- School health services
- Social work services in schools
- Speech-language pathology services
- Transportation

If a child needs a particular related service in order to benefit from special education, the related service professional should be involved in developing the IEP. He or she may be invited by the school or parent to join the IEP team as a person "with knowledge or special expertise about the child."

Transition Services

Transition refers to activities meant to prepare students with disabilities for adult life. This can include developing postsecondary education and career goals, getting work experience while still in school, setting up linkages with adult service providers such as the vocational rehabilitation agency—whatever is appropriate for the student, given his or her interests, preferences, skills, and needs. Statements about the student's transition needs must be included in the IEP after the student reaches a certain age.

Transition planning, for students beginning at age 14 (and sometimes younger) involves helping the student plan his or her courses of study (such as advanced placement or vocational education) so that the classes the student takes will lead to his or her post-school goals.

Transition services, for students beginning at age 16 (and sometimes younger) involves providing the student with a coordinated set of services to help the student move from school to adult life. Services focus upon the student's needs or interest in such areas as: higher education or training, employment, adult services, independent living, or taking part in the community.

Writing the IEP

To help decide what special education and related services the student needs, generally the IEP team will begin by looking at the child's evaluation results, such as classroom tests, individual tests given to establish the student's eligibility, and observations by teachers, parents, paraprofessionals, related service providers, administrators, and others. This information will help the team describe the student's "present levels of educational performance"—in other words, how the student is currently doing in school. Knowing how the student is currently performing in school will help the team develop annual goals to address those areas where the student has an identified educational need.

The IEP team must also discuss specific information about the child. This includes:

- the child's strengths;
- the parents' ideas for enhancing their child's education;
- the results of recent evaluations or reevaluations; and
- how the child has done on state and district-wide tests.

It is important that the discussion of what the child needs be framed around how to help the child:

- advance toward the annual goals;
- be involved in and progress in the general curriculum;
- participate in extracurricular and nonacademic activities; and
- be educated with and participate with other children with disabilities and nondisabled children.

Based on the above discussion, the IEP team will then write the child's IEP. This includes the services and supports the school will provide for the child. If the IEP team decides that a child needs a particular device or service (including an intervention, accommodation, or other program modification), the IEP team must write this information in the IEP. As an example, consider a child whose behavior interferes with learning. The IEP team would need to consider positive and effective ways to address that behavior. The team would discuss the positive behavioral interventions, strategies, and supports that the child needs in order to learn how to control or manage his or her behavior. If the team decides that the child needs a particular service (including an intervention, accommodation, or other program modification), they must include a statement to that effect in the child's IEP.

Special Factors to Consider

Depending on the needs of the child, the IEP team needs to consider what the law calls special factors. These include:

- If the child's behavior interferes with his or her learning or the learning of others, the IEP team will consider strategies and supports to address the child's behavior.
- If the child has limited proficiency in English, the IEP team will consider the child's language needs as these needs relate to his or her IEP.
- If the child is blind or visually impaired, the IEP team must provide for instruction in Braille or the use of Braille, unless it determines after an appropriate evaluation that the child does not need this instruction.
- If the child has communication needs, the IEP team must consider those needs.

- If the child is deaf or hard of hearing, the IEP team will consider his or her language and communication needs. This includes the child's opportunities to communicate directly with classmates and school staff in his or her usual method of communication (for example, sign language).

- The IEP team must always consider the child's need for assistive technology devices or services.

Will Parents Need an Interpreter in Order to Participate Fully?

If the parents have a limited proficiency in English or are deaf, they may need an interpreter in order to understand and be understood. In this case, the school must make reasonable efforts to arrange for an interpreter during meetings pertaining to the child's educational placement. For meetings regarding the development or review of the IEP, the school must take whatever steps are necessary to ensure that parents understand the meetings—including arranging for an interpreter. This provision should help to ensure that parents are not limited in their ability to participate in their child's education because of language or communication barriers.

Therefore, if parents need an interpreter for a meeting to discuss their child's evaluation, eligibility for special education or IEP, they should let the school know ahead of time. Telling the school in advance allows the school to make arrangements for an interpreter so that parents can participate fully in the meeting.

Deciding Placement

The child's placement (where the IEP will be carried out) must be decided. The placement decision is made by a group of people, including the parents and others who know about the child, what the evaluation results mean, and what types of placements are appropriate. In some states, the IEP team serves as the group making the placement decision. In other states, this decision may be made by another group of people. In all cases, the parents have the right to be members of the group that decides the educational placement of the child.

Placement decisions must be made according to IDEA's least restrictive environment requirements—commonly known as LRE. These requirements state that, to the maximum extent appropriate, children with disabilities must be educated with children who do not have disabilities. The law also clearly states that special classes, separate schools, or other removal of children with disabilities from the regular educational environment may occur only if the nature or severity of the child's disability is such that education in regular classes with the use of supplementary aids and services cannot be achieved satisfactorily.

What Type of Placements Are There?

Depending on the needs of the child, his or her IEP may be carried out in the regular class (with supplementary aids and services, as needed), in a special class (where every student in the class is receiving special education services for some or all of the day), in a special school, at home, in a hospital and institution, or in another setting. A school system may meet its obligation to ensure that the child has an appropriate placement available by:

- providing an appropriate program for the child on its own;

- contracting with another agency to provide an appropriate program; or

- utilizing some other mechanism or arrangement that is consistent with IDEA for providing or paying for an appropriate program for the child.

The placement group will base its decision on the IEP and which placement option is appropriate for the child. Can the child be educated in the regular classroom, with proper aids and supports? If the child cannot be educated in the regular classroom, even with appropriate aids and supports, then the placement group will talk about other placements for the child.

After the IEP Is Written

When the IEP has been written, parents must receive a copy at no cost to themselves. The IDEA also stresses that everyone who will be involved in implementing the IEP must have access to the document. This includes the child's:

- regular education teacher(s);

- special education teacher(s);

359

- related service provider(s) (for example, speech therapist); or

- any other service provider (such as a paraprofessional) who will be responsible for a part of the child's education.

Each of these individuals needs to know what his or her specific responsibilities are for carrying out the child's IEP. This includes the specific accommodations, modifications, and supports that the child must receive, according to the IEP.

Parents' Permission

Before the school can provide a child with special education and related services for the first time, the child's parents must give their written permission.

Implementing the IEP

Once the IEP is written, it is time to carry it out—in other words, to provide the student with the special education and related services as listed in the IEP. This includes all supplementary aids and services and program modifications that the IEP team has identified as necessary for the student to advance appropriately toward his or her IEP goals, to be involved in and progress in the general curriculum, and participate in other school activities.

Every individual involved in providing services to the student should know and understand his or her responsibilities for carrying out the IEP. This will help ensure that the student receives the services that have been planned, including the specific modifications and accommodations the IEP team has identified as necessary.

Teamwork plays an important part in carrying out the IEP. Many professionals are likely to be involved in providing services and supports to the student. Sharing expertise and insights can help make everyone's job a lot easier and can certainly improve results for students with disabilities. Schools can encourage teamwork by giving teachers, support staff and/or paraprofessionals time to plan or work together on such matters as adapting the general curriculum to address the student's unique needs. Teachers, support staff, and others providing services for children with disabilities may request training and staff development.

Communication between home and school is also important. Parents can share information about what is happening at home and build upon what the child is learning at school. If the child is having difficulty at school, parents may be able to offer insight or help the school explore possible reasons as well as possible solutions.

It is helpful to have someone in charge of coordinating and monitoring the services the student receives. In addition to special education, the student may be receiving any number of related services. Many people may be involved in delivering those services. Having a person in charge of overseeing that services are being delivered as planned can help ensure that the IEP is being carried out appropriately.

The regular progress reports that the law requires will help parents and schools monitor the child's progress toward his or her annual goals. It is important to know if the child is not making the progress expected or if he or she has progressed much faster than expected. Together, parents and school personnel can then address the child's needs as those needs become evident.

Reviewing and Revising the IEP

The IEP team must review the child's IEP at least once a year. One purpose of this review is to see whether the child is achieving his or her annual goals. The team must revise the child's individualized education program, if necessary, to address:

- the child's progress or lack of expected progress toward the annual goals and in the general curriculum;

- information gathered through any reevaluation of the child;

- information about the child that the parents share;

- information about the child that the school shares (for example, insights from the teacher based on his or her observation of the child or the child's classwork);

- the child's anticipated needs; or

- other matters.

Although the IDEA requires this IEP review at least once a year, in fact the team may review and revise the IEP more often. Either the parents or the school can ask to hold an IEP meeting to revise the child's IEP. For example, the child may not be making progress toward his or her IEP goals, and his or her teacher or parents may become concerned. On the other hand, the child may have met most or all of the goals in the IEP, and new ones need to be written. In either case, the IEP team would meet to revise the IEP.

Look at Those Factors Again

When the IEP team is meeting to conduct a review of the child's IEP and, as necessary, to revise it, members must again consider all of the factors discussed. This includes:

- the child's strengths,

- the parents' ideas for enhancing their child's education,

- the results of recent evaluations or reevaluations, and

- how the child has done on state and district-wide tests.

What If Parents Don't Agree with the IEP?

There are times when parents may not agree with the school's recommendations about their child's education. Under the law, parents have the right to challenge decisions about their child's eligibility, evaluation, placement, and the services that the school provides to the child. If parents disagree with the school's actions—or refusal to take action—in these matters, they have the right to pursue a number of options.

They may try to reach an agreement. Parents can talk with school officials about their concerns and try to reach an agreement. Sometimes the agreement can be temporary. For example, the parents and school can agree to try a plan of instruction or a placement for a certain period of time and see how the student does.

Ask for mediation. During mediation, the parents and school sit down with someone who is not involved in the disagreement and try to reach an agreement. The school may offer mediation, if it is available as an option for resolving disputes prior to due process.

Ask for due process. During a due process hearing, the parents and school personnel appear before an impartial hearing officer and present their sides of the story. The hearing officer decides how to solve the problem. (Note: Mediation must be available at least at the time a due process hearing is requested.)

File a complaint with the state education agency. To file a complaint, generally parents write directly to the SEA and say what part of IDEA they believe the school has violated. The agency must resolve the complaint within 60 calendar days. An extension of that time limit is permitted only if exceptional circumstances exist with respect to the complaint.

OSEP Monitoring

The U.S. Department of Education's Office of Special Education Programs (OSEP) regularly monitors states to see that they are complying with IDEA. Every two years OSEP requires that states report progress toward meeting established performance goals that, at a minimum, address the performance of children on assessments, dropout rates, and graduation rates. As part of its monitoring, the Department reviews IEPs and interviews parents, students, and school staff to find out:

- whether, and how, the IEP team made the decisions reflected in the IEP;

- whether those decisions and the IEP content are based on the child's unique needs, as determined through evaluation and the IEP process;

- whether any state or local policies or practices have interfered with decisions of the IEP team about the child's educational needs and the services that the school would provide to meet those needs; and

- whether the school has provided the services listed in the IEP.

Chapter 41

Student Diversity and Learning Needs

Student Diversity

To successfully reach out to a diversity of learners requires substantial support. Although budget-minded critics will argue that such support is costly, they need to be reminded that an investment in prevention today will eliminate or lessen the expense of remediation tomorrow. Not surprisingly, educators who receive substantial help are more effective when carrying out worthwhile innovations that increase all students' potential for success. This notion of support is vitally important because student with the tendency to be at risk will not disappear and because the government and educational community continue to believe in the efficacy of raising academic standards. This chapter will discuss some sources of support intended as a complement to and a scaffold for teachers and administrators who experiment with different ways of meeting a diversity of learning needs.

Curricular Congruence

At-risk learners benefit from instructional activities that are carefully planned and mutually supported by classroom teachers and learning center staff (Nelson, 1994). Unfortunately, many schools provide separate instruction in both settings. For example, in the English

Text in this chapter is from "Student Diversity and Learning Needs," by Joseph Sanacore, *ERIC Digest*, ERIC Identifier: ED412527, 1997; and "Curriculum Access and Universal Design for Learning," by Raymond Orkwis, *ERIC/OSEP Digest* #E586, ERIC Identifier: ED437767, 1999.

classroom, students may explore the theme of good and evil by reading and discussing William Golding's, *Lord of the Flies*, whereas in the learning center, at-risk students may complete workbook exercises and other fragmented activities unrelated to the instructional theme. Clearly, at-risk learners are more likely to be successful when classroom and learning center teachers provide them with congruent goals, resources, strategies, and skills.

A model that can be adapted to both push-in and pull-out efforts represents an ambitious approach, but it can be a major source of support for at-risk learners (Sanacore, 1988). Specifically, these learners receive language arts instruction 7 periods a week. Twice a week, the majority of students experience a double period of instruction, while the at-risk learners are enriched with activities that support the language arts program. If *Lord of the Flies* is being highlighted, the classroom teacher might immerse students in interactive activities concerning important themes, concepts, and vocabulary of the novel. Meanwhile, the learning center teacher might engage individuals in a similar instructional focus, while providing support through a prereading plan, structured overview, semantic mapping, or semantic feature analysis.

An important part of this classroom/learning center connection is cooperative planning time that is built into the teaching assignments of the English staff (Raywid, 1993). These professionals are scheduled weekly for 20-minute periods of teaching and for one period of mutual planning with the learning center staff. During the planning session, the key players discuss their community of learners and organize congruent activities that support effective learning.

Creating a closer link between the classroom and the learning center makes sense. This approach increases transfer of learning and simultaneously lessens the incidence of fragmented, reductionistic teaching. Thus, at-risk learners have more opportunities to engage in cohesive instruction directly related to their learning strengths and needs. Although curricular congruence is not a cure-all, it is a serious source of support for helping at-risk learners to be successful and independent.

Special Education Teacher as Team Teacher

Similar to the intent of curricular congruence is the changing role of the special education teacher serving as a team teacher. This inclusionary perspective helps learners with mild, moderate, and severe disabilities to be successful in the heterogeneous classroom and, thus, to be genuine members of the learning community. In a chapter of Villa and Thousand's *Creating an Inclusive School* (1995), middle grades science teacher Nancy Keller and special educator Lia Cravedi-Cheng describe their bonding as team teachers, which led to the social and academic growth of themselves and their students. Initially, the key players decided to meet at least one period each week for mutual planning. During this time, they focused on building a trusting relationship as they defined and redefined professional roles, discussed content to be covered, planned related instructional activities, and assessed student outcomes. These and other planning agendas set the stage for continued growth with a variety of joint responsibilities (i.e., having parent conferences, managing student behavior). While reflecting on their professional growth, Keller and Cravedi-Cheng realized that successful inclusion occurs when both teachers and students receive support. Planning cooperatively, developing goals, maintaining personal accountability helped the teachers to merge their talents, to reaffirm their commitment to all students, and to reach their audience academically and socially. As was expected, both special needs students and their nondisabled peers became contributing members of the learning community.

Cheryl Jorgensen (1995) describes an interdisciplinary program at Souhegan High School in New Hampshire. The learning environment for grades 9 and 10 involves 2 teams for each grade level, with approximately 85 students in each team. Social studies, science, English, and special education teachers share daily blocks of time morning and afternoon, and these professionals may organize instruction in a variety of ways to accommodate students' learning needs. An important part of these efforts is collaborative planning time for content area teachers and special educators.

Interestingly, special needs students at Souhegan High do not usually require instructional modifications in their heterogeneously grouped classes; however, when support is needed for nurturing full participation, it may be provided by peers, adults, adapted resources, or assistive technology. Individuals also benefit from modified expectations—for example, a physically disabled learner may have his or her lines in a play tape-recorded by a classmate. When the lines are to be spoken aloud, the disabled learner leans on a pressure switch which then activates the lines.

Volunteers and Paraprofessionals

Another source of help for students and teachers in a heterogeneous learning environment is an extra set of hands. In *The Reading*

Resource Handbook for School Leaders (1996), Patty, Maschoff, and Ransom provide useful insights about parent volunteers and teacher aides supporting the language arts program. Specifically, these individuals may nurture learning by functioning as effective role models, reading to students, listening to them read, listening to their retellings after silent reading, asking challenging questions concerning their reading, coaching their efforts, sharing and monitoring reading and writing, developing instructional materials, administering interest and attitude inventories, organizing a classroom newspaper, assisting with bulletin boards and classroom displays that encourage reading and writing, and serving as a resource during field trips.

Volunteers and aides can make valuable contributions to the classroom context, and their support is vitally needed to accommodate the diversity of learning needs which has increased markedly in recent years. Well-constructed questionnaires surveying parents and potential volunteers can provide useful information that can lead to a functional plan of action for eliciting, managing, and developing effective volunteers and aides.

Instructional Resources

Students' journey toward success also involves natural immersion in authentic resources. All learners, including those at risk of failing, benefit from literacy-rich classrooms cluttered with paperbacks, anthologies, fiction and nonfiction works, dramas and comedies, poetry, illustrated books, how-to manuals, bibliotherapeutic stories, talking books, large-print books, dictionaries, magazines, newspapers, and pamphlets. Students are more apt to respond positively to these materials when they are permitted to choose from a wide variety of options, when they observe teachers respecting their choices, and when they are encouraged to read at their own comfortable pace in the classroom.

Being sensitive to students' interests and strengths will also help them to meet content area expectations, especially if teaching and learning are organized around important themes and concepts. For example, if the instructional unit concerns the Civil War, an individual may demonstrate his or her preferred learning style by reading illustrated materials and by creating a flow chart showing important battles. Others may respond to thematic and conceptual aspects of the study unit in ways that represent their unique styles, as the teacher guides them to focus on instructional outcomes that fulfill curricular expectations. These flexible considerations not only provide immediate learning benefits, but also promote a lifelong love of learning.

Not surprisingly, this flexibility also applies to technological resources, which play a major role in helping students to be successful. Disabled learners, in particular, may benefit from adaptive hardware, such as seating devices, switches, electronic communication aids, and computers that scan printed materials and read the text aloud. Although appropriate instructional resources can facilitate learning in heterogeneous classrooms, a problematic economy has caused school administrators to allocate budgets for the basic curricula. Administrators need to work with parents and the community to provide a wide variety of resources to support students and teachers (Mendez-Morse, 1991). This effort increases the chances that special needs students and their nondisabled classmates will respond positively to literacy learning and will use it throughout their lives.

Curriculum Access and Universal Design for Learning

Under the 1997 IDEA re-authorization, all students, regardless of their abilities, must be given the opportunity to become involved with and progress in the general education curriculum. Every student must have access to what is being taught. Providing access, however, involves much more than supplying every student with a textbook or a computer. Teachers must ensure that students are actively engaged in learning; that is, the subject matter is cognitively challenging them, regardless of their developmental level.

Students with disabilities can be blocked from this interaction because of an inflexible text that may inadvertently create physical, sensory, affective, or cognitive barriers. Even though they may have the same tools as everyone else, they do not truly have equal access to the curriculum. But there are several strategies educators can employ to give these students access, including using a curriculum that has been universally designed for accessibility.

What Is Universal Design for Learning?

To accommodate students' individual needs and to give them the opportunity to progress in content areas, educators traditionally have adapted or altered the textbook or tests. Typical accommodations are Braille or recorded texts for visually impaired students, captioned materials for hearing-impaired students, and customized supplementary materials or alternative texts that address cognitive disabilities.

In most classrooms, these accommodations are added to the standardized curriculum much as a wheelchair ramp is added to a building where stairs formerly provided the only access.

Just as after-the-fact architectural accommodations are often awkward and expensive, after-the-fact curriculum adaptations can be time consuming to design and difficult to implement in classrooms of diverse learners. A more efficient way to provide student access is to consider the range of user abilities at the design stage of the curriculum and incorporate accommodations at that point. This built-in access for a wide range of users, those with and without disabilities, is the underlying principle in universal design.

In terms of curriculum, universal design implies a design of instructional materials and activities that allows learning goals to be attainable by individuals with wide differences in their abilities to see, hear, speak, move, read, write, understand English, attend, organize, engage, and remember. Such a flexible, yet challenging, curriculum gives teachers the ability to provide each student access to the subject area without having to adapt the curriculum repeatedly to meet special needs.

The essential features of universal design for learning have been formulated by the Center for Applied Special Technology (CAST) into three principles:

- The curriculum provides multiple means of representation. Subject matter can be presented in alternate modes for students who learn best from visual or auditory information, or for those who need differing levels of complexity.

- The curriculum provides multiple means of expression to allow students to respond with their preferred means of control. This accommodates the differing cognitive strategies and motor-system controls of students.

- The curriculum provides multiple means of engagement. Students' interests in learning are matched with the mode of presentation and their preferred means of expression. Students are more motivated when they are engaged with what they are learning.

How Is Universal Design for Learning Being Implemented?

Teachers who want to begin implementing universal design must begin by using curricular materials that are flexible. Although digital materials are not the only way to deliver a universally designed curriculum, they allow the greatest flexibility in presentation. They can be easily customized to accommodate a wide range of student abilities, but the teacher and the students must know how to use them. The mere presence of good software programs in the classroom does not guarantee that they will provide needed access.

The access provided by universal design for instructional materials does not mean that students are accommodated by lowering the standards, finding the least common denominator, or otherwise dumbing down the curriculum. In fact, the curriculum must remain at a sufficient level of difficulty if students are to progress in it. For example, a software program for beginning readers can have different settings for the speed at which the information is presented and highlighted (multiple representations). It can be controlled with vocal commands, single switch controls, or alternate keyboards (multiple expressions). It can request different levels of feedback from students, from having them repeat the sounds of letters and words to creating their own stories using the vocabulary words they've learned (multiple engagements). These accommodations allow the necessary flexibility for student access and the necessary challenge for learning.

Is There Support for a Universal Design Curriculum?

Many teachers are already working in environments with varying degrees of inclusiveness, effectively teaching students with and without disabilities in the same classroom. Many general and special educators now collaborate on curriculum and prepare adaptations for special needs in their classes. These teachers have already taken the first step toward implementing universal design goals in their classrooms.

As the demographics of classrooms continue to change and there is more need for adapted materials, curriculum developers, particularly those who produce instructional software, are considering the advantages of universal design. With the federal government and states pushing for schools to incorporate more technology-based teaching tools in the classroom, understanding the foundations of universal design for curriculum access can help guide teachers into implementation.

References

Jorgensen, Cheryl (1995). Essential Questions—Inclusive Answers. *Educational Leadership*, 52(4), 52-55. [EJ 496 170]

Mendez-Morse, Sylvia (1991). The Principal's Role in the Instructional Process: Implications for At-Risk Students. *SEDL Issues about Change*, 1(3), 1-4. [ED 363 967]

Nelson, Carol (1994). Organizing for Effective Reading Instruction. *ERIC Digest*. Bloomington, IN: ERIC Clearinghouse on Reading, English, and Communication. [ED 369 034]

Patty, Del, et al (1996). *The Reading Resource Handbook for School Leaders*. Norwood, MA: Christopher-Gordon.

Raywid, Mary Anne (1993). Finding Time for Collaboration. *Educational Leadership*, 51(1), 30-34. [EJ 488 684]

Sanacore, Joseph (1988). Needed: A Better Link between the Reading Center and the Classroom. *Clearing House*, 62(2), 57-60. [EJ 386 881]

Villa, Richard A., ed., and Jacqueline S. Thousand, ed. (1995). Creating An Inclusive School. Alexandria, VA: Association for Supervision and Curriculum Development. [ED 396 505]

Chapter 42

Learning Strategies

Teaching Students with Learning Disabilities to Use Learning Strategies

Learning is the process of acquiring—and retaining—knowledge so it may be applied in life situations. Learning is not a passive process. As any teacher can attest, students are not vessels into which new information is poured and then forever remembered. Rather, learning new information and being able to recall and apply it appropriately involves a complex interaction between the learner and the material being learned. Learning is fostered when the learner has opportunities to practice the new information, receive feedback from an expert, such as a teacher, and apply the knowledge or skill in familiar and unfamiliar situations, with less and less assistance from others.

To each new learning task, students bring their own ideas, beliefs, opinions, attitudes, motivation, skills, and prior knowledge; they also bring with them the strategies and techniques they have learned in order to make their learning more efficient. All these aspects will contribute directly to the students' ability to learn, and to remember and use what has been learned.

Excerpted from "Interventions for Students with Learning Disabilities," by Neil Sturomski, from the National Information Center for Children and Youth with Disabilities (NICHCY), *NICHCY News Digest,* #ND25, August 1997. Despite the older date of this article, it contains timeless information about teaching children with learning disabilities become more effective learners.

The focus of this chapter is on helping students become more efficient and effective learners by teaching them how to learn. By equipping them with a repertoire of strategies for learning—ways to organize themselves and new material; techniques to use while reading, writing, and doing math or other subjects; and systematic steps to follow when working through a learning task or reflecting upon their own learning—teachers can provide students with the tools for a lifetime of successful learning.

The Learning Difficulties of Students with Learning Disabilities

It is no secret that many students find learning a difficult and painful process. Learning may be made more difficult by any number of factors, including inadequate prior knowledge, poor study skills, problems with maintaining attention, cultural or language differences, and—as is the focus of this chapter—the presence of a learning disability. Students who have learning disabilities are often overwhelmed, disorganized, and frustrated in learning situations. Learning can become a nightmare when there are memory problems, difficulties in following directions, trouble with the visual or auditory perception of information, and an inability to perform paper-and-pencil tasks (i.e., writing compositions, note taking, doing written homework, taking tests).

Another aspect of learning that presents difficulties for students who have learning disabilities is why they think they succeed or fail at learning. Due to their history of academic problems, such students may believe that they cannot learn, that school tasks are just too difficult and not worth the effort, or that, if they succeed at a task, they must have gotten lucky. They may not readily believe that there is a connection between what they do, the effort they make, and the likelihood of academic success. These negative beliefs about their ability to learn, and the nature of learning itself, can have far-reaching academic consequences.

The Need to Be Strategic Learners

Notwithstanding the difficulties that students with learning disabilities often experience with learning, they have the same need as their peers without disabilities to acquire the knowledge, skills, and strategies—both academic and nonacademic—that are necessary for functioning independently on a day-to-day basis in our society. Perhaps one of the most important skills they need to learn is how to learn.

Knowing that certain techniques and strategies can be used to assist learning, knowing which techniques are useful in which kinds of learning situations, and knowing how to use the techniques are powerful tools that can enable students to become strategic, effective, and lifelong learners.

Surprisingly, many learners know little about the learning process, their own strengths and weaknesses in a learning situation, and what strategies and techniques they naturally tend to use when learning something new. Yet, we all use various methods and strategies to help us learn and remember new information or skills. For example, when encountering a new word while reading, some of us may try to guess its meaning from the context of the passage and be satisfied with an approximate idea of what it means, while others may look the word up in the dictionary or ask someone nearby what it means. Still others may go a step further and write the new word down or try to use the word in a sentence before the day is through. Some of these methods are more effective than others for learning and remembering new information, and some of us are more conscious of our own learning processes than others.

Because of the nature of their learning difficulties, students with learning disabilities need to become strategic learners, not just haphazardly using whatever learning strategies or techniques they have developed on their own, but becoming consciously aware of what strategies might be useful in a given learning situation and capable of using those strategies effectively. Teachers can be enormously helpful in this regard. They can introduce students to specific strategies and demonstrate when and how the strategies are used. Students can then see how a person thinks or what a person does when using the strategies. Teachers can provide opportunities for students to discuss, reflect upon, and practice the strategies with classroom materials and authentic tasks. By giving feedback, teachers help students refine their use of strategies and learn to monitor their own usage. Teachers may then gradually fade reminders and guidance so that students begin to assume responsibility for strategic learning.

What, Exactly, Are Learning Strategies?

Learning strategies are "techniques, principles, or rules that facilitate the acquisition, manipulation, integration, storage, and retrieval of information across situations and settings" (Alley & Deshler, 1979, p. 13). Strategies are efficient, effective, and organized steps or procedures used when learning, remembering, or performing.

More simply put, learning strategies are the tools and techniques we use to help ourselves understand and learn new material or skills; integrate this new information with what we already know in a way that makes sense; and recall the information or skill later, even in a different situation or place. When we are trying to learn or do a task, our strategies include what we think about (the cognitive aspect of the strategy) and what we physically do (the behavioral or overt action we take).

Strategies can be simple or complex, unconsciously applied or used with great awareness and deliberation. Simple learning strategies that many of us have used, particularly in school settings, include: note taking, making a chart, asking the teacher questions, asking ourselves questions, re-reading when something does not make sense, looking at the reading questions before beginning reading, checking our work, making an outline before beginning to write, asking a friend to look over our composition, rehearsing a presentation aloud, making up a goofy rhyme to remember someone's name, using resource books, drawing a picture that uses every new vocabulary word we have to learn, or mapping in sequence the events of a story. Complex strategies tend actually to be a set of several different strategies that are used in tandem (and recursively) to accomplish a complex learning task such as writing a composition or reading a passage and answering questions.

For example, a complex set of strategies for writing a composition might involve three recursive stages: planning, writing, and revising. Each of these stages can involve using many different strategies. When planning, for instance, we might think hard about the audience that will be reading what we've written (e.g., what do they need or want to know, or how can we best capture and hold their attention?), write an outline, and identify points where we need to gather more information in order to write effectively. When actually writing, we might focus on stating our main ideas well, supporting them with appropriate details, and summarizing our main points in the conclusion. Revising may have several mini-stages: looking back while writing to make sure we're following our outline (or deciding to abandon parts of the outline), laying aside the composition for a day, then re-reading it with a fresh eye. We might also check to make sure we've used correct punctuation and grammar, consult a dictionary or other resource guide when we're uncertain, and ask someone else to read what we've written and give us feedback. We also move back and forth between these three stages—thinking and planning, writing for a while, re-reading to see how we're doing, thinking of how to fix mistakes or add new information, writing again—and on until we're finished.

The research literature abounds with descriptions of these strategy sets, often called strategy interventions, which are intended to make learners highly aware of what they doing, thus making their approach to completing specific tasks more purposeful, systematic, and, according to the research findings, more effective. The writing intervention called DEFENDS is an example of such a strategy set (see Table 42.1). The name is actually an acronym; each letter stands for one of the steps in the strategy. Remembering the acronym helps students remember the steps they are to use when writing.

Strategies can also be categorized in many different ways. Distinctions have been made, for instance, between cognitive and metacognitive strategies. Cognitive strategies help a person process and manipulate information—examples include taking notes, asking questions, or filling out a chart. Cognitive strategies tend to be very task-specific, meaning that certain cognitive strategies are useful when learning or performing certain tasks. Metacognitive strategies are more executive in nature. They are the strategies that a student uses when planning, monitoring, and evaluating learning or strategy performance. For this reason, they are often referred to as self-regulatory strategies.

The use of metacognitive strategies indicates that the student is aware of learning as a process and of what will facilitate learning. Taking the time to plan before writing, for example, shows that the student knows what is involved in writing a good composition. Similarly, he or she might monitor comprehension while reading and take action when something does not make sense—for example, look back in the text for clarification or consciously hold the question in mind while continuing to read. Evaluating one's work, learning, or even strategy use is also highly metacognitive in nature, because it shows that a learner is aware of—and thinking about—how learning takes place.

Metacognitive strategies are at the core of self-regulated learning, which, in turn, is at the core of successful and lifelong learning. Self-regulation involves such strategies as goal setting, self-instruction, self-monitoring, and self-reinforcement (Graham, Harris, & Reid, 1992). It's easy to see why self-regulated learners tend to achieve academically. They set goals for learning, talk to themselves in positive ways about learning and use self-instruction to guide themselves through a learning problem, keep track of (or monitor) their comprehension or progress, and reward themselves for success. Just as students can be helped to develop their use of cognitive, task-specific strategies, they also can be helped to use self-regulatory, metacognitive ones as well. In fact, the most effective strategy interventions combine the use of cognitive and metacognitive strategies.

Strategies have also been categorized by their purpose or function for the learner (Lenz, Ellis, & Scanlon, 1996). Is a strategy being used to help the student initially learn new information or skills? Such strategies are acquisition strategies. Is a strategy being used to help the student manipulate or transform information so that it can be effectively placed in memory? These types of strategies are storage strategies. Is a strategy being used to help the learner recall or show what he or she has learned? Such strategies are demonstration and expression of knowledge strategies.

What Strategies Might We Help Students Learn? Examples from the Reading Field

Decades of research into reading has resulted in a substantial knowledge base about how we learn to read, what effective readers do, what not-so-effective readers do and don't do, and how good reading skills might be fostered or poor reading skills remediated. Much of this knowledge base has been put to use in the form of strategy instruction—helping beginning readers, and those whose skills need remediating, develop the strategies the good reader uses. Good readers, for example, successfully construct understanding and meaning through interacting with the text using learning strategies, including thinking about what they already know on the topic, being aware when they are not understanding something in the text, and taking some sort of corrective action to clear up the difficulty (Pressley, Brown, El-Dinary, & Afflerbach, 1995). They also paraphrase or summarize as they go along, and they ask questions of themselves or others to maximize their comprehension. Studies have shown that children with learning disabilities and other low-achievers can master the learning strategies that improve reading comprehension skills (e.g., Deshler, Shumaker, Alley, Clark, & Warner, 1981; Idol, 1987; Palincsar & Brown, 1987; Schunk & Rice, 1989; Wong & Jones, 1982). Techniques that help students learn to ask questions and to paraphrase and summarize what they are reading have been shown to help them develop higher level reading comprehension skills. For students with learning problems, learning to use questioning strategies is especially important, since these students do not often spontaneously self-question or monitor their own reading comprehension (Bos & Filip, 1984).

This section looks briefly at some of the strategies that researchers and teachers have focused their attention upon, with the purpose of illustrating concretely what strategies might be helpful to students, particularly those with learning disabilities.

Questioning and Paraphrasing. Several strategic approaches have been designed to foster student interaction with the text being read. Reciprocal teaching is one such approach (Brown & Palincsar, 1988). In reciprocal teaching, students interact deeply with the text through the strategies of questioning, summarizing, clarifying, and predicting. Organized in the form of a discussion, the approach involves one leader (students and teacher take turns being the leader) who, after a segment of the text is read, frames a question to which the group responds. Participants can then share their own questions. The leader then summarizes the gist of the text. Participants comment or elaborate upon that summary. At any point in the discussion, either the leader or participants may identify aspects of the text or discussion that need to be clarified, and the group joins together to clarify the confusion. Finally, the leader indicates it's time to move on when he or she makes or solicits predictions about what might come up next in the text.

Paraphrasing, self-questioning, and finding the main idea are the strategies used in an approach developed and researched by Deshler, Schumaker, Alley, Clark, and Warner (1981). Students divide reading passages into smaller parts such as sections, subsections, or paragraphs. After reading a segment, students are cued to use a self-questioning strategy to identify main ideas and details. The strategy requires students to maintain a high level of attention to reading tasks, because they must alternate their use of questioning and paraphrasing after reading each section, subsection, or paragraph.

Questioning to Find the Main Idea. Wong and Jones (1982) developed a self-questioning strategy focused primarily on identifying and questioning the main idea or summary of a paragraph. They first taught junior high students with learning disabilities the concept of a main idea. A self-questioning strategy was then explained. Students then practiced the self-questioning strategy, with cue card assistance, on individual paragraphs. Following the practice, students were provided with immediate feedback. Eventually, following successful comprehension of these short paragraphs, students were presented with more lengthy passages as the cue card use was removed. Continuing to give corrective feedback, Wong and Jones (1982) finished each lesson with a discussion of students' progress and of strategy usefulness. Their results indicated that students with learning disabilities who were trained in a self-questioning strategy performed significantly higher (i.e., demonstrated greater comprehension of what was read) than untrained students.

Story-mapping. Idol (1987) used a story-mapping strategy to help students read a story, generate a map of its events and ideas, and then answer questions. In order to fill in the map, students had to identify the setting, characters, time and place of the story, the problem, the goal, the action that took place, and the outcome. Idol modeled for students how to fill in the map, then gave them extensive opportunities to practice the mapping technique for themselves and receive corrective feedback. She stated that if comprehension instruction provides a framework for understanding, conceptualizing, and remembering important story events, students will improve their comprehension of necessary information. Idol further recognized that comprehension improves only through direct teacher instruction on the use of the strategy, high expectation of strategy use, and a move toward students independently using the strategy.

This is just a sampling of the strategies that can be used by students to improve their reading comprehension technique. Many other strategies can be used in reading, and there are also many strategies designed for math, writing, and other academic and non-academic areas.

The Research Base for Learning Strategies

As our knowledge has grown regarding the learning strategies that help us learn new information and perform various tasks, so has our knowledge regarding how to teach those strategies to students. In the last 20 years, a sizeable research base has developed that demonstrates the usefulness of directly teaching students how to use strategies to acquire skills and information and how to apply those strategies, skills, and information in other settings and with other materials (known as generalization).

Researchers at the University of Kansas have been deeply involved in researching learning strategies since the 1970s and have done much to define and articulate the benefits of strategy instruction in general and for individuals with learning disabilities in particular. Chief among the benefits is the fact that instruction in learning strategies helps students with learning disabilities approach and complete tasks successfully and provides them with techniques that promote independence in acquiring and performing academic skills (Ellis, Deshler, Lenz, Schumaker, & Clark, 1991).

The work at the University of Kansas has also resulted in one of the most well researched and well articulated models for teaching students to use learning strategies. This model has been known for years as the Strategies Intervention Model, or SIM, and was recently renamed the Strategies Integration Model. The SIM is designed as a series of steps that a teacher can use to effectively teach students to use any number of strategies or strategic approaches. The SIM is not the only model available to guide how teachers provide students with strategy instruction; not surprisingly, researchers around the country tend to advocate similar methods, drawing from what is known about effective teaching methodology and about learning.

Table 42.1. Example of a Strategy Intervention

DEFENDS is the acronym for a strategic approach that helps secondary students write a composition in which they must take a position and defend it (Ellis, 1994). Each letter stands for a strategic step, as follows:

D ecide on audience, goals, and position

E stimate main ideas and details

F igure best order of main ideas and details

E xpress the position in the opening

N ote each main idea and supporting points

D rive home the message in the last sentence

S earch for errors and correct

In a nutshell, teaching methods need to provide students with the opportunity to observe, engage in, discuss and reflect upon, practice, and personalize strategies that can be used with classroom and authentic tasks now and in the future (Rosenshine & Stevens, 1986). In using these teaching methods, teachers promote student independence in use of the strategies. Research makes it clear, however, that if students are to use learning strategies and generalize their strategic knowledge to other academic and nonacademic situations, teachers must understand both the strategies that provide students with the necessary learning tools and the methods that can be used to effectively teach those learning strategies to students.

Effective Teaching Methods

Just as there are effective approaches to learning, there are effective approaches to teaching. A great deal of research has been conducted into the nature of effective teaching, and much has been learned. Educational researchers (e.g., Englert, 1984; Nowacek, McKinney & Hallahan, 1990; Rosenshine & Stevens, 1986; Sindelar, Espin, Smith, and Harriman, 1990) have concluded, for example, that a systematic approach to providing instruction greatly improves student achievement.

These researchers also state that teachers can learn the specific components of an effective, systematic approach to providing instruction and can modify and thereby enhance their teaching behavior. Using such a systematic approach with whatever is being taught can only help to further improve educational opportunities for all students, especially those who have learning disabilities.

Rosenshine and Stevens (1986) have identified common teaching practices of successful teachers, such as teaching in small steps, practicing after each step, guiding students during initial practice, and providing all students with opportunities for success. Englert (1984) pointed out that successful teachers use lesson strategies to provide students with both direct instruction and the opportunity for practice. Lesson strategies include: communicating the rules and expectations of the lesson, stating instructional objectives and linking them to previous lessons, providing numerous examples, prompting student responses, and providing drill and further practice immediately following incorrect responses. Sindelar, Espin, Smith, and Harriman (1990) add that the more time an actively engaged educator spends in the instructional process, the more positive student behavior and achievement will be. Sindelar et al. (1990) suggest that effective teachers limit seatwork activities, provide ample opportunities for student over learning through teacher questioning, and allow time to socially interact with students. They conclude that encouraging higher levels of student participation, providing effective classroom transitions (i.e., concluding one activity and moving on to another), and bringing lessons to a close by providing assignments for further practice are consistent with teacher-directed learning.

Nowacek, McKinney, and Hallahan (1990) indicate that teacher-directed, rather than student-directed, activities provide for an effective educational experience that is more likely to improve student achievement. Higher levels of student achievement occur because teachers, using a systematic approach, are more organized, have

clearer expectations, maintain student attention, and provide immediate, corrective, and constructive feedback. Because their instruction
is highly structured, these teachers provide a positive environment
in which to learn.

Using a systematic approach to teaching does not suggest that
teacher and student creativity is not a vital part of the process. It
merely lays out an organizational framework that provides a means
for enhanced, successful, and efficient learning.

Teaching Students to Use Learning Strategies

As with the basic tenets of effective teaching, much has been
learned through research regarding effective learning strategy instruction. As mentioned earlier, a well articulated, strategies instructional approach known as the Strategies Integration Model (SIM) has
emerged from the research conducted at the University of Kansas.
Based on cognitive behavior modification, the SIM is one of the field's
most comprehensive models for providing strategy instruction. It can
be used to teach virtually any strategic intervention to students.

First, of course, the teacher must select a strategy—most likely, a
set of strategies—to teach to students. The decision of what strategy
to teach, however, should not be arbitrary. Rather, the strategy should
be clearly linked to (i.e., useful in completing) the tasks that students
need to perform and where they need to perform them. When the strategy instruction is matched to student need, students tend to be more
motivated to learn and use the strategy.

Once the teacher has decided upon what strategy or approach to
teach, he or she may find the steps of the SIM particularly useful for
guiding how the actual instruction should proceed.

*Pretest Students and Get Them Interested in Learning the Strat-
egy.* Although the teacher may not wish to call this step testing, it is
nonetheless important to know how much the students already know
about using the strategy and to secure their commitment to learning
the strategy from top to bottom. As Lenz, Ellis, and Scanlon (1996)
remark, "Short of standing over students with a gun, you cannot force
them to be strategic against their will" (p. 85).

Letting students know that gains in learning can occur when the
strategy is used effectively is one of the keys to motivating them. Studies have shown that it is important to tell students directly that they
are going to learn a strategy that can help them in their reading,
writing, or whatever skill is being addressed through the strategy.

They also need to know that their effort and persistence in learning and in using the strategy can bring them many learning benefits. In a study by Shunk and Rice (1989), for example, students were put into three groups and taught the strategy of finding the main idea of a reading passage. The groups, however, were given different goals for their work. One group was told that the goal of the activity was to learn the strategy, which would help them answer several reading questions. Another group was told that the goal was to answer several reading questions; the third group was simply told to do their best. Results indicated that students whose learning goal was to learn the strategy performed the best when post tested. Understanding, knowing, and applying a strategy that assisted comprehension, Shunk and Rice (1989) reported, gave students a sense of control over their learning outcomes and, therefore, encouraged students to use the strategy. Use of the strategy also fostered a sense of task involvement among students. These results indicate the importance of overtly teaching students both the strategy and the power of the strategy—i.e., making sure they understand that the strategy can help them learn, and how it can help.

The pretest can be instrumental in helping students see the need to learn the strategy. To this end, it is critical that the teacher pretest students using materials and tasks that are similar to the materials and tasks that the students actually encounter in their classes. The strategy should also be useful when working with those materials and tasks—in other words, students will find it easier to work with those materials or perform those tasks if they apply the strategy.

The pretest should be primarily focused on completing the task (e.g., reading a passage and answering questions). Following the pretest, the class should discuss results. How did students do? Were they able to perform the task successfully? What types of errors did they make? What did they do, or think about, to help themselves while taking the pretest? What difficulties did they have, and how did they address those difficulties? If students did not perform particularly well, the teacher then indicates that he or she knows of a strategy or technique that will help students perform that task more successfully in the future.

Obtaining a commitment from students to learn the strategy, according to the SIM model, can involve any number of approaches, including discussing the value of the strategy, the likelihood that success will not be immediate upon learning the strategy but will come if the student is willing to persevere and practice the strategy, and the teacher's own commitment to helping the students learn the strategy (Lenz,

Ellis, & Scanlon, 1996). (With elementary school students, student-teacher collaboration in use of the strategy is especially important; teachers need to discuss and practice strategies with these young students frequently.) Commitments can be verbal or in writing, but the idea here is to get the students involved and to make them aware that their participation in learning and using the strategy is vital to their eventual success.

Describe the Strategy. In this stage, teachers "present the strategy, give examples, and have students discuss various ways the strategy can be used" (Day & Elksnin, 1994, p. 265). A clear definition of the strategy must be given, as well as some of the benefits to learning the strategy. The teacher should also identify real assignments in specific classes where students can apply the strategy and ask students if they can think of other work where the strategy might be useful. Students should also be told the various stages involved in learning the strategy, so they know what to expect.

Once this type of overview is provided and the teacher feels that students are ready to delve more deeply into hearing about and using the strategy, instruction must become more specific. Each separate step of the strategy must be described in detail. It is important that the strategy is presented in such a way that students can easily remember its steps. Many strategies have been given an acronym to help students remember the various steps involved. (An example is listed in the Table 42.2, and another, DEFENDS, in Table 42.1.) Students may also benefit from having a poster or chart about the strategy and its steps displayed in plain view.

Table 42.2. An Example of an Acronym Designed to Help Students Remember the Steps in Using a Strategy

COPS is the acronym for a strategic approach that helps students detect and correct common writing errors. Each letter stands for an aspect of writing that students need to check for accuracy (Shannon & Polloway, 1993).

C Capitalization of appropriate letters

O Overall appearance of paper

P Punctuation used correctly

S Spelling accuracy

During the description stage, the class may also discuss how this new approach to a specific task differs from what students are currently using. The stage should conclude with a review of what has been said.

Model the Strategy. Modeling the strategy for students is an essential component of strategy instruction. In this stage, teachers overtly use the strategy to help them perform a relevant classroom or authentic task, talking aloud as they work so that students can observe how a person thinks and what a person does while using the strategy, including: deciding which strategy to use to perform the task at hand, working through the task using that strategy, monitoring performance (i.e., is the strategy being applied correctly, and is it helping the learner complete the work well?), revising one's strategic approach, and making positive self-statements. An example of such a think aloud is provided in the box at the right.

The self-talk that the teacher provides as a model can become a powerful guide for students as responsibility for using the strategy transfers to them. In fact, Lenz, Ellis, and Scanlon (1996) suggest that teachers model the strategy intervention more than once and involve students in these subsequent modelings by asking questions such as "What do I do in this step?" Teachers can prompt this type of student involvement by asking "Now what's next? How do we do that step? What questions should you be asking yourself?" Student responses will help the teacher determine how well the students understand when and where they might use the strategy intervention, as well as the steps involved in the intervention.

Practice the Strategy. Repeated opportunities to practice the strategy are important as well. The more students and teachers collaborate to use the strategy, the more internalized the strategy will become in students' strategic repertoire. Initial practice may be largely teacher-directed, with teachers continuing to model appropriate ways of thinking about the task at hand and deciding (with increasing student direction) which strategy or action is needed to work through whatever problems arise in completing the task.

Students may also be called upon to think aloud as they work through the practice tasks, explaining the problems they are having, decisions they are making, or physical actions they are taking, and what types of thoughts are occurring to them as they attempt to solve the problems, make the decisions, or take the physical actions. These student think alouds should increasingly show the strategy being used to help them complete the task successfully. While these think alouds may initially be part of teacher-directed instruction, students may benefit greatly from practicing as well in small groups, where they listen to each other's think alouds and help each other understand the task, why the strategy might be useful in completing the task, and how to apply the strategy to the task. Practice opportunities should eventually become self-mediated, where students work independently to complete tasks while using the strategy.

In the beginning, students should practice using the strategy with materials that are at or slightly below their comfort level, so they do not become frustrated by overly difficult content. Using materials that are well matched to the strategy is also important, because then students can readily see the strategy's usefulness. As time goes by and students become more proficient in using the strategy, materials that are more difficult should be used.

Provide Feedback. The feedback that teachers give students on their strategy use is a critical component in helping students learn how to use a strategy effectively and how to change what they are doing when a particular approach is not working. Much of the feedback can be offered as students become involved in thinking aloud about the task and about strategy use, in the modeling and practice steps described above. It is also important to provide opportunities for students to reflect upon their approach to and completion of the task. What aspects of the task did they complete well? What aspects were hard? Did any problems arise, and what did they do to solve the problems? What might they do differently the next time they have to complete a similar task?

How Teachers Might Model a Strategy by Thinking Aloud

One strategy that is vital when reading, particularly for students with learning disabilities, is comprehension monitoring. Comprehension monitoring "is the active awareness of whether one is understanding or remembering text being processed" (Pressley, Brown, El-Dinary, & Afflerbach, 1995, p. 218).

After explaining to students that good readers constantly monitor how well they are understanding what they read, the teacher might show students an example of how we think when we monitor. She puts up a sample text entitled "Grizzly Bears," reads it aloud, and thinks aloud as she's reading. Note that the think aloud following illustrates some of the corrective actions (e.g., asking questions, looking back in

387

the text, thinking about what we already know, reading on) good readers might take to clear up any confusion.

The text the teacher reads: "Grizzly bears are found in western Canada and in Alaska, living in forests on mountain sides. They have shaggy fur, humped shoulders, sharp teeth and long, sharp claws...Grizzlies usually live alone. Each bear has its own area of land, called a "home range." It leaves scents on the bark of trees all the way around its home range to let other bears know where it lives." [Wood, J. (1989). *My First Book of Animals* (p. 34). Boston, MA: Little, Brown.]

The teacher's think aloud might be as follows:

> Let's see. This is about grizzly bears, I can tell that from the title. I know a little bit about grizzly bears—they're big and have sharp claws and teeth, and sometimes they come into people's campsites and try to get the food. I guess they're not all Gentle Ben...okay, "...found in western Canada and in Alaska," places it's cold, yeah, that makes sense because they hibernate in winter, I remember that now... "...living in forests on mountain sides. They have shaggy fur..." I guess that's good, because they live where it's cold.
>
> "...humped shoulders..." Humped shoulders? What do they mean by that? Oh, maybe when they're down on all fours, yeah, their backs are kind of like a hump then, okay, I get it "...and have sharp claws and teeth..." see! I knew that!
>
> "Grizzlies usually live alone..." I wonder why that is. Don't they like one another? Maybe they don't want to share the food they find, or maybe they fight over territory...Let me look back and see if I missed something...[re-reads] no, I still don't have a clue. Maybe they'll tell me in a bit why bears don't live together in little groups, let's see.
>
> "Each bear has its own area of land...[reads to end], no, no answer, at least not real clear. I can see they probably do defend their territory, though, if they mark the trees with their scent. They must be like dogs then, dogs do that, mark things with their scent, to warn other dogs off. Sort of like a fence around your yard! I wonder how they leave the scent, though—maybe they go on the tree or rub up against it, against the bark. I also wonder how big an area a bear gets. As big as he wants, I guess, with all those claws and teeth!"

Promote Generalization. It is important for students to be able to apply the strategy in novel situations and with novel tasks. Surprisingly, many students will not recognize that the strategy they have been learning and practicing may be ideal for helping them to complete a learning task in a different classroom or learning situation; this is particularly true of students with learning disabilities (Borkowski, Estrada, Milstead & Hale, 1989). Thus, mere exposure to strategy training appears insufficient for both strategy learning and strategy utilization (Wood, Rosenburg, & Carran, 1993). Consistent, guided practice at generalizing strategies to various settings and tasks is, therefore, vital for students with learning disabilities (Pressley, Symons, Snyder & Cariglia-Bull, 1989), as are repeated reminders that strategies can be used in new situations (Borkowski, Estrada, Milstead & Hale, 1989).

Therefore, teachers need to discuss with students what generalization is and how and when students might use the strategy in other settings. An important part of this discussion will be looking at the actual work that students have in other classes and discussing with students how the strategy might be useful in completing that work. Being specific—actually going through the steps of the strategy with that work—is highly beneficial. Students can also be called upon to generate their own lists of instances where they might apply the strategy in other classes. Additionally, teachers may wish to coordinate between themselves to promote student use of strategies across settings, so that the strategies being taught in one classroom are mentioned and supported by other teachers as well. All of these approaches will promote student generalization of the strategy.

The Importance of Positive Self-Statements

Teachers may find that it's important to address the negative feelings that many students with learning disabilities have about learning and about themselves. Often, these students believe that they cannot learn, that the work is simply too difficult, or that any success they might achieve is due to luck. They may not readily believe they can achieve success in learning through their own effort and strategic activities and thoughts, and so they may not persist in using strategies.

Just as teachers can help students develop strategic approaches to learning, teachers can help students learn to attribute success in learning to their own effort and use of strategies. Modeling positive self-statements, and encouraging students to use such self-talk, are essential.

Examples of positive self-statements that attribute success to effort and not to luck include: "I can probably do this problem because

I've done similar ones successfully." "I'm usually successful when I work carefully and use the learning strategy correctly." "If I make a mistake, I can probably find it and correct it." (Corral & Antia, 1997, p. 43) Changing students' perceptions about themselves and about the connection between effort and success can be a vital element in their willingness to keep trying in the face of challenge, using learning strategies as a valuable tool.

Other Approaches to Strategy Instruction

The steps given previously have been drawn primarily from research conducted at the University of Kansas and represent one strong approach to teaching the wide range of strategies that learners can use to tackle challenging learning situations. Other approaches to strategy instruction exist as well, with most recommending many of the steps articulated in the SIM. Much effort has gone into defining, testing, and refining their components, and in validating their effectiveness in promoting student achievement.

While the SIM and other strategy instruction models present educators with an overall structure for teaching students about learning and about learning strategies and techniques, the research literature also abounds with descriptions of specific strategies that students can use to enhance their reading, writing, and math skills. There are also many descriptions of strategies designed for use in specific academic (e.g., science) and non-academic (e.g., social skills) areas.

Some strategy interventions are designed for use at the elementary level, while others are appropriate for secondary students. While much is known about strategy instruction, new instruction and instructional methodology continues to unfold, as does our understanding of

Table 42.3. Student-Generated List of Opportunities to Use COPS

Love letters	Written math problems
Homework assignments	Health questions
Spelling practice	History exam questions
Job applications	Friendly letters
English papers	Written instructions

(Shannon & Polloway, 1993, p. 161)

both strategies and strategy instruction. Therefore, strategy techniques and instruction should not be looked upon as a cure-all when working with students who have learning disabilities but as another possible approach to meeting learners' needs.

Conclusion

Learning strategy instruction appears to hold great educational potential, especially for students who have learning disabilities. This is because strategy training emphasizes helping students learn how to learn and how to use strategies found to be effective in promoting successful performance of academic, social, or job-related tasks. Students need these skills not only to cope with immediate academic demands but also to address similar tasks in different settings under different conditions throughout life. Strategies are, thus, skills that empower. They are resources for an individual to use, especially when faced with new learning situations.

Good strategy instruction makes students aware of the purposes of strategies, how they work, why they work, when they work, and where they can be used. To accomplish this, teachers need to talk about strategies explicitly, describe and name them, model how they are used by thinking aloud while performing tasks relevant to students, provide students with multiple opportunities to use the strategies with a variety of materials, and provide feedback and guidance to help students refine and internalize strategy use. Ultimately, responsibility for strategy use needs to shift from teacher to students, so that students can become independent learners with the cognitive flexibility necessary to address the many learning challenges they will encounter in their lives.

Of course, no single technique or intervention can be expected to address the complex nature of learning or the varied needs of all learners. When working with students with learning disabilities, teachers will find it highly beneficial to have a variety of interventions and techniques with which to foster student success. Strategies are one such technique—and a powerful one at that. When students are given extensive and ongoing practice in using learning strategies within the context of day-to-day school instruction, they become better equipped to face current and future tasks. Learning how to learn provides them with the ability to be independent lifelong learners, which is one of the ultimate goals of education. When students learn, they grow and change intellectually. They acquire more than knowledge. They enhance their sense of competence and their ability to achieve.

References

Alley, G.R. and Deshler, D.D. (1979). *Teaching the Learning Disabled Adolescent: Strategies and Methods*. Denver: Love.

Borkowski, J.G.; Estrada, M.; Milstead, M.; and Hale, C. (1989). General problem-solving skills: Relations between metacognition and strategic processing. *Learning Disabilities Quarterly*, 12, 57-70.

Bos, C.S. and Filip, D. (1984). Comprehension monitoring in learning disabled and average students. *Journal of Learning Disabilities*, 17(4), 229-233.

Brown, A.L. and Palincsar, A.S. (1982). Including strategic learning from texts by means of informed, self-control training. *Topics in Learning and Learning Disabilities*, 2(1), 1-17.

Corral, N. and Antia, S.D. (1997, March/April). Self-talk: Strategies for success in math. *TEACHING Exceptional Children*, 29(4), 42-45.

Day, V.P. and Elksnin, L.K. (1994). Promoting strategic learning. *Intervention in School and Clinic*, 29(5), 262-270.

Deshler, D.D.; Shumaker, J.B.; Alley, G.R.; Clark, F.L.; and Warner, M.M. (1981). Paraphrasing strategy. University of Kansas, Institute for Research in Learning Disabilities (Contract No. 300-77-0494). Washington, DC: Bureau of Education for the Handicapped.

Ellis, E.S. (1994). DEFENDS: A strategy for defending a position in writing. Unpublished manuscript.

Ellis, E.S.; Deshler, D.D.; Lenz, K.; Schumaker, J.B.; and Clark, F.L. (1991). An instructional model for teaching learning strategies. *Focus on Exceptional Children*, 23(6), 1-24.

Englert, C.S. (1984). Effective direct instruction practices in special education settings. *Remedial and Special Education*, 5(2), 38-47.

Graham, S.; Harris, K.R.; and Reid, R. (1992). Developing self-regulated learners. *Focus on Exceptional Children*, 24(6), 1-16.

Idol, L. (1987). Group story mapping: A comprehension strategy for both skilled and unskilled readers. *Journal of Learning Disabilities*, 20(4), 196-205.

Lenz, B.K.; Ellis, E.S.; and Scanlon, D. (1996). Teaching learning strategies to adolescents and adults with learning disabilities. Austin, TX: PRO-ED.

Meichenbaum, D. (1977). *Cognitive-Behavior Modification: An Integrative Approach*. New York: Plenum.

Nowacek, E.; McKinney, J.; and Hallahan, D. (1990). Instructional behaviors of more and less beginning regular and special educators. *Exceptional Children*, 57, 140-149.

Page-Voth, V. and Graham, S. (1993). The application of goal setting to writing. *LD Forum*, 18(3), 14-17.

Palincsar, A.S. and Brown, A. (1987). Enhancing instructional time through attention to metacognition. *Journal of Learning Disabilities*, 20(2), 66-75.

Palincsar, A.S. and Brown, A. (1988). Teaching and practicing thinking skills to promote comprehension in the context of group problem solving. *Remedial and Special Education*, 9(1), 53-59.

Pressley, M.; Symons, S.; Snyder, B.L.; and Cariglia-Bull, T. (1989). Strategy instruction research comes of age. *Learning Disabilities Quarterly*, 12, 16-30.

Pressley, M.; Brown, R.; El-Dinary, P.B.; and Afflerbach, P. (1995, Fall). The comprehension instruction that students need: Instruction fostering constructively responsive reading. *Learning Disabilities Research & Practice*, 10(4), 215-224.

Rosenshine, B. and Stevens, R. (1986). Teaching functions. In M. Wittrock (Ed.)., *Handbook of Research on Teaching* (pp. 376-393). New York: Macmillan.

Schumaker, J.B.; Deshler, D.D.; Alley, G.R.; and Warner, M.M. (1983). Toward the development of an intervention model for learning disabled adolescents: The University of Kansas Institute. *Exceptional Education Quarterly*, 4(1), 45-74.

Schunk, D.H. and Rice, J.M. (1989). Learning goals and children's reading comprehension. *Journal of Reading Behavior*, 21(3), 279-293.

Shannon, T.R. and Polloway, E.A. (1993). Promoting error monitoring in middle school students with LD. *Intervention in School and Clinic*, 28, 160-164.

Sindelar, P.T.; Espin, C.; Smith, M.; and Harriman, N. (1990). A comparison of more and less effective special education teachers in elementary level programs. *Teacher Education and Special Education*, 13, 9-16.

Wong, B.Y.L. and Jones, W. (1982). Increasing metacomprehension in learning disabled and normally achieving students through self-questioning training. *Learning Disability Quarterly*, 5, 409-414.

Wood, D.; Rosenburg, M.; and Carran, D. (1993). The effects of tape-recorded self-instruction cues on the mathematics performance of students with learning disabilities. *Journal of Learning Disabilities*, 26(4), 250-258, 269.

Chapter 43

Homework Strategies for Teaching Students with Learning Disabilities

Homework is one aspect of the general education curriculum that has been widely recognized as important to academic success. Teachers have long used homework to provide additional learning time, strengthen study and organizational skills, and in some respects, keep parents informed of their children's progress. Generally, when students with disabilities participate in the general education curriculum, they are expected to complete homework along with their peers. But, just as students with disabilities may need instructional accommodations in the classroom, they may also need homework accommodations.

Many students with disabilities find homework challenging, and teachers are frequently called upon to make accommodations for these students. What research supports this practice? This chapter describes five strategies that researchers have identified to improve homework results for students with disabilities.

Strategy 1. Give Clear and Appropriate Assignments

Teachers need to take special care when assigning homework. If the homework assignment is too hard, is perceived as busy work, or takes too long to complete, students might tune out and resist doing

"Five Homework Strategies for Teaching Students with Disabilities," by Cynthia Warger, from ERIC Clearinghouse on Disabilities and Gifted Education, *ERIC/OSEP Digest* E608, ERIC Identifier: ED452628, 2001.

it. Never send home any assignment that students cannot do. Homework should be an extension of what students have learned in class.

To ensure that homework is clear and appropriate, consider the following tips from teachers for assigning homework:

- Make sure students and parents have information regarding the policy on missed and late assignments, extra credit, and available adaptations. Establish a set routine at the beginning of the year.

- Assign work that the students can do.

- Assign homework in small units.

- Explain the assignment clearly.

- Write the assignment on the chalkboard and leave it there until the assignment is due.

- Remind students of due dates periodically.

- Coordinate with other teachers to prevent homework overload.

Students concur with these tips. They add that teachers can:

- Establish a routine at the beginning of the year for how homework will be assigned.

- Assign homework toward the beginning of class.

- Relate homework to class-work or real life (and/or inform students how they will use the content of the homework in real life).

- Explain how to do the homework, provide examples and write directions on the chalkboard.

- Have students begin the homework in class, check that they understand, and provide assistance as necessary.

- Allow students to work together on homework.

Strategy 2. Make Homework Accommodations

Make any necessary modifications to the homework assignment before sending it home. Identify practices that will be most helpful to individual students and have the potential to increase their involvement, understanding, and motivation to learn. The most common homework accommodations are to:

- Provide additional one-on-one assistance to students.

- Monitor students' homework more closely.

- Allow alternative response formats (e.g., allow the student to audiotape an assignment rather than handwriting it).

- Adjust the length of the assignment.

- Provide a peer tutor or assign the student to a study group.

- Provide learning tools (e.g., calculators).

- Adjust evaluation standards.

- Give fewer assignments.

It is important to check out all accommodations with other teachers, students, and their families. If teachers, students, or families do not find homework accommodations palatable, they may not use them.

Strategy 3. Teach Study Skills

Both general and special education teachers consistently report that homework problems seem to be exacerbated by deficient basic study skills. Many students, particularly students with disabilities, need instruction in study and organizational skills. Here is a list of organizational strategies basic to homework:

- Identify a location for doing homework that is free of distractions.

- Have all materials available and organized.

- Allocate enough time to complete activities and keep on schedule.

- Take good notes.

- Develop a sequential plan for completing multi-task assignments.

- Check assignments for accuracy and completion before turning them in.

- Know how to get help when it is needed.

- Turn in completed homework on time.

Teachers can enhance homework completion and accuracy by providing classroom instruction in organizational skills. They should talk with parents about how to support the application of organizational skills at home.

Strategy 4. Use a Homework Calendar

Students with disabilities often need additional organizational support. Just as adults use calendars, schedulers, lists, and other devices to self-monitor activities, students can benefit from these tools as well. Students with disabilities can monitor their own homework using a planning calendar to keep track of homework assignments. Homework planners also can double as home/school communication tools if they include a space next to each assignment for messages from teachers and parents.

Here's how one teacher used a homework planner to increase communication with students' families and improve homework completion rates:

> Students developed their own homework calendars. Each page in the calendar reflected one week. There was a space for students to write their homework assignments and a column for parent-teacher notes. The cover was a heavy card stock that children decorated. Students were expected to take their homework planners home each day and return them the next day to class.

> In conjunction with the homework planner, students graphed their homework return and completion rates—another strategy that is linked to homework completion and improved performance on classroom assessments. The teacher built a reward system for returning homework and the planners. On a self-monitoring chart in their planner, students recorded each time they completed and returned their homework assignment by:

- Coloring the square for the day green if homework was completed and returned.
- Coloring the square for the day red if homework was not done.
- Coloring one-half of the square yellow and one-half of the square red if homework was late.

If students met the success criterion, they received a reward at the end of the week, such as 15 extra minutes of recess. The teacher found that more frequent rewards were needed for students with emotional and behavioral disabilities.

Strategy 5. Ensure Clear Home/School Communication

Homework accounts for one-fifth of the time that successful students invest in academic tasks, yet students complete homework in environments over which teachers have no control—which, given the fact that many students experience learning difficulties, creates a major dilemma. Teachers and parents of students with disabilities must communicate clearly and effectively with one another about homework policies, required practices, mutual expectations, student performance on homework, homework completion difficulties, and other homework-related concerns.

Recommended ways that teachers can improve communications with parents include:

- Encourage students to keep assignment books.

- Provide a list of suggestions on how parents might assist with homework. For example, ask parents to check with their children about homework daily.

- Provide parents with frequent written communication about homework (e.g., progress reports, notes, letters, forms).

- Share information with other teachers regarding student strengths and needs and necessary accommodations.

Ways that administrators can support teachers in improving communications include:

- Supply teachers with the technology needed to aid communication (e.g., telephone answering systems, e-mail, homework hotlines).

- Provide incentives for teachers to participate in face-to-face meetings with parents (e.g., release time, compensation).

- Suggest that the school district offer after school and/or peer tutoring sessions to give students extra help with homework.

Summary

The five strategies to help students with disabilities get the most from their homework are:

1. Give clear and appropriate assignments.

2. Make accommodations in homework assignments.

3. Teach study skills.

4. Use a homework planner.

5. Ensure clear home/school communication.

Resources

Bryan, T.; Nelson, C.; and Mathur, S. (1995). Homework: A survey of primary students in regular, resource, and self-contained special education classrooms. *Learning Disabilities Research & Practice*, 10(2), 85-90.

Bryan, T. and Sullivan-Burstein, K. (1997). Homework how-to's. *TEACHING Exceptional Children*, 29(6), 32-37.

Epstein, M.; Munk, D.; Bursuck, W.; Polloway, E. and Jayanthi, M. (1999). Strategies for improving home-school communication about homework for students with disabilities. *The Journal of Special Education*, 33(3), 166-176.

Jayanthi, M.; Bursuck, W.; Epstein, M.; and Polloway, E. (1997). Strategies for successful homework. *TEACHING Exceptional Children*, 30(1), 4-7.

Jayanthi, M.; Sawyer, V.; Nelson, J.; Bursuck, W.; and Epstein, M. (1995). Recommendations for homework-communication problems: From parents, classroom teachers, and special education teachers. *Remedial and Special Education*, 16(4), 212-225.

Klinger, J. and Vaughn, S. (1999). Students' perceptions of instruction in inclusion classrooms: Implications for students with learning disabilities. *Exceptional Children*, 66(1), 23-37.

Polloway, E.; Bursuck, W.; Jayanthi, M.; Epstein, M.; and Nelson, J. (1996). Treatment acceptability: Determining appropriate interventions within inclusive classrooms. *Intervention In School and Clinic*, 31(3), 133-144.

Chapter 44

Cooperative Teaching: General and Special Education Teachers

Historically, teachers have worked in isolation—one teacher to a classroom. As children with disabilities entered the public schools in the 1970s, they were taught in separate classrooms with their own teachers. Over the past 25 years, these students have slowly moved into the flow of the regular classroom, thus the use of the term "mainstreaming." However, students were mainstreamed for selected subjects or parts of the day; they were not considered part of the typical class. Now the philosophy is to include all students in the same class, which has brought about teams of general education and special education teachers working collaboratively or cooperatively to combine their professional knowledge, perspectives, and skills.

The biggest change for educators is in deciding to share the role that has traditionally been individual: to share the goals, decisions, classroom instruction, responsibility for students, assessment of student learning, problem solving, and classroom management. The teachers must begin to think of it as "our" class. This chapter explores the facets of this collaboration between general and special education teachers.

What Is Cooperative Teaching?

Cooperative teaching was described in the late 1980s as:

"Collaboration between General and Special Education Teachers," by Suzanne Ripley, from *ERIC Digest*, Educational Resources Information Center, ERIC Identifier: ED409317, 1997. Despite the older date of the article, it will be informative to the reader.

"an educational approach in which general and special educators work in co-active and coordinated fashion to jointly teach heterogeneous groups of students in educationally integrated settings....In cooperative teaching both general and special educators are simultaneously present in the general classroom, maintaining joint responsibilities for specified education instruction that is to occur within that setting" (Bauwens, Hourcade, & Friend, 1989, p. 36).

The distinctive feature of cooperative teaching, which differs from earlier approaches, is that it is direct collaboration with the general education and special education teachers working together in the same classroom most of the day.

An effective team of teachers will work together as equal partners in interactive relationships, with both involved in all aspects of planning, teaching, and assessment. Areas for this collaboration will include curricula and instruction, assessment and evaluation, and classroom management and behavior. As one team teacher says:

"the key to making co-teaching work is joint planning. You must both know all the curriculum so that you can switch back and forth and support each others efforts. If you don't know the curriculum you are not a co-teacher, you are just an assistant" (Crutchfield, M. in press).

"In developing and implementing cooperative teaching, school professionals experience great changes in the way they go about their daily work. To overcome the inevitable fears and stresses associated with change, the educators involved must feel that they are responsible for the change and that its success or failure lies directly with them" (Bauwens & Hourcade, 1995, p. 189).

What Role Does Each Teacher Play?

In a collaborative model the general education and special education teachers each bring their skills, training, and perspectives to the team. Resources are combined to strengthen teaching and learning opportunities, methods, and effectiveness. "The one point that clearly developed from this relationship was that both of us had expertise in many areas, and combining these skills made both teachers more effective in meeting the needs of all students" (Dieker & Barnett, 1996, p. 7).

Typically the primary responsibility of general education teachers is to use their skills to instruct students in curricula dictated by the

402

school system. Typically the primary responsibility of special education teachers is to provide instruction by adapting and developing materials to match the learning styles, strengths, and special needs of each of their students. In special education situations, individual learners' needs often dictate the curricula.

General educators bring content specialization, special education teachers bring assessment and adaptation specializations. Both bring training and experience in teaching techniques and learning processes. Their collaborative goal is that all students in their class are provided with appropriate classroom and homework assignments so that each is learning, is challenged, and is participating in the classroom process.

Planning for Effective Collaboration

Collaboration involves commitment by the teachers who will be working together, by their school administrators, by the school system, and by the community. It involves time, support, resources, monitoring, and, above all, persistence. However, the biggest issue is time—time for planning, time for development, and time for evaluating. Planning should take place at the district and the building levels, as well as at the classroom level.

District planning helps ensure that all resources will be available, including time, money, and professional assistance. District-level planning will take into consideration the effect change in one place will have on other settings. Building-level planning will assist the teams in being sure adequate support is in place to sustain new initiatives. Principals play an extremely important leadership role in facilitating collaborative efforts by instructional personnel.

Both district- and building-level planning should provide staff development opportunities to encourage teachers and administrators to participate in classes, workshops, seminars, and/or professional conferences on cooperative teaching. Motivation is an important ingredient for success, but additional skills will be needed to realize the goals teachers set for themselves and their classes.

Planning also is a factor in selecting the students who will be part of the collaborative process. It is important to keep natural proportions of typical students, students identified as being at risk, and students who have been found to have disabilities. Achieving a balanced classroom is easier at the elementary and middle school levels than at the secondary level, where a certain amount of grouping takes place with course selection.

A major consideration is in arranging planning times for co-teachers. Co-planning must take place at least once a week, according to studies. "Planning sessions were viewed as priorities by both teachers; they refused to let other competing responsibilities interfere with their planning sessions" (Walther-Thomas, Bryant, & Land, 1996, p. 260). The planning must be ongoing to allow teachers to review progress on a regular basis, make adjustments, evaluate students, and develop strategies to address problems either in discipline or learning.

Walther-Thomas and her colleagues (1996) found that five planning themes were identified by co-teachers who considered themselves to be effective co-planners:

* confidence in partner's skills;

* design of learning environments for both the educators and students that require active involvement;

* creation of learning and teaching environments in which each person's contributions are valued;

* development of effective routines to facilitate in-depth planning; and

* increased productivity, creativity, and collaboration over time. Participants in collaborative programs agreed that the time required for planning does not decrease during the year, but the quality of instruction continues to improve.

Teacher Education and Professional Development

Collaboration should also be part of teacher preparation programs. This begins with the understanding that all teachers will be working with both typical and special needs students. Every teacher needs to study teaching techniques, subject area(s), disability, individualization, accommodation, and skills for collaboration in the classroom.

Time away from the classroom for consultation, professional conferences, and additional training is vital to the success of any program. Teachers, related service providers, and administrators will benefit from research findings on collaborative teaching, inclusion, and related subjects.

Results

Research findings on schools where collaborative teaching has been practiced indicate student benefits for both special education students and their typical peers. Walther-Thomas and others conducted a study of inclusion and teaming in 1996 to assess collaboration between general education and special education staff. Improvements were attributed to more teacher time and attention, reduced pupil-teacher ratios generally, and more opportunities for individual assistance. Students with disabilities developed better self-images, became less critical and more motivated, and recognized their own academic and social strengths. Their social skills improved and positive peer relationships developed.

Low-achieving students showed academic and social skills improvements. All students gained a greater understanding of differences and acceptance of others. All developed a stronger sense of self, a new appreciation of their own skills and accomplishments, and all learned to value themselves and others as unique individuals.

Staff reported professional growth, personal support, and enhanced teaching motivation. Collaboration brought complementary professional skills to planning, preparation, and delivery of classroom instruction.

Conclusion

The concepts of individualized instruction, multiple learning styles, team teaching, weekly evaluation, and detailed planning are all of direct benefit to students. The purpose of the collaboration is to combine expertise and meet the needs of all learners.

It is important that teachers receive preparation and classroom support. It is also important that planning time continues to be available throughout the school year. "Most important, all students win by being challenged by collaborating teachers who believe that they are responsible for all children in the classroom" (Angle, 1996, p.10).

References

References identified with an *EJ* or *ED* number have been abstracted and are in the ERIC database. Journal articles (*EJ*) should be available at most research libraries; most documents (ED) are available in microfiche collections at more than 900 locations. Documents can also be ordered through the ERIC Document Reproduction Service (800-443-ERIC).

Angle, B. (1996). Five steps to collaborative teaching and enrichment remediation. *TEACHING Exceptional Children*, 29(1), 8-10. EJ 529 434.

Bauwens, J. and Hourcade, J. J. (1995). Cooperative teaching: Rebuilding the schoolhouse for all students. Austin, TX: Pro-Ed. *ED* 383 130.

Bauwens, J.; Hourcade, J. J.; and Friend, M. (1989). Cooperative teaching: A model for general and special education integration. *Remedial and Special Education*, 10(2), 17-22. EJ 390 640.

Crutchfield, M. (in press). Who's teaching our children? *NICHCY News Digest*.

Dieker, L. A. and Barnett, C. A. (1996). Effective co-teaching. *TEACHING Exceptional Children*, 29(1), 5-7. *EJ* 529 433 Friend, M. & Cook, L. (1996). Interactions. White Plains, NY: Longman.

Walther-Thomas, C. S.; Bryant, M.; and Land, S. (1996). Planning for effective co-teaching: The key to successful inclusion. *Remedial and Special Education*, 17(4), 255-264. EJ 527 660.

Chapter 45

Public Charter Schools and Students with Disabilities

Charter schools are a relatively new component of the public education system in the United States. At the start of the 2000-2001 school year, 37 states in the United States had adopted legislation permitting charter schools, and over 2,000 charter schools were in operation with approximately 500,000 students. This chapter examines the unique nature of these schools, explains their obligations in relation to serving students with disabilities, and presents the results of current research on special education in charter schools.

What Are Charter Schools?

A charter school is most often described as a new or converted public school founded by parents, teachers, or others, and operated with various levels of autonomy from state or local rules or policies. Charter schools are selected by parents for their children to attend, so they are considered schools of choice. Each charter school has a written charter or contract issued by an authorizing body in accordance with state law. However, because each state law is different, it is impossible to give a uniform definition of charter schools or to generalize about details of their operation.

"Public Charter Schools and Students with Disabilities," by Eileen Ahern, from the Educational Resources Information Center (ERIC), *ERIC Digest,* #609, ERIC Identifier: ED455656, 2001.

Do Charter Schools Serve Students with Disabilities?

Although public charter schools are afforded some level of exemption from state or local laws or requirements, they must conform to all federal laws and regulations including the Individuals with Disabilities Education Act (IDEA), Section 504 of the Rehabilitation Act, and the Americans with Disabilities Act (ADA). A charter school is prohibited by law from discriminating in admissions and must accept every student who applies or hold a lottery if there are more applicants than the school can accommodate. Recruitment and admissions are addressed in a set of questions and answers regarding the application of federal civil rights laws to public charter schools published by the U. S. Department of Education's Office of Civil Rights (2000).

What Are Some of the Issues Related to Special Education in Public Charter Schools?

The legal identity of the charter school under state law largely determines the specific responsibilities it has for its students with disabilities. There are two extremes: the charter school may be its own separate district, usually referred to as a local education agency (LEA); or the charter school may be one of the schools of a traditional district. There are also charter schools that have ties with LEAs that fall between these two extremes. If the charter school is its own LEA, it is responsible for all aspects of special education including evaluations, programs, and related services. By contrast, in some states, the LEA of the child's residence is responsible for special education for all its students even if they attend charter schools operated independently from the district.

Thus, there are profound legal, financial, and operational implications in the legal identity of a public charter school. It is critical that charter schools understand the nature of their linkage with the local district and/or intermediate unit, especially with respect to their responsibilities for providing a free appropriate public education to children with disabilities.

Charter schools are also affected by many of the same pressures faced by other public schools, such as finding appropriate special education staff, accessing fiscal resources, and integrating special education into the overall program of the school.

What Does Research Reveal about Students with Disabilities in Charter Schools?

The U.S. Department of Education has funded two studies to examine special education in charter schools. The first study, conducted by the research firm Westat, is called Charter Schools and Students with Disabilities: A National Study (Fiore, Harwell, Blackorby, & Finnigan, 2000). It involved visits to 32 charter schools where parents, teachers and students were interviewed about why the parents chose to enroll their children with disabilities in a charter school, the ways charter schools serve those students, and how successful charter schools have been in meeting their goals.

The study found that:

- Enrollment of students with more significant disabilities in charter schools is relatively rare, except in schools specifically designed for these students.

- Parents of students with disabilities enroll their child in a charter school for a combination of reasons related to attractive features of the charter school and negative experiences with the previously attended school.

- Staff at some charter schools may counsel parents of students with disabilities against enrolling in the charter school. However, other schools are specifically designed to serve these students and other at-risk learners.

- Most charter schools use the term inclusion to describe their approach to serving students with disabilities. The meaning of the term varies across schools.

- By almost all accounts, students with and without disabilities receive more individualized attention at the charter school than they did at their previous school.

- Although accountability is a central feature of charter schools, most of them have little data to document the impact of their program on students with disabilities. However, parents and students themselves are confident about the students' success at charter schools. Factors identified as supporting student success include caring and dedicated teachers and small schools and classes.

- Some barriers encountered include lack of adequate funding, strained relationships with local districts, lack of extracurricular activities, and transportation.

The second federally funded study was supported by a field-initiated grant to the National Association of State Directors of Special Education (NASDSE). The study, Project SEARCH: Special Education As Requirements in Charter Schools (2001), focused on the implementation of special education policy in the nation's public charter schools. Some of the Project SEARCH findings follow:

- There is much variability and a great need for defining specific roles and responsibilities of state education agencies (SEAs), LEAs and other administrative units, and individual charter schools in relation to special education.

- Charter school application and contracting processes often provide little more than assurances that special education services will be provided; they generally do not require demonstration of the capacity to meet those obligations.

- Most charter school operators have limited understanding of federal/state/local sources of special education funding and how to access these resources.

- Charter schools often have difficulty locating appropriate special education staff, including teachers and related services personnel.

- A charter school's philosophy and curricular orientation can cause conflict between the school's goals and special education requirements.

Two critical policy conflicts that underlie many of the specific findings of the study were identified:

- Team decision-making vs. parental choice-the tension between the special education principle of individualized educational decision-making through a team and the primacy of parental choice, a major characteristic of charter schools, and

- Autonomy vs. regulation-conflict that arises from the compliance and procedural regulation associated with special education and the principle of autonomy that is so central to the charter school concept.

What Is Needed to Increase the Capacity of Charter Schools to Provide Special Education?

To ensure appropriate compliance, school districts employ an administrator of special education who is knowledgeable about legal requirements, proper procedure, and the delivery of services. Since most charter schools are very small and their funding is limited, their staffs seldom include such an individual. Yet, for purposes of implementing IDEA, charter schools need to be connected in some way with a special education infrastructure. This could be accomplished through an existing LEA, the SEA, a cooperative organized to provide special education support, or some other structure. Access to the necessary expertise, provided in a way that does not compromise the autonomy of the charter school and its mission, is essential to ensure appropriate services for students with disabilities and protect the charter schools from the serious consequences of avoidable non-compliance.

Research has revealed that everyone involved with charter schools-authorizers, state and district officials, operators and charter school staff-needs to understand the policy conflicts that surround the implementation of special education in charter schools and their need for a supportive connection to special education expertise. Such understanding will contribute significantly to the improvement of results for students with disabilities who attend public charter schools.

References

Ahearn, E. M.; McLaughlin, M. J.; Lange, C. M.; and Rhim, L. M. (in press). Project SEARCH: A national study of special education in charter schools. Alexandria, VA: National Association of State Directors of Special Education.

Fiore, T. A.; Harwell, L. M.; Blackorby, J.; and Finnigan, K. S. (2000). Charter schools and students with disabilities: A national study. Washington, DC: U. S. Department of Education, Office of Educational Research and Improvement.

Nelson, B.; Berman. P.; Ericson, J.; Kamprath, N.; Perry, R.; Silverman, D.; and Solomon, D. (2000). The state of charter schools 2000: Fourth-year report. Washington, DC: U.S. Department of Education, Office of Educational Research and Improvement. *ED* 437 724.

U.S. Office for Civil Rights. (2000, December). Applying federal civil rights laws to public charter schools. Washington, DC: U.S. Department of Education. *ED* 443 233.

Chapter 46

Special Education in Alternative Education Programs

With the 1997 Amendments to the Individuals with Disabilities Education Act (PL 105-17), the mission of alternative programs has expanded from the education of youth who have dropped out, or who were at risk for dropping out, to students with disabilities whose behavior warrants special attention outside the general education setting. These programs now provide alternative programming, including flexible curricula that can address the unique social, behavioral, emotional, cognitive, and vocational needs of the individual student. In contrast to the traditional alternative settings where students were sent away, many communities are offering alternative programs within the public school setting.

While there are numerous models for serving students with disabilities in alternative programs, there are seven essential elements of effective programs (Quinn & Rutherford, 1998; Rutherford, Nelson, & Wolford, 1985: (1) functional assessments; (2) functional curriculum; (3) effective and efficient instructional techniques; (4) programming for effective and efficient transitions; (5) comprehensive systems; (6) appropriate staff, resources, and procedural protections for students with disabilities (Rutherford & Howell, 1997); and (7) educational climates that are supportive of the student's social/emotional needs (Quinn, Osher, Hoffman, & Hanley, 1998).

"Special Education in Alternative Education Programs," by Mary Magee Quinn, Robert B. Rutherford Jr., and David M. Osher, from the Educational Resources Information Center (ERIC), *ERIC Digest,* E585, ERIC Identifier: ED436054, 1999.

Functional Assessment

Assessment of student needs for the development of educational and treatment plans is essential to successful alternative programs. Functional assessment procedures identify student strengths and skill deficits that interfere with educational achievement and social/emotional adjustment. This form of assessment is based on identifying students' needs in relationship to the curriculum and to their individualized education program (IEP), rather than on global achievement and/or ability measures.

Functional assessment is also a continuous process, not static, and results can be used to make systematic adjustments in the student's educational program (Howell, Fox, & Morehead, 1993). Assessment procedures should include curriculum-based evaluation and measurement procedures to monitor overall student performance and improvement. To accomplish this assessment, the academic and social skills curricula for the student must be clarified and implemented.

Functional Curriculum

A functional educational curriculum allows the program to meet a student's individual academic, vocational, social, and behavioral needs. Such a curriculum focuses on the student's general curriculum and IEP. In addition to academic skills, this curriculum can include developing functional job-related skills, daily-living skills, and social skills. While most alternative education programs do not have comprehensive vocational programs on site, the development of basic work skills tied to job-related social- and life-skills training is often an important component of a student's IEP. Effective alternative programs sometimes provide the opportunity for part-time employment and access to vocational training in the community.

In addition, the student's IEP team should review and revise the IEP to include goals that directly relate to the behaviors that warranted the placement in the alternative setting. These goals should be based on a functional behavioral assessment and should lead to a positive behavior intervention plan.

Effective and Efficient Instruction

Functional instruction uses positive and direct student-centered instructional strategies, which are aligned with functional assessment measures and the curriculum. In this situation, instruction specifically addresses the short-term objectives in the student's IEP that are based on the results of the functional assessment, as well as the standards specified in the general education curriculum. Student progress toward mastery of these objectives and standards is monitored using ongoing data collection procedures.

Effective and efficient instruction can also involve the use of behavior strategies for meaningful intervention in alternative classrooms. Behavioral interventions include a variety of procedures to teach acceptable replacement behaviors, enhance and support appropriate behaviors, and reduce inappropriate behaviors.

Transition

The transition of students and their educational records into and out of alternative settings is important. Staff in the public and alternative settings can make a major contribution to the transition process by providing comprehensive information concerning the strengths and needs of their students and assuring that there is follow-up and continued support for students in the new settings. It also is important to include the results of any functional behavioral assessment and the positive behavioral intervention and support plan that addresses the specific behaviors that warranted the placement in the alternative setting.

The public school, the alternative setting, and other community-based or residential program staff must share the responsibility for transition of students into and out of alternative education programs. Planning for transition as soon as the student enters the alternative setting ensures that the student is taught the necessary skills and is provided with the necessary supports. Further, functional transition plans and meaningful transition objectives should be a part of the student's IEP.

Comprehensive Systems

Comprehensive systems provide coordinated special education services to eligible students in alternative settings. Alternative programs can offer a continuum of education and treatment services (e.g., direct instruction, pull-out programs, therapeutic programs) to best meet the individual needs of students who qualify for special education.

In alternative programs with separate education and treatment functions, it is important that staff develop common goals and objectives for student success. In addition, coordinated and comprehensive linkages must be developed among the public schools, the alternative education program, the student's family, and social service agencies. Unless agencies collaborate, programs often lead to fragmented services for these youth. Educational, social service, juvenile justice, and mental health agencies must be linked by providing a system of wraparound programming (Eber, 1997) where coordinated, cooperative, and comprehensive services are implemented to serve students with disabilities. Wraparound programming is a process for developing realistic behavior plans linking the student, the alternative program staff, families, public school personnel, and staff of the different social service agencies (Woodruff et al., 1998).

Appropriate Staff, Resources, and Procedural Protections for Students with Disabilities

The 1997 Amendments to IDEA contain new regulations about sending students to alternative educational settings for drugs, weapons, or "substantial evidence that maintaining the current placement of the child is substantially likely to result in injury to the child or to others..." (Section 300.521) As a result, the number of students in alternative programs could increase. Therefore, some of the education staff of alternative programs should have special education certification, and support staff should have extensive training in how to serve students with disabilities. Multidisciplinary education and treatment teams also must be established in alternative schools and programs.

In addition, special education programs in alternative settings must provide a full continuum of educational services, including instruction in academics, independent living skills, social skills, and work related skills, and assure procedural protections, including parental notification of evaluation and parental involvement in the review and revision of IEPs.

Supportive Climate

Since students and staff are more productive in environments where they feel welcome, safe, and valued (Gottfredson, 1997), alternative settings should actively provide each person with the skills and supports necessary to create safe, productive, caring environments. In effective alternative settings, everyone is treated with respect and problem behavior is viewed as an opportunity to teach new skills (Quinn et al., 1998).

Summary

It is still unclear how alternative programs will translate the policies promulgated by the 1997 Amendments to IDEA into practice. It is certain, however, that alternative programs around the country will have to make some significant changes to their operating procedures. Without a doubt, when alternative programs focus on providing the seven essential elements of effective alternative programs as discussed in this chapter, they are more effective at meeting students' needs.

References

Eber, L., (1997). Improving school-based behavioral interventions through use of the wraparound process. *Reaching Today's Youth*, 1 (2), 32-36.

Gottfredson, D. C. (1997). School-based crime prevention. In L. Sherman, D. Gottfredson, D. Mackenzie, J. Eck, P. Reuter, & S. Bushway (Eds.), *Preventing Crime: What Works, What Doesn't, What's Promising*. College Park, MD: Department of Criminology and Criminal Justice.

Howell, K. W., Fox, S. S., & Morehead, M. K., (1993). *Curriculum-Based Evaluation (2nd Ed.)*. Belmont, CA: Brooks/Cole.

Individuals with Disabilities Education Act Amendments (1997). P.L. 105-17.

Quinn, M. M., & Rutherford, R.B., (1998). Alternative Programs for Students with Social, Emotional, and Behavioral Problems. Reston, VA: Council for Children with Behavioral Disorders.

Quinn, M. M., Osher, D., Hoffman, C. C., & Hanley, T. V., (1998). Safe, drug-free, and effective schools for all students: What works! Washington, DC: American Institutes for Research.

Rutherford, R. B., & Howell, K. W., (1997). Education Program Assessment: MacLaren Children's Center School. Los Angeles: Los Angeles County Department of Child and Family Services, 1997.

Rutherford, R. B., Nelson, C. M., & Wolford, B. I. (1985). Special education in the most restrictive environment: Correctional/special education. *Journal of Special Education*, 19(1), 59-7.

Woodruff, D. W., Osher, D., Hoffman, C. C., Gruner, A., King, M. A., Snow, S. T., & McIntire, J. C., (1998). The role of education in a system of care: Effectively serving children with emotional or behavioral disorders. *Systems of Care: Promising Practices in Children's Mental Health, 1998 Series, Volume III*. Washington, DC: Center for Effective Collaboration and Practice, American Institutes for Research.

Chapter 47

Learning Disabilities and the Individuals with Disabilities Education Act (IDEA)

What Disabilities Entitle a Child to Special Education?

The Education for All Handicapped Children Act (P.L. 94-142) of 1975 and the Individuals with Disabilities Education Act (IDEA) (P. L. 101-476) identified specific categories of disabilities under which children may be eligible for special education and related services. As defined by IDEA, the term "child with a disability" means a child:

> "with mental retardation, hearing impairments (including deafness), speech or language impairments, visual impairments (including blindness), serious emotional disturbance, orthopedic impairments, autism, traumatic brain injury, other health impairments, or specific learning disabilities; and who, by reason thereof, needs special education and related services."

The most recent legislation, the IDEA Amendments of 1997 (P.L. 105-17), allows states and local education agencies to apply the term "developmental delay" for children ages 3-9. Previously, this definition applied to children ages 3-5.

> "For children ages 3 through 9, the term 'child with a disability' may, at the discretion of the state and the local education agency, include children who are experiencing developmental

"IDEA's Definition of Disabilities," by Bernadette Knoblauch and Barbara Sorenson, from the Educational Resources Information Center (ERIC), *ERIC Digest,* E560, ERIC Identifier: ED429396, 1998.

delays in one or more of the following areas: physical development, cognitive development, communication development, social or emotional development, or adaptive development...."

Thus, children must meet two criteria in order to receive special
education: (1) the child must have one or more of the disabilities listed
following, and (2) he or she must require special education and related services. Not all children who have a disability require special
education; many are able to and should attend school without any
program modifications. Following are the disabilities included in the
definition.

Autism: A developmental disability significantly affecting verbal
and nonverbal communication and social interaction, generally evident
before age 3, that adversely affects a child's educational performance.
Other characteristics often associated with autism are engagement
in repetitive activities and stereotyped movements, resistance to environmental change or change in daily routines, and unusual responses to sensory experiences. The term does not apply if a child's
educational performance is adversely affected primarily because the
child has a serious emotional disturbance as defined following. Autism was added as a separate category of disability in 1990 under P.L.
101-476. This was not a change in the law so much as it is a clarification. Students with autism were covered by the law previously, but
now the law identifies them as a separate and distinct class entitled
to the law's benefits.

Deafness: A hearing impairment so severe that the child cannot
understand what is being said even with a hearing aid.

Deaf-Blindness: A combination of hearing and visual impairments
causing such severe communication, developmental, and educational
problems that the child cannot be accommodated in either a program
specifically for the deaf or a program specifically for the blind.

Hearing Impairment: An impairment in hearing, whether permanent or fluctuating, that adversely affects a child's educational performance but that is not included under the definition of deafness as
listed previously.

Mental Retardation: Significantly subaverage general intellectual
functioning existing concurrently with deficits in adaptive behavior.

And manifested during the developmental period that adversely affects a child's educational performance.

Multiple Disabilities: A combination of impairments (such as mental retardation and blindness, or mental retardation and physical disabilities) that causes such severe educational problems that the child cannot be accommodated in a special education program solely for one of the impairments. The term does not include deaf-blindness.

Orthopedic Impairment: A severe orthopedic impairment that adversely affects educational performance. The term includes impairments such as amputation, absence of a limb, cerebral palsy, poliomyelitis, and bone tuberculosis.

Other Health Impairment: Having limited strength, vitality, or alertness due to chronic or acute health problems such as a heart condition, rheumatic fever, asthma, hemophilia, and leukemia, which adversely affect educational performance.

Serious Emotional Disturbance: A condition exhibiting one or more of the following characteristics, displayed over a long period of time and to a marked degree that adversely affects a child's educational performance:

• An inability to learn that cannot be explained by intellectual, sensory, or health factors

• An inability to build or maintain satisfactory interpersonal relationships with peers or teachers

• Inappropriate types of behavior or feelings under normal circumstances

• A general pervasive mood of unhappiness or depression

• A tendency to develop physical symptoms or fears associated with personal or school problems

This term includes schizophrenia, but does not include students who are socially maladjusted, unless they have a serious emotional disturbance. P.L. 105-17, the IDEA Amendments of 1997, changed "serious emotional disturbance" to "emotional disturbance." The change has no substantive or legal significance. It is intended strictly to eliminate any negative connotation of the term "serious."

Specific Learning Disability: A disorder in one or more of the basic psychological processes involved in understanding or in using language, spoken or written, that may manifest itself in an imperfect ability to listen, think, speak, read, write, spell, or do mathematical calculations. This term includes such conditions as perceptual disabilities, brain injury, minimal brain dysfunction, dyslexia, and developmental aphasia. This term does not include children who have learning problems that are primarily the result of visual, hearing, or motor disabilities; mental retardation; or environmental, cultural or economic disadvantage.

Speech or language impairment: A communication disorder such as stuttering, impaired articulation, language impairment, or a voice impairment that adversely affects a child's educational performance.

Traumatic brain injury: An acquired injury to the brain caused by an external physical force, resulting in total or partial functional disability or psychosocial impairment, or both, that adversely affects a child's educational performance. The term applies to open or closed head injuries resulting in impairments in one or more areas, such as cognition; language; memory; attention; reasoning; abstract thinking; judgment; problem-solving; sensory, perceptual and motor abilities; psychosocial behavior; physical functions; information processing; and speech. The term does not apply to brain injuries that are congenital or degenerative, or brain injuries induced by birth trauma. As with autism, traumatic brain injury (TBI) was added as a separate category of disability in 1990 under P.L. 101-476.

Visual impairment, including blindness: An impairment in vision that, even with correction, adversely affects a child's educational performance. The term includes both partial sight and blindness.

What If a Child Is Thought to Have a Disability?

Children suspected of having a disability are evaluated by a multidisciplinary team that includes at least one teacher or other specialist with knowledge in the area of the suspected disability. Following a full individual evaluation of the child's educational needs, the team determines whether or not the child requires special education and related services. If the evaluation confirms that a child has one or more disabilities and requires special education and related services because of the disabilities, then states and localities must provide a free, appropriate public education for that child.

The new IDEA (P. L. 105-17) sends a strong message about the school's responsibility to include students with disabilities in the general education classroom and curriculum, with accommodations when necessary; "...to be involved and progress in the general curriculum...and to participate in extracurricular and other nonacademic activities; and...to be educated and participate with other children with disabilities and nondisabled children..."[Section 614(d)(1)(A)(iii)]. Schools may place children with disabilities in separate classrooms or schools only when supports and services are not enough to help the child learn in a regular classroom.

References

Final Regulations for Part B of IDEA, 57 C.F.R. 300.7 (1992).

Individuals with Disabilities Education Act Amendments of 1997 (P.L. 105-17), 111 Stat. 37-157 (1997).

Nineteenth Annual Report to Congress on the Implementation of the Individuals with Disabilities Act. (1997). (ED412721). ERIC Document Reproduction Service (EDRS), 7420 Fullerton Road, Suite 110, Springfield, VA 22153-2852. 800-443-3742. 381pp.

Part Six

Accommodations and Assistive Devices

Chapter 48

Test Accommodations for the Learning Disabled

Testing Accommodations

Accommodations on exams and quizzes are sometimes necessary to allow a person with a disability to demonstrate proficiency in the material being tested. For example, a student with a physical impairment may write too slowly or a person with a cognitive impairment may process information too slowly to allow them to take exams effectively within the time limits established for non-disabled individuals. Testing accommodations may consist of use of special adaptive equipment, a change in exam format (e.g., oral vs. written) or print size, or simply the provision of additional time or a distraction-free environment.

Typically, a student who uses testing accommodations should be expected to take exams at the same time as the rest of the class. There are, however, some exceptions to this rule.

The instructor is responsible for making certain that the student has the exam in the necessary format, at the proper time, and in the appropriate location. Completed exams must be graded within a reasonable amount of time: like all other students, students with disabilities are eager to learn the results of their efforts.

The information in this chapter is excerpted from "Testing Accommodations," provided by the Office of Disability, Re-Entry, and Veterans Services at Montana State University, Bozeman, MT. © 2000 Montana State University-Bozeman. Reprinted with permission. Although some of the information in this chapter applies specifically to Montana State University-Bozeman, similar types of test accommodations are also available elsewhere.

Any of the following methods may be used by instructors to transport exams to and from an alternative testing site.

- The instructor or his/her designee may deliver and pick up the exam.

- The student may carry the exam in a sealed envelope.

- The exam may be faxed or e-mailed to Disabled Student Services

Exam Accommodation Procedures

Extended Exam Time: Extending time on exams and quizzes for qualified students with disabilities is a means of reducing or removing the effect of disability on test and quiz performance. The minimum, and most common extension is time-and-a-half, although some students may require double or even triple time to complete the exam. The approved time extension and the types of exams for which the accommodation is approved appears on the student's Disabled Student Services Certification Card. If extended time is the only exam accommodation approved for the student, the instructor is typically expected to make this arrangement without assistance from Disabled Student Services.

The student will usually begin the exam at the same time as the rest of his or her class. However, exceptions to this may be necessary if the Testing Service or Disabled Student Services is closed during class time.

On occasion, a student will insist upon unlimited time in which to complete an exam. Unlimited time is, however, not viewed by Disabled Student Services as a reasonable accommodation.

Distraction-Free Testing Environment: Some students with disabling psychological impairments, learning disabilities and traumatic brain injuries are very easily distracted by noise or by the slightest bit of activity. To compensate for this limitation, these students are offered a relatively distraction-free environment in which to take exams. An instructor must make certain that the exam room is free from noise and activity.

The Use of Readers, Scribes, or Assistive Technology: Most students who require these services will take their exams in the Disabled Student Services office, although some assistive devices, such as electronic spellers and calculators, may be used by a student in a classroom during an exam.

Tape Recorded Exams: A visually impaired student or a student with a severe learning disability who is unable to read an exam may be provided with an audio taped version of the exam. When it is necessary for Disabled Student Services to record an exam, the instructor is asked to deliver the exam at least one work day before the exam is scheduled to be taken. The student and Disabled Student Services, via the DSS Exam Proctoring Setup Sheet, notify the instructor well in advance when this accommodation is needed.

Please Note: If the exam contains language, technical jargon, or discipline-specific symbols that DSS staff are unable to read effectively, the instructor may be asked to assist in identifying a competent person to read the exam. If necessary, DSS will pay the reader.

Chapter 49

Accommodating All Learners

The goal for every student is to learn, but not every child learns in the same way. Kids with learning differences may have an especially difficult time with traditional classroom materials. Today, your child's teachers compensate for variation among their students by adapting how they present information, structure assignments, and test for understanding. In the future, the adaptations may be built into the curriculum materials, thanks to Universal Design for Learning (UDL). UDL uses computer technology to create an educational environment that allows all students, including those with learning differences, to succeed in general education classrooms with minimal use of assistive technology (AT).

Universal Design has its roots in architecture and urban planning. Ramps, automatic doors, and curb cuts were created to provide access to people with physical disabilities but actually ease access for everyone. Think of the last time you pushed a stroller or luggage cart and the broader value of ramps is instantly apparent.

UDL embraces the concept of improved access for everyone and applies it to curriculum materials and teaching methods. Rather than rely on AT to bridge the gap between the material and the student's learning needs, materials designed using UDL concepts have built-in accommodations. Add-on technology is less often needed to translate the material into a mode that enables learning.

From "Accommodating All Learners," by Nancy Firchow. © 2002 SchwabLearning.org. Reprinted with permission of Schwab Learning. For more information, please visit www.schwablearning.org.

Principles of UDL

UDL stretches beyond accessibility for the disabled, however. A teacher's goal is for students to learn skills and understand the subject. Traditional curriculum materials tend to offer only limited flexibility for meeting that goal—often requiring students to adapt to the curriculum. Universally designed curriculum overcomes limitations by incorporating three principles of flexibility into the design:

- Multiple methods of presentation

- Multiple options for participation

- Multiple means of expression

This built-in flexibility provides into a wider range of options for students to choose from—meaning the curriculum adapts to the student, rather than the other way around.

Let's consider each of these principles and the impact they could have in your child's classroom.

Multiple Methods of Presentation

Flexibility in presentation allows the same concepts to be taught using a variety of methods, media, or materials. How would this look in a classroom?

- Content could be presented using multiple media, such as oral lectures, textbooks, charts or diagrams, audio tapes, and videos.

- The same content could be changed from one medium to another, such as oral output for students with reading difficulties or pictures and illustrations for students who need a visual image.

- Materials would have adjustable presentation characteristics—changeable font style and size, highlighting of main concepts, or variable volume and speed controls.

- Material could be adjusted to match students' cognitive styles. For example, students who prefer sequential, factual information might learn a history lesson from a timeline-style presentation. Students who learn better with a base of broader concepts might choose to have the same lesson presented from a big picture, or cause-and-effect perspective, with dates and facts filled in later.

Multiple Options for Participation

Since one task or teaching method may engage and motivate some kids but bore or frustrate others, UDL allows flexibility in how students interact with the material. It also lets teachers tailor the level of difficulty of assignments, ensuring that each student is sufficiently challenged while meeting the overall goals of the lesson. How would this look in a classroom?

- Students would choose their preferred method of learning new material. One child might learn vocabulary by playing a game in a race against the clock; another might create stories or even artwork to incorporate the new words.

- Content would be tailored to match kids' interests. For example, math principles could be taught using topics ranging from hockey to horses.

- Materials would provide extra support where students need it. For reading practice, independent readers could read silently from a book. Students needing more support might read computer-based stories where they could click on a troublesome word to hear it pronounced or have the entire text read aloud.

- Materials might have adjustable challenge levels, such as educational computer games with several levels of difficulty.

- Materials might allow students to add their own words, images, or ideas, such as reading software that encourages learners to customize the stories or illustrations.

- Assignments could be varied according to each child's skills. If the goal of a project is to learn research skills, more advanced students might be required to produce a longer report or cite more references. Students with less developed research skills might gain as much from creating a report using fewer references to cover a limited number of key points.

Multiple Means of Expression

With UDL, students are not limited to one way of completing assignments. Instructors can match the curriculum to each child's strengths. How would this look in a classroom?

- Assignments would be accepted in various formats. A student who finds written expression difficult might show his knowledge orally; another might turn in a report, write a play, or develop a project to demonstrate learning.

- Paper and pencil exercises could become computer and printer exercises for students who are slowed down by the physical effort of writing, or for any student who prefers using a keyboard.

UDL in the Classroom

To create a UDL environment in general or special education classrooms, teachers need materials and methods that incorporate these three principles. Curriculum materials in an electronic format are the cornerstone of UDL and offer a great deal of flexibility. Electronic materials can be used on and manipulated by computers, making it easy to alter content to meet the needs of different students.

Variations in presentation can make the same text more accessible to all students, especially those with LD. For example, a social studies text in electronic format:

- Can be read aloud using screen reading software (useful for students with reading problems)

- Can include dialogue, music, sound effects, and video clips (helpful to students who learn through more sensory involvement)

- Can be changed to different print sizes, colors, spacing, or highlighting (helpful for students to see and remember)

- Can be printed as a personalized copy (helpful for most students)

- Can be copied and pasted into outlining or graphic organizers (particularly useful for students who find organizing information difficult)

Strategies That Follow UDL Principles

But with or without computer-based curriculum materials, you can work with your child's teachers to apply UDL principles to his schoolwork. These accommodations are just a few that keep the focus on material to be learned, rather than on the method of presentation or format of response, and offer choices to students:

- If traditional textbooks bog your child down, discuss using a video documentary, audio tapes, or computer programs that cover the same material.

434

- If your child is struggling to complete an assignment, talk to his teacher about alternate ways for him to show what he's learned—such as creating a website, preparing a slide show, presenting an oral report, building a model, etc.

- If a particular subject fails to spark your child's interest, try relating it to something he's interested in and passionate about.

Because UDL assumes each learner brings individual strengths, needs, interests, and limitations to the classroom, flexibility in curriculum and teaching methods increases access to learning—just like curb cuts and ramps increase physical access.

Universal Design for Learning is a concept developed by CAST, a leading authority on Universal Design for Learning and whose mission is to expand educational opportunities for individuals with disabilities through the development and innovative uses of technology. Their innovative concepts and research on UDL have been used as a reference in writing this chapter. For more information about CAST and UDL visit http://www.cast.org/udl/.

About the Author

Nancy Firchow is a freelance writer and former librarian for Schwab Learning. She has a Masters degree in Library Science and has also worked as a medical research librarian.

Chapter 50

Considering Your Child's Need for Assistive Technology

The 1997 revision of the Individuals with Disabilities Education Act (IDEA) included many new requirements for school districts. One of those new requirements is the group of special factors which each IEP team must consider. Assistive technology is one of those special factors. The requirement states simply,

> "...the IEP Team shall...consider whether the child requires assistive technology devices and services."

Although school districts have been required to provide assistive technology devices and services if they are needed for a child to receive a free and appropriate public education (FAPE) since 1990, in many cases assistive technology was treated as a special area that was separate from the general delivery of services. In some cases assistive technology was only thought about for children with very severe disabilities or only for those with physical and speech disabilities. The passage of IDEA '97 is the first time that each IEP team in every school district has been specifically required to focus on the need for assistive technology. This is the first time that every IEP team developing programs for children with learning disabilities must ask the question, "Does this child need assistive technology in order to

"Considering Your Child's Need for Assistive Technology," © 2000 LD Online/WETA. Available online at http://www.LDOnLine.org/ld_indepth/technology/bowzer_reed.html. Reprinted with permission. For more information go to http://www.LDOnLine.org.

accomplish the educational goals we have set?" So what is assistive technology? How can it help children with learning disabilities?

Assistive Technology for Children with Learning Disabilities

Assistive technology is defined in IDEA as follows:

300.5 Assistive technology device. As used in this part, Assistive technology device means any item, piece of equipment, or product system, whether acquired commercially off the shelf, modified, or customized, that is used to increase, maintain, or improve the functional capabilities of a child with a disability. (Authority: 20 U.S.C. 1401(1))

Students with learning disabilities most often have difficulty with functional capabilities such as writing, reading, studying, listening, accessing the curriculum and organizing. While this is a fairly long list of very important skills, the list includes tasks for which most of us already use some kind of technology. The assistive technology devices that might help a student with learning disabilities are often not specialized devices designed for people with disabilities, but are simply readily available technology that might not be commonly used in classrooms or technology that might not be introduced as early as it is needed by a student with learning disabilities. Because the legal definition of assistive technology is very broad, there is sometimes confusion about what is assistive technology as opposed to what is instructional technology. Assistive technology is not technology that helps students practice new skills they are learning. It is not software to practice spelling words or math facts. However, if the child's problem is handwriting, assistive technology might be technology that allows him to keyboard to produce more legible spelling tests or math problems. When technology is used as assistive technology, it helps a child to do a task that he either cannot perform without it or cannot perform as well without it.

Assistive technology often can be used in a variety of environments and can help a child with a task that might be done at school, at home or out in the community. Technology that can be used by students with learning disabilities to compensate for their skill deficits is the most rapidly developing area of assistive technology today. There are literally hundreds of products available. In addition, more products are coming out of the general technology realm with built in accessibility features. Products with voice output or voice recognition such as Microsoft Word and Dragon Dictate are being purchased for general use in school districts and can become assistive technology for a child with a learning disability. The inclusion of these accessibility features is called universal design (UD). Any product with universal design features:

- Provides multiple representations of the information being presented.

- Provides multiple or modifiable means of expression and control.

- Provides multiple or modifiable means of motivating and engaging students.

A Historical Perspective

The field of assistive technology is a relative newcomer in education. As soon as electronics and home computers came on the market, people began to see ways that these technologies might help children and adults with severe disabilities to do things that most of us take for granted. They saw that technology might help to overcome the barriers of hands that could not write or voices that could not speak. The problems to be solved were complicated and so was the technology, so many school districts set up specialized services which required referral to assistive technology specialists in order to identify and access needed assistive technology. The problem with the specialized or expert system is that it only allows the IEP team to do two things; 1) decide that there is no need or 2) make a referral to an expert. With this model, children with learning disabilities were often left out of the assistive technology assessment system because their problems didn't seem as critical as those of children who could not walk or see or hear.

One other historical factor has limited the use of assistive technology for children with learning disabilities. The families and teachers of children with learning disabilities were sometimes unwilling to allow them to use assistive technology tools to help compensate for a problem. They worried that if a student used a calculator to do math assignments, they would never learn math facts and processes. They worried that if a student used a computer to produce written work, they would never learn to spell or write with a pencil. The focus was on teaching the child compensatory skills to overcome the disability.

Today, research tells us that assistive technology can be a tool to help children acquire the more difficult concepts which they can understand, but which their deficits in reading, writing or processing have prevented them from learning.

The assessment systems developed to take advantage of the skills of experts are often closed systems. They require that if you have an assistive technology question, you go elsewhere to get an assessment. If an expert system is used exclusively, it can sometimes actually make it harder to address the needs of students with learning disabilities. A more open system in which the student's educational team works together to identify problems and look for assistive technology tools makes it easier to address the needs of students with learning disabilities. You and the other members of your child's educational team can probably already identify some tools that are appropriate to your child's educational needs and useful in overcoming the limitations caused by your child's learning disabilities. An open system provides on going information and training about the myriad of assistive technology devices and the rapidly appearing new additions to the field.

Common Uses of Assistive Technology for Students with Learning Disabilities

The assistive technology devices that are most often needed by students with learning disabilities fall into five categories. The categories include the following.

Writing: Handwriting and written communication goals are the most common goals found on IEPs across the nation. When a child has been unsuccessful in learning to put thoughts and words on paper using a pencil or a pen, the IEP team may decide that an assistive technology tool is needed. For examples of assistive technology devices that can be used to help a child improve written communication.

Reading: When a student with learning disabilities has difficulty reading, there are many tools which can help to identify single words, phrases or even read an entire document to the child.

Math: If your child is having trouble with calculations but understands how math may can be used to solve problems, there are a variety of tools which may make calculation easier or may even do basic calculations for him.

Studying/Organizing: Many students with learning disabilities have difficulty keeping track of assignments, identifying the most important information to learn and/or organizing thoughts to show what they know.

Listening/Note Taking: When writing is difficult, a student may have a great deal of trouble getting notes on paper. When students are distractible or especially sensitive to noise, even listening can be a problem.

Access to the Curriculum: For some students with learning disabilities, reading can be such a problem that reading difficulties keep the child from getting information that is available to other students. Sometimes an alternative to reading is needed.

What to Expect when Assistive Technology Is Considered

What should be different in your IEP meeting now that your IEP team is required to consider your child's need for assistive technology? Following are some things that you can expect.

In your IEP meeting at some point there should be a discussion about assistive technology. Generally, this should come after you have agreed upon the goals that your child will be expected to attain in the next twelve months. It is really not possible to make a decision about assistive technology until you can talk about the specific tasks that your child will be trying to accomplish. Remember, the definition of assistive technology is, "any item, piece of equipment, or product system, whether acquired off the shelf, modified, or customized, that is used to increase, maintain, or improve functional capabilities of children with disabilities" (20 USC, 1401, Section 602 (1)). The functional capabilities of the child in any situation are directly related to the tasks that he or she is trying to accomplish. There may be different assistive technology to be considered for your child in meeting an arithmetic goal than in meeting a writing goal.

When you do consider assistive technology, the consideration should involve some discussion and examination of potential assistive technology tools. Consideration should not be someone saying, "Assistive technology? No, he doesn't need that." with no discussion. Consideration is defined in the *American Heritage Dictionary* as "to think carefully about, to form an opinion about, or to look at thoughtfully." We believe that Congress did not choose that word by accident, but clearly intended that there would be some thought about whether assistive technology may be needed by each child. So one thing that should be different, is that assistive technology should be discussed from now on at each IEP meeting.

This thoughtful look should certainly include at least a brief discussion of which assistive technology devices are useful for children with disabilities like the ones your child experiences and whether your child needs tools like those. Someone on the IEP team will need to be sufficiently knowledgeable about assistive technology to help lead the discussion. So another thing that may be different in your child's IEP meeting is that someone may bring along specific resource information about assistive technology to help all of you focus on what assistive technology exists for the tasks that are challenging to your child. That information might be books, catalogs, printouts from a web site, or actual hardware or software for you to see. Whether they bring something or not, one thing that you should expect is a brief discussion of assistive technology during which at least one person displays some knowledge about relevant assistive technology.

During an IEP meeting, this discussion should be brief. It should last at least a minute or two, but no more than 15 to 20 minutes. Congress intended that we could do this within the confines of an IEP meeting, so it should not add appreciably to the length of that meeting. If understanding and agreement cannot be reached in twenty minutes, then it is possible that there are questions that need to be addressed at another time. Your IEP team may decide to complete an assistive technology assessment if you feel that you do not have enough information. If that is the decision, it should be written into the IEP with an anticipated date of initiation and completion.

If your IEP team decides that your child will be using assistive technology, you should also expect to talk about assistive technology services. The consideration requirement requires IEP teams to consider the support services a student will need in order to use assistive technology which has been included in the IEP. Specific assistive technology services may include:

- an evaluation of your child's need for assistive technology;

- training of your child, members of your family or staff on how to use the assistive technology;

- technical assistance about its operation or use;

- modification or customization of the assistive technology; and

- other supports to the school personnel that might be necessary for the assistive technology to be appropriately used.

The supports your child might need are not specified in the law. They could include anything that is needed, for example, printing assignments your child has completed on a portable word processor, scanning new materials into a software program that reads the text or the planning about how and when these things will happen.

Finally, you should expect that someone on the IEP team will know how to locate assistive technology devices and services within your school district. In a small district it may be that the direct service providers who work with your child (i.e. the teachers, therapists, and aides) will need to provide all of the services themselves. In a larger district, there may be individuals whose entire job is assistive technology. They may need to be contacted through appropriate channels so they can help become a part of your child's educational team.

Preparing for the IEP Meeting

A lot of information should be collected before assistive technology is actually included as a part of your child's daily educational program. If questions of assistive technology are raised for the first time during the IEP meeting and you feel your child might need assistive technology, it is a good idea to use the time during the IEP meeting to begin to plan trial periods or an assistive technology assessment rather than to make a final decision. Including assistive technology that your child has never tried in an IEP is very likely to create frustration for you and for your child.

Once evaluation and trial period data has been collected, the team probably has enough information to develop a plan that can succeed. Sometimes the data shows that the assistive technology you tried is not an appropriate solution to the problem. If this happens, your child's team might decide to try other things.

When assistive technology will be considered during your child's IEP meeting, you can prepare for the meeting by asking yourself questions like these.

Do I feel that we have information that points us in the direction of assistive technology that might help my child?

If I believe that assistive technology that can help my child has been identified, do I believe that my child needs to use this assistive technology at home as well as at school? For what specific tasks would it be used? If I believe my child needs assistive technology at home to accomplish IEP goals, how will the use of assistive technology at home impact our family?

Do I need to know how to use the assistive technology my child is using? How much do I need to know?

Using a Form to Guide Consideration of Assistive Technology

Many school districts and other groups have developed specific forms to assist the IEP team as they consider each child's need for assistive technology. One example is the Assistive Technology Evaluation Guide for Students with Learning Disabilities. This form was developed as a tool that IEP teams could use to guide them through the consideration process. It asks the team to answer these questions:

What difficulties is the student experiencing in the school environment for which assistive technology intervention is needed?

What strategies, materials, equipment and technology tools has the student already used to address the concerns?

What new or additional assistive technology or accommodations should be tried?

What will the criteria be for determining whether or not the students needs are being met while using assistive technology during the trial period?

Another example is the *AT Consideration Guide* that can be downloaded from the Wisconsin Assistive Technology Initiative's website.

Your role as a parent in developing the assistive technology portion of the IEP is to express your ideas and feelings about the assistive technology being considered. You can contribute information about what you see at home and bring up any concerns you have. It is important that every IEP team member keeps in mind the long-term vision for your child and takes steps toward that vision.

When assistive technology is included in the IEP, you can help clarify the specifics. You can ask questions like the following as the team develops a plan.

For what specific tasks will my child use the assistive technology at school?

When and how often will my child use the assistive technology during the school day?

How long should I expect to wait for the assistive technology to be provided?

What related services, if any, will my child need in order to use the technology effectively?

What other support services will my child need in order to use the technology effectively?

When my child uses this assistive technology in school, what will I have to do to support him/her?

If my child uses assistive technology only at school, how will I know if it is working?

What about Skill Development? A Note of Caution

When you have the computer speak the text, the child is not necessarily reading along. When you have the computer write through word prediction or voice recognition, the child is no longer writing in the same way. Even when you decide to use assistive technology, it is important to make sure that the focus doesn't get pulled totally away from skill development. In other words, don't stop teaching and holding the child accountable to learn new skills.

What about Statewide Assessments?

Assistive technology is a major issue in accommodating for the disabilities of students with disabilities in statewide and district wide assessments. Each state varies somewhat in its guidelines. It is important to know the rules related to using assistive technology in assessments and how that use will impact your child's assessment scores. More important, assistive technology should never be used during assessment until it has been proven effective during routine class assignments. It's unfair to a child to add a new tool to the stresses involved in a testing situation.

What about Assistive Technology Use at Home?

IDEA '97 guarantees that AT must be sent home if it is needed. However, the determination of need is based on its relationship to goals and objectives in the IEP. It is within the rights of the school district to provide arrangements to complete tasks at school if they can be completed at school. For example, if your child has social studies homework, the school district could provide extra time on a computer at school so there is no need for your child to do homework. The school district could provide an Alphasmart 2000 or some other less expensive portable word processor. There is never a specific requirement to provide a computer for your home unless there is no other way for your child to do something required on the IEP.

If assistive technology is sent home with your child, it is your responsibility to ensure that it is used appropriately and kept in good condition. Be prepared to report technical problems and any difficulties you experience to your child's teacher as soon as you can so that the use of assistive technology at home does not become a barrier to your child's achievement rather than a help.

Summary

The requirement for every IEP team to consider the need for assistive technology is a step forward. In many cases a giant step forward, because it has caused school districts to break out of the box and begin to think about assistive technology for many children who had previously been overlooked in the provision of assistive technology. It is also an opportunity. It is an opportunity for parents to encourage a thoughtful discussion of the potential use of assistive technology for their child.

It's important to remember that the development of a plan is only the beginning of your child's journey with assistive technology. Learning to use the technology is just like learning to read. It takes time and effort and support from you and your child's teachers. As you begin the journey, we hope the information contained in this chapter provides you with a useful road map.

Resources

Bowser, G. and Reed, P., Education Tech Points; A Framework for Assistive Technology Planning, Winchester, OR: Coalition for Assistive Technology in Oregon.

Council for Exceptional Children, Ensuring Access to the General Education Curriculum, Individuals with Disabilities Education Act, Amendments of 1997, Public Law No. 105-17, 602, U.S.C. 1401.

Reed, P. and Bowser, G. Assistive Technology Pointers for Parents, Winchester, OR: Coalition for Assistive Technology in Oregon, (2000).

Reed, P. (ed) Assessing Students' Need for Assistive Technology, Oshkosh, WI: Wisconsin Assistive Technology Initiative, 1998.

Cumley, Judi and Marcia Obukowicz, Science for Everyone: It Can Be Done, conference reference *CTG*, 1999.

Chapter 51

Computer-Based Assistance for the Learning Disabled

Secondary students with learning disabilities often find the challenges of an academic curriculum more than they can handle. Faced with a text-centered world, they are frequently encumbered by an inability to read and write with sufficient fluency and legibility to meet the expectations of their teachers. Faced with a fast-paced curriculum, they are frequently hampered by minimal organizational skills and slowed by the additional time that even simple assignments can demand when the student has a learning disability. Faced with low self-confidence and a history of poor achievement, they frequently choose (or are advised to take) courses with minimal intellectual content and limited utility as preparation for postsecondary education. Faced with academic frustration and the constant threat of failure, they frequently drop out of high school before completing the requirements for graduation.

Although the challenges faced by secondary students with learning disabilities are real, academic frustration and school failure are not axiomatic. We all know students with learning disabilities who find the stamina and self-will to persist and succeed in secondary school in spite of their difficulties. Many learn or develop strategies

Reprinted with permission from "Computer-Based Solutions for Secondary Students with Learning Disabilities: Emerging Issues," by Lynne Anderson-Inman, Ph.D., *Reading and Writing Quarterly*, Volume 15, Number 3, pages 239-249 (June 1999), published by Taylor & Francis, Ltd. For more information about *Reading and Writing Quarterly*, visit http://www.tandf.co.uk/journals. © 1999 Taylor and Francis, Ltd.

to overcome the negative impact of their learning disabilities. They find ways to acquire information and to study that take advantage of their individual, and sometimes unique, learning strengths. They devise personally useful ways to remember information and to prepare for tests. They create or adopt techniques to stay organized and get assignments in on time. More than anything else, they maintain confidence in their abilities to succeed and take responsibility for their own learning. Because of this, they persevere and, more often than not, they reach their academic goals.

Unfortunately, this picture of success is not the rule. Furthermore, achieving success usually requires an enormous amount of experimentation and, not uncommonly, extraordinary levels of support and advice from parents as well as teachers. In spite of a vast and well supported system of special education for students with learning disabilities, many (if not most) still reach high school unprepared for the academic rigors they find and unskilled in strategies for overcoming their learning difficulties. This usually leads to academic frustration at the secondary level, failure to pursue postsecondary education or training, and a loss of human potential for the community.

The Center for Electronic Studying has been investigating ways in which computers and other forms of advanced technology can be used to support students' efforts to succeed in school. Specifically, they have explored ways in which computer technology can be used to minimize the negative impact of students' disabilities and maximize the potential of their learning strengths. They describe their approach of supporting students through the use of computer technology as electronic studying, that is, use of the computer to enhance students' abilities to read, write, and think in ways that promote learning and success in school. By focusing on the processes of learning (rather than on the learning of specific content), they have worked to uncover strategies for using the computer as a study tool that have relevance to almost all content areas.

Over the last 10 years the Center for Electronic Studying has been fortunate in obtaining considerable federal funding to support their efforts to develop and evaluate strategies and materials for electronic studying. Many of these projects have enabled them to focus on the needs of students who are educationally at risk, including students with learning disabilities. For example, they conducted a 3-year study investigating the use of computer-based outlining as a study tool for various types of students (Anderson-Inman, Redekopp, & Adams 1992). One of the things learned in this project was that strategies for using computer-based outlining were particularly helpful when used by students with learning disabilities (Adams, 1992, Adams & Anderson-Inman, 1991). A subsequent project, therefore, focused exclusively on teaching computer-based information organization strategies to students with learning disabilities, using tools such as electronic outlining and concept mapping programs (Anderson-Inman, Knox-Quinn, & Horney, 1996) Additional projects have helped them to explore (a) other approaches to electronic studying (Anderson-Inman & Horney, 1998; Knox-Quinn & Anderson-Inman 1996); (b) applications of electronic studying to meet the needs of other populations (e.g., at-risk students, students with hearing impairments, students who speak English as a second language); and (c) the utility of electronic studying for students at the postsecondary level (Anderson-Inman, Knox-Quinn & Szymanski, in press).

In total, they have explored computer-based solutions for three types of academic problems: reading difficulties, writing (as well as spelling) difficulties, and learning difficulties. Two examples of strategies designed to address the reading difficulties of students include a three-step process for textbook notetaking (Anderson-Inman, 1995) and the use of embedded resources or supported text in hypermedia versions of students' content-area reading materials (Anderson-Inman & Horney, 1997). With respect to students' writing difficulties, strategies for using computer-based writing aids and organizing ideas with electronic outliners and concept mappers, as well as taking notes from lectures and discussions has been explored (Knox-Quinn & Anderson-Inman, 1996). To address the learning difficulties of students, they have found effective ways to help them use computer technology to organize and manage their time, manipulate information in search of patterns and meaning, and study for tests (Anderson-Inman et al., 1996).

The purpose of this chapter is to share a number of observations about implementation issues that have emerged during the efforts to find and evaluate computer-based solutions for students' learning and studying problems. These issues fall into five topic areas: access issues, motivational issues, curriculum integration issues, labeling issues, and funding issues.

Access Issues

By definition, studying and learning that rely on computer-based tools require a high degree of student access to computer technology. Although student computer ratios in schools have improved greatly over the last decade, the national average is still 10 students for each computer, with high schools faring slightly better at an average of 8.4 students per computer (Coley, Cradler, & Engel, 1997). However, as schools invest more of their technology dollars in telecommunications and networks, the pace of new computer purchases has slowed. Unfortunately, this is occurring at the same time that teachers are discovering more and more ways to integrate the technology into their curricula. In other words, over the next few years there will be vastly increasing demand for a minimally increasing number of computers.

In general, we have found that even well-equipped secondary schools do not provide students with sufficient access to computers for electronic studying to be implemented in a way that is maximally effective for students with learning disabilities. In an ideal world, secondary and postsecondary students with learning disabilities would all have 24-hr access to, at the very least, a notebook size computer. This level of access enables computer technology to support learning and studying whenever and wherever the student needs it. In many of our projects we have been able to solve the access issue by providing students with a laptop computer for use in their classes and at home. This increased the amount of time and the number of ways in which students could be expected to integrate computer-based studying into their lives. It also facilitated the students' finding novel ways to partner with the machines to accomplish school tasks.

Even a relatively low-level computer (in today's terms) can support most of the procedural tasks associated with school assignments (such as recording assignments and notetaking) as well as some of the cognitive tasks (such as calculating, spell checking, and synthesizing information). For example, students in our projects are still often provided with a now-extinct Macintosh PowerBook 145. This laptop computer contains only 4 megabytes of RAM and a hard disk of only 40 megabytes. There is no color, no CD-ROM drive, and memory limitations make it incapable of supporting most of today's browsers for the World Wide Web. Nonetheless, if loaded with a few key pieces of commercially available software, even a relatively spartan computer such as the Macintosh 145 can empower students to implement a broad array of computer-based study strategies. Supported by no more than this level of computing power, we have seen secondary students with learning disabilities who were on the verge of dropping out of high school turn their lives around academically, graduate with good grades, and move on to college.

One of the keys, however, is sufficient access, and sufficient access means as close to constant access as possible. Not only does this provide students with computing power at critical times (e.g., to take legible notes in class), it also creates an environment in which students can personalize the hardware and software for their unique learning needs. For example, screenshots of the computer desktop and file organization styles adopted by students in one of our projects revealed vastly different approaches to organizing and storing information. These differences presumably reflect personal preferences, perhaps influenced by course expectations and instructor style. Shared computers, even shared laptop computers, would not permit this level of customization. When used in the way I describe, portable computers are analogous to other types of assistive technology. In the words of one of our students, the computer is a "wheelchair for the mind." Just as we would never expect 5-10 students with orthopedic impairments to share a single wheelchair, we should not expect 5-10 students with learning disabilities to share a single computer.

Motivational Issues

Studying is hard work. It takes effort, frequently sustained effort, over a long period of time. Students who study effectively believe that the effort will pay off and are therefore willing to engage in the process (Grabbe, 1988). It is therefore not surprising that motivation is an important variable affecting the extent to which students are willing to engage in a program of computer-supported studying. Although the computer itself is somewhat motivating to many students, its interest value alone is not sufficient in the long run. In our studies on students with learning disabilities, we have found numerous factors related to motivation that influenced students' behavior and their level of success. Some of these factors appeared to be personal, whereas others seemed to be more environmental.

For example, implementing a program of computer-supported studying for students with learning disabilities is based on the premise that the students want to succeed in school. For the vast majority of students with whom we have worked, this premise turned out to be true. The students were still trying to play the school game, albeit with varying degrees of success, and they still believed that academic achievement was a worthwhile goal. Most of these students worked to learn the strategies we were teaching and tried to implement them in their classes. Even though there were differences in adoption level (Anderson-Inman et al., 1996), the approach was generally embraced by students as worthwhile.

However, we also have worked with students for whom success in school no longer seemed to be a motivating factor. Although they volunteered to be in one of our projects, their reasons for doing so were often inconsistent with the project's goals. One student, for example, saw our computer-supported studying project as an easy way to get increased access to a computer. He was extremely computer literate (more so than any other student in the project) and consistently used the computer for personal activities rather than school-related assignments. He was not motivated to apply what we taught to subjects in which he was experiencing failure, and our continued insistence on this eventually led him to drop out of the project.

In our investigations, successful implementation of computer supported studying often has revolved around finding a personally meaningful solution to a student's difficulties in school. For example, one of our students was faced with writing a paper that required synthesizing information from multiple sources. She felt overwhelmed by the task. Learning a computer-based strategy for synthesizing information (Anderson-Inman & Zeitz, 1994) resulted in both an A on the paper and her conversion to computer-supported studying as a way to get through school. For this type of motivational transformation to occur, the student must believe that there is a problem that needs to be solved and that the proposed computer-based solution is effective. There have been numerous occasions when we found ourselves proposing computer-based solutions to situations that students did not see as problems. The students were either content with the status quo (e.g., minimal comprehension of the textbook) or unwilling to put forth the effort required to change the status quo. For many, a long history of school failure had led to an attitude of learned helplessness, or at least one of learned wariness, toward novel attempts by school personnel to affect their academic achievement.

For some students, the day-to-day experiences of living in a dysfunctional home or hanging out with an antisocial peer group appeared to overshadow any personal motivation they might have had to succeed in school. Being introduced to computer-supported studying, and even achieving initial success in implementing computer-based study strategies, was not sufficiently compelling or rewarding for these students to reject the strong environmental influences that, in our view, were detrimental to their adjustment in school. For example, parental ridicule or abuse, frequent absences to hang out with the gang, and homelessness were all conditions that interfered with students putting forth effort in school. Computer supported studying is a not silver bullet. It can flourish as a solution to academic difficulties only if planted in fertile ground. Motivation to succeed in school, at least on some minimal level, appears to be a prerequisite.

Curriculum Integration Issues

Secondary-level classrooms are often high-speed, complicated places of learning. For computer-supported studying to be integrated into the curriculum, the strategies proposed to and adopted by students must be compatible with the frenzy and fast-paced schedule in which they are expected to survive. This means that computer-based solutions have to reflect the actual demands of the curriculum and also have to be implementable without too much difficulty.

In our work in middle schools and high schools, we have uncovered numerous small hurdles that had to be overcome by students and teachers in order for them to successfully adopt a program of computer-supported studying. For example, students who took portable computers into their classes for taking notes or writing assignments and tests often had difficulty arranging for printing. Printers in schools are most often in a computer laboratory and, especially in large schools, that can mean a long walk to the laboratory and back. Teachers may expect an assignment or test to be turned in at the end of the period, so there may be a problem if the student has to hike to and from the laboratory to get it printed. Teachers may feel uncomfortable with students not turning in their tests immediately, and students may resent the time crunch caused by having to accomplish this before going to the next class. In our studies, students who were successful adopters of computer-supported studying found ways to get around these types of hurdles (Anderson Inman et al., 1996), often resolving the problem in different ways with different teachers. For example, a teacher resolved the printing problem in one class by having the student turn in a disk copy of the test immediately after class and then return with the printed version later in the day. In another class it was resolved by a teacher who made arrangements for the student to use a printer in the departmental office, even though the printer was attached to a computer normally reserved for teachers.

Successful integration of computer-supported studying often relies on the good will and support of teachers. When one or more students start bringing portable computers into their classrooms, it is understandable that teachers will have concerns. In general, however, we have found teachers to be outstandingly supportive, once they understood the rationale underlying this type of assistance for students with learning disabilities. We realize, however, that it is important for students to be skilled enough in using their computers that they do not require assistance from their classroom teachers, many of whom expressed concern that they would be called on to resolve a technical problem in the middle of teaching.

It also was helpful if teachers communicated their course expectations in advance. This allowed the person responsible for implementing a study skills curriculum to provide students with prior instruction on the software and study strategies most needed for success in any given class. This was particularly important during the initial stages, when students were less likely to have a large repertoire of computer-based study strategies and were less likely to have the skills to determine which strategies are most suited to which types of assignments. Unfortunately, many teachers seem to have a very short lead time in their planning. This makes advanced preparation of students extremely difficult. This in turn leads to implementation issues associated with curricular velocity—the speed at which the curriculum moves—and the need to develop computer based study skills for quickly changing expectations.

Labeling Issues

Students in our projects have been found eligible for special education services using standard statewide procedures for diagnosing learning disabilities. This particular diagnosis, however, hinges on the assumption that students with learning disabilities fail to achieve in school commensurate with their aptitude, as indicated by IQ tests. In other words, for students to be diagnosed with learning disabilities, there must be a significant discrepancy between achievement and aptitude, and this discrepancy must not be explainable by other factors.

Computer-based solutions for students with learning disabilities, however, minimize and sometimes even eliminate this discrepancy. With sufficient access to supportive technology, and sufficient instruction on how to use it for the purposes of studying and learning across the curriculum, students with learning disabilities can achieve up to normal expectations. If they are now successful in school (and in some cases our students were identified by teachers as the best students in class), do they still have learning disabilities?

This is not an idle question. Students' rights to special education services, including the technology and instruction provided by our projects, depend on them being certified as having a learning disability. If they are no longer thought to have a learning disability, they are no longer eligible to receive special education assistance. This may be a high price to pay for success in school. For example, after 2 years in one of our projects, approximately half of the participating students in an area middle school were decertified—that is, no longer found eligible for special education services. With the support of the technology we provided, they were performing at or above grade level. Decertification for these students meant they went on to high school without the benefit of special education support and without the benefit of the computers on which they had come to rely.

Funding Issues

Computer technology, like other forms of special education assistance, is not cheap. Furthermore, it cannot be used as a study tool without intensive instruction on how and when to use technology to maximize educational gains. When I present results from our projects at national conferences, one of the first questions from the audience always revolves around how to obtain funding to purchase the technology. There is, of course, no magic answer. Although technology funding for our research has come largely from the federal government, we have worked with students, families, and school districts in an effort to help them obtain the funds to purchase the computers they need to participate in or implement a curriculum of computer-supported studying. Following below are some options for educators and parents to consider:

1. Legally, schools should provide the equipment a student with learning disabilities needs to achieve in the general education curriculum. The recently rewritten Individuals with Disabilities Education Act (IDEA 97) legislation guarantees students with disabilities a free public education (P.L. 105-17) and makes provisions for guaranteeing students the assistive technology necessary for education in general education classes if provisions are written in the student's individualized education program. Parent and teachers should advocate for students' rights to appropriate assistive technology and expert district support for these students' needs.

2. Unfortunately, this process takes times and may even result in disagreement over the extent to which technology is needed. For these and other reasons, personal purchase of computers may be the answer. Prices for computer technology are falling daily. If parents can possibly afford to purchase a computer for their son or daughter with learning disabilities, it could be a lifesaving investment. Furthermore, used equipment is increasingly available at very reasonable rates. Fancy

features are not necessary, so much of the available used equipment has the necessary power and capability.

3. The office of Vocational Rehabilitation is charged with assisting individuals with disabilities in obtaining work, or education, leading to employment. Over the years, we have developed a good relationship with our Vocational Rehabilitation office, and their counselors have been impressed with the results achieved by clients who have participated in our projects. Vocational Rehabilitation has funds earmarked for equipment that can be documented as necessary for success during education or vocational training. These funds can be a great resource, especially for students moving into programs at local community colleges or technical institutes.

Concluding Remarks

Computer-based solutions represent the future in educators' efforts to help students with learning disabilities achieve in school up to their potential. It is not hard to imagine a time when students with learning disabilities are automatically supplied with computers and the instruction necessary for them to adopt and implement strategies that minimize their disabilities and maximize their learning strengths. None of this is magical and, as the foregoing discussion illustrates, there are very real issues that must be addressed and solved. Nonetheless, computers and other forms of advanced technology hold great promise, especially when combined with systematic efforts to identify and teach strategies for computer-based learning and studying.

References

Adams, V. (1992). Comparing paper-based and electronic outlining as a study strategy for mainstreamed students with learning disabilities. Unpublished doctoral dissertation, University of Oregon.

Adams, V. and Anderson-Inman, L. (1991). Electronic outlining: A computer-based study strategy for handicapped students in regular classrooms. In J. Marr & G. Tindall (Eds.), *The Oregon Conference Monograph* 1991, 86-92. Eugene: University of Oregon.

Anderson-Inman, L. (1995). Computer-assisted outlining: Information organization made easy. *Journal of Adolescent and Adult Literacy*, 40, 302-306.

Anderson-Inman, L. and Horney, M. (1997). Electronic books for secondary students. *Journal of Adolescent and Adult Literacy*, 40, 486-491.

Anderson-Inman, L. and Horney, M. (1998). Transforming text for at-risk readers. In D. Reinking, L. Labbo, M. McKenna, and R. Kieffer (Eds.), *Handbook of Literacy and Technology: Transformations in a Post-Typographic World*, (pp. 1543). Mahwah, NJ: Erlbaum.

Anderson-Inman, L.; Knox-Quinn, C.; and Horney, M. A. (1996). Computer-based study strategies for students with learning disabilities: Individual differences associated with adoption level. *Journal of Learning Disabilities*, 29,461-484.

Anderson-Inman, L.; Knox-Quinn, C.; and Szymanski, M. (in press). Computer-Supported Studying: stories of successful transition to post secondary education. *Career Development for Exceptional Individuals*.

Anderson-Inman, L.; Redekopp, R.; and Adams, V. (1992). Electronic studying: Using computer-based outlining programs as study tools. *Reading & Writing Quarterly: Overcoming Learning Difficulties*, 8, 337-358.

Anderson-Inman, L. and Zeitz, L. (1994). Beyond notecards: Synthesizing with electronic study tools. *Computing Teacher*, 21, 21-25.

Coley, R. J.; Cradler, J.; and Engel, P. K. (1997). Computers and classrooms: The status of technology in U.S. schools. Princeton, NJ: Educational Testing Service.

Grabbe, M. (1988). Technological enhancement of study behavior: On-line activities to produce more effective learning. *Collegiate Microcomputer*, 6, 253-259.

Knox-Quinn, C. and Anderson-Inman, L. (1996, April). Using portable wireless networks and synchronous collaborative software to support the content-area-literacy of mainstream students with disabilities. Paper presented at the American Educational Research Association Annual Conference, New York.

Chapter 52

Reading Software for Students with Learning Disabilities

The fourth grade boy sits at the computer ready to read his book. It is a CD-ROM program, a talking storybook. He starts the program and turns to the first page of the story. The screen comes alive with color, sound, animation, and speech. The characters in the illustrations move and speak as the narrator reads the text aloud. Then, it's the boy's turn to interact with the text and graphics. "Neat," he says.

Hypermedia-based children's literature programs, sometimes called talking storybooks, are one of the most popular types of software today. These programs read stories aloud to students in realistic digitized speech, colorful graphics accompany the text, and students often can interact with both text and graphics. Examples are the programs in series such as *Living Books*, *Disney's Animated Storybooks*, *Reader Rabbit's Reading Development Library*, *Discis Books*, *Magic Tales*, and *WiggleWorks*.

Project LITT, Literacy Instruction Through Technology, is a three-year research project funded by the U.S. Office of Special Education. The overall purpose of Project LITT is investigation of the effectiveness of hypermedia-based children's literature software in improving the reading skills of students with learning disabilities. This chapter

Reprinted with permission from "Reading Software for Students with Learning Disabilities: Hypermedia-Based Children's Literature," by Rena B. Lewis, Ph.D., Professor of Special Education, San Diego, CA. © 1998. The complete text of this article is available at http://www.ldonline.org/ld_indepth/technology/lewis_rdgsftware.html.

describes the project, the body of software under study, and prelimi-nary results from several empirical studies.

The Potential of Hypermedia-Based Children's Literature Software

Hypermedia-based children's literature has several potential ad-vantages for students with learning disabilities who are struggling to acquire basic reading skills. First is the motivational appeal of this body of software. With its dazzling graphics, realistic sound, and plen-tiful opportunities for interactions between the learner and the task, this type of software has the capability to capture and hold students' attention. As Erickson and Staples (1995) reported, even students with autism respond to the attractiveness of these programs with increased attention to the reading task. This level of motivational value may increase the probability that reluctant readers will persevere in their interactions with text. This would be a particularly valuable outcome because repeated readings of the same text have been found to be of value for students with learning disabilities (Sindelar, 1987).

Also, hypermedia-based children's literature offers students text that is speech-enhanced. Speech makes the text more accessible to readers or, in the words of Boone, Higgins, Falba, and Langley (1993), more cooperative.

In addition, this software is a computer translation of children's literature. When transformed into computer-mediated books, the qual-ity of the texts and illustrations are preserved. Texts are typically heavily illustrated; also, they are often predictable and include nar-rative features such as repeated lines and rhymes. These features, like software speech enhancements, increase the cooperativeness of the text. Comprehension is aided because of the graphical cues and the predictability of the text. Also, if a computer-mediated book is used as a springboard for instruction in skills such as decoding, that in-struction is easily anchored, as Hasselbring and his colleagues (e.g., Bottge & Hasselbring, 1993) use the term, to the student's experiences with that piece of children's literature.

Moreover, hypermedia-based children's literature programs offer new opportunities to students with learning disabilities whose first lan-guage is Spanish, rather than English. Many programs allow students to hear the story read aloud in either language; some, like the *Discis Books* series, provide Spanish assistance in English word-reading tasks. Researchers such as Ruiz (1989, 1995) suggest that the commu-nicative competence of bilingual exceptional students can be enhanced when the classroom context emphasizes communication, centers on students' background knowledge and experiences, allows for student initiations and student-directed discourse, and involves whole texts, rather than fragments. Hypermedia-based children's literature in English and Spanish could certainly contribute to establishing a more optimal learning environment for these students.

Finally, the vast majority of this software is general education software. Because it is widely used in typical classrooms, it reflects the reading experiences of typical children. Use of this software as a means to ameliorate the reading problems of students with learning disabilities would allow them to participate in the same types of reading activities as their peers. And, when students with learning disabilities are educated in inclusionary settings, instruction with talking storybooks would call less attention to their reading difficulties than similar efforts with special software. Armstrong, Brand, Glass, and Regan (1995) recognized these advantages when they included hypermedia-based children's literature among their recommended general education software titles for students with special needs.

It is also important to recognize that there are several potential disadvantages to hypermedia-based children's literature software for students with learning disabilities. First, these programs rely on discovery learning. Because they are hypermedia, the programs do not lead the student through a carefully sequenced series of instructional activities. Students choose their own paths through the programs, and their interactions with text elements may be quite limited. Unfortunately, mere exposure to text is unlikely to increase the reading proficiency of students with learning disabilities. As observed by Lewis and Doorlag (1999), these students "will likely require explicit instruction in skills such as decoding" (p. 246). Thus, it is likely that students with learning disabilities will require instructional support in order to maximize the benefits they might derive from this type of software.

Second, the very elements of hypermedia-based children's literature that make it appealing and motivating to young readers may decrease its usefulness for students with learning disabilities. There is wide variation in the degree of emphasis this software places on the reading task. In some programs, students can virtually ignore the text and concentrate on interacting with its illustrations. However, as Lewis (1998) points out, "10 seconds of reading followed by 10 minutes of play is not a good use of instructional time" (p. 22). In addition, some students with learning disabilities are characterized by their distractibility (Reid, Maag, & Vasa, 1994); poor skills in marshaling attentional resources will not assist students as they attempt to navigate through programs filled with highly entertaining distractions. These limitations underscore the need for instructional support in the use of this type of software.

Third, students with learning disabilities may encounter difficulty in the use of speech-enhanced text to support the reading process. As MacArthur and Haynes (1995) and Wise and Olson (1994) observed, students with learning disabilities do not consistently take advantage of the support provided by speech-enhanced text. In Olofsson's (1992) study (as reported by Lundberg, 1995), students with disabilities used speech supports less often than typical readers, despite the fact that they were less skilled in the decoding process. Again, instructional support, above and beyond the cooperative text provided by the software, is required to optimize the benefits that students with learning disabilities may obtain from hypermedia-based children's literature.

Fourth, because this software is designed for general education audiences, it is geared to the interest levels of students achieving at grade level. Students with learning disabilities, however, typically read below grade level. To match their interest levels with their reading skills, high-interest low-vocabulary reading materials are required. Unfortunately, there is a scarcity of high-interest low-vocabulary reading software in the talking storybook format.

In summary, hypermedia-based children's literature has many potential advantages for improving the reading performance of students with learning disabilities. It is appealing general education software that presents high quality children's books in an interactive format. In addition, it includes a variety of features that support the reading process including graphical cues, predictable text, and speech enhancements in both English and Spanish.

However, there are potential drawbacks and many of these center around the interactive nature of this type of software. Because it is hypermedia-based, the student directs the flow of interactions with the text and other elements of the program. However, interactive graphics may compete with text for students' attention. And, when students do attend to the text, they may fail to take full advantage of the speech enhancements available to support them in the reading process. Students with learning disabilities may lack the strategies needed to successfully negotiate hypermedia-based children's literature software in order to improve their reading skills.

At present, it is unclear whether the potential advantages of hypermedia-based children's literature as an instructional tool for students with learning disabilities outweigh its possible disadvantages. Final judgments must be postponed until research evidence becomes available. Project LITT's purpose is to gather the data needed to determine the instructional usefulness of talking storybooks for students with learning disabilities.

The Software Search: What's Available?

In order to study the effectiveness of hypermedia-based children's literature, Project LITT began by conducting a nationwide software search. The goal was to identify and evaluate all commercially available talking storybook programs. As of October 1998, we have located more than 300 titles. Project staff reviewed each program, story texts were evaluated for readability, and students with learning disabilities and their teachers critiqued a sample of representative programs. Programs were included in the collection if they were CD-ROM based, they included text, and that text could be read aloud. Excluded were programs with nonfiction text (e.g., science, social studies) and those with estimated readability levels higher than grade 8.

The first major conclusion that can be drawn from the software search is that there is a large number of talking storybook programs currently available. In planning the project, we had estimated that 50 to 75 such programs existed; our estimates were clearly too low. In 1996-97, more than 250 programs were identified; in the next year, approximately 50 additional programs were located. However, the rate at which new programs appear on the market seems to be slowing; in the summer of 1998, for example, fewer than 5 new programs were published.

The second major conclusion from the software search is that this body of software is extremely heterogeneous. Talking storybooks vary in several ways including their length, difficulty level, and the types and numbers of opportunities they provide to students to interact with text, graphics, and activities. The paragraphs that follow describe the body of software in an attempt to point out the areas in which variability occurs along with some of the commonalities among programs.

Titles. All types of stories are available in CD-ROM format. Some talking storybooks are software adaptations of award-winning children's books, others are traditional children's stories and fairy tales, and some are new texts especially written for the software format. Several duplicate titles were located in the software search, and the most common were traditional tales such as *Jack and the Beanstalk* and *Goldilocks* and the *Three Bears*.

Computer platform and price. Most talking storybook CD-ROMs (72%) are dual platform, i.e., available for both Windows and Macintosh computers. Most are relatively inexpensive (less than $50) (79%). Prices do vary, however, from programs costing less than $20 to one multi-CD-ROM instructional package costing almost $2,000.

Intended market. Talking storybooks are produced for both home and school markets. Home programs tend to be less expensive, more likely to include many opportunities for interactions with graphics, and more likely to contain game activities. School programs, in contrast, typically offer instructionally relevant features such as glossaries, word processing activities, and reading skill lessons.

Length of stories. There is enormous variability in the length of on-screen stories. Some stories are very brief, including fewer than 50 words. Others contain texts of more than 12,000 words.

Availability of print books. About one-fourth of programs (27%) include a print book along with the CD-ROM. However, there are often differences in the text and illustrations between the print and software versions. In many cases, the on-screen story is a shortened version of the original book. For example, the *Living Books CD-ROM Stellaluna* contains 343 words whereas the print book contains 1,201.

Estimated readability level. The readability level of the on-screen text may be different from the print book, and it may also be inconsistent with the age or grade levels recommended by the publisher. We used the Grammatik program to compute estimated Flesch-Kincaid readability levels for all stories in the Project LITT collection. Estimated reading levels ranged from grade 1 through grade 8. On-screen stories were fairly equally distributed between the grade 1-2 range (28%), the grade 3-4 range (39%), and the grade 5-6 range (27%).

Age-appropriateness. The age-appropriateness of programs is related not only to readability but also to factors such as story content and the program's appearance. Stories that are likely to interest and appeal to younger elementary grade students may be written at higher grade levels. For example, *Winnie the Pooh and the Honey Tree*, one of the programs in *Disney's Animated Storybook* series, is recommended by the publisher for ages 3 to 8; its estimated readability level is grade 7. Also, some programs incorporate music, cartoon characters, and children's voices that make them most appropriate for young

466

students, even though the story content and reading levels may make more sense for older students.

Availability of languages other than English. Some talking storybooks are bilingual or multilingual (23%). When languages other than English are available, Spanish is the most common although some books provide French, German, and Japanese versions. In some multilingual programs, the story appears in its entirety in each language addressed. For example, there may be a version of the story in English and a separate version in Spanish. However, some programs provide only limited support in a language other than English. For example, students may be able to click on a word in the English text to hear (but not see) its Spanish translation.

Text interactivity. The programs in the Project LITT collection allow students to interact with the text and hear that text read aloud (programs without that feature were excluded). In all programs, students can hear the entire on-screen page read aloud. In more than half of the programs (56%), students can also hear individual words read aloud, and these programs were rated high in text interactivity.

Interactivity with graphics. Much more variability among programs was seen in the amount of graphics interactivity. The range extended from programs with no opportunities for interactions with graphics to those with literally dozens of opportunities (hot spots) on each page. Thirty-eight percent of the talking storybooks offered no opportunities for interactions with graphics, and these tended to be programs designed for school markets (e.g., *WiggleWorks*, *Multimedia Literature*). In 17% of programs, there were more than 15 hot spots per page, on average; these programs were rated high in graphics interactivity. In most cases, students clicked on hot spots to see animations of the graphics and hear speech, music, and/or sound effects. In some program series (e.g., *Discis Books*, *Top Hat Tales*), clicking on a hot spot produces a picture label. For example, if the student clicks on the picture of a duck within the story illustration, a label with the word duck appears and the word is pronounced.

Features and activities. Many talking storybook programs offer features and activities that support the development of literacy skills. The most typical literacy activity is a word processing feature, provided by 55% of the programs. Reading mini-lessons or activities were found in 38% of programs and word definitions and/or glossaries in

38%. Programs designed for the home market were more likely to contain games and activities such as matching, concentration, mazes, and the like. For example, *Hunchback of Notre Dame*, one of the titles in *Disney's Animated Storybook* series, contains five activities including arcade-type games such as "Gargoyles vs. Soldiers" and "Climbing Down the Walls."

Teachers' and Students' Views of Talking Storybook Software

Students with learning disabilities and their teachers were asked to view representative talking storybook programs and share their views on the usefulness of these programs for improving reading skills. Focus group discussions were held with 42 special education teachers and 13 students with learning disabilities.

Students' Views

The students with learning disabilities who participated in the focus groups were in grades 2 through 7. Students were very enthusiastic about the talking storybook programs they viewed. All liked the programs and, when asked what they liked best, students identified features related to the interactivity of the software. For example, several students commented on the animated graphics that brought story illustrations to life. One sixth grade girl said, "It looked like it was really happening." A fourth grade boy observed, "It moves instead of a book that just stays." Students also talked about text interactivity. As one fourth grader said, "I can find a word and it says it." In most cases, students were not able to identify aspects of the programs that they did not like. However, two second graders who viewed a program with no graphics interactivity complained that the pictures didn't move. Students were asked whether they thought that talking storybook programs would help them to read better. Most students felt these programs would improve their reading skills because the story is read aloud, "it shows the words and you can read along with it," and "you can click on a word and it will say it."

Teachers' Views

Teachers had generally positive reactions to the talking storybook programs they viewed during the focus group discussions. However, they were critical of program features that they felt detracted from instructional goals, and they had strong opinions about which features software developers should include when designing programs to enhance students' reading skills. In addition to pointing out that clear directions are essential for student success, teachers' discussions centered around three main areas: the text presented in the stories, the graphics components of the software, and program features related to instruction and individualization.

Text considerations. Many of the programs evaluated by the teachers were based on print books and, in some cases, the books were included with the software package. Teachers felt this was a good practice because it gave students the opportunity to interact with both the traditional print and software versions of the story. Teachers preferred programs that did not deviate substantially from the text of the book. Unfortunately, many children's books are quite long and the text is condensed when the software version is created.

Teachers viewed programs very positively if they offered versions of the story in languages other than English. Spanish is the language other than English that is most often available in talking storybook programs, and the teachers felt this choice was the best for the population of students they served. Programs offering only English text were considered much less desirable than multilingual programs.

Several factors related to the appearance of the text on the screen were considered important by teachers. They preferred text styles and fonts that were familiar to children and easy to read. They believed text should be large enough for it to be seen easily, and there should not be too much text on any one screen page. The color of the text should be chosen so that the words stand out from the background, particularly when the background is a busy graphical illustration. Even more preferable is text on a plain white or neutral background. Several teachers commented on the placement of the text on the screen. In most cases, teachers wanted the text placed in a logical location (e.g., at the bottom of the screen) and preferred that text remain in the same location from screen to screen. Teachers particularly liked programs where the on-screen displays resembled books (e.g., the *Reader Rabbit's Reading Development Library Series*).

Teachers preferred programs where the text is highlighted as it is read aloud. In general, teachers wanted text highlighted either word by word (to direct learners' attention to individual text elements) or phrase by phrase (to encourage more fluent reading and better comprehension). Less desirable were programs that highlighted entire sentences or each line of text. Least liked were programs where text was not highlighted because teachers believed that students with learning disabilities would not be able to keep their place in the text. The method used to highlight text was also important. Teachers criticized programs where colored highlighting made text more difficult to see.

In all of the programs that teachers reviewed, the text on the screen was read aloud. Teachers considered this feature essential for instruction but voiced some concerns. Although teachers wanted the programs to move along at a brisk pace to keep students' interest, one common complaint was that the narrator read too quickly. Teachers feared that students would have difficulty keeping up and would become lost. Teachers preferred narrators who read with expression and criticized those with monotone or boring voices. Also, teachers felt that juvenile or babyish voices would be unattractive to older students.

Most programs viewed by the teachers allowed students to hear the text read aloud again (after the narrator had read the page in its entirety). Teachers liked this capability, particularly when students were able to select individual words rather than sentences, paragraphs, or the entire selection on the page. Also highly rated were programs that provided information about word meanings. Included in the software sample were examples of programs that offered definitions and explanation of words in a variety of modes including text, text accompanied by speech, multimedia presentations with brief video clips, drawings or illustrations (for nouns), and animated graphics sequences (for verbs).

Teachers were very sensitive to the content of the story, its value as literature, its appeal to students, and its fit with the goals of the curriculum. Several programs were praised for their inclusion of diverse groups and their multicultural themes. Teachers also carefully examined the structure of the language used in the stories, and those working with less able readers favored predictable and repetitive texts and ones that included rhyming words and high frequency vocabulary.

One major concern was the appropriateness of the programs given the discrepancy between their students' ages and the grade levels at which they were able to read. Teachers criticized stories they perceived as too juvenile in content. They were also concerned that the reading level of some stories might be too high. The stories in the programs reviewed by teachers ranged in readability level from grade 1 to grade 6. However, even some of the stories with the lowest readability levels were considered too difficult for some elementary grade students.

Considerations related to graphics. Teachers evaluated the illustrations accompanying the stories in terms of their appeal to students, age appropriateness, and general quality. Teachers expressed individual preferences for some illustrations; for example, some professionals liked more realistic depictions of the characters in the story rather than cartoon-style drawings. Teachers were particularly concerned that illustrations not be too primary and that the age level to which they appealed be congruent with the content of the story and the readability of the text.

The programs that teachers viewed ranged from those with no capacity for interaction with the graphics on the screen to others with very large numbers of interaction opportunities. One way to quantify this is by the numbers of hot spots per screen. A hot spot is a screen location which, when selected by a student, produces some type of result. Examples are: (a) the appearance of a picture label (e.g., the word "dog" appears next to a graphic of a dog and the word is read aloud), (b) a short animation sequence involving one of the objects on the screen and sound effects (e.g., a flower sways to music or a dresser drawer opens and bangs shut), and (c) a more prolonged animation sequence in which characters in the story move, speak, and interact accompanied by sound effects and/or music. The programs used in the demonstrations varied from some with no hot spots to those with more than 40 hot spots per screen, on average.

On one hand, teachers were enthusiastic about programs with interactive graphics because they felt they'd be highly motivating to students. Comments included "It makes learning fun," "Grabs kids," and "high interest level." On the other hand, teachers were highly critical of programs that contained "too many" hot spots and those where selecting the hot spots disrupted the continuity of the story. Teachers seemed to prefer programs in which the graphical interaction related to the story (e.g., *The Living Books Series*), the interactions retold the story (*Reader Rabbit's Reading Development Library*), or the interactions were simple picture labels rather than animation sequences (e.g., *Top Hat Tales, Discis Books*). Teachers also liked the *WiggleWorks* series which offers no graphics interactions. As one teacher remarked, "I like that this focuses on actually teaching reading."

Another concern raised by teachers related to long action sequences that preceded and/or followed the oral reading of the text on the screen. Most felt that, although these sequences related to the story, they distracted students from the reading task.

Other considerations. Three other areas were repetitive themes in teachers' discussions of the programs: games and other activities, instructional features of the programs, and options for individualization.

In general, teachers were not impressed with games and other types of activities embedded within the stories. They felt they disrupted the continuity of the story line and, although entertaining, were too much of a distraction. Most criticized was the *Disney's Animated Storybooks* series designed for use at home, not school. Teachers' observations included "Too gimmicky," "more for entertainment than education," and "students would go to game before choosing to read text on their own."

The instruction-related features of the programs typically were adjunct activities which students (or their teachers) could choose to select. Overall, teachers were pleased with these features and felt they contributed to the educational value of the programs. Most common were writing activities such as blank books where students could write and illustrate a story. Also available were more structured writing tasks such as the letter writing activity in *Reader Rabbit's Reading Development Library* (students choose sentence endings) or the "Let Me Write" activity in *Arthur's Reading Race* from the *Living Books* series (students modify sentences by selecting objects on the screen).

Teachers also liked programs that provided or collected lists of words to which students could refer. For example, the *Discis Books* keep a record of each word the student selects. The *WiggleWorks* programs allow students to build a "My Words" list as they read a story, and those words can then be used in the programs' writing activities.

Other popular features were the ability for students to tape-record their voices as they read stories aloud (e.g., the *WiggleWorks* series) and activities or options that promote comprehension skills. For example, the *Reader Rabbit's Reading Development Library* series offers two comprehension features. At the start of each story, the student selects the narrator (e.g., in *"The Three Little Pigs,"* a traditional storyteller, the second pig, or the wolf), and the story then is told from the point of view of that narrator. Also available is a Story Map activity where students put pictures of the events in the story in order.

Art activities were available as part of the writing activities in several programs, but teachers did not regard these as important features. However, teachers were enthusiastic about *The Art Lesson*, one of two programs in *MECC's Stories that Click* series. This is an autobiographical story read aloud by Tomie de Paola, the author and illustrator. It includes 14 art activities embedded with the story, and teachers felt these would motivate students, particularly those with interest and talent in art. Teachers also liked the two extension activities in the program, an interview with the author/artist and a tour of his studio, both of which include brief video tape segments.

Teachers liked programs that gave them some control over instructional parameters and enabled them to customize program features to the needs of individual students. Examples of customization options available in some programs are the ability to change the size, style, and color of text; to turn the highlighting on or off, to modify the speed with which text is read aloud; and to determine what portion of the text is read aloud automatically (e.g., the entire selection or individual sentences). Unfortunately, only a few software series offer features such as these, and no program allowed teachers to control the elements they found most intrusive to the learning process: games embedded within the story and the number of hot spots per page. Teachers also expressed a desire for record keeping capabilities within programs to help in monitoring student progress; again, no program offered this feature.

Teachers' recommendations. Teachers recommended that great care be taken in selecting talking storybook programs for use in teaching reading skills to students with learning disabilities. The suggestions that follow summarize their major points:

- Talking storybooks are typically rich and engaging programs that appeal to students, keep their attention, and motive them. However, beware of programs with more entertainment than educational value.

- Select programs that are enhanced versions of excellent storybooks for children. Don't settle for poor or mediocre children's literature because it is found on a CD-ROM disc.

- Give preference to programs where the focus is on the story (rather than on dazzling graphics, superfluous hot spots, or unrelated activities).

- Choose programs that are appropriate for students' ages in content, text, graphics, and narration. Avoid programs where one element (e.g., the content of the story) is clearly discrepant from another element (e.g., the graphics).

- Consider the readability level of the story and other characteristics of the text (e.g., appearance, interactivity).

- Carefully evaluate the graphical components of the program and whether they enhance or diminish the reading experience.

- Whenever possible, select programs that are both age-appropriate and skill-appropriate for students.

- Select programs with useful instructional features such as writing activities; avoid programs where game-like activities interfere with the story.

- Look for programs where teachers can control important instructional parameters such as the size of the text and the speed at which text is read aloud.

Observational Studies of Students with Learning Disabilities

The second phase of Project LITT focused on the ways in which students with learning disabilities interacted with hypermedia-based children's literature programs and the gains in reading skills that resulted from these interactions. In the first study, students were observed as they engaged in unstructured interactions with the software. In the second study, increasing levels of instructional support were introduced to determine if such support could result in improved reading performance.

Students' Unstructured Interactions with Talking Storybooks

Six elementary grade students with learning disabilities were introduced to a range of hypermedia-based children's literature programs, then observed as they interacted with these programs under unstructured classroom conditions. Programs were carefully chosen to represent the heterogeneity of this body of software. Included were:

Type 1: 6 programs with high text interactivity, no embedded games or activities, and varying interactivity with graphics

Type 2: 6 programs with varying text interactivity and games and activities embedded within the story

Type 3: 6 programs with varying text interactivity, definitions or glossary features, and picture label hot spots

Each student interacted with three different programs of one type, each for a total of 2 hours over 4 days. Students were observed as they worked at the computer and videotaped. Before each intervention began, students' reading skills were assessed by asking them to read aloud 50 words selected from the story in the software program. At the end of each intervention, students read the words again, retold the story in their own words, and answered questions about their perceptions of the software.

The intervention in this study included a range of software programs because we hypothesized that some types of programs contained greater numbers of attractive nuisances than other types. When students with learning disabilities interacted with programs with many opportunities for interactions with graphics and those with game-like activities, we believed students would be more likely to be distracted from the reading task and thus less likely to learn new words. This did not prove to be the case.

Preliminary analyses of the data from this study suggest two important findings:

- Students with learning disabilities chose nonreading activities over reading activities when interacting with all types of talking storybook programs.

- In unstructured interactions with talking storybook programs, students with learning disabilities did not show appreciable gains in reading skills.

Analyses of videotapes indicate that students spent at least 40% of each 2-hour instructional period engaged in nonreading activities such as interacting with hot spots in the graphics, playing games, and engaging in other types of activities. Nonreading time ranged from 42.8% to 70.3% of the time, with an average across 12 programs of 64.6%. Given those results, it is not surprising that students as a group gained an average of only 2.4 words per program.

Instructional Interventions

In the second observational study, students interacted with the same types of talking storybook programs but increasing amounts of instructional support were imposed. The purpose of this support was to focus students' attention on the reading task in order to maximize opportunities for gaining reading skills.

One important aspect of the support conditions was to limit the amount of time students spent in nonreading activities. However, because these types of activities appear to be highly motivating to students, they were not totally eliminated. On each page of a storybook, students were allowed to access two hot spots in the graphics. Also, at the end of each instructional session, students were given 5 minutes of free time when they could reread the story, interact with hot spots, or play games or other activities.

Each of the six students in the study interacted with 4 talking storybook programs, the first two under moderate instructional support conditions and the second two under high instructional support conditions. In the moderate support condition, students were asked to read each page of the story aloud. In the high support condition, students were required to read each page aloud until they reached a criterion of 90% accuracy.

In both conditions, storybooks with two types of text interactivity were used. Stories with medium text interactivity allow students to hear the entire page read aloud. Those with high text interactivity allow student to hear not only the entire page but also individual words read aloud. These variations in text interactivity allowed students to experience four different levels of instructional support:

- Moderate support, whole page only: Students read each page aloud once.

- Moderate support, whole page and individual words: Students read each page aloud once, after reading 3 individual words on the page.

- High support, whole page only: Students read each page aloud to criterion.

- High support, whole page and individual words: Students read each page and 3 individual words per page to criterion.

Analyses of the data from this study are currently underway. However, preliminary results suggest that, as the level of support increases, students are more likely to show gains in reading skill. Table

Table 52.1. Average Number of Words Gained from Pretest to Posttest

Condition	Type of Support	Page/Words	Reading Gains
1	Moderate	page	4.8 words
2	Moderate	page, words	6.8 words
3	High	page	8.8 words
4	High	page, words	9.6 words

52.1 presents the average number of words gained from pretest to posttest for the 6 students in this study. Clearly, there appears to be an increase in word recognition gains as the students progressed through the four levels of support. These results are even more interesting when it is recalled that students in unstructured interactions with the software gained an average of 2.4 words.

References

Armstrong, K.; Brand, J.; Glass, G.; and Regan, L. (1995, October). Special software for special kids. *Technology & Learning*, 16, 56-61.

Boone, R.; Higgins, K.; Falba, C.; and Langley, W. (1993). Cooperative text: Reading and writing in a hypermedia environment. *LD Forum*, 18, 28-37.

Bottge, B. A. and Hasselbring, T. S. (1993). A comparison of two approaches for teaching complex, authentic mathematics problems to adolescents in remedial math classes. *Exceptional Children*, 59, 556-566.

Erickson, K. and Staples, A. (1995, October). Living Books and talking book strips: Interactive reading lessons for children with developmental disabilities. Paper presented at the Closing the Gap Microcomputer Technology in Special Education and Rehabilitation Conference, Minneapolis, MN.

Lewis, R. B. (1998). Assistive technology and learning disabilities: Today's realities and tomorrow's promises. *Journal of Learning Disabilities*, 31, 16-25, 54.

Lewis, R. B. and Doorlag, D. H. (1999). *Teaching Special Students in General Education Classrooms (5th Ed.)*. Upper Saddle River, NJ: Merrill.

Lundberg, I. (1995). The computer as a tool of remediation in the education of students with learning disabilities—A theory-based approach. *Learning Disability Quarterly*, 18, 89-99.

MacArthur, C. A. and Haynes, J. B. (1995). Student Assistant Learning from Text (SALT): A hypermedia reading aid. *Journal of Learning Disabilities*, 28, 150-159.

Olofsson, Å. (1992). Can dyslexia be compensated for by computer-aided reading and synthetic speech? Fourth International ISAA Conference, Stockholm.

Reid, R.; Maag, J. W.; and Vasa, S. F. (1993). Attention deficit hyperactivity disorder as a disability category: A critique. *Exceptional Children*, 60, 198-214.

Ruiz, N. T. (1989). An optimal learning environment for Rosemary. *Exceptional Children*, 56, 130-144.

Ruiz, N. T. (1995). The social construction of ability and disability: II. Optimal and at-risk lessons in a bilingual special education classroom. *Journal of Learning Disabilities*, 28, 491-502.

Sindelar, P. T. (1987). Increasing reading fluency. *Teaching Exceptional Children*, 19(2), 59-60.

Wise, B. W. and Olson, R. K. (1994). Computer speech and the remediation of reading and spelling problems. *Journal of Special Education Technology*, 12, 207-220.

Chapter 53

Integrating Assistive Technology into the Standard Curriculum

Assistive technology (AT) is defined as any item, piece of equipment, or product, whether acquired commercially, off the shelf, modified, or customized, that is used to increase, maintain, or improve the functional capabilities of individuals with disabilities. (P.L. 101-407, The Technology Related Assistance Act of 1988).

The 1997 reauthorization of the Individuals with Disabilities Education Act (IDEA) emphasizes the importance of technology and the need to share cutting-edge information about advances in the field. The law requires that assistive technology devices and services be considered for all children identified as having an exceptional education need. These amendments mark a significant shift in how educators view assistive technology which previously had been viewed almost exclusively within a rehabilitative or remediative context. Now, within the context of planning individualized education plans (IEP), technology is being considered as a viable tool for expanding access to the general education curriculum. However, there is still much work to be done to ensure that IEP teams consider the maximum benefits of technology use.

Considering Assistive Technology in the IEP

The new requirements in IDEA '97 to consider assistive technology (AT) devices and services for all students with disabilities creates

"Integrating Assistive Technology into the Standard Curriculum," by Cynthia Warger, from *ERIC/OSEP Digest*, E568, Educational Resources Information Center (ERIC), ERIC Identifier ED426517, 1998.

a massive task for school districts. Already, special educators across the country are reporting an increased number of referrals for children with mild disabilities in which the issue is access to the curriculum and productivity once in the curriculum. School-based professionals are finding that the fix-it approach taken with traditional assistive technology applications is not appropriate for these new types of technology referrals. More often than not, instructional issues are at the heart of these referrals—they require educators to start with the curriculum and then ask how tools might assist students in achieving the outcomes.

Thus, school districts are searching for tools that they can use to ensure that IEP teams meet the intent and the spirit of the law. To assist school districts with this goal, Gayl Bowser and Penny Reed have developed the Education TECH Point system which educators can use as a tool to develop effective assistive technology delivery systems. The TECH Point system offers educators a strategy for identifying specific points in the planning process where AT should be considered. The TECH Points are:

- Initial referral question.
- Evaluation questions.
- Extended assessment questions.
- Plan development questions.
- Implementation questions.
- Periodic review questions.

At each point, questions are posed which reflect issues that must be addressed. The TECH Point structure provides a way to effectively organize and monitor AT utilization while enabling programs to tailor activities to match each student's needs.

State Level Support for Assistive Technology

States can support local education agencies in meeting these new requirements to consider assistive technology in each child's IEP. To ensure that technology benefits children with disabilities, states need to implement policies and practices that support its effective use. Louis Danielson, Director of the Division of Research to Practice at OSEP, suggests that state directors of special education put into place a clear policy on assistive technology that includes:

- A statement of desired AT outcomes.

- Policies for delivering AT services.
- Staff development and technical assistance policies.
- Verification that the technology plan includes research-based practices.
- Mechanisms for interdisciplinary involvement.
- Policies for purchasing, using, and managing equipment.
- Strategies for obtaining adequate funding.
- Strategies for communicating these policies.

Promoting Access to the Curriculum: Promising Practices

As a result of the new law, technology is increasingly being recommended to help students with cognitive disabilities achieve in a challenging curriculum. Technology that supports students in accessing the curriculum does not need to be expensive or complicated to make a difference in learning. Both low tech and high tech applications have been used successfully to ensure students' success in the general education curriculum. What do we know about the positive benefits of using technology in academic subject areas to help children with disabilities achieve to high standards? The following research-based applications have been selected to show how technology is being integrated into curriculum and instruction to support a wide range of student abilities.

Enhancing Literacy Goals

Michigan State University researcher Carol Sue Englert has developed a web-based curriculum for elementary students with mild disabilities that enhances literacy learning, particularly writing. The web site called TELE-Web (which stands for Technology-Enhanced Learning Environments on the Web) serves as a literacy development environment. The web site provides tools that help students develop performance abilities in reading and writing, in addition to independent learning skills.

TELE-Web is set up in the classroom as four central environments—writing room, reading room, library, and publishing room. In each environment, students are able to receive cognitive and social support. The following example shows how TELE-Web was integrated into a fourth grade unit on castles:

481

TELE-Writing Room. A KWL (what I know, want to know, have learned about) activity on castles; retelling stories in one's own words; creating cognitive webs play writing; story writing.

TELE-Reading Room. Castle spelling words; castle chat.

TELE-Library. Internet search on castles; castle word-sort; email to people knowledgeable about castles in Poland and Scotland.

TELE-Publishing Room. Stories for editing and comments; journal of castle life contrasts. Preliminary research suggests that with TELE-Web children are more motivated to write, and that they are writing longer and more descriptive stories.

Improving Access to the Science Curriculum

Judy Zorfass at the Education Development Center, Inc., in Massachusetts is finding that technology tools can be integrated into challenging science curriculum and instruction to ensure access for students with disabilities. Zorfass' Project ASSIST (All Students in Supported Inquiry-Based Science with Technology) brings together teachers, science specialists, special educators, and technology specialists on a regular basis to plan, act, and reflect upon student learning in science, in inclusive classrooms, supported by technology. To support educators in talking about children's science learning, Zorfass and her colleagues created an action reflection process. The team cycles and then re-cycles through these phases:

Plan activities. During the planning phase the classroom teacher and the specialists develop a lesson containing clear science learning goals. The lesson is related to the science standards, includes modifications for students with disabilities, and is supported by technology where appropriate.

Implement instruction. The teacher implements the lesson, however, some of the team members also participate. Their role is to closely observe and gather data on children's responses to the lesson, as well as assist with instruction when appropriate.

Reflect on progress. The reflection phase occurs soon after the lesson. Each team member shares the data he or she has gathered regarding student learning. The teacher and the specialists describe, interpret, and reflect on the students' work as it relates to the criteria that have been set.

Improving Concept Development in Mathematics

John Woodward of the University of Puget Sound in Washington has been studying how technology can be integrated into mathematical problem-solving activities to provide access to students with cognitive disabilities.

Unlike traditional math story problem lessons where students read a problem in text and are expected to calculate answers, Woodward uses computer-based spreadsheet programs in conjunction with real-life problems. Spreadsheets are an excellent tool because they model or provide visual representations of the problem, crunch the calculations—which is a tedious turn-off for many youngsters, but especially true for students with disabilities—and thereby focus the students' attention on understanding the mathematical operations in a real-life context. Spreadsheets free students, who heretofore had difficulty with math, to keep asking questions, to continue analyzing the visual representations of the data, and eventually to use their higher level thinking skills to formulate conclusions.

Woodward has successfully field tested numerous lessons using his research-based approach.

Elements to Consider in Implementing Technology

- Locate equipment where instruction and learning are taking place.
- Technology needs to be in the classroom and accessible to the child.
- Select low tech applications whenever possible.
- Integrate the use of technology into lessons in a purposeful and meaningful way.
- Have the same equipment used in the classroom available in the child's home to promote continuity of learning, if possible.
- Offer training and technical support to classroom teachers initially.
- When the technology is available in the home, provide training to family members.

- View the initial fiscal and human resources as an investment that the child will continue to benefit from in subsequent years.

- Don't reinvent the wheel each year—when possible use the technology that is already in place.

Conclusion

The potential of assistive technology to improve and enhance the lives of individuals with disabilities is virtually unlimited. Now, with the help of current Federal laws, assistive technology will provide more children with the opportunity to maximize their learning in a challenging curriculum.

Resources

Behrmann, M. (January 1995). Assistive technology for students with mild disabilities. *ERIC Digest* E529.

Readings on the use of technology for individuals with disabilities. ERIC Mini-Bib EB16. (July 1996).

Resources on the use of technology for individuals with disabilities. ERIC Mini-Bib EB17. (July 1996).

Woodward, J. Redoing the numbers: Using technology to enhance mathematical literacy in secondary classrooms. *TEACHING Exceptional Children*.

Woodward, J. and Baxter, J. (1997). The effects of an innovative approach to mathematics on academically low achieving students in inclusive settings. *Exceptional Children*, 63(3), 373-388.

Zorfass, J. (1998). Successful Science for Every Student: How Technology Helps (video-based professional development package). Newton, MA: Education Development Center, Inc.

Chapter 54

Job Accommodations for People with Learning Disabilities

As a person with dyslexia, you are entitled to reasonable accommodations from your employer if they are covered by the Americans with Disabilities Act. Before asking for help, do what you can on your own. Many people with dyslexia get help from their co-workers, spouses and friends. Some find ways to accommodate themselves. Many dyslexic sales people have found ways to get their customers to write the order.

If you wish to request help from your employer, decide whether or not you wish to disclose your disability. Disclosure is becoming easier as the stigma lessens, but discrimination is not yet cleansed from our country. If you do not wish to disclose your dyslexia, explain what you want using positive terms. Many times, a productivity argument has won the day. Examples:

> Have you seen XYZ software? It gets the computer to talk so that you can hear what's on the screen. Since my job requires so much detailed reading it would be wonderful if I could hear it. Then there would be less errors.

From "Accommodations for People with Dyslexia: Coping in the Workplace," by Dale S. Brown. This article originally appeared in the Fall 1996 issue of *Perspectives*," the newsletter of the International Dyslexia Association. © 1996 International Dyslexia Association. Reprinted with permission. Despite the older date of this article, it contains information that will be helpful to those seeking to learn about the job accommodations and strategies available to the learning disabled.

I need Mary to proof my work before you see it. That way we can both pay more attention to the content and not worry about the way it's typed.

Regardless of the strategy you take, consider practicing the conversation beforehand with a friend or coworker. Your accommodation request must be well-thought out, and the easier it is for your employer, the more likely your success. You may have to disclose your dyslexia, particularly if the accommodation you need is difficult to obtain or against the culture of where you work. If you work for a big company and you have reason to believe that your boss will not be open minded, you may want to visit the human resource department. They are often knowledgeable about the Americans with Disabilities Act and usually consider it part of their job to help employees with disabilities. Following are some problems which are common to people with dyslexia and suggested solutions. Use them to think about possible accommodations or to start a discussion with your employer.

If you find that you need help in thinking about your situation, call the President's Committee Job Accommodation Network (JAN). Describe your disability to the consultant who answers the phone and he or she will help you think about accommodation options. Their phone number is 800-526-7234.

Problem: You have severe difficulty reading. As a matter of fact, someone is reading this article to you.

Suggested Solutions

1. Ask another employee to read to you.

2. Get written menus placed on your voice mail.

3. Your boss tells you what needs to be done rather than writing down directions.

4. Someone highlights important information and you read that material first.

5. A reading machine is bought for you.

6. Voice input is added to your work computer.

7. You phone people instead of writing them.

Problem: Your reading, problem is not severe, but it is still hard for you to read large amounts of material.

Suggested Solutions

1. Discuss the material with coworkers. Obtain their ideas and summaries.

2. Find other ways besides reading to obtain the same information.

3. Manage your work so that you have the time to read slowly and complete the task.

4. Get information through drawings, diagrams, and flow charts. Your supervisor or team members may be able to organize some of your information in this way.

5. Voice output on your computer may assist you.

Problem: You have visual perceptual problems, causing you to have difficulty locating objects, so you lose things frequently.

Suggested Solutions

1. Keep your work area well organized. Your supervisor and team should assure that common areas such as tool stations, files, and bookshelves stay neat.

2. Color code items.

3. Keep items on shelves, bulletin boards or other places where you can see them.

4. Put important objects, such as keys, in the same place each time you put them down.

5. Assure that you have sufficient light.

Problem: You have auditory perceptual problems, giving you difficulty in following verbal directions.

Suggested Solutions

1. Ask people to give you instructions slowly and clearly in a quiet location.

2. Ask people to write down important information.

3. Ask people to show you what needs to be done and then watch you do it.

4. Take notes as you hear directions. Ask a person who heard those directions to review your notes.

5. Repeat instructions back to people. Make sure they listen to you and confirm that you understand.

6. Tape record important procedure and instructions. Play back and review.

7. On complicated projects, write a memorandum to your supervisor that outlines your understanding of what you are to do. Get their sign off before you proceed.

Problem: You have difficulty understanding the hidden meanings of what is said.

Suggested Solutions

1. Ask people to talk to you directly and not hint.

2. In some cases, you may want to make hidden meanings explicit and say, for example, "Are you trying to tell me to be neater?"

Problem: You have difficulty with remembering and sticking to deadlines.

Suggested Solutions

1. Use a daily calendar and alarm feature on your work computer. Some software will ring and put a written reminder on your computer screen.

2. Use a signal watch.

3. Use a tickler file. This file has a section for each month and a section for each day. You can put follow-up reminders in the file. Get in the habit of reviewing the file each day for the deadlines.

4. Ask your supervisor to remind you of important deadlines or to review priorities on a regular basis.

Problem: You have difficulty with handling interruptions. Each interruption interferes with your ability to get started again.

Suggested Solutions

1. Use a "Do not disturb sign."

2. When interrupted, pause and write down what you were doing so that you remember it when you need to resume your work.

3. Do one task at a time. Start new tasks only when the earlier one is complete.

4. Initiate as many calls as possible avoid interruptions from callbacks by telling the receptionist you will call back, and hang up if you get an answering machine.

5. Arrange your time so that you are available for interruptions for part of the day and have quiet time during the rest of the day. If you stick to a routine, people will often respect it.

6. When someone who is not your boss tries to interrupt you, keep your eyes on your work and don't engage in conversation.

Problem: You have difficulty with the physical act of writing.

Suggested Solutions

1. Use typewriters and computer keyboards as a substitute for handwriting.

2. Have an assistant hand write when necessary.

3. Teach others to read your writing.

Problem: You can write, but there are frequent grammatical errors and misspellings.

Suggested Solutions

1. Use spell check and grammar check software.

2. Obtain clerical support.

3. Ask co-workers, friends, or family to proof your work before you turn it in.

Problem: You reverse numbers frequently as you calculate figures.

Suggested Solutions

1. State numbers aloud when you write them down or touch the calculator key. Pause and assure that you have written it correctly.

2. Use a piece of paper with a hole punched out of it to check your numbers.

3. Use a talking calculator.

Problem: You have difficulty with left and right. You have been known to get lost in your own office building.

Suggested Solutions

1. Use maps.

2. Find people who will go with you and navigate.

3. Stay late and practice going from one place to another.

4. After you have been on the job a while, offer to put up pictures or find ways to place cues in public space so that there is a visual distinction between left and right. Get maps up on the walls.

Problem: You are easily distracted and the work is done in open space with systems furniture.

Suggested Solutions

1. Ask for a private place to work.

2. Arrange to work at home on occasion.

3. Negotiate for the quietest and least distracting location (usually along comers away from doors).

4. Arrange to use libraries, file rooms, private offices, store rooms, and other enclosed spaces when they are not in use.

Problem: You have trouble remembering details such as names, numbers and specific facts, particularly the first time the information is presented. This is usually due to short term memory problems.

Suggested Solutions

1. Use mnemonic devices and acronyms such as remembering the color of the rainbow by syllables. For example, ROY G BIV are the initials of the colors of the rainbow (Red, Orange, Yellow, Green, Blue, Indigo, Violet.).

2. Organize details on paper so that they can be quickly looked up through diagrams, flow charts, or cheat sheets.

3. Develop ways of drilling yourself on the new material.

4. Use your computer software. Sometimes well-designed menus and help features can assist you.

5. Have your supervisor check with you to be sure that you understand.

Remember, if you need assistance, you may call the President's Committee job Accommodation Network at 1-800-526-7234.

Part Seven

Coping Strategies

Chapter 55

Parents: Helping Yourself and Your Learning Disabled Child

Parents: Helping Yourself and Your Child

Parents of children with learning disabilities are faced with many challenges. These challenges can be emotional, intellectual, and even financial. Parents must become knowledgeable about the educational assessment process, special education services, and education law. They must also master a new vocabulary that enables them to work cooperatively with clinicians and school personnel. All of these challenges can contribute to pressures that upset the family equilibrium. The following may help parents to meet these challenges more successfully, support school success, and promote quality family time.

Acknowledging the Problem

Acknowledgement begins with understanding. As children's first teachers and role models, parents have a unique perspective from which to understand and report strengths, weaknesses, interests, and patterns of learning and development.

- Pay close attention to your child's behavior, especially as it relates to school and learning related issues.

"Parents: Helping Yourself and Your Child," "Understanding Your Children's Learning Needs," "Parents as Advocates," "Choosing a Tutor for Your Child," and "Promoting Confidence." © 2001 National Center for Learning Disabilities. Reprinted with permission. For more information from the National Center for Learning Disabilities, visit their website at http://www.ncld.org.

- Be prepared to share information about the nature and scope of any problems or concerns (be specific).

- Gather information from others who work with your child. Try to keep an open mind and avoid becoming overwhelmed, frightened, or adversarial. The more meaningful information you can collect from a variety of perspectives, the better an advocate you will be during any decision making process.

Finding Information

Finding accurate information depends upon knowing what questions to ask and to whom they should be addressed. The language of special education can be confusing, and parents, should request clarification of terms and ask that any recommended educational practices or interventions be explained.

- Seek assistance from the proper school district personnel; learn how to request services, accommodations, evaluations, and initiate meetings or facilitate communication among those involved in your child's education.

- As appropriate, seek help from qualified professionals outside of the school system: tutors, educational therapists, psychologists, social workers, speech/language pathologists, and occupational and physical therapists.

- Organize your questions and concerns; be ready to address sensitive issues; try to anticipate questions and concerns that might be raised by others in the decision-making process.

- Clarify roles and responsibilities of all those who are involved in your child's education, understand the routines and expectations set for classroom participation, and identify key personnel (resource room teacher, teaching assistant) who will be able to monitor progress and provide feedback on a regular basis.

- Do not rely on hearsay or on someone else's past experience; every student's situation is unique and should be considered individually.

- Beware of what you hear or read in the media; educational issues in general, and learning disabilities specifically, receive a lot of attention from the press. Controversy about legislation, medication, special education practices, and teacher training and certification are common. Verify information with reliable sources.

- Know your rights; become familiar with your entitlements and the protections that are granted under Federal and state law. Evaluation procedures, the individualized educational planning process (IEP, IFSP), and the delivery of educational services, are all carefully regulated. Remember that parents and school district personnel are equal partners in educational planning, and are bound by the same mandate—to afford every child the benefits of appropriate educational opportunities.

Becoming an Advocate

Parents are encouraged to be active participants in all aspects of educational planning. Be familiar with the rights and safeguards (due process) incorporated into law which assure your access to and participation in educational decision-making.

- Enlist the help of others who might be able to assist in planning or in decision making; this includes any caregivers, professionals, or friends who can provide information or support.

- Children should be helped to understand the nature of their disability, the types of strategies and accommodations that might be helpful, and how to seek assistance in meeting their specific needs.

- Parents should encourage children to believe in their own potential and to be aware of their areas of relative strength and weakness. This will promote their ability to be academically and socially successful and to become better self-advocates.

- Realistic expectations should be set; matching children's interests and abilities with the resources available in school and in the community will greatly enhance progress.

- Parents, teachers, and children should be ready to face frustrations and unexpected challenges; don't allow discouragement to undermine your hard work. Progress and change are sometimes slow in coming, but with creativity, flexibility, determination, and commitment, positive outcomes are often achieved.

Getting Support

Parent support groups can be great sources of information and emotional support. Networking with other parents and professionals can also be helpful. Many organizations provide support, training and

497

information to parents. Some groups help parents locate other parents with similar concerns. Attorneys, educational advocates, representatives from educational organizations, teachers, other school personnel and parents are all potential sources of useful information.

Understanding Your Children's Learning Needs

Each of us has a unique learning style. We all take in new information and acquire new skills differently. Understanding the particular circumstances in which children learn best can help parents work more effectively and become better partners with teachers and other professionals.

Although evaluations can provide information about academic strengths and weaknesses as well as optimal teaching approaches and educational settings, parents can gather important information about their children's learning needs during their daily interactions.

The following guidelines can assist parents in identifying how to help their children learn best.

Consider Time of Day

Try to identify when your children:

- Are best able to sustain focus and attention
- Have the necessary energy to work
- Are least likely to be distracted by other events or circumstances

Select Preferred Place(s) to Work

Try to identify a space where:

- Work is most easily accomplished
- Adults can be close by
- Materials are readily available
- Distractions are minimized
- Your children are comfortable

Understand How Information Is Best Learned

Think about how your children prefer:

- To have new information presented (seeing, hearing, reading)
- To have information reinforced (repetition, elaboration)

Encourage Work with Others

Try to identify:

- The type of information, or tasks, where others can be of help
- Opportunities for your children to work with others in one-to-one settings, as well as in small groups

Increase Motivation

Try to understand:

- What motivates your children
- The types of rewards and consequences that will be meaningful to your children

Encourage Independence

Try to understand:

- How you can support your children to become independent learners
- How your children organize materials and work space, and track assignments and projects

Communicate with Your Children

Talk with your children directly about their feelings regarding:

- Their learning strengths and areas of need
- Strategies that have been helpful in the past
- Preferred settings, and ways, to work with others
- Functional workspace and necessary materials

Use Assistive Technology

Consider accessible devices that could be of help, including:

- Word processing, graphics, database, and spreadsheet programs for the computer

- Text-to-speech and speech-to-text software programs
- electronic organizers, schedulers, and address books
- Hand-held electronic spellers
- Portable tape recorders

Help Provide Access to Good Information

Encourage your children to make use of:

- Textbooks/reference books
- Internet and World Wide Web sites
- Libraries
- Materials from helping organizations and information clearinghouses

Parents as Advocates

Many parents, upon discovering that their child has a learning disability, become anxious (or even angry), and wonder what they can do. Gathering information, networking with others (parents and professionals), and becoming advocates are ways for parents to help children reach their potential.

Know Your Legal Rights

When parents and school personnel suspect the presence of an educationally disabling condition, Federal law offers children and parents a wide range of guarantees including the right to a free evaluation and the provision of appropriate services or accommodations in the least restrictive settings.

Become Involved with the School

Regular and ongoing communication with your child's teacher is an important way to monitor progress and to insure that concerns are addressed in a timely manner. Be sure to share your own observations with teachers; knowing more about your child's strengths, weakness, and behaviors at home can provide a valuable framework for teachers to understand behaviors observed at school.

Maintaining open avenues of communication with school personnel reinforces the message to both your child and to school staff that your child's education is of great importance; it also affirms your willingness to be an active partner in your child's school career.

Modifications and Accommodations

Once your child is identified as having a learning disability, a number of services can be provided. These provisions are meant to equalize opportunities, and to assure that appropriate educational opportunities are afforded to your child, and not to lower academic standards.

Whether or not your child qualifies for special education services, you are encouraged to meet with teachers to identify (and if possible, to implement) helpful modifications or changes in classroom routines.

Listen to Your Child

Whether or not children go bounding off to school in the morning, their feelings about school may provide valuable insights about the level of difficulty, ease, and satisfaction with which they experience school. Frequent complaints of boredom or illness (headaches, stomach aches) often mask other school difficulties.

Learn about Learning Disabilities

Read as much as you can about LD and related issues. (Note: Beware of what you read or hear in the media. When in doubt, verify reports with reliable expert sources.)

Seek Support

Information, guidance, and support are available through a wide network of agencies, organizations, and informal parent networks. Contact your State Education Department and local school district for printed material about regulations that exist under state or local law. Advocacy organizations and support groups (national, local) can provide personal comfort as well as information about your rights and available resources.

Choosing a Tutor for Your Child

Many parents seek additional help for their children by having them work with tutors. Tutors can provide individualized and specialized assistance that will enhance children's learning skills and support their teacher's instructional work in the classroom. Following are a few suggestions for parents to help ensure a good match between a student and tutor.

- Identify your child's needs

    Determine the specific subject areas of need.

    Make note of learning strategies, strengths, and weaknesses.

    Assess organizational and study skills.

- Include your child in the selection process.

    Discuss the goals of tutoring.

    Assess attitude and motivation about working with a tutor.

    Find out whether your child has a preference for the gender of the tutor.

- Include your child's teacher in the decision-making.

    Confirm the need for extra help.

    Prioritize the work that the tutor and your child will cover.

    Make sure that the teacher will work collaboratively with the tutor.

    Formulate a plan for increased feedback from the teacher regarding your child's progress.

    Request information and materials that will help students link their new skills to classroom success.

- Identify options.

    Look into private tutors (experienced teachers with advanced degree, undergraduate or graduate students, high school students, volunteers).

    Look into after-school programs (which can provide a structured learning environment and adult assistance).

- Ask about credentials and previous experience of potential tutors.

    Discuss their formal academic training.

    Discuss their previous teaching experience.

    Discuss their previous tutoring experience (work with children of the same age, experience with the specific issues that need to be addressed).

- Discuss the format and structure of tutoring sessions.

    Decide on the number of sessions per week.

    Find a convenient location for tutoring (one that will allow work to be done effectively).

    Assess costs (regular fees, additional costs for materials or transportation).

- Determine the nature of work to be covered.

    Decide how much time will be devoted to the direct support of school work (homework, book reports, term papers, writing assignments, studying for tests).

    Decide how much time will be devoted to independent skill building (learning and study skills, reading, writing, research).

- Determine how the tutor will coordinate with others.

    Formulate a plan for the tutor to have regular communication with school personnel.

    Formulate a plan for the tutor to have ongoing communication with parents (including the assessment and reporting of progress and proposed modifications to the teaching approach).

Finding the right match between a student and a tutor (or after-school program) can be a time-consuming process that requires careful thought and planning. The rewards, as measured by improved schoolwork and increased self-confidence, are well worth the effort.

Promoting Confidence

Students with learning disabilities face special challenges, not only in the areas of learning and skill mastery, but also in the areas of self-esteem and self-actualization. These students are often prone to attribute their successes to luck or chance, and are quick to blame others for poor grades or for incomplete work. The process of teaching these students to be more aware of their limitations and more confident in their abilities extends throughout the course of their educational careers, and is likely to open windows of opportunity in school as well as in the world of work.

Encourage Risk-Taking

- Help students to clarify goals and strategies.

- See that goals set are realistic and attainable.
- Be prepared to evaluate outcomes.
- Encourage students to own their successes.
- Establish learning environments that are flexible and allow for spontaneity and change.
- Reward good effort and perseverance, not just success.

Help Students to Learn from Their Frustrations

- Provide immediate feedback that is instructive and non-punitive.
- Offer feedback that is both general and specific, and include information within the social/behavioral domains.

Recognize Individual Differences

- Remember that no two people are alike, and each of us needs different amounts and types of feedback to learn effectively.
- Some people like to study in a quiet room; others prefer to listen to music; the right way is the way that works best.

Be Patient and Understanding

- Offer praise, positive reinforcement and constructive feedback for self-correction.
- Be respectful of the students' rights to privacy.
- Be a good listener.

Maintain a Sense of Humor and Don't Be Afraid to Show It

- Humor can be an effective tool to diffuse bad feelings and soften disappointment.
- Real-life events are filled with teachable moments; use imagination and be creative.

Teach Students the Benefits of Negotiation

- Help students to understand that teachers and parents are not mind-readers and that being able to ask for help is a strength.

- Encourage students to appreciate the power of conversation; at the same time emphasize the importance of clarifying their needs before they turn to someone for help.

- Don't overlook opportunities to teach about feelings during this process, and help them to understand the benefits of compromise.

Be a Good Role Model

- Think aloud when making decisions.

- Don't be afraid to make mistakes and self-correct; repair strategies are wonderful tools that are best taught in real-life situations.

- Parents need to be partners with school personnel; positive communication between parents, teachers, and other staff will give students permission to do their best.

Acknowledge Students' Rights

- Children may not always be insightful thinkers, but they often have strong opinions that drive their language and behavior; help them to understand feelings and clarify wishes.

- Discuss problems and concerns objectively, and share issues with the school personnel who can effect change.

Maintain High Expectations

- Be sure that there is consensus among parents, children, and teachers about academic and behavioral goals.

- Special care should be taken to assure that expectations are age and developmentally appropriate.

Chapter 56

Tips for Developing Self-Esteem in Your Learning Disabled Child

Most parents are aware that their child's feelings of self-worth are linked with their success socially and academically. But, sometimes parents are unaware of how easy it is to damage their child's self-esteem without even realizing it. Research shows that children with learning disabilities are more likely to suffer from lack of self-esteem than their peers. The Coordinated Campaign for Learning Disabilities, along with Dr. Robert Brooks, have compiled a list of ways parents can develop positive feelings of self-worth in their children.

Help your child feel special and appreciated. Research indicates that one of the main factors that contributes to a child developing hope and becoming resilient is the presence of at least one adult who helps the child to feel special and appreciated; an adult who does not ignore a child's problems, but focuses energy on a child's strengths. One way for parents to do this is to set aside special time during the week alone with each child in the household. If the child is young, it is even helpful for the parent to say, "When I read to you or play with you, I won't even answer the phone if it rings." Also, during these special times, focus on things that your child enjoys doing so that he/she has an opportunity to relax and to display his/her strengths.

Reprinted with permission from "Tips for Developing Self-Esteem," by the Coordinated Campaign for Learning Disabilities (CCLD), a collaboration of leading U.S. nonprofit learning disabilities organizations. © 2000 Coordinated Campaign for Learning Disabilities. All Rights Reserved.

Help your child to develop problem-solving and decision-making skills. High self-esteem is associated with solid problem-solving skills. For example, if your child is having difficulty with a friend, you can ask him/her to think about a couple of ways of solving the situation. Don't worry if your child can't think of solutions immediately, you can help him/her reflect upon possible solutions. Also, try role-playing situations with your child to help demonstrate the steps involved in problem solving.

Avoid comments that are judgmental and, instead, frame them in more positive terms. For example, a comment that often comes out in an accusatory way is, "try harder and put in more of an effort." Many children do try hard and still have difficulty. Instead say, "we have to figure out better strategies to help you learn." Children are less defensive when the problem is cast as strategies that must be changed rather than as something deficient with their motivation. This approach also reinforces problem-solving skills.

Be an empathetic parent. Many well-meaning parents, out of their own frustration, have been heard to say such things as, "Why don't you listen to me?!" or "why don't you use your brain?" If your child is having difficulty with learning, it is best to be empathetic and say to the child that you know he/she is having difficulty; then the parent can cast the difficulty into a problem to be solved and involve the child in thinking about possible solutions.

Provide choices for your child. This will also minimize power struggles that may arise. For example, ask your child if he/she would like to be reminded 5 or 10 minutes before bedtime to get ready for bed. These beginning choices help to set the foundation for a feeling of control of one's life.

Do not compare siblings. It is important not to compare siblings and to highlight the strengths of all children in the family.

Highlight your child's strengths. Unfortunately, many youngsters view themselves in a negative way, especially in terms of school. Make a list of your child's islands of competence or areas of strength. Select one of these islands and find ways of reinforcing and displaying it. For example, if your child is a wonderful artist, display his/her artwork.

Provide opportunities for children to help. Children seem to have an inborn need to help others. Providing opportunities for children to help is a very concrete way of displaying their islands of competence and of highlighting that they have something to offer their world. Involving your child in charitable work is just one possible example. Helping others certainly boosts their self-esteem.

Have realistic expectations and goals for your child. Having realistic expectations provides the child with a sense of control. The development of self-control goes hand-in-glove with self-esteem.

If your child has a learning disability, demystify or help your child to understand the nature of his/her learning disability. Many children have fantasies and misconceptions about their learning problems that add to their distress (for example, one child said he was born with half a brain). Having realistic information provides that child not only with a sense of control, but also with a feeling that things can be done to help the situation.

Chapter 57

Stress and Students with Learning Disabilities

Stress, the perception of a threat to one's well being and the apprehension that one is unable to cope with the perceived threat, is brought about by the continual adjustments and demands that individuals place upon themselves as they react to given stimuli. As the individual is called upon to adjust to changing situations, the greater the stress which is acquired. Stress is a combination of factors that affect each individual differently. That which is stressful to one person, may not be so to another, and reactions to stressors vary among individuals. "Stress," according to one expert, "is a non-specific response of the body to a demand" (Kopolow, 1987). In the complicated worlds of our students, these demands can come from a variety of directions: academic, social, financial, familial, and others. Stress can manifest itself in ways psychological, physiological and behavioral.

For all the negative publicity it receives, stress is not necessarily a bad thing. It is not always harmful and can result from pleasant experiences as well as unpleasant ones. The human body perceives excitement in much the same way it perceives fear. Both emotions produce stress, which in turn affords the body an extra boost of energy. The physical attributes of stress, which include elevated heart and breathing rates, together with increased adrenaline flow, improve

Reprinted with permission from "Stress and Students with Learning Disabilities," by Daniel J. Berkowitz, M.A. This article originally appeared in the *Learning Assistance Association of New England Newsletter,* 11(2), 1, 4-6 (1998). © Daniel Berkowitz. Daniel Berkowitz is currently Assistant Director of the Office of Disability Services, Boston University.

muscle strength and energy levels. Physiologically, stress sharpens an individual's awareness and boosts overall energy levels just when they are needed the most. Having the knowledge and ability to harness this stress energy can help students meet physical challenges, solve problems, complete assignments, and meet their goals.

The problem here is that the human body is unable to distinguish positive stress from negative stress. Positive stress can become negative stress as the excitement of being in college turns into the fear of being in college. When negative stress becomes excessive or out of control, it becomes harmful. Physically, improved muscle strength may lead to increased muscle contractions and strain. This manifests itself through head and backaches, soreness and stiff necks, digestive problems, and spasms. If left unchecked, increased adrenaline flow can lead to an inability to concentrate, lack of sleep or constant fatigue, an unwillingness to eat or continual hunger, and a variety of nervous symptoms (e.g., grinding teeth, tapping fingers, clenching fists). Stress can also cause physiologically behavioral changes such as emotional distress, fear, forgetfulness, panic attacks, general irritability, and either an inability to communicate or excessive talking.

Students often experience a variety of difficulties making the transition from a structured, supervised high school context to a relatively unstructured college or university. For students with learning disabilities, this transition, coupled the negative effects of stress, can be especially troubling. Students with learning disabilities are more likely to feel the effects of stress in the educational environment and are more likely to exhibit signs of tension and anxiety (Brinckerhoff, Shaw, McGuire, 1993). Learning disabled students making the transition to postsecondary education may feel increased pressure to perform at the same level as their non-learning disabled peers. The increased academic expectations of college may lead some students to believe that they are incapable of living up to personal, peer, and parental expectations. Looking beyond the individual's disability, consistently high levels of stress may result not from the students current academic involvement, but from growing up in a stressful family environment (Brinckerhoff, Shaw, McGuire, 1993), parental stress brought about by unrealistic expectations for the child or a denial or ambivalence about the child's disability (Dyson 1996), or peer pressure leading to a heightened state of anxiety (Huntington & Bender, 1993).

Stress management, the ability to effectively deal with stress and stressful situations, involves a variety of coping strategies, lifestyle or behavioral changes, and methods of short term stress release. Positive coping strategies for the individual involve learning how to prioritize activities, setting realistic goals, using positive self-talk and self-hypnosis, and making time for play. Lifestyle changes involve effectively using time management strategies, maintaining good physical health (including eating and sleeping properly), and learning about what stressors most impact upon the individual. Short term stress release methods include such things as taking study breaks and going for a walk, doing regular breathing exercises, taking short mental vacations, and popping sealed air capsules (i.e., bubble paper) (Dillon, 1992), just to name a few. Wach (1989), recommends that students keep a daily journal tracking how they manage their time and which may provide clues about events which trigger stress symptoms.

It is important for learning specialists and service providers, to be able to recognize the outward signs of stress overload in students. These stress signals may include; 1) a sudden dramatic increase or decrease in academic efforts, 2) major changes in attitude or temperament (irritability, lack of enthusiasm, carelessness), 3) withdrawal or outbursts, 4) overactive or distracting behaviors (fidgeting, nervous tics, jumping from task to task, showing difficulty in concentrating, being prone to accidents, and sighing), 5) complaints of fatigue and vague illnesses, 6) problems sleeping, 7) headaches or stomachaches, 8) drug and/or alcohol use or abuse, 9) increase in allergic or asthmatic attacks, 10) avoidance of school or testing situations by direct refusal or convenient illness, 11) loss of appetite or excessive eating, and 12) antisocial or disruptive behaviors (Rubenzer, 1988).

Unfortunately, when compared to their non-disabled peers, students with learning disabilities tend to lack appropriate coping strategies for dealing with stress. This may be caused by a delay in cognitive development which could result in lower metacognitive abilities. In other words, students with learning disabilities are less likely to recognize that they have a problem for which they need help (Geisthardt & Munsch, 1996). Many learning disabled students rely on denial as a strategy for coping with stress. It is important for professional staff to help students understand that actively dealing with school-related problems is a more productive long-term strategy, and help them identify methods with which to exercise some control over their academic pursuits (Geisthardt & Munsch, 1996). Seeking the support of peers is another common coping method which may not always be appropriate for students with learning disabilities. Geisthardt & Munsch (1996) studied the coping strategies of students both with and without learning disabilities. They found that not only are learning disabled students less likely to discuss their problems with peers, but that these students also generally have smaller peer groups to turn to. In addition, the peer groups of students with learning disabilities usually include mostly other learning disabled students. In an unstructured environment (i.e., simply crying on each other's shoulder), this form of peer support may negate any potentially positive aspects of the relationship. Therefore, organizing and maintaining a professionally led student support group may prove very beneficial to students dealing with stress and other issues.

As if stress itself is not harmful enough, students engage in the abuse of a number substances which act as stress enhancers. In fact, many students believe that these substances help them to relax. Caffeine and cigarettes, with the nicotine and other chemicals they contain, work as stimulants on the body. Caffeine and cigarettes may rob the body of certain vitamins and minerals, which the body must then replace. Additionally, the cost of cigarettes may lead to additional concerns over personal finances. Although quitting smoking or decreasing one's caffeine intake may be very stressful processes, the long term mental and physical health benefits make it worthwhile. Excessive sugar intake may also have physical effects on the body and should be avoided. Eating too many sugary foods will leave students less hungry for more nutritious ones, and they may end up missing valuable vitamins and minerals. The brief energy boost that accompanies the intake of sugar is quickly replaced by a longer shortage of energy.

Drugs and alcohol also work as stress enhancers. Many students hold the mistaken belief that drugs and alcohol will relieve their stressors and help them to relax. Addiction, and subsequent negative health issues, may develop within a relatively short amount of time. A preliminary study by Rhodes and Jasinski (1990) found that learning disabilities may be related to the development of alcoholism. In the study, they found that some of the subjects "turned to alcohol as an escape from the stress of their problems, rather than because of an inherited predisposition" (p. 555).

Stress affects everyone, but it can be especially detrimental to students with learning disabilities. It is important for learning specialist and service providers, to have a solid understanding of both the effects of stress on students and be able to recognize stress within them. If students can learn to cope with and prevent stress in themselves, they will be able to more efficiently accomplish goals they have set for themselves.

Sources

Brinckerhoff, Loring C.; Shaw, Stan F.; and McGuire, Joan M. (1993). *Promoting Postsecondary Education for Students with Learning Disabilities: A Handbook for Practitioners*. Pro-Ed: Austin, TX.

Dillon, Kathleen M. (1992). Popping Sealed Air-Capsules to Reduce Stress. *Psychological Reports*, 71, 243-246.

Geisthardt, Cheryl and Munsch, Joyce. (1996). Coping with School Stress: A Comparison of Adolescents With and Without Learning Disabilities. *Journal of Learning Disabilities*, 29(3), 225-336.

Huntington, Deborah D. and Bender, William N. (1993). Adolescents with Learning Disabilities at Risk? Emotional Well-Being, Depression, Suicide. *Journal of Learning Disabilities*, 26(3), 159-166.

Kopolow, Louise E. (1987). Plain Talk About Handling Stress. U.S. Department of Health and Human Services, National Institute of Mental Health, Division of Communication and Education.

Rhodes, Sharyn S. and Jasinski, Donald R. (1990). Learning Disabilities in Alcohol Dependent Adults: A Preliminary Study. *Journal of Learning Disabilities*, 23(9), 551-556.

Rubenzer, Ronald L. (1988). Stress Management and the Learning Disabled. ERIC Document Reproduction Service, ED295396.

Chapter 58

Siblings of Children with Learning Disabilities

"In a way he's a handicap and in a way he's everything I'd ever want," wrote a twelve-year old girl about her brother with learning disabilities. Sibling relationships in any family are complex and ambivalent, but when one child in the family has a handicap, even more intense feelings are aroused. According to one study (Trevino, 1979) this is particularly true in families where there are two children of the same sex who are close in age, or where the non-handicapped child is the youngest in the family or the oldest girl. Even more significant than birth order, though, is the family atmosphere and the attitudes that prevail.

Neglect Can Be a Concern

There are three issues which seem to be of particular concern to siblings of youngsters with learning disabilities. The first of these is neglect—real or imaged. Actually, the child with a problem usually requires more than his equal share of parental time and attention. Transportation to therapists and tutors, help with homework and

From "My Brother Is Different: Sibling Relationships," by Betty B. Osman, Ph.D. This article appeared in the 1988 issue of *Their World,* a magazine published by the National Center for Learning Disabilities. © National Center for Learning Disabilities. Reprinted with permission. Despite the older date of this document, this timeless information will be helpful to the reader. For more information from the National Center for Learning Disabilities, visit their website at http://www.ncld.org.

soothing hurt feelings after school represent an investment of time, money and energy for parents. Some I have known focused so much attention to their LD child that there was little left over for their other children. As long as they seemed to be getting along all right, they were left to grow like topsy—until they began to imitate their LD sibling, to get their share of equal time, as it were. Only when they began to fail in school or became depressed did their parents realize the extent of their neglect.

Handling Responsibility

Responsibility is a second issue affecting many siblings of children with learning disabilities. Parents tend to expect more from the child without problems. Good manners, appropriate social behavior and caretaking responsibilities may be taken for granted. Because they seem more capable, parents may rely on them to make life easier at home. At 12, Barbara became a miniature parent to her nine year-old brother. She took him with her when she went to play with friends and scolded him when he stayed up too late or didn't do his homework. But eventually she resented the responsibility and so did her brother who already had two parents, enough for any child.

Even when parents are sensitive to the role of the well functioning child in the family and don't push beyond capabilities, siblings are likely to assume additional responsibilities on their own. Joey did. He walked the dog without being asked, conscientiously did his homework, and got up early to fix breakfast and get his brother ready for school. All this on top of his being number one in his class. He worked hard to become the super-child in the family, as if to compensate for the disappointment and frustration his brother was causing. But his drive to excel was exhausting.

Finally, responsibility for the future of the LD child is a matter of concern for sibling. "When my parents are no longer around, I'll have to take care of her. Will I be able to handle it and how will it affect my own future life? Will my children have learning disabilities too?" These are only a few of the questions many children ponder, but may not express. They need to be dealt with openly by parents and/or professionals.

Guilt Feelings

A third issue is the guilt that siblings of handicapped children feel so keenly. It is normal for children in any family to resent their sibling some of the time, and even wish them the worst. But when those fantasies become real, as in the case of a child with a problem that doesn't go away overnight, the guilt can be overwhelming. Some children are even afraid to excel in school for fear of surpassing the LD child in the family; the guilt is too great. "Why him and not me?" they ask. Such children sometimes develop problems unconsciously to be more on a par with their sib.

Another source of guilt is the embarrassment and social discomfort of having a brother or sister who acts different. It is hard to explain to one's friends why Billy acts so dumb or weird at times, particularly if one hasn't really been told. Brothers and sister are not usually included in conferences about a child's handicap and are left to guess or fantasize about what is wrong. With knowledge and understanding though, a boy or girl can become an unexpected ally and friend to his LD sibling.

Deal Openly with LD Problems

The following are a few suggestions for parents who have a child with a learning disability—and other children who may be suffering the consequences.

Discuss the problem openly with the other children in the family, encouraging questions and reactions. A sib's learning disability is a fact of life to be dealt with in the family, not avoided. Family secrets only lead to denial and the pretense that things are not what they seem.

Acknowledge your own negative feelings as well as the natural resentment sibs may feel. It will help them to know they are not alone with their anger. And the recognition that it is hard to love, and even to play with, a sister or brother who is being obnoxious will alleviate some of their guilt.

Don't try to discipline children equally. Fair doesn't always mean equal. Children in a family need to know they are separate people with needs and capabilities of their own. But don't be too harsh with the child without problems because he should know better. He's a child too, after all, even though he may seem exceptionally mature for his years.

On a positive note, try to find ways for each child to gain recognition and a feeling of self-worth. A child who feels respected and appreciated will be able to appreciate others, even with handicaps.

519

Accepting Parents a Basic Influence

Finally, the ways in which parents view and respond to their LD child is the most important basic influence on sibling reactions. Parents who are accepting of their child enable siblings to respond similarly. Having a child with a handicap affects the experience of each person in the family, but along with the frustration and difficult times, parents can offer each child opportunities for growth, understanding and love. With these, a sibling can honestly day, "He's not heavy. He's my brother."

Chapter 59

Communicating with Your Family about Learning Disabilities

Talking to Family Members

From "Communicating with Your Family about LD" by Ann Muilenburg. © Copyright 2001 SchwabLearning.org. Reprinted with permission of Schwab Learning. For more Information, please visit www.schwablearning.org.

"I'm having a hard enough time coping with Jason's LD myself, so why do I have to talk to my family about it, too? They think I'm just being overprotective. I really don't think they'll understand. Couldn't it make things worse at home for Jason?"

Why should you talk to family members?

Coping with a child's learning difference (LD) is stressful for any parent, and the last thing you need is another demand on your time and energy. But avoiding talk about your child's LD can send a message to well-meaning family members that you're hiding something—feeling ashamed, embarrassed, or guilty. Telling the secret often produces great relief for everyone involved. And since LD often is inherited, it may even help other family members understand the reasons they may have had problems when they were in school.

This chapter includes text from two documents that are reprinted with permission from Schwab Learning. Citation information is provided at the beginning of each article.

Here are more reasons why educating your family about LD can help your child and you personally.

- To break down barriers that separate families because of misinformation or misunderstanding.
- To provide a common knowledge of how your child learns—his strengths, as well as challenges—and why he acts as he does.
- To exchange harmful labels—dumb, lazy, inattentive—for terms that describe his talents and help to build self-esteem—creative thinker, star athlete, skilled at math.
- To help set realistic expectations.
- To reduce feelings of isolation.
- To expand the home support system for you and your child.

Who should you speak to? Who should you educate about your child's LD?

Grandparents, extended family, and siblings all need to know.

How should you educate these people?

The message needs to be open, honest, and fit the audience. Your elderly grandmother may need a very different level of detail than your sister-in-law who is a teacher. So you can't speak to everyone in one group at the same time, and you'll need to speak to different people in different ways.

What should you say?

Keep information simple, and avoid using educational jargon. Help family members identify some strategies to help your child succeed in his interactions with them.

Remember how overwhelming even basic information was when you first began learning about LD? Give everyone a chance to think about what you've shared. It won't be easy if the person is in denial—doesn't believe or accept what you're saying. Then you'll need lots of patience and an outside support system to get you through the process.

For most of the family, education isn't something that can be done effectively in one talk. As questions arise, take advantage of the opportunity to answer thoughtfully. Some people may want to learn more on their own, so be ready to provide resources for them—articles, educational programs, support groups, and Web sites, such as SchwabLearning.org.

Remember to include your child in discussions so he has a chance to tell his own story, in his own way. It's probably better if you do this after you know how others will respond to him. Are they likely to doubt what he's telling them, or will they understand and be able to offer him support? Remember to have him talk about his strengths and talents, as well as his LD.

Talking to the brother or sister of your child with LD may be the hardest job of all. Siblings often feel jealous of all the extra attention a child with LD needs—extra help on homework, tutoring, time spent at school—and may be quick to express anger or make comments that can hurt. Parents have to balance the demands of all their children, not just those with special needs.

When speaking to a sibling, consider the age of the child, use language that's easy to understand, and speak positively and factually. Reassure all your children that each one is special and loved and find ways to show them you mean what you say. The structure and positive discipline that help kids with LD function better can benefit all kids in the family. So have routines apply to everyone, and that way no one will feel singled out or left out.

When should you do it?

While it's important to educate family members about your child's LD as soon as you comfortably can, do it on your own timetable—when it feels right for you.

About the Author

Ann Muilenburg is a Marriage and Family Therapist in private practice.

Enlisting Family Support

From "Enlisting Family Support," by Kristin Stanberry, SchwabLearn ing.org. © Copyright 2001 SchwabLearning.org. Reprinted with permission of Schwab Learning. For more information, please visit www.schwablearning.org.

Soon after your child is identified with a learning problem, you'll want to explain the situation to your family and ask for their support. How will they take the news? Some will accept the problem and offer support right away. Others may disagree or deny there's a problem at all. And some may even blame you or your child.

If you find yourself in this frustrating, sometimes maddening, situation, know you're not alone. Take a deep breath and read on for some tips on how to work with family members who resist or deny your child's LD.

Finding Your Allies

Begin by talking to those in your family who understand and accept the situation. Together, you can decide how to work with resistant relatives. You and your child can depend on these allies to support you and reinforce the message with other family members.

Dealing with Denial

You may feel sure a certain family member loves your child. So why can't she understand his special needs? You may gain insight if you ask yourself some questions about the person who's in denial. Is she afraid for your child? Does she find it too upsetting to think about the problem and how it might affect your child's chances for success? Does she feel guilty because she wasn't sympathetic enough to your child's struggles in the past? How was she brought up as a child? How were individual differences recognized and addressed in her family? Did she have trouble learning as a child, too? Since LD often runs in families, will she now have to face her own problem? Did you overwhelm her with too much information? Some family members don't need to understand every detail in order to help.

As you reflect on possible reasons for a person's reaction, you'll think of better ways to approach her. For instance, if your mother sometimes cares for your child after school, she may want to know some basic tips for helping him with his homework. But explaining your child's Individualized Education Program (IEP) may overwhelm her.

Remember that you had to work through your own feelings—some of them painful—to face your child's LD. Allow family members time and space to work through their feelings, too.

Getting Dad's Support

If your husband denies the problem, it can put distance between your child and him. Your child may feel rejected if his dad accuses him of being lazy or stupid. Or your husband may blame the problem on your family or your parenting skills. Either of these reactions can have a harmful effect on your child and your marriage.

If your husband can't accept what you're telling him, perhaps another family member or a trusted teacher could help him understand. If communication about your child's problem doesn't improve, consider professional marriage and/or family counseling right away.

Once your husband seems receptive, help him learn what LD is and what it is not. When he seems ready, help him discover ways to get involved.

Highlighting Your Child's Strengths

Would it be easier for certain family members to focus on what your child does well, rather than what he struggles with? If so, praise them for wanting to boost your child's self-esteem. Then ask how each person would like to support your child's skills, talents, and interests. For example:

- Does your child share a love of science with his dad? They might go to a science museum or build a project for the science fair together.

- Reassure aunts, uncles, and grandparents that showing interest in your child's hobbies and activities is a great gift. Simple gestures, such as showing interest in the child's opinions or sharing secret jokes, will help him feel special.

- Encourage your other children to cheer their brother on at games and remind him what he's good at. Some siblings resent this responsibility, so rewarding their efforts is very important.

Aiming for Acceptance

Communicating with your family about LD is an ongoing process. It will take time for each family member to feel comfortable in a new role with your child. Don't be discouraged if some never fully understand his LD. As long as they give him their love, acceptance, and attention, he'll feel special. In time, each person can find positive ways to support and interact with him—either in his struggles or in his strengths.

About the Author

In her role as Writer/Editor for Schwab Learning, Kristin Stanberry provides information, insight, strategies, and support for parents whose children have learning differences. She combines a professional background developing consumer health and wellness publications with her personal experience of coaching family members with learning differences.

Chapter 60

Dealing with Learning Disabilities in Relationships

Learning disabilities may present many challenges to the individual other than the obvious. They can have a great impact on relationships and personal interactions. The effects are experienced by persons with learning disabilities and their partners. The problems can manifest themselves in a variety of situations.

A person with learning disabilities may be frustrated about the way a partner provides assistance. When too much is routinely provided, the perception is that he or she is stupid or treated as a child creates anxiety and frustrations. Also, he or she may feel unfairly blamed for relationship problems, such as not listening or not trying hard enough, which may be due to his/her learning disabilities.

The partner without learning disabilities may experience resentment at having to continually tend to the needs of the other, while many of his/her needs may seem to go unmet.

As everyone has good and bad days, so do persons with learning disabilities, but their peaks and valleys may be more pronounced and frequent. Their capabilities can vary widely from day to day without any predictable patterns or identifiable causes.

"Dealing with Learning Disabilities in Relationships," by Britta Miller and the National Institute for Literacy. This article originally appeared in *Linkages,* the newsletter of the National Adult Literacy and Learning Disabilities Center ,Volume 2, Number 1, 1995. For more information please visit www.nifl.gov. Despite the older date of this article, the information will be helpful to the reader.

Since learning disabilities are often invisible, both partners may have difficulty understanding and accepting the limitations they create. No matter who has the disability, the problems must be worked out together. It is important to distinguish between difficulties which can be overcome (using strategies and accommodations) and those which are not likely to change.

The following are some helpful tips that may be useful for partners who have learning disabilities:

- Have a good understanding of the way in which the learning disability affects your ability to process information, communicate, etc.

- Explain to your partner how the learning disabilities interfere with many aspects of everyday life.

- Request accommodations in a direct manner without feeling guilty or giving excuses.

- To maintain credibility with others, avoid "crying wolf." Accept that some tasks may take longer.

- Be as self-reliant as possible by finding alternatives to overburdening your partner.

These tips may be useful for the partner of a person who has a learning disability:

- Try to recognize, specifically, how the learning disability impacts on your partner's ability to: pay attention, comprehend, conceptualize, visualize, communicate, be organized, follow conversations, interpret body language, etc.

- Be aware that what appears to be a simple and logical way to carry out a task for you may not be the most logical way for the person with learning disabilities. Persuading the partner to "just do it this way" is not necessarily helpful. Conversely, you should accept that what seems like a roundabout method may, in fact, be the easiest way for your partner to complete the task.

- Remember that the learning disability thought process may manifest itself in a nonlinear fashion, which may seem confusing.

- Refrain from demanding that your partner try harder to correct a disability. This would be like expecting a deaf person to hear by trying harder.

- Be aware that symptoms of learning disabilities may be more apparent at the end of the day or when your partner is fatigued.

Socially constructed gender roles may compound the effects of learning disabilities. For instance, men have traditionally been designated as breadwinners. This has not been realistic for some men with learning disabilities who have had difficulties with job stability and career advancement. A couple can reduce the stress they feel by creating more realistic expectations and redefining their roles according to each person's abilities, rather than tradition.

Although couples may feel that learning disabilities are a unique problem, they are shared by a great number of people. Due to the close interaction of a relationship, the effects of learning disabilities are often greatly magnified, thus creating additional stress for the couple. It is only with hard work and a lot of understanding that these problems may be resolved.

Chapter 61

Marriage Under Pressure: Help for Couples with Learning Disabled Children

Raising a child who has a learning difference (LD) requires a lot of time and energy from parents. At times, the whole family may be caught up in the whirlwind of adjusting to life with LD. In this situation, it's easy to neglect your marriage. Remember it's essential to nurture your relationship during such challenging times. Partners who understand and support each other can better help their children and each other. Having a strong, healthy marriage also gives your children a sense of security.

Follow Your Tracks

When focusing on your marriage, you may find it useful to imagine two different tracks running parallel to each other. Track one includes a couple's outward behavior and actions—things that are easy to observe track two runs parallel to track one but involves deeper feelings under the surface. For every behavior on track one, there are corresponding emotions at work on track two.

Track One: Watch for Warning Signs

When a child has LD, his relationship with one or both parents can intensify. This is normal and expected. However, pouring extra energy

From "Marriage Under Pressure," by Kristin Stanberry, SchwabLearning.org. © Copyright 2001 SchwabLearning.org. Reprinted with permission of Schwab Learning. For more information, please visit www.schwablearning.org.

into your child's well being can make it easy to ignore signs of stress in your marriage. Try to stay aware of how you and your spouse are behaving. There are some common warning signs to be aware of. For example, do you or your spouse:

- Devote most of your time, energy, and attention to your child and have nothing left for yourself or your partner?
- Avoid being at home and find excuses to stay away?
- Seem to be addicted to drugs, alcohol, food, work, or exercise?
- Have trouble communicating with your partner without blame, anger, defensiveness, or frustration?

It's best not to ignore signs like these, hoping they'll disappear. Try to face problems together and resolve them as soon as possible. It takes courage to ask your partner about his behavior. It can be even harder to admit to your own shortcomings.

There are many ways to improve how you behave with each other and your family. Often, a licensed marriage counselor or clergy member can help you change the patterns you've fallen into. Let's explore some steps you can take right now.

Work as a Team

It's critical that you and your partner both understand your child's LD—and how you can help him. Whenever possible, participate in these activities together:

- Back-to-school night and Open House
- Parent-teacher conferences
- IEP (Individualized Education Program) meetings
- Your child's medical appointments
- Seminars about learning differences

Doing this allows each of you to hear information directly and ask questions. You'll also get a clear sense of what's involved. That way, you can make better decisions as a team. If you handle the day-to-day management of your child's LD, your spouse will better understand the work you're doing.

As the father of a second grade student explains, "By attending the parent-teacher conferences with my wife, I found there were some tasks I was comfortable volunteering for. I offered to complete most of the paperwork, which I'm good at. That left my wife more time to help our daughter with her homework."

- Give each other some space—it takes energy to help your child and maintain your marriage. To stay healthy, you and your partner may need time away from each other and your responsibilities. Try to give each other a break from parenting duties on a regular basis. Then, use your free time to enjoy activities, hobbies, or social plans that help you relax and recharge.

When you and your partner are together, be sensitive to each other's need for space and privacy. One stay-at-home mom cringes when she describes how she used to greet her husband when he returned home from work. "He was barely in the door when I'd unload all the problems I'd had with the kids that day," she admits. "He'd give me the silent treatment all evening." After several arguments about this, she realized he needed to settle in before helping her. She found that if she let him unwind for a while, then he was happy to play with the kids while she fixed dinner. They learned to wait and discuss problems at less hectic times of the day.

Rediscover Each Other

When your child's needs demand your time and energy, romance may be the last thing on your mind. But rekindling your relationship is critical if you and your partner are to stay strong and happy. Make it a point to schedule regular dates with each other. Your time together can be as simple as taking a walk after dinner or as special as the two of you getting away for the weekend. Use this time together to rediscover each other. Avoid talking about your child's problems. To accomplish this, hire a sitter or enlist help from other family members.

Track Two: When Actions and Feelings Don't Match

Often, a person's behavior reflects what he feels inside. But if you and your partner are stressed and have lost touch with each other, one or both of you may behave in a way that hides your true feelings. From there, communication often breaks down and your marriage suffers. There are steps you can take to understand each other better.

Understanding Your Partner

If your partner's behavior frustrates or confuses you, there may be a disconnect between outward behavior (track one) and inner feelings (track two). One woman recalls how her husband's silence bothered her as she struggled to help their son who has AD/HD. She thought back to another time when her husband seemed aloof and unconcerned. It was before she had surgery. "He didn't seem to care about my operation. Months later he admitted how afraid he had been that something would happen to me during surgery. He couldn't tell me at the time."

That memory prompted her to ask him how he really felt about the current situation with their son. Professional counseling helped him sort through and express his emotions. "It turned out my husband felt guilty because he couldn't solve all of our son's problems," she explains.

This story is not uncommon. Like many men in our culture, her husband needed encouragement to verbalize his feelings. And when he did speak up, he expressed a sense of inadequacy for not being able to protect his wife during surgery, or end their son's struggle. Men often prefer to look for immediate solutions rather than learn to understand and manage a problem over time.

Finally, consider the different emotions you've felt about your child's LD. Your spouse may be processing his feelings in a different way. And his past experiences may influence his reaction to your child's LD.

Helping Your Partner Understand You

Sharing information honestly and in ways that are comfortable will help you and your spouse understand each other better. Try expressing your feelings to your spouse in an honest, non-threatening way. Remember your partner is not a mind reader. Make it clear to your partner what you do—and don't—expect from him. For instance, you might tell him you want to talk about your feelings, but you don't expect him to give you answers. In general, women tend to verbalize their feelings more than men do. Women are comfortable thinking out loud and appreciate being heard. Often, all a woman wants is an outlet, not the solution to a problem.

If your partner seems to have a hard time hearing you talk about feelings, try writing him a note to express yourself. This will help you focus on what's important and give him time to consider your concerns without having to respond right away.

Looking to the Future

Working to repair and strengthen your marriage can be hard work. The path to a better marriage is seldom smooth; you'll encounter bumps and detours along the way. But if you and your partner agree on your overall goal, the journey will be a bit easier. "Some of the couples I counsel make a clear commitment to stay married," a therapist relates. "Once they set that as their goal, then the other pieces fall into place."

Your marriage is a union of two people with individual needs. Your child and family situation are also unique to you. Working together, you and your partner will find the best path to take. The reward comes when your understanding and love for each other deepens. There's a good chance your marriage and family will not only survive—but also thrive—from the challenging experience you are going through.

About the Author

In her role as Writer/Editor for Schwab Learning, Kristin Stanberry provides information, insight, strategies, and support for parents whose children have learning differences. She combines a professional background developing consumer health and wellness publications with her personal experience of coaching family members with learning differences.

Part Eight

Additional Help and Information

Chapter 62

Glossary of Related Terms

This glossary is a compilation of terms and definitions adapted from a number of sources, which are duly noted. All definitions not otherwise attributed have been written by the Learning Disabilities Council's Handbook Writing Committee.

Academic Classes: Classes in basic subjects such as reading, arithmetic, science, and social studies at elementary level; and English, history, science, and math at secondary level.[1]

Accommodation: Adaptations and modifications of printed materials, teaching approaches and techniques, etc., designed to enable students with learning disabilities to accomplish school work with greater ease and effectiveness. The accommodations also help students participate in and benefit from classroom activities.

Achievement Test: A test that measures the extent to which a person has acquired certain information or mastered certain skills, usually as a result of planned instruction or training. These tests are often called educational tests.

From *Understanding Learning Disabilities: A Parent Guide and Workbook, 3rd Edition,* edited by Mary Louise Trusdell and Inge W. Horowitz. Copyright 2002 by the Learning Disabilities Council, P.O. Box 8451, Richmond, VA. 23226. Book orders should be addressed to York Press, Inc., P.O. Box 504, Timonium, MD 21094, www.yorkpress.com, or 1-800-962-2763.

ADA (Americans with Disabilities Act): A law which applies to persons with a physical or mental impairment that substantially limits one or more of life's activities. Such persons are protected from discrimination by the ADA and Section 504. ADA prohibits discrimination solely on the basis of a disability.

Adaptive Physical Education: A special physical education program developed to fit the limits and disabilities of persons with handicaps.[2]

ADD (Attention Deficit Disorder): A term frequently used to describe the academic and behavioral problems of children who have difficulty focusing and maintaining attention.

ADHD (Attention Deficit Hyperactivity Disorder): Characterized by difficulty sitting still, paying attention, or controlling impulsive behavior. For some people, the problem is so pervasive and persistent that it interferes with their daily lives, including home, academic, social, and working settings.[3] Some people use ADD when they are referring to this condition.

Age of Eligibility: All eligible children with disabilities, who have not graduated from high school, who are in need of special education and related services, and who are between the ages two to 21, inclusive.[4]

Amphetamines: A group of drugs used to stimulate the cerebral cortex of the brain. Sometimes used to treat hyperactivity. (See also Dexedrine and Ritalin.)[2]

Anoxia: Deficient amount of oxygen in the tissues of a part of the body or in the bloodstream supplying such part.[3]

Aptitude Test: A test designed to measure a person's ability to learn and the likelihood of success in future school work or in a specific career.

Articulation (Speech): Refers to the production of speech sounds resulting from the movements of the lips, jaw, and tongue as they modify the flow of air.[1]

Assistive Technology: Equipment that enhances the ability of students and employees to be more efficient or successful. For individuals with learning disabilities, computer grammar checkers, and overhead projector used by a teacher, or the audiovisual information delivered through a CD-ROM would be typical examples.[6]

Association: Ability to relate concepts presented through the senses (visual, auditory, tactile, or kinesthetic).[4]

Attention Span: The length of time an individual can concentrate on a task without being distracted or losing interest. (See also Distractibility.)[2]

Auditory Discrimination: Ability to detect differences in sounds; may be gross ability, such as detecting the differences between the noises made by a cat and dog, or fine ability, such as detecting the differences made by the sounds of letters "m" and "n."

Auditory Figure-Ground: Ability to attend to one sound against a background of sound (e.g., hearing the teacher's voice against classroom noise).[8]

Auditory Memory: Ability to retain information which has been presented orally; may be short term memory, such as recalling information presented several seconds before; long term memory, such as recalling information presented more than a minute before; or sequential memory, such as recalling a series of information in proper order.

Basic Skill Area: Includes such subjects as reading, writing, spelling, mathematics.[1]

Behavior Modification: A technique intended to change behavior by rewarding desirable actions and ignoring or "negatively rewarding" undesirable actions.[2]

Benchmarks: The measurements that are taken at equal increments of time during the year and provide a marker or gauge that tells how well the student is doing in relation to the annual goal. Is same as short-term objectives.

Binocular Fusion: The blending of separate images from each eye into a single meaningful image.[2]

BIP (Behavioral Intervention Plan): A plan that utilizes positive behavioral interventions and supports to address behaviors that interfere with the learning of students with disabilities or with the learning of others, or behaviors that require disciplinary action.[4]

Blending: See Sound Blending.[1]

Body Image: The concept and awareness of one's own body as it relates to space, movement, and other objects.[5]

Brain Damage: Any actual structural (tissue) damage due to any cause or causes. This means verifiable damage, not neurological performance that is indicative of damage.

Catastrophic Reaction: Extreme terror, grief, frustration, or anger without apparent cause. May be triggered by changes in routine, unexpected events, or over stimulation. Children reacting in this manner may throw or break things, scream uncontrollably, or burst into tears.[2]

CEC: Council for Exceptional Children[2]

Central Auditory Processing Problem: The inability to understand spoken language in a meaningful way in the absence of what is commonly considered a hearing loss.[9]

Central Nervous System (CNS): The brain and spinal cord.[2]

Cerebral Cortex: The outer layer of the brain; controls thinking, feeling, and voluntary movement.[2]

Channel: The routes through which the content of communication flows. It includes both the modalities through which impression is received and the form of expression through which the response is made. Ex: Auditory—Vocal Channel.[4]

Child Study Committee: Is located in each school building to receive and act upon referrals of students suspected of being handicapped. The membership of this committee usually consists of at least three persons, including the school principal or a person chosen by the principal, the teacher or teachers, specialists, and the referring source if appropriate.

CNS: See Central Nervous System.

Cognition: The act or process of knowing; the various thinking skills and processes are considered cognitive skills.[10]

Cognitive Ability: Intellectual ability; thinking and reasoning skills.

Cognitive Style: A person s typical approach to learning activities and problem solving. For example, some people carefully analyze each task, deciding what must be done and in what order. Others react impulsively to situations.[2]

Collaborative Consultation: The student participates in the general education classroom. The special educator serves as consultant to general education teachers, collaborating with them in planning and implementing instructional accommodations in regular classrooms.

Compensation: Process in which a person is taught how to cope with his learning problems, how to work around skills or abilities which may be lacking; emphasis is placed on using the individual's strengths. (See Remediation.)

Conceptual Disorder: Disturbances in thinking, reasoning, generalizing, memorizing.

Conceptualization: The process of forming a general idea from what is observed. For example, seeing apples, bananas, and oranges and recognizing that they are all fruit.[2]

Configuration: The visual shape or form of words; may be used as a cue in word-attack skills.[11]

Congenital: A condition existing at birth or before birth. Congenital does not imply that a condition is hereditary.[2]

Contingency Self-Management: A student manages his or her own behavior with checklists or other cues and is rewarded or not based on his or her performance.

Continuum: A graded series of program options to serve students with differing levels of need of special education and related services.[12]

Coordination: The harmonious functioning of muscles in the body to perform complex movements.[2]

Co-Teaching: The student participates in the general education classroom. The special educator and general educator teach the class together, both planning and delivering instruction.

Criterion Referenced Test: Designed to provide information on specific knowledge or skills possessed by a student. Such tests usually cover relatively small units of content and are closely related to instruction. Their scores have meaning in terms of what the student knows or can do, rather than their relation to the scores made by some external reference group.

Cross-Categorical: Refers to a system in which a teacher addresses more than one handicapping condition within one instructional period. (for example, a student with learning disabilities may receive instruction in the same special education classroom as a student with an emotional/behavioral disorder). Also called multi-categorical.

Cross Dominance: A condition in which the preferred eye, hand, or foot are not on the same side of the body. For example, a person may be right-footed and right-eyed but left-handed. Also called mixed dominance.[2]

Decoding: The process of getting meaning from written or spoken symbols. (See Receptive Language.)[2]

Developmental Lag: A delay in some aspect of physical or mental development.[2]

Dexedrine: Trade name for one of several stimulant drugs often given to modify hyperactivity in children.[2]

Directionality: The ability to know right from left, up from down, forward from backward, and direction and orientation.[13]

Disability: Any physical and/or mental problem that causes a person to have difficulty in doing certain tasks such as walking, seeing, hearing, speaking, learning, or working.

Discrepancy: Significant difference; defined differently by different school districts.

Discrimination: Process of detecting differences between and/or among stimuli.[1]

Disinhibition: Lack of restraint in responding to a situation. A child exhibiting disinhibition reacts impulsively and often inappropriately.[2]

Distractibility: The shifting of attention from the task at hand to sounds, sights, and other stimuli that normally occur in the environment.[2]

Due Process: The application of law to ensure that an individual's rights are protected. When applied to children with learning disabilities, due process means that parents have the right to request a full review of any educational program developed for their child. A due process hearing may be requested to ensure that all requirements of Public Law 94-142 have been met.[2]

Dysarthria: A disorder of the speech muscles that affects the ability to pronounce words.[2]

Dyscalculia: Difficulty in understanding or using mathematical symbols or functions. A child with dyscalculia may be able to read and write but have difficulty in performing mathematical calculations.

Dysfunction: Any disturbance or impairment in the normal functioning of an organ or body part.[2]

Dysgraphia: Difficulty in producing legible handwriting with age-appropriate speed.

Dyslexia: Impairment of the ability to deal with language (speaking, reading, spelling, writing). A dyslexic may see letters, syllables, or words upside down, reversed, blurred, backwards, or otherwise distorted.

Dysnomia: Difficulty in remembering names or recalling appropriate words to use in a given context.

Dyspraxia: Difficulty in performing fine motor acts such as drawing, buttoning, etc. A person with dyspraxia has difficulty producing and sequencing the movements necessary to perform these kinds of tasks.

Early Intervention Program: A program specially designed to assist developmentally delayed infants and preschool children. The purpose of this type of program is to help prevent problems as the child matures.[2]

Educational Consultant/Diagnostician: An individual who may be familiar with school curriculum and requirements at various grade levels: may or may not have a background in learning disabilities; may conduct educational evaluations.

Educational Evaluation: The evaluation generally consists of a battery of educational tests along with an analysis of class work designed to determine the current levels of achievement in areas such as reading, math, spelling, etc.

Educational Psychologist: See School Psychologist.

Electroencephalogram (EEG): A graphic recording of electrical currents developed in the cerebral cortex during brain functioning. Sometimes called a Brain wave test." A machine called an electroencephalograph records the pattern of these electrical currents on paper.[2]

Eligibility: A team determines (1) whether a child has a handicapping condition which requires special education and, in some cases, related services such as speech and language therapy; (2) whether the child needs special education.

Encoding: The process of expressing language (i.e., selecting words; formulating them into ideas; producing them through speaking or writing). (See Expressive Language.)[1]

ESY (Extended School Year Services): Special Education and Related Services that are provided to a child with a disability beyond the normal school year, in accordance with the child's IEP, and at no cost to the parents of the child. ESY services must meet standards established by the LEA or SEA.[4]

Etiology: The study of the cause or origin of a condition or disease.[2]

Expressive Language: Communication through writing, speaking, and/or gestures.[2]

Eye-Hand Coordination: The ability of the eyes and hands to work together to complete a task. Examples are drawing and writing.[2]

FAPE: See Free Appropriate Public Education.

Far Point Copying: Writing while copying from a model some distance away, e.g., copying from the blackboard.

FBA (Functional Behavioral Assessment): A process to determine the underlying cause or functions of a child's behavior that impede the learning of a child with a disability or the learning of the child's peers.[4]

FCLD: Foundation for Children with Learning Disabilities. (Now known as NCLD—The National Center for Learning Disabilities.)

Figure-Ground Discrimination: The ability to sort out important information from the surrounding environment. For example, hearing a teacher s voice while ignoring other classroom noises (air conditioners, heaters, etc.) or seeing a word among others on a crowded page.[2]

Fine Motor: The use of small muscles for precision tasks such as writing, tying bows, zipping a zipper, typing, doing puzzles.[2]

Free Appropriate Public Education (FAPE): A guarantee given by IDEA to all eligible students with disabilities. It refers to specialized instruction, provided to a student at no cost to the parents, that addresses the student's needs and provides educational benefit.

Full-Time Special Class (Self-Contained): The student spends the majority of his or her day in a separate classroom with a smaller group of students who receive intensive instruction from a special educator in areas of need. The students may spend a portion of their day in regular classrooms but most of their instruction occurs in this special class.

General Education: All education not included under Special Education. (See Regular Education.)

Gross Motor: The use of large muscles for activities requiring strength and balance. Examples are walking, running, and jumping.[2]

Haptic Sense: Combined kinesthetic and tactile senses.[1]

Homebound Instruction: Homebound instruction is usually used for short, temporary periods of time when a student cannot attend school. In this situation, a teacher comes to the home and provides instruction there.

Hyperactivity (or Hyperkinesis): Disorganized and disruptive behavior characterized by constant and excessive movement. A hyperactive child usually has difficulty sticking to one task for an extended period and may react more intensely to a situation than a normal child.[2]

Hyperkinesis: Another term for hyperactivity.[1]

Hypoactivity: Underactivity; child may appear to be in a daze, lacking energy.

IAES (Interim Alternative Educational Setting): An assignment which may be used for a maximum of 45 days when disciplinary action is needed.

IDEA: See Individuals with Disabilities Education Act.

IEP: See Individualized Education Plan (or Program).

Impulsivity: Reacting to a situation without considering the consequences.[2]

Inclusion: The idea that students with disabilities should be included in the general education program at their school. Can be partial inclusion (the student is in general education classes for some subjects) or full inclusion (the student is in all general education classes).

Individuals with Disabilities Education Act (IDEA): Public Law 101-476, the Individuals with Disabilities Education Act. This law strengthens the rights of children with disabilities—and their parents. It builds upon the achievements gained under Public Law 94-142. Further clarification was provided in 1997 with Public Law 105-17.

Individualized Education Plan (IEP): A written educational prescription developed for each handicapped (including learning disabled) child. Sometimes called an Individualized Education Program. School districts are required by law to develop these plans, in cooperation with parents.[2]

Informal Tests: Task-oriented tests to provide information concerning specific skills. Are not standardized.[1]

Insertions: In reading/ spelling, or math, the addition of letters or numbers which do not belong in a word or numeral, e.g., sinceare for sincere.

International Dyslexia Association: Formerly The Orton Dyslexia Society. An organization of professionals, scientists, and parents in the field of LD.

Inversions: In reading, spelling, or math, confusion of up-down directionality of letters or numbers, e.g., m for w, 6 for 9, etc.

I.Q. (Intelligence Quotient): A standard score which usually has a mean of 100 and a standard deviation of 15. Such a score is obtained from an individual's performance on a standardized test of intelligence, such as the Wechsler Intelligence Scale for Children (WISC).

Itinerant Teacher: Special Education teacher who is shared by more than one school.[11]

Kinesthetic: Pertaining to the muscles.[2]

Kinesthetic Method: A way of teaching words by using the muscles. For example, a student might trace the outline of a word with a finger while looking at the word and saying aloud the word or its letters, in sequence.[2]

Laterality: The tendency to use the hand, foot, eye, and ear on a particular side of the body. For example, many people use their right hand when eating and their right foot when kicking.[2]

LD: Learning disability, learning disabled, learning disabilities.[2]

LEA: Local Education Agency (a school division).

Learning Disabilities (LD): Disorders of the basic psychological processes that affect the way a child learns. Many children with learning disabilities have average or above average intelligence. Learning disabilities may cause difficulties in listening, thinking, talking, reading, writing, spelling, or arithmetic. Included are perceptual handicaps, dyslexia, and developmental aphasia. Excluded are learning difficulties caused by visual, hearing, or motor handicaps, mental retardation, emotional disturbances, or environmental disadvantage.[2]

Learning Disorder: Damage or impairment to the nervous system that results in a learning disability.[2]

Learning Style: The channels through which a person best understands and retains learning. All individuals learn best through one or more channels: vision, hearing, movement, touching, or a combination of these.

Lesion: Abnormal change in body tissue due to injury or disease.[2]

Licensed Clinical Psychologist: A psychologist who is competent to apply the principles and techniques of psychological evaluation and psychotherapy to individual clients for the purpose of ameliorating problems of behavioral and/or emotional maladjustment.[14]

Licensed Clinical Social Worker: A social worker who, by education and experience, is professionally qualified to provide direct diagnostic, preventive and treatment services where functioning is threatened or affected by social and psychological stress or health impairment.[14]

Licensed Professional Counselor: A person trained in counseling and guidance services with emphasis on individual and group guidance and counseling; assists individuals in achieving more effective personal, social, educational, and career development and adjustment.[14]

Linguistic Approach: Method for teaching reading (decoding skills) which emphasizes use of Sword families. For example, the child is taught to read at and then subsequently is taught to decode words such as "cat," "bat," "sat," "mat," etc. Early stories adhere strictly to the words which have been taught previously and so may sometimes seem nonsensical, e.g., "Sam sat on a mat. The cat sat on a mat. The cat is fat," etc.

Location: This term indicates where the special education and related services included in the IEP will be provided—such as the regular classroom, resource room, a combination of locations. Location is a general description, it does not need to be specific such as Mr. Smith's class or Virginia Elementary School.[12]

Mainstreaming: The practice of placing handicapped children with special educational needs into regular classrooms for at least a part of the children's school programs.[2]

Manifestation Determination: In all suspension or expulsion cases over 10 days, the school must conduct an IEP team meeting (with other qualified personnel) to determine if the behavior was a manifestation of the student's disability.

Maturation Lag: Delayed maturity in one or several skills or areas of development.[2]

Mediation: Mediation is a process by which you or the school invite a third, impartial party to hear both sides of your argument in an informal fashion.

Mental Age: The age for which a given score on a mental ability test is average or normal. The term is most appropriately used at the early age levels where mental growth is rapid.

Milieu Therapy: A clinical technique designed to control a child's environment and minimize conflicting and confusing information.[2]

Minimal Brain Dysfunction (MBD): A broad and unspecific term formerly used to describe learning disabilities.[2]

Mixed Dominance: See cross dominance.

Mixed Laterality or Lateral Confusion: Tendency to perform some acts with a right side preference and others with a left, or the shifting from right to left for certain activities.[15]

Modality: The sensory channel used to acquire information. Visual, auditory, tactile, kinesthetic, olfactory (odors), and gustatory (taste) are the most common modalities.[2]

Motor: Pertaining to the origin or execution of muscular activity.[3]

Multi-Categorical: A special education classroom model in which students with more than one handicapping condition are assigned to a special education teacher. (Also called Cross-Categorical.)[1]

Multisensory: Involving most or all of the senses.[2]

NCLD: National Center for Learning Disabilities.

Near Point Copying: Writing while copying from a model close at hand, e.g., copying from a textbook.

Neurological Examination: Testing of the sensory or motor responses to determine if there is impairment of the nervous system.[2]

Noncategorical: Refers to a system of grouping handicapped children together without reference to a particular label or category of exceptionality.[10]

Norm-Referenced Test: See Standardized Test.[2]

Norms: Statistics that provide a frame of reference by which meaning may be given to test scores. Norms are based upon the actual performance of pupils of various grades or ages in the standardization group for the test. Since they represent average or typical performance, they should not be regarded as standards or universally desirable levels of attainment. The most common types of norms are standard scores such as stanines or deviation IQ, percentile rank, grade or age equivalents.

Ombudsman: An official appointed to investigate complaints and speak for individuals with grievances.[2]

Oral Language: Those verbal communication skills needed to understand (listen) and to use (speak) language.

Organicity: A disorder of the central nervous system; brain damage.[2]

Orton Dyslexia Society: Organization of professionals in the field of LD as well as scientists and parents.

Orton-Gillingham Approach: An approach to teaching individuals with learning disabilities. The technique, devised by Dr. Samuel Orton, Anna Gillingham, and Bessie Stillman, stresses a multisensory, phonetic, structured, sequential approach to learning.

Part-Time Special Class (Resource): The special educator takes students needing special education services into a special class for instruction only in specific areas in which they have difficulties.

Perceptual Abilities: The abilities to process, organize, and interpret the information obtained by the five senses; a function of the brain.

Perceptual Handicap: Difficulty in ability to process and organize as well as interpret information through the senses.

Perceptual Speed: Specific meaning of this term varies, depending upon the manner in which a given test measures this ability. May refer to motor speed, how fast something is copied or manipulated, or to visual discrimination, (how quickly identical items in a given series are identified).

Perseveration: The repeating of words, motions, or tasks. A child who perseverates often has difficulty shifting to a new task and continues working on an old task long after classmates have stopped.[2]

Phonics Approach: Method for teaching reading and spelling in which emphasis is placed on learning the sounds which individual and various combinations of letters make in a word. In decoding a word, the child sounds out individual letters or letter combinations and then blends them to form a word.

Phonological Awareness: The awareness of the sounds of speech ad how they relate to print, including sequence of sounds within words, awareness of word boundaries, discrimination blending, segmentation, deletion, rhyming.[16]

Procedural Safeguards: Section 1415 of IDEA which includes the rules of procedure that attempt to level the playing field between schools and parents. These safeguards include the opportunity to examine the child's records, to have advance notice before any significant actions are taken, the right to pursue mediation and litigation, the right to view exhibits and to know the names of witnesses in advance of a hearing, the right to confront and cross-examine witnesses, the right to a fair hearing and, for parents, the right to possible reimbursement of reasonable attorney's fees.[12]

Program: The special education and related services, including accommodations, modifications, supplementary aids and services, as determined by a child's IEP.[17]

Program Modifications: Included in this term are any modifications needed by the student in order (1) to advance appropriately toward attaining each of the annual goals; (2) to be involved and progress in the general curriculum, and to participate in extracurricular and other nonacademic activities; and (3) to be educated and participate with other students with and without disabilities.[12]

Psychiatrist: An individual who treats behavioral or emotional problems. Is a licensed medical doctor (M.D.), so is permitted to use medications in treating a problem.

Psychological Examination: An evaluation by a certified school or clinical psychologist of the intellectual and behavioral characteristics of a person.[1]

Psychomotor: Pertaining to the motor effects of psychological processes. Psychomotor tests are tests of motor skill which depend upon sensory or perceptual motor coordination.[5]

Public Law (P.L.) 94-142: The federal Education for All Handicapped Children Act that became law in 1975. P.L. 94-142 requires each state to provide free and appropriate public education to all handicapped children from birth through age 21. The law also requires that an Individualized Education Plan be prepared for each handicapped child, that parents must have access to their child's school records, and are entitled to a due process hearing if they are dissatisfied with the educational plan.[2]

Readiness: Acquisition of skills considered prerequisite for academic learning.[11]

Reasoning Ability: Specific meaning of this term varies, depending upon the manner in which a given test measures this ability; generally refers to nonverbal, deductive, inductive, analytical thinking.

Receptive Language (Decoding): Language that is spoken or written by others and received by the individual. The receptive language skills are listening and reading.[11]

Referral: A request made for special education evaluation to the school principal or special education coordinator.

Regrouping: In arithmetic, the processes traditionally known as carrying in addition or borrowing in subtraction.

Regular Education: All education not included under Special Education (See General Education).

Rehabilitation Act of 1973: The Civil Rights Act for the Handicapped. The act prohibits discrimination on the basis of physical or mental handicap in all federally-assisted programs. Section 504 of the act provides further guarantees.

Related Services: Services including transportation and such developmental, corrective, and other supportive services as may be required to assist a child with a disability to benefit from special education. These services may include speech-language pathology and audiology services, physical and occupational therapy, psychological services, recreation (including therapeutic recreation), social work services, counseling services (including rehabilitation and psychological counseling), medical services for diagnostic and evaluation purposes, and parent counseling and training. Included may be developmental, corrective, or supportive services such as artistic and cultural programs, and art, music and dance therapy if they are required to assist a child with a disability to benefit from special education.[4]

Remediation: Process in which an individual is provided instruction and practice in skills which are weak or nonexistent in an effort to develop/strengthen these skills.

Resource Teacher: A specialist who works with handicapped students; may also act as a consultant to other teachers.[1]

Reversals: Difficulty in reading or reproducing letters alone, letters in words, or words in sentences in their proper position in space or in proper order. May also refer to reversal of mathematical concepts (add/subtract. multiply/divide) and symbols (>; x+). See also Transposition.[1]

Ritalin: Trade name for one of several stimulant drugs often given to modify hyperactivity in children.[2]

Scatter: Variability in an individual's test scores.[18]

School Psychologist: A person who specializes in problems manifested in and associated with educational systems and who uses psychological concepts and methods in programs which attempt to improve learning conditions for students.[14]

SEA: State Education Agency (the state Department of Education).

Section 504: See Rehabilitation Act of 1973.[12]

Self-Concept: How a person feels and thinks about himself or herself. Sometimes called self-image.[2]

Self-Contained: See Full-Time Special Class.

Semantics: The meaning or understanding given to oral or written language.

Sensorimotor: Relationship between sensation and movement. Sometimes spelled sensory-motor.[2]

Sensory Acuity: The ability to respond to sensation at normal levels of intensity.[5]

Sequence: The detail of information in its accustomed order (for example, days of the week, the alphabet, etc.).[1]

Service Plan: An individualized educational plan designed for students with special needs who are enrolled in a private school setting.

Short Term Objectives: See Benchmarks.

Sight Word Approach: Also known as whole word approach; method for teaching reading which relies heavily upon a child's visual memory skills, with minimal emphasis on sounding out a word; child memorizes the word based on its overall configuration.

Sight Words: Words a child can recognize on sight without aid of phonics or other word-attack skills.[11]

SLD: Specific learning disability. Difficulty in certain areas of learning is contrasted with a general learning disability, (i.e., difficulty in all areas of learning). Also sometimes interpreted as Specific Language Disability.

Slingerland Method: A highly structured, multisensory teaching method designed for group instruction of persons with specific learning disabilities. Named for its developer, Beth Slingerland.[2]

Social Perceptions: The ability to interpret stimuli in the social environment and appropriately relate such interpretations to social situations.

Socio-Cultural: Combined social and cultural factors as they affect the development of a child in all areas of life.[1]

Soft Neurological Signs: Neurological abnormalities that are mild or slight and difficult to detect, as contrasted with the gross or obvious neurological abnormalities.[10]

Sound Blending: The ability to combine smoothly all the sounds or parts of a word into the whole.[11]

Spatial Orientation: Awareness of space around the person in terms of distance, form, direction, and position.[5]

Spatial Relationships: The ability to perceive the relationships between self and two or more objects and the relationships of the objects to each other.[5]

Special Education: Specially designed instruction to meet the needs of students with disabilities.

Specific Language Disability (SLD): Difficulty in some aspect of learning how to read, write, spell, or speak. Is also called Specific Language Learning Disability. (SLD sometimes refers to Specific Learning Disability.)

Standardized Test: A test that compares a child's performance with the performance of a large group of similar children (usually children of the same age). Also called a norm-referenced test. IQ tests and most achievement tests are standardized.[2]

Structural Analysis: Using syllabication, prefix, suffix, and root word clues, etc. to read or spell a word.

Structure: Consistent use of rules, limits, and routines. The use of structure reassures a child with learning disabilities that the environment is somewhat predictable and stable.[2]

Substitution: in reading, spelling, or math, interchanging a given letter, number, or word for another, e.g., sereal for cereal.

Supplementary Aids and Services: Aids, services, and other supports that are provided in regular education classes or other education-related settings to enable a child with disabilities to be educated with children without disabilities to the maximum extent appropriate.[4]

Supports for School Personnel: This refers to any needed support for the regular education teacher in order for the student with LD to be able to participate in and progress in the general education curriculum. This may include assistance in providing program modifications as well as specific training in strategies and skills that will assist the teacher in working with the student in the classroom.[12]

Survival Skills: Minimal skills needed for a student to cope with everyday society.[1]

Syndrome: A set of symptoms that indicates a specific disorder.[2]

Syntax: Grammar, sentence structure, and word order in oral or written language.

Tactile: Having to do with the sense of touch.[2]

Task Analysis: The technique of carefully examining a particular task to discover the elements it comprises and the processes required to perform it.[10]

Thematic Maturity: Ability to write in a logical, organized manner that easily and efficiently conveys meaning.

Thinking Skills: Refers to the manner in which humans acquire, interpret, organize, store, retrieve, and employ knowledge.[1]

Transition Plan: The part of the IEP that outlines what transition services are necessary to help the student move from school to the next step in their life.

Transition Services: Component of the IEP, beginning by the time a student with a disability reaches age 14. The term identifies a co-ordinated set of activities for the student, designed within an outcome-oriented process, that promotes movement from school to post-school activities. Transition goals may include post-secondary education, vocational training, integrated employment (including supported employment), continuing and adult education, adult services, independent living, or community participation.[4]

Transposition: In reading, spelling, or math, confusion of the order of letters in a word or numbers in a numeral, e.g., sliver for silver, 432 for 423, etc.

VAKT: Acronym for visual-auditory-kinesthetic-tactile; multisensory teaching approach which emphasizes using all of the senses to teach skills and concepts.

Verbal Ability: Specific meaning of this term varies, depending upon the manner in which a given test measures this ability. Generally refers to oral or spoken language abilities.

Visual Association: Ability to relate concepts which are presented visually, through pictures or written words. For example, given a picture of a dog, house, flower and bone, the child is able to indicate that the dog and bone go together.

Visual Closure: Ability to see only the outline of an item or picture, or a partially completed picture, and still be able to indicate what it is.

Visual Discrimination: Ability to detect similarities and/or differences in materials which are presented visually, e.g., ability to discriminate h from n, o from c, b from d, etc.

Visual Figure-Ground: Ability to focus on the foreground of material presented visually, rather than background. Those who have difficulty with this may find it hard to keep their place while copying or reading, may find a crowded page of print or illustrations confusing, etc.

Visual Memory: Ability to retain information which is presented visually; may be short term memory, such as recalling information presented several seconds before; long term memory, such as recalling information presented more than a minute before; or sequential memory, such as recalling a series of information in proper order.

Visual Motor: Ability to translate information received visually into a motor response. Difficulties are often characterized by poor handwriting, etc.

Visual Perception: Ability to correctly interpret what is seen. For example, a child sees a triangle and identifies it as a triangle.[2]

Word Attack Skills: Ability to analyze unfamiliar words visually and phonetically.[2]

Word Recognition: Ability to read or pronounce a word; usually implies that the word is recognized immediately by sight and that the child does not need to apply word analysis skills. Does not imply understanding of the word.

Written Language: Encompasses all facets of written expression, e.g., handwriting, capitalization, punctuation, spelling, format, ability to express one's thoughts in sentences and paragraphs, etc.

References

1. Virginia Department of Education. *Guidelines for Programs for Students with Specific Learning Disabilities in Virginia's Public Schools.* 1980.

2. Foundation for Children with Learning Disabilities. *The FCLD Learning Disabilities Resource Guide.* New York. 1985.

3. www.CHADD.org

4. Virginia Department of Education. *Regulations Governing Special Education Programs for Children with Disabilities in Virginia.* 2000.

5. Myers, P. and Hammill, D. *Methods for Learning Disorders, (Second Edition).* New York: John Wiley & Sons, Inc. 1976.

6. www.ldanatl.org

7. Kirk, S. A. and Kirk, W. D. *Psycholinguistic Learning Disabilities: Diagnosis and Remediation.* Urbana, IL: University of Illinois Press. 1971.

8. *SLD Gazette.* Massachusetts Association for Children and Adults with Learning Disabilities. March 1977.

9. Learning Disabilities Association of America, *Fact Sheet,* Jan. 1996.

10. Lerner, J.W. *Children with Learning Disabilities. 2ⁿᵈ Edition.* Boston: Houghton Mifflin Co., 1976.

11. Wallace, G. *Characteristics of Learning Disabilities: A Television Series.* Richmond, VA. The Learning Disabilities Council, 1975.

12. Tomey, H.A., III. *Individualized Education Program: The Process.* Richmond, VA. Virginia Department of Education, 2000.

13. Valett, R.E. *The Remediation of Learning Disabilities.* Palo Alto, CA. Fearon Publishers, 1967.

14. Virginia Department of Health Regulatory Boards. *Code of Virginia* (Chapter 28—Behavioral Science Professions).

15. Lerner, J.W. *Learning Disabilities: Theories, Diagnosis and Teaching Strategies.* Boston. Houghton Mifflin Co., 1971.

16. Cicci, R. Pre-Conference Symposium Handout, "Language, Learning, and Literacy." Virginia Department of Education, Arlington, VA. April 19, 1991.

17. Wright, P.W.D., and Wright, P.D. *Wrightslaw: Special Education Law,* Hartsfield, VA. Harbor House Law Press, 1999.

18. Bryan, T. and Bryan, J. *Understanding Learning Disabilities, 2ⁿᵈ Edition,* Sherman Oaks, CA. Alfred Publishing Co., 1978.

Chapter 63

Learning Disabilities Professionals

Being a parent isn't easy. Parenting a child with LD is even more challenging because you may be involved with a variety of professionals during your child's education. Following is a brief list of some of them and an explanation of the services they provide.

Attorney: provides legal assistance to parents about issues pertaining to federal and state special education laws and regulations.

Advocate: represents parents in legal issues related to special education but may not have legal training.

Audiologist: assesses for degree of hearing loss and advises on devices for hearing amplification.

Child psychiatrist: specializes in the assessment and treatment of behavior and emotional aspects of infants, children, and adolescents; medical doctor who can prescribe medication.

Clinical psychologist: provides non-medical diagnosis and therapeutic treatment of emotional and behavioral problems for individuals or groups.

From "Specialists in the LD Field," by Jan Baumel, SchwabLearning.org. © Copyright 2000 SchwabLearning.org. Reprinted with permission of Schwab Learning. For more information, please visit www.schwablearning.org.

Developmental behavioral pediatrician: focuses on the diagnosis and treatment of developmental disorders in children; medical doctor who can prescribe medication.

Educational psychologist: administers psychological and educational assessments, prepares written report that interprets test results and behavior, and consults regarding education and behavior.

Educational therapist: assesses educational needs; develops and carries out programs for school-related behavior and learning problems, especially LD.

Neurologist: specializes in diagnosis and treatment of disorders of the brain and nervous system; medical doctor who can prescribe medication.

Neuropsychologist: assesses brain functioning and its relationship to learning and behavior through psychological tests.

Occupational therapist: assesses for and provides training to improve muscular strength, motor, or sensory coordination and functioning.

Pediatrician: specializes in the primary care of infants, children, and adolescents; medical doctor who can prescribe medication.

Social worker: provides counseling for individuals and families.

Speech and language therapist: provides assessment and training to improve communication skills.

Tutor: provides instructional support in academic areas; no specific training requirements; may or may not be a credentialed teacher.

About the Author

Jan Baumel, M.S., Licensed Educational Psychologist, spent 35 years in education as a teacher, school psychologist, and special education administrator before joining Schwab Learning 6 years ago. She also serves as a consultant to local school districts and university field supervisor for student teachers. Areas of specialty include learning and child development, assessment, and compliance issues.

Chapter 64

National Organizations on Learning Disabilities

Serving All Ages

National Center for Learning Disabilities (NCLD)

381 Park Avenue South, Suite 1401
New York, NY 10016
Toll Free: 888-575-7373
Tel: 212-545-7510
Fax: 212-545-9665
Internet: http://www.ld.org

National non-profit organization that offers a free Information & Referral Service, conducts educational programs, raises public awareness of LD, and advocates for improved legislation and services for those with LD.

Learning Disabilities Association of America (LDA)

4156 Library Road
Pittsburgh, PA 15234
Toll Free: 888-300-6710
Tel: 412-341-1515
Fax: 412-244-0224

"National Organizations on Learning Disabilities," © 2001 National Center for Learning Disabilities. Available online at http://www.ld.org/resources/natl_orgs.cfm. Resources verified August 2002. For more information from the National Center for Learning Disabilities, visit their website at http://www.ncld.org.

Learning Disabilities Association of America (LDA) *(continued)*
Internet: http://www.ldaamerica.org
E-Mail: info@lda@ladamerica.org

National non-profit membership organization, with state and local chapters, that conducts an annual conference and offers information and various publications.

International Dyslexia Association
Chester Building
8600 La Salle Road
Suite 382
Baltimore, MD 21204
Toll Free: 800-ABC-D123
Tel: 410-296-0232
Fax: 410-321-5069
Internet: http://www.interdys.org

International non-profit membership organization that offers training in language programs and provides publications relating to dyslexia. Chapters are located in most states.

Division for Learning Disabilities (DLD) of the Council for Exceptional Children (CEC)
1110 North Glebe Road
Suite 300
Arlington, VA 22201-5704
Toll Free: 888-CEC-SPED
Tel: 703-620-3660
TTY: 703-264-9446 (text only)
Fax: 703-264-9494
Internet: http://www.teachingld.org

CEC is a non-profit membership organization that has seventeen specialized divisions. DLD is the division dedicated to LD. Both CEC and DLD provide free information and hold conferences.

Council for Learning Disabilities (CLD)
P.O. Box 40303
Overland Park, KS 66204
Tel: 913-492-8755
Fax: 913-492-2546
Internet: http://www.cldinternational.org

National membership organization dedicated to assisting professionals who work in the field of learning disabilities. The *Learning Disabilities Quarterly*, a professional publication is available through CLD.

Learning Disabilities Association of Canada (LDAC)
323 Chapel Street
Suite 200
Ottawa, Ontario, Canada K1N 7Z2
Tel: 613-238-5721
Fax: 613-235-5391
Internet: http://www.ldac-taac.ca
E-Mail: information@ldac-taac.ca

Non-profit membership organization with provincial and territorial offices that conducts programs and provides information for LD children and adults. Resources include books and pamphlets that may be useful to U.S. residents.

National Information Center for Children and Youth with Disabilities (NICHCY)
P.O. Box 1492
Washington, DC 20013-1492
Tel: 800-695-0285
Fax: 202-884-8441
Internet: http://www.nichcy.org
E-Mail: nichcy@aid.org

Information clearinghouse that provides free information on disabilities and disability-related issues.

Schwab Foundation for Learning
1650 South Amphlett Boulevard
Suite 300
San Mateo, CA 94402-2516
Toll Free: 800-230-0988
Tel: 650-655-2410
Fax: 650-655-2411
Internet: http://www.schwablearning.org

Non-profit organization that provides information and referral to national and local resources as well as research and guidance for parents, teachers, clinicians, and others who work with children who have learning differences.

Adult Resources

HEATH Resource Center
One Dupont Circle
Suite 800
Washington, DC 20036
Toll Free: 800-544-3284
Tel: 202-973-0904
Fax: 202-973-0908
Internet: http://www.heath.gwu.edu
E-Mail: askheath@heath.gwu.edu

National clearinghouse that provides free information on postsecondary education and related issues.

The National LINCS Literacy & Learning Disabilities Special Collection
1775 I Street NW
Suite 730
Washington, DC 20006
Tel: 202-233-2039
Fax: 202-233-2050
Internet: http://www.nifl.gov/lincs

A collection of Web-based and other resources on issues affecting adults with learning disabilities and their families, as well as literacy practitioners and other human resource service providers who work with these persons.

National Association for Adults with Special Learning Needs (NAASLN)
4300 Forbes Boulevard
Lanham, MD 20706
Toll Free: 800-496-9222
Internet: http://www.naasln.org

Non-profit organization comprised of professionals, advocates, and consumers, whose purpose is to educate adults with special learning needs. Publishes a newsletter and holds annual conferences.

Web Sites

LD OnLine
http://www.ldonline.org

Comprehensive on-line resource offering information on learning disabilities for parents, educators, as well as children and adults with learning disabilities. Features include basic and in-depth information, national events calendar, bulletin boards, audio clips from LD experts, extensive resource listings with hyperlinks, and a special section just for kids. Artwork and writing by young people with learning disabilities are featured weekly.

National Association of State Directors of Special Education, Inc. (NASDE)
King Station I
1800 Diagonal Road
Suite 320
Alexandria, VA 22314
Tel: 703-519-3800
TDD: 703-519-7008
Fax: 703-519-3808
Internet: http://www.nasdse.org/home.htm

Not-for-profit corporation that promotes and supports educational programs for students with disabilities and holds annual meetings.

National Institute for Child Health and Human Development (NICHD)
31 Center Drive
Bldg. 31, Room 2A32, MSC 2425
Bethesda, MD 20892-2425
Toll Free: 800-370-2943
Tel: 301-496-5733
Internet: http://www.nichd.nih.gov
E-Mail: NICHDClearinghouse@mail.nih.gov

Provides reviews of literature and information related to NICHD research.

National Center to Improve the Tools of Educators (NCITE)

805 Lincoln
Eugene, OR 97401
Tel: 503-683-7543
Internet: http://idea.uoregon.edu/~ncite
E-Mail: ncite@darkwing.uoregon.edu

Center funded by the U.S. Department of Education. Dedicated to the improvement of instructional methods and materials. Publishes articles on educational practices.

National Association of School Psychologists (NASP)

4340 East West Highway, Suite 402
Bethesda, MD 20814
Tel: 301-657-0270
Internet: http://www.naspweb.org/index2.html
E-Mail: center@naspweb.org

International not-for-profit membership association of school psychologists. Provides a nationally recognized certification system, promotes children's rights, produces videos, and sponsors conferences. Publishes books, a newspaper, and the quarterly *School Psychology Review*.

Chapter 65

Financial Aid for Students with Disabilities

What Is Financial Aid?

Financial aid is designed to help individuals meet their educational expenses when their own resources are not sufficient. A student who believes that his or her own and family resources are not sufficient to pay for all the costs of attendance (tuition, room and board, books, transportation, campus activities, etc.) should apply for financial aid through the financial aid office of the institution he or she plans to attend. Four types of aid are available:

1. Grants—Aid that generally does not have to be repaid.

2. Loans—Money borrowed to cover school costs, which must be repaid (usually with interest) over a specified period of time (usually after the student has left school or graduated).

Reprinted with permission from *Creating Options: a Resource on Financial Aid for Students with Disabilities,* (2001), published by the HEATH Resource Center of the George Washington University School of Education and Human Development, the national clearinghouse on postsecondary education for individuals with disabilities. This publication was prepared under Cooperative Agreement Number H326H98002, awarded to the American Council on Education by the U.S. Department of Education. The full text of this document is available online at http://www.heath.gov.edu/PDFs/financialaid.pdf. For additional information about the HEATH Resource Center, visit www.heath.gwu.edu.

3. Work-study—Employment that enables a student to earn money toward a portion of school costs during or between periods of enrollment.

4. Scholarships—Gifts and awards based on a student's academic achievement, background, or other criteria.

What Expenses Are Considered Disability Related?

The student with a disability is often faced with additional expenses not incurred by other students. These may include:

• Special equipment (related to the disability) and its maintenance.

• Cost of services for personal use or study, such as readers, interpreters, note takers, or personal care attendants.

• Transportation, if traditional means are not accessible.

• Medical expenses not covered by insurance that relate directly to the individual's disability.

Students should be sure to inform the aid administrator of disability-related expenses that may previously have been covered by the family budget. These may include food and veterinary bills for guide dogs, batteries for hearing aids and a Typed Text (TTY) (previously called a Telecommunication Device for the Deaf (TDD)), or the cost of recruiting and training readers or personal care attendants. Leaving home often necessitates the purchase of new or additional equipment that will allow the student to be independent at college. For example, the student's secondary school may have furnished an adapted computer or other disability-related equipment, but that equipment belongs to and remains at the high school after the student graduates. Students with disabilities should seek assistance from the Office of Disability Support Services and/or the Financial Aid Office to determine disability-related expenses.

Financial Aid Resources on the Internet

Students with Internet access will find a wealth of information about grants and scholarships for which they may apply. The following World Wide Web addresses are listed to facilitate an electronic search. Note that many web sites offer additional links to other related sites.

Easy Access for Students and Institutions (EASI)
Internet: http://www.easi.ed.gov

Offers information about the financial aid system.

Financial Aid for Students, through the U.S. Department of Education's Office of Postsecondary Education
Internet: http://www.ed.gov/offices/OPE/students

Offers information and links relating to federal student assistance programs.

The Financial Aid Information Page
Internet: http://www.finaid.org

A comprehensive resource that will connect students with mailing lists, news groups, loan information, and scholarships for special interest groups such as females, minorities, veterans, etc.

FAFSA Express
Internet: http://www.ed.gov/offices/OPE/express.html

Allows students to download, complete, and file the FAFSA electronically. Or call the FAFSA Express Customer Service Line for more information at (800) 801-0576.

College Board Home Page
Internet: http://www.collegeboard.org

Includes an instant profile search of available grants and scholarships.

FastWEB (Financial Aid Search Through the WEB)
Internet: http://www.fastweb.com

A searchable database of more than 180,000 private-sector scholarships, fellowships, grants, and loans. Used by colleges across the United States, FastWEB is now available to you at no charge through the World Wide Web, courtesy of the Financial Aid Information Page and Student Services, Inc.

CASHE (College Aid Sources for Higher Education)
Internet: http://www.salliemae.com

Provided free through Sallie Mae's Online Scholarship Service, is a database of more than 180,000 scholarships, fellowships, grants, loans, internships, competitions, and work-study programs sponsored by more than 3,600 organizations.

CollegeNET MACH25
Internet: http://www.collegenet.com/mach25

A free Web version of the Wintergreen/Orchard House Scholarship Finder database. This database contains listings of more than 500,000 private-sector awards from 1,570 sponsors. The database is updated annually.

The National Association of Student Financial Aid Administrators' (NASFAA)
Internet: http://www.nasfaa.org

Includes two free downloadable publications for students and their parents, Cash for College and TIPS: Timely Information for Parents and Students. The site also contains links to other financial aid-related web sites.

College Quest
Internet: http://www.collegequest.com

A comprehensive site devoted to the process of searching, choosing, applying, and paying for college that contains a database of more than 850,000 scholarships and grants for postsecondary study.

Chapter 66

The Education Resources Information Center (ERIC)

Have you heard of the ERIC database but never used it? Have you tried to search the ERIC database on the Internet and been confused by what you found? Have you used ERIC but wondered if you found everything on your topic? Here are some tips for new and experienced ERIC users that will help you get the most out of the world's largest education database.

What Is ERIC?

The Educational Resources Information Center (ERIC) is a federally funded information network designed to provide users with ready access to education literature. Papers, curriculum and teaching guides, conference proceedings, literature reviews, along with articles from nearly 800 education-related journals, are indexed and abstracted for the ERIC database.

Although the ERIC system consists of 16 clearinghouses and several support components at various locations around the United States, there is only one ERIC database. Whether you access ERIC on the Internet (World Wide Web) or through a public library, college library, or other information center, you are searching the same database of educational information.

"How to Use ERIC to Search Your Special Education Topic," by Kathleen McLane and Barbara Sorensen. From the Educational Resources Information Center (ERIC), *Eric Digest,* E573, ERIC Identifier: ED434465, 1999.

ERIC and Students with Exceptionalities

Currently, more than 74,000 documents and journal articles in ERIC relate to the education of individuals who have disabilities and/or who are gifted. Virtually all of these were added by the ERIC Clearinghouse on Disabilities and Gifted Education.

What Will You Get from an ERIC Search?

The result of the search will be an annotated bibliography of the journal and document literature on your topic. After you have received and screened your search, you can readily obtain the full text of most of the materials. Microfiche or paper copies of materials are available from many ERIC service providers or from the ERIC Document Reproduction Service (EDRS); and EDRS provides the full text of many documents in the ERIC database. Journal articles can be found in many libraries, and reprints can be ordered from article reprint services.

Find the Best Way for You to Access ERIC

The ERIC database is available at a number of World Wide Web sites, at university libraries, and at many public and professional libraries. If you have a personal computer and access to the Internet, you can search the ERIC database through a variety of computer networks and services like the Internet, OCLC's First Search, DIALOG, Dataware Technologies, and other online services. Before you decide where to search ERIC, ask these questions:

1. How much will it cost?

   You may have free or inexpensive access to ERIC, for example, through your school or college library or through your own Internet account. If not, you may have to pay for connect time on some computer systems or order a search through a search service.

2. How much of the ERIC database is available?

   Some services provide access to only the most recent five or ten years of ERIC, which may be all you need. Decide whether you want to limit your search by date; remember that the database was started in 1966.

3. How long will it take?

    Turnaround time can vary greatly, from a few minutes if you have direct access to ERIC on a personal computer, to several days or longer if you have to order a search that someone else will run for you.

4. How much flexibility does the search system offer?

    Many different software systems are used to search ERIC. Some menu-driven search systems make it easy for a first-time user, but limit your opportunities to make changes to your search question. If you try searching ERIC and feel you cannot locate exactly what you are looking for, ask your librarian for help or call an ERIC clearinghouse.

For help in locating the ERIC resource collection nearest you, call ACCESS ERIC at 1-800-LET-ERIC (800-538-3742).

Use the Thesaurus of ERIC Descriptors

Every one of the nearly 1 million articles and documents in the ERIC database has been given subject indexing terms called descriptors. Before you run an ERIC search, it is important to take a few minutes to find the ERIC descriptors that best capture your topic. For example, articles and documents about regular class placement are indexed under the descriptor mainstreaming or inclusive schools. If you want resources about developing children's social skills, the best descriptor is interpersonal competence.

Many web sites and search devices have the Thesaurus online so that you can consult it as you are searching. If you are using ERIC at a library, ask for a copy of the Thesaurus of ERIC Descriptors for help with your strategy. (Note: If you are searching a relatively new concept for which there is no descriptor, free text searching is available on most systems. Free text searching means you can look for the word or concept anywhere in the abstract.)

Know Your "Ands" and "Ors"

Although the software used to search ERIC will depend on which system you use, all searching is based on Boolean logic. The computer creates sets of information based on the way you tell it to combine words, including subject terms (descriptors).

For example, if you wanted ideas on how computers can be used to improve the writing skills of students with learning disabilities, you could use the Thesaurus to find these subject descriptors:

- learning disabilities

- computer assisted instruction

- writing instruction

To search ERIC for records that are indexed under all three of your concepts, you would combine these descriptors with ANDs (learning disabilities AND computer assisted instruction AND writing instruction) to create a search based on Boolean logic.

If you wanted to expand your search to find additional relevant materials on this topic, you could add descriptors to your writing and computer sets using the OR operator. Remember, ORs expand or add more to your search, ANDs limit and help focus your search.

How to Use the ERIC Search Planning Sheet

The previous example shows how a special education question can be converted to a strategy for searching the ERIC database. Use a blank worksheet to plan your search as follows:

1. Write your topic in your own words.

2. Divide the topic into two or three basic concepts.

3. Use the Thesaurus of ERIC Descriptors to locate the descriptors (subject terms) that best represent the concepts in your topic.

4. Combine the descriptors using ANDs and ORs, keeping in mind that ANDs limit and focus your search and ORs expand your search.

Note: If you cannot locate an ERIC Thesaurus, call the ERIC Clearinghouse on Disabilities and Gifted Education for help (800-328-0272).

Index

Index

Page numbers followed by 'n' indicate a footnote. Page numbers in *italics* indicate a table or illustration.

A

academic classes, defined 539
academic skills disorders
  described 7–8
  women 52
acalculia, described 229
"Accommodating All Learners" (Firchow) 431n
accommodations
  defined 501, 539
  dyslexia 485–91
  homework assignments 396–97
  multiple chemical sensitivity/ environmental illness 260–61
  recommendations 290
  tests 427–29
  Tourette syndrome 271–74
"Accommodations for People with Dyslexia: Coping in the Workplace" (Brown) 485n
Achenbach Child Behavior Checklist 40
achievement test, defined 539

ADA *see* Americans with Disabilities Act
"Adapting Mathematics Instruction in the General Education Classroom for Students with Mathematics Disabilities" (Lock) 121n
adaptive physical education, defined 540
ADD *see* attention deficit disorder
AD/HD *see* attention deficit hyperactivity disorder
adolescents
  attention deficit hyperactivity disorder 193
  learning disorders diagnosis 291–92
  tobacco use, pregnancy 38
  XXY males 240–41
"Adults with Learning Disabilities" (Kerka) 55n
advocate, defined 561
age of eligibility, defined 540
agraphia, described 229
AHEAD *see* The Association on Higher Education and Disability
Ahern, Eileen 407n
alcohol use, pregnancy 33–34, 39–41
  see also fetal alcohol syndrome
alcohol-related neurodevelopmental disorder (ARND) 40–42

allergic reactions *see* multiple chemical sensitivity/environmental illness
alternative education programs 413–
18
American Academy of Audiology, contact information 115
The American Academy of Pediatrics,
contact information 69
American Psychiatric Association
(APA), mental disorders publication
5, 51–52
American Sign Language (ASL) 250
American Speech-Language-Hearing
Association (ASLHA)
contact information 69, 115, 246
learning disabilities publication
71n
Americans with Disabilities Act
(ADA; 1990)
defined 540
described 23
dyslexia 155
job accommodations 485–91
learning disabilites 285
multiple chemical sensitivity/
environmental illness 259
public charter schools 408
specific learning disabilities 56
amniocentesis, XXY males 233
amphetamines, defined 540
Anderson-Inman, Lynne 449n
animal studies
fetal nicotine exposure 35
lead exposure 12
learning disabilities 25
prenatal tobacco exposure 37
anoxia, defined 540
APA *see* American Psychiatric Association
APD *see* auditory processing disorder
aphasia
described 52, 229
overview 99–103
"Aphasia" (NIDCD) 99n
"Aphasia: Recent Research" (NIDCD)
99n
apraxia *see* dyspraxia
aptitude test, defined 540

ARND *see* alcohol-related
neurodevelopmental disorder
art therapy, learning disabilities 306
articulation
defined 540
described 77, 82
articulation disorders, described 88
ASL *see* American Sign Language
ASLHA *see* American Speech-
Language-Hearing Association
"Asperger Syndrome" (Lord) 183n
Asperger syndrome, overview 183–88
assessments *see* tests
assistive technology (AT)
accommodations 431
consideration 437–47
defined 438, 540–41
described 58, 300–302, 499–500
hearing impairments 252–53
standard curriculum 479–84
Tourette syndrome 270–71
association, defined 541
The Association on Higher Education
and Disability (AHEAD), learning
disabilities publication 285n
AT *see* assistive technology
attention, learning disabilities warning signs 28–29, 30, 31
attention deficit disorder (ADD) 270
attention deficit hyperactivity disorder (AD/HD)
coping measures 19–20
defined 540
described 9, 189
diagnosis 190–
dyslexia 153
gifted children 47–48
heredity 191
maternal tobacco use 35
research 195
symptoms 190
Tourette syndrome 270
treatment 193–95
"Attention Deficit Hyperactivity Disorder (AD/HD) - Questions and Answers" (NIMH) 189n
attention disorders, described 9
attention span, defined 541
attorney, defined 561

590

Q

Health Reference Series
COMPLETE CATALOG

Adolescent Health Sourcebook

Basic Consumer Health Information about Common Medical, Mental, and Emotional Concerns in Adolescents, Including Facts about Acne, Body Piercing, Mononucleosis, Nutrition, Eating Disorders, Stress, Depression, Behavior Problems, Peer Pressure, Violence, Gangs, Drug Use, Puberty, Sexuality, Pregnancy, Learning Disabilities, and More

Along with a Glossary of Terms and Other Resources for Further Help and Information

Edited by Chad T. Kimball. 658 pages. 2002. 0-7808-0248-9. $78.

"A good starting point for information related to common medical, mental, and emotional concerns of adolescents." — *School Library Journal, Nov '02*

"This book provides accurate information in an easy to access format. It addresses topics that parents and caregivers might not be aware of and provides practical, useable information." — *Doody's Health Sciences Book Review Journal, Sep-Oct '02*

"Recommended reference source."
— *Booklist, American Library Association, Sep '02*

■

AIDS Sourcebook, 1st Edition

Basic Information about AIDS and HIV Infection, Featuring Historical and Statistical Data, Current Research, Prevention, and Other Special Topics of Interest for Persons Living with AIDS

Along with Source Listings for Further Assistance

Edited by Karen Bellenir and Peter D. Dresser. 831 pages. 1995. 0-7808-0031-1. $78.

"One strength of this book is its practical emphasis. The intended audience is the lay reader . . . useful as an educational tool for health care providers who work with AIDS patients. Recommended for public libraries as well as hospital or academic libraries that collect consumer materials."
— *Bulletin of the Medical Library Association, Jan '96*

"This is the most comprehensive volume of its kind on an important medical topic. Highly recommended for all libraries." — *Reference Book Review, '96*

"Very useful reference for all libraries."
— *Choice, Association of College and Research Libraries, Oct '95*

"There is a wealth of information here that can provide much educational assistance. It is a must book for all libraries and should be on the desk of each and every congressional leader. Highly recommended."
— *AIDS Book Review Journal, Aug '95*

"Recommended for most collections."
— *Library Journal, Jul '95*

AIDS Sourcebook, 2nd Edition

Basic Consumer Health Information about Acquired Immune Deficiency Syndrome (AIDS) and Human Immunodeficiency Virus (HIV) Infection, Featuring Updated Statistical Data, Reports on Recent Research and Prevention Initiatives, and Other Special Topics of Interest for Persons Living with AIDS, Including New Antiretroviral Treatment Options, Strategies for Combating Opportunistic Infections, Information about Clinical Trials, and More

Along with a Glossary of Important Terms and Resource Listings for Further Help and Information

Edited by Karen Bellenir. 751 pages. 1999. 0-7808-0225-X. $78.

"Highly recommended."
— *American Reference Books Annual, 2000*

"Excellent sourcebook. This continues to be a highly recommended book. There is no other book that provides as much information as this book provides."
— *AIDS Book Review Journal, Dec-Jan 2000*

"Recommended reference source."
— *Booklist, American Library Association, Dec '99*

"A solid text for college-level health libraries."
— *The Bookwatch, Aug '99*

Cited in *Reference Sources for Small and Medium-Sized Libraries, American Library Association, 1999*

■

Alcoholism Sourcebook

Basic Consumer Health Information about the Physical and Mental Consequences of Alcohol Abuse, Including Liver Disease, Pancreatitis, Wernicke-Korsakoff Syndrome (Alcoholic Dementia), Fetal Alcohol Syndrome, Heart Disease, Kidney Disorders, Gastrointestinal Problems, and Immune System Compromise and Featuring Facts about Addiction, Detoxification, Alcohol Withdrawal, Recovery, and the Maintenance of Sobriety

Along with a Glossary and Directories of Resources for Further Help and Information

Edited by Karen Bellenir. 613 pages. 2000. 0-7808-0325-6. $78.

"This title is one of the few reference works on alcoholism for general readers. For some readers this will be a welcome complement to the many self-help books on the market. Recommended for collections serving general readers and consumer health collections."
— *E-Streams, Mar '01*

"This book is an excellent choice for public and academic libraries."
— *American Reference Books Annual, 2001*

"Recommended reference source."
— *Booklist, American Library Association, Dec '00*

"Presents a wealth of information on alcohol use and abuse and its effects on the body and mind, treatment, and prevention." — *SciTech Book News, Dec '00*

"Important new health guide which packs in the latest consumer information about the problems of alcoholism." — *Reviewer's Bookwatch, Nov '00*

SEE ALSO *Drug Abuse Sourcebook, Substance Abuse Sourcebook*

■

Allergies Sourcebook, 1st Edition

Basic Information about Major Forms and Mechanisms of Common Allergic Reactions, Sensitivities, and Intolerances, Including Anaphylaxis, Asthma, Hives and Other Dermatologic Symptoms, Rhinitis, and Sinusitis

Along with Their Usual Triggers Like Animal Fur, Chemicals, Drugs, Dust, Foods, Insects, Latex, Pollen, and Poison Ivy, Oak, and Sumac; Plus Information on Prevention, Identification, and Treatment

Edited by Allan R. Cook. 611 pages. 1997. 0-7808-0036-2. $78.

■

Allergies Sourcebook, 2nd Edition

Basic Consumer Health Information about Allergic Disorders, Triggers, Reactions, and Related Symptoms, Including Anaphylaxis, Rhinitis, Sinusitis, Asthma, Dermatitis, Conjunctivitis, and Multiple Chemical Sensitivity

Along with Tips on Diagnosis, Prevention, and Treatment, Statistical Data, a Glossary, and a Directory of Sources for Further Help and Information

Edited by Annemarie S. Muth. 598 pages. 2002. 0-7808-0376-0. $78.

"This second edition would be useful to laypersons with little or advanced knowledge of the subject matter. This book would also serve as a resource for nursing and other health care professions students. It would be useful in public, academic, and hospital libraries with consumer health collections." — *E-Streams, Jul '02*

■

Alternative Medicine Sourcebook, 1st Edition

Basic Consumer Health Information about Alternatives to Conventional Medicine, Including Acupressure, Acupuncture, Aromatherapy, Ayurveda, Bioelectromagnetics, Environmental Medicine, Essence Therapy, Food and Nutrition Therapy, Herbal Therapy, Homeopathy, Imaging, Massage, Naturopathy, Reflexology, Relaxation and Meditation, Sound Therapy, Vitamin and Mineral Therapy, and Yoga, and More

Edited by Allan R. Cook. 737 pages. 1999. 0-7808-0200-4. $78.

"Recommended reference source."
— *Booklist, American Library Association, Feb '00*

"A great addition to the reference collection of every type of library." — *American Reference Books Annual, 2000*

Alternative Medicine Sourcebook, 2nd Edition

Basic Consumer Health Information about Alternative and Complementary Medical Practices, Including Acupuncture, Chiropractic, Herbal Medicine, Homeopathy, Naturopathic Medicine, Mind-Body Interventions, Ayurveda, and Other Non-Western Medical Traditions

Along with Facts about such Specific Therapies as Massage Therapy, Aromatherapy, Qigong, Hypnosis, Prayer, Dance, and Art Therapies, a Glossary, and Resources for Further Information

Edited by Dawn D. Matthews. 618 pages. 2002. 0-7808-0605-0. $78.

"An important alternate health reference."
— *MBR Bookwatch, Oct '02*

■

Alzheimer's, Stroke & 29 Other Neurological Disorders Sourcebook, 1st Edition

Basic Information for the Layperson on 31 Diseases or Disorders Affecting the Brain and Nervous System, First Describing the Illness, Then Listing Symptoms, Diagnostic Methods, and Treatment Options, and Including Statistics on Incidences and Causes

Edited by Frank E. Bair. 579 pages. 1993. 1-55888-748-2. $78.

"Nontechnical reference book that provides reader-friendly information."
— *Family Caregiver Alliance Update, Winter '96*

"Should be included in any library's patient education section." — *American Reference Books Annual, 1994*

"Written in an approachable and accessible style. Recommended for patient education and consumer health collections in health science center and public libraries." — *Academic Library Book Review, Dec '93*

"It is very handy to have information on more than thirty neurological disorders under one cover, and there is no recent source like it." — *Reference Quarterly, American Library Association, Fall '93*

SEE ALSO *Brain Disorders Sourcebook*

■

Alzheimer's Disease Sourcebook, 2nd Edition

Basic Consumer Health Information about Alzheimer's Disease, Related Disorders, and Other Dementias, Including Multi-Infarct Dementia, AIDS-Related Dementia, Alcoholic Dementia, Huntington's Disease, Delirium, and Confusional States

Along with Reports Detailing Current Research Efforts in Prevention and Treatment, Long-Term Care Issues, and Listings of Sources for Additional Help and Information

Edited by Karen Bellenir. 524 pages. 1999. 0-7808-0223-3. $78.

"Provides a wealth of useful information not otherwise available in one place. This resource is recommended for all types of libraries."
— *American Reference Books Annual, 2000*

"Recommended reference source."
— *Booklist, American Library Association, Oct '99*

■

Arthritis Sourcebook

Basic Consumer Health Information about Specific Forms of Arthritis and Related Disorders, Including Rheumatoid Arthritis, Osteoarthritis, Gout, Polymyalgia Rheumatica, Psoriatic Arthritis, Spondyloarthropathies, Juvenile Rheumatoid Arthritis, and Juvenile Ankylosing Spondylitis

Along with Information about Medical, Surgical, and Alternative Treatment Options, and Including Strategies for Coping with Pain, Fatigue, and Stress

Edited by Allan R. Cook. 550 pages. 1998. 0-7808-0201-2. $78.

". . . accessible to the layperson."
— *Reference and Research Book News, Feb '99*

■

Asthma Sourcebook

Basic Consumer Health Information about Asthma, Including Symptoms, Traditional and Nontraditional Remedies, Treatment Advances, Quality-of-Life Aids, Medical Research Updates, and the Role of Allergies, Exercise, Age, the Environment, and Genetics in the Development of Asthma

Along with Statistical Data, a Glossary, and Directories of Support Groups, and Other Resources for Further Information

Edited by Annemarie S. Muth. 628 pages. 2000. 0-7808-0381-7. $78.

"A worthwhile reference acquisition for public libraries and academic medical libraries whose readers desire a quick introduction to the wide range of asthma information."
— *Choice, Association of College & Research Libraries, Jun '01*

"Recommended reference source."
— *Booklist, American Library Association, Feb '01*

"Highly recommended."   — *The Bookwatch, Jan '01*

"There is much good information for patients and their families who deal with asthma daily."
— *American Medical Writers Association Journal, Winter '01*

"This informative text is recommended for consumer health collections in public, secondary school, and community college libraries and the libraries of universities with a large undergraduate population."
— *American Reference Books Annual, 2001*

Attention Deficit Disorder Sourcebook

Basic Consumer Health Information about Attention Deficit/Hyperactivity Disorder in Children and Adults, Including Facts about Causes, Symptoms, Diagnostic Criteria, and Treatment Options Such as Medications, Behavior Therapy, Coaching, and Homeopathy

Along with Reports on Current Research Initiatives, Legal Issues, and Government Regulations, and Featuring a Glossary of Related Terms, Internet Resources, and a List of Additional Reading Material

Edited by Dawn D. Matthews. 470 pages. 2002. 0-7808-0624-7. $78.

■

Back & Neck Disorders Sourcebook

Basic Information about Disorders and Injuries of the Spinal Cord and Vertebrae, Including Facts on Chiropractic Treatment, Surgical Interventions, Paralysis, and Rehabilitation

Along with Advice for Preventing Back Trouble

Edited by Karen Bellenir. 548 pages. 1997. 0-7808-0202-0. $78.

"The strength of this work is its basic, easy-to-read format. Recommended."
— *Reference and User Services Quarterly, American Library Association, Winter '97*

■

Blood & Circulatory Disorders Sourcebook

Basic Information about Blood and Its Components, Anemias, Leukemias, Bleeding Disorders, and Circulatory Disorders, Including Aplastic Anemia, Thalassemia, Sickle-Cell Disease, Hemochromatosis, Hemophilia, Von Willebrand Disease, and Vascular Diseases

Along with a Special Section on Blood Transfusions and Blood Supply Safety, a Glossary, and Source Listings for Further Help and Information

Edited by Karen Bellenir and Linda M. Shin. 554 pages. 1998. 0-7808-0203-9. $78.

"Recommended reference source."
— *Booklist, American Library Association, Feb '99*

"An important reference sourcebook written in simple language for everyday, non-technical users. "
— *Reviewer's Bookwatch, Jan '99*

■

Brain Disorders Sourcebook

Basic Consumer Health Information about Strokes, Epilepsy, Amyotrophic Lateral Sclerosis (ALS/Lou Gehrig's Disease), Parkinson's Disease, Brain Tumors, Cerebral Palsy, Headache, Tourette Syndrome, and More

Along with Statistical Data, Treatment and Rehabilitation Options, Coping Strategies, Reports on Current Research Initiatives, a Glossary, and Resource Listings for Additional Help and Information

Edited by Karen Bellenir. 481 pages. 1999. 0-7808-0229-2. $78.

"Belongs on the shelves of any library with a consumer health collection." — *E-Streams, Mar '00*

"Recommended reference source."
— *Booklist, American Library Association, Oct '99*

SEE ALSO Alzheimer's Disease Sourcebook, 2nd Edition

Breast Cancer Sourcebook

Basic Consumer Health Information about Breast Cancer, Including Diagnostic Methods, Treatment Options, Alternative Therapies, Self-Help Information, Related Health Concerns, Statistical and Demographic Data, and Facts for Men with Breast Cancer

Along with Reports on Current Research Initiatives, a Glossary of Related Medical Terms, and a Directory of Sources for Further Help and Information

Edited by Edward J. Prucha and Karen Bellenir. 580 pages. 2001. 0-7808-0244-6. $78.

"Recommended reference source."
— *Booklist, American Library Association, Jan '02*

"This reference source is highly recommended. It is quite informative, comprehensive and detailed in nature, and yet it offers practical advice in easy-to-read language. It could be thought of as the 'bible' of breast cancer for the consumer." — *E-Streams, Jan '02*

"The broad range of topics covered in lay language make the *Breast Cancer Sourcebook* an excellent addition to public and consumer health library collections."
— *American Reference Books Annual 2002*

"From the pros and cons of different screening methods and results to treatment options, *Breast Cancer Sourcebook* provides the latest information on the subject."
— *Library Bookwatch, Dec '01*

"This thoroughgoing, very readable reference covers all aspects of breast health and cancer.... Readers will find much to consider here. Recommended for all public and patient health collections."
— *Library Journal, Sep '01*

SEE ALSO Cancer Sourcebook for Women, 1st and 2nd Editions, Women's Health Concerns Sourcebook

Breastfeeding Sourcebook

Basic Consumer Health Information about the Benefits of Breastmilk, Preparing to Breastfeed, Breastfeeding as a Baby Grows, Nutrition, and More, Including Information on Special Situations and Concerns Such as Mastitis, Illness, Medications, Allergies, Multiple Births, Prematurity, Special Needs, and Adoption

Along with a Glossary and Resources for Additional Help and Information

Edited by Jenni Lynn Colson. 388 pages. 2002. 0-7808-0332-9. $78.

SEE ALSO Pregnancy & Birth Sourcebook

Burns Sourcebook

Basic Consumer Health Information about Various Types of Burns and Scalds, Including Flame, Heat, Cold, Electrical, Chemical, and Sun Burns

Along with Information on Short-Term and Long-Term Treatments, Tissue Reconstruction, Plastic Surgery, Prevention Suggestions, and First Aid

Edited by Allan R. Cook. 604 pages. 1999. 0-7808-0204-7. $78.

"This is an exceptional addition to the series and is highly recommended for all consumer health collections, hospital libraries, and academic medical centers."
— *E-Streams, Mar '00*

"This key reference guide is an invaluable addition to all health care and public libraries in confronting this ongoing health issue."
— *American Reference Books Annual, 2000*

"Recommended reference source."
— *Booklist, American Library Association, Dec '99*

SEE ALSO Skin Disorders Sourcebook

Cancer Sourcebook, 1st Edition

Basic Information on Cancer Types, Symptoms, Diagnostic Methods, and Treatments, Including Statistics on Cancer Occurrences Worldwide and the Risks Associated with Known Carcinogens and Activities

Edited by Frank E. Bair. 932 pages. 1990. 1-55888-888-8. $78.

Cited in *Reference Sources for Small and Medium-Sized Libraries, American Library Association, 1999*

"Written in nontechnical language. Useful for patients, their families, medical professionals, and librarians."
— *Guide to Reference Books, 1996*

"Designed with the non-medical professional in mind. Libraries and medical facilities interested in patient education should certainly consider adding the *Cancer Sourcebook* to their holdings. This compact collection of reliable information . . . is an invaluable tool for helping patients and patients' families and friends to take the first steps in coping with the many difficulties of cancer."
— *Medical Reference Services Quarterly, Winter '91*

"Specifically created for the nontechnical reader . . . an important resource for the general reader trying to understand the complexities of cancer."
— *American Reference Books Annual, 1991*

"This publication's nontechnical nature and very comprehensive format make it useful for both the general public and undergraduate students."
— *Choice, Association of College and Research Libraries, Oct '90*

New Cancer Sourcebook, 2nd Edition

Basic Information about Major Forms and Stages of Cancer, Featuring Facts about Primary and Secondary Tumors of the Respiratory, Nervous, Lymphatic, Circulatory, Skeletal, and Gastrointestinal Systems, and Specific Organs; Statistical and Demographic Data; Treatment Options; and Strategies for Coping

Edited by Allan R. Cook. 1,313 pages. 1996. 0-7808-0041-9. $78.

"An excellent resource for patients with newly diagnosed cancer and their families. The dialogue is simple, direct, and comprehensive. Highly recommended for patients and families to aid in their understanding of cancer and its treatment."
— *Booklist Health Sciences Supplement, American Library Association, Oct '97*

"The amount of factual and useful information is extensive. The writing is very clear, geared to general readers. Recommended for all levels." — *Choice, Association of College & Research Libraries, Jan '97*

■

Cancer Sourcebook, 3rd Edition

Basic Consumer Health Information about Major Forms and Stages of Cancer, Featuring Facts about Primary and Secondary Tumors of the Respiratory, Nervous, Lymphatic, Circulatory, Skeletal, and Gastrointestinal Systems, and Specific Organs

Along with Statistical and Demographic Data, Treatment Options, Strategies for Coping, a Glossary, and a Directory of Sources for Additional Help and Information

Edited by Edward J. Prucha. 1,069 pages. 2000. 0-7808-0227-6. $78.

"This title is recommended for health sciences and public libraries with consumer health collections."
— *E-Streams, Feb '01*

"... can be effectively used by cancer patients and their families who are looking for answers in a language they can understand. Public and hospital libraries should have it on their shelves."
— *American Reference Books Annual, 2001*

"Recommended reference source."
— *Booklist, American Library Association, Dec '00*

■

Cancer Sourcebook for Women, 1st Edition

Basic Information about Specific Forms of Cancer That Affect Women, Featuring Facts about Breast Cancer, Cervical Cancer, Ovarian Cancer, Cancer of the Uterus and Uterine Sarcoma, Cancer of the Vagina, and Cancer of the Vulva; Statistical and Demographic Data; Treatments, Self-Help Management Suggestions, and Current Research Initiatives

Edited by Allan R. Cook and Peter D. Dresser. 524 pages. 1996. 0-7808-0076-1. $78.

". . . written in easily understandable, non-technical language. Recommended for public libraries or hospital and academic libraries that collect patient education or consumer health materials."
— *Medical Reference Services Quarterly, Spring '97*

"Would be of value in a consumer health library. . . . written with the health care consumer in mind. Medical jargon is at a minimum, and medical terms are explained in clear, understandable sentences."
— *Bulletin of the Medical Library Association, Oct '96*

"The availability under one cover of all these pertinent publications, grouped under cohesive headings, makes this certainly a most useful sourcebook." — *Choice, Association of College & Research Libraries, Jun '96*

"Presents a comprehensive knowledge base for general readers. Men and women both benefit from the gold mine of information nestled between the two covers of this book. Recommended."
— *Academic Library Book Review, Summer '96*

"This timely book is highly recommended for consumer health and patient education collections in all libraries." — *Library Journal, Apr '96*

■

Cancer Sourcebook for Women, 2nd Edition

Basic Consumer Health Information about Gynecologic Cancers and Related Concerns, Including Cervical Cancer, Endometrial Cancer, Gestational Trophoblastic Tumor, Ovarian Cancer, Uterine Cancer, Vaginal Cancer, Vulvar Cancer, Breast Cancer, and Common Non-Cancerous Uterine Conditions, with Facts about Cancer Risk Factors, Screening and Prevention, Treatment Options, and Reports on Current Research Initiatives

Along with a Glossary of Cancer Terms and a Directory of Resources for Additional Help and Information

Edited by Karen Bellenir. 604 pages. 2002. 0-7808-0226-8. $78.

"Highly recommended for academic and medical reference collections." — *Library Bookwatch, Sep '02*

"This is a highly recommended book for any public or consumer library, being reader friendly and containing accurate and helpful information."
— *E-Streams, Aug '02*

"Recommended reference source."
— *Booklist, American Library Association, Jul '02*

SEE ALSO *Breast Cancer Sourcebook, Women's Health Concerns Sourcebook*

Cardiovascular Diseases & Disorders Sourcebook, 1st Edition

Basic Information about Cardiovascular Diseases and Disorders, Featuring Facts about the Cardiovascular System, Demographic and Statistical Data, Descriptions of Pharmacological and Surgical Interventions, Lifestyle Modifications, and a Special Section Focusing on Heart Disorders in Children

Edited by Karen Bellenir and Peter D. Dresser. 683 pages. 1995. 0-7808-0032-X. $78.

". . . comprehensive format provides an extensive overview on this subject." — *Choice, Association of College & Research Libraries, Jun '96*

". . . an easily understood, complete, up-to-date resource. This well executed public health tool will make valuable information available to those that need it most, patients and their families. The typeface, sturdy non-reflective paper, and library binding add a feel of quality found wanting in other publications. Highly recommended for academic and general libraries. " — *Academic Library Book Review, Summer '96*

SEE ALSO *Healthy Heart Sourcebook for Women, Heart Diseases & Disorders Sourcebook, 2nd Edition*

■

Caregiving Sourcebook

Basic Consumer Health Information for Caregivers, Including a Profile of Caregivers, Caregiving Responsibilities and Concerns, Tips for Specific Conditions, Care Environments, and the Effects of Caregiving

Along with Facts about Legal Issues, Financial Information, and Future Planning, a Glossary, and a Listing of Additional Resources

Edited by Joyce Brennfleck Shannon. 600 pages. 2001. 0-7808-0331-0. $78.

"Essential for most collections." — *Library Journal, Apr 1, 2002*

"An ideal addition to the reference collection of any public library. Health sciences information professionals may also want to acquire the *Caregiving Sourcebook* for their hospital or academic library for use as a ready reference tool by health care workers interested in aging and caregiving." — *E-Streams, Jan '02*

"Recommended reference source." — *Booklist, American Library Association, Oct '01*

■

Colds, Flu & Other Common Ailments Sourcebook

Basic Consumer Health Information about Common Ailments and Injuries, Including Colds, Coughs, the Flu, Sinus Problems, Headaches, Fever, Nausea and Vomiting, Menstrual Cramps, Diarrhea, Constipation, Hemorrhoids, Back Pain, Dandruff, Dry and Itchy Skin, Cuts, Scrapes, Sprains, Bruises, and More

Along with Information about Prevention, Self-Care, Choosing a Doctor, Over-the-Counter Medications, Folk Remedies, and Alternative Therapies, and Including a Glossary of Important Terms and a Directory of Resources for Further Help and Information

Edited by Chad T. Kimball. 638 pages. 2001. 0-7808-0435-X. $78.

"A good starting point for research on common illnesses. It will be a useful addition to public and consumer health library collections." — *American Reference Books Annual 2002*

"Will prove valuable to any library seeking to maintain a current, comprehensive reference collection of health resources. . . . Excellent reference." — *The Bookwatch, Aug '01*

"Recommended reference source." — *Booklist, American Library Association, July '01*

■

Communication Disorders Sourcebook

Basic Information about Deafness and Hearing Loss, Speech and Language Disorders, Voice Disorders, Balance and Vestibular Disorders, and Disorders of Smell, Taste, and Touch

Edited by Linda M. Ross. 533 pages. 1996. 0-7808-0077-X. $78.

"This is skillfully edited and is a welcome resource for the layperson. It should be found in every public and medical library." — *Booklist Health Sciences Supplement, American Library Association, Oct '97*

■

Congenital Disorders Sourcebook

Basic Information about Disorders Acquired during Gestation, Including Spina Bifida, Hydrocephalus, Cerebral Palsy, Heart Defects, Craniofacial Abnormalities, Fetal Alcohol Syndrome, and More

Along with Current Treatment Options and Statistical Data

Edited by Karen Bellenir. 607 pages. 1997. 0-7808-0205-5. $78.

"Recommended reference source." — *Booklist, American Library Association, Oct '97*

SEE ALSO *Pregnancy & Birth Sourcebook*

■

Consumer Issues in Health Care Sourcebook

Basic Information about Health Care Fundamentals and Related Consumer Issues, Including Exams and Screening Tests, Physician Specialties, Choosing a Doctor, Using Prescription and Over-the-Counter Medications Safely, Avoiding Health Scams, Managing Common Health Risks in the Home, Care Options for Chronically or Terminally Ill Patients, and a List of Resources for Obtaining Help and Further Information

Edited by Karen Bellenir. 618 pages. 1998. 0-7808-0221-7. $78.

"Both public and academic libraries will want to have a copy in their collection for readers who are interested in self-education on health issues."
— *American Reference Books Annual, 2000*

"The editor has researched the literature from government agencies and others, saving readers the time and effort of having to do the research themselves. Recommended for public libraries."
— *Reference and User Services Quarterly, American Library Association, Spring '99*

"Recommended reference source."
— *Booklist, American Library Association, Dec '98*

■

Contagious & Non-Contagious Infectious Diseases Sourcebook

Basic Information about Contagious Diseases like Measles, Polio, Hepatitis B, and Infectious Mononucleosis, and Non-Contagious Infectious Diseases like Tetanus and Toxic Shock Syndrome, and Diseases Occurring as Secondary Infections Such as Shingles and Reye Syndrome

Along with Vaccination, Prevention, and Treatment Information, and a Section Describing Emerging Infectious Disease Threats

Edited by Karen Bellenir and Peter D. Dresser. 566 pages. 1996. 0-7808-0075-3. $78.

■

Death & Dying Sourcebook

Basic Consumer Health Information for the Layperson about End-of-Life Care and Related Ethical and Legal Issues, Including Chief Causes of Death, Autopsies, Pain Management for the Terminally Ill, Life Support Systems, Insurance, Euthanasia, Assisted Suicide, Hospice Programs, Living Wills, Funeral Planning, Counseling, Mourning, Organ Donation, and Physician Training

Along with Statistical Data, a Glossary, and Listings of Sources for Further Help and Information

Edited by Annemarie S. Muth. 641 pages. 1999. 0-7808-0230-6. $78.

"Public libraries, medical libraries, and academic libraries will all find this sourcebook a useful addition to their collections."
— *American Reference Books Annual, 2001*

"An extremely useful resource for those concerned with death and dying in the United States."
— *Respiratory Care, Nov '00*

"Recommended reference source."
— *Booklist, American Library Association, Aug '00*

"This book is a definite must for all those involved in end-of-life care." — *Doody's Review Service, 2000*

Depression Sourcebook

Basic Consumer Health Information about Unipolar Depression, Bipolar Disorder, Postpartum Depression, Seasonal Affective Disorder, and Other Types of Depression in Children, Adolescents, Women, Men, the Elderly, and Other Selected Populations

Along with Facts about Causes, Risk Factors, Diagnostic Criteria, Treatment Options, Coping Strategies, Suicide Prevention, a Glossary, and a Directory of Sources for Additional Help and Information

Edited by Karen Belleni. 602 pages. 2002. 0-7808-0611-5. $78.

■

Diabetes Sourcebook, 1st Edition

Basic Information about Insulin-Dependent and Non-insulin-Dependent Diabetes Mellitus, Gestational Diabetes, and Diabetic Complications, Symptoms, Treatment, and Research Results, Including Statistics on Prevalence, Morbidity, and Mortality

Along with Source Listings for Further Help and Information

Edited by Karen Bellenir and Peter D. Dresser. 827 pages. 1994. 1-55888-751-2. $78.

". . . very informative and understandable for the layperson without being simplistic. It provides a comprehensive overview for laypersons who want a general understanding of the disease or who want to focus on various aspects of the disease."
— *Bulletin of the Medical Library Association, Jan '96*

■

Diabetes Sourcebook, 2nd Edition

Basic Consumer Health Information about Type 1 Diabetes (Insulin-Dependent or Juvenile-Onset Diabetes), Type 2 (Noninsulin-Dependent or Adult-Onset Diabetes), Gestational Diabetes, and Related Disorders, Including Diabetes Prevalence Data, Management Issues, the Role of Diet and Exercise in Controlling Diabetes, Insulin and Other Diabetes Medicines, and Complications of Diabetes Such as Eye Diseases, Periodontal Disease, Amputation, and End-Stage Renal Disease

Along with Reports on Current Research Initiatives, a Glossary, and Resource Listings for Further Help and Information

Edited by Karen Bellenir. 688 pages. 1998. 0-7808-0224-1. $78.

"An invaluable reference." — *Library Journal, May '00*

Selected as one of the 250 "Best Health Sciences Books of 1999." — *Doody's Rating Service, Mar-Apr 2000*

"This comprehensive book is an excellent addition for high school, academic, medical, and public libraries. This volume is highly recommended."
— *American Reference Books Annual, 2000*

"Provides useful information for the general public."
— *Healthlines, University of Michigan Health Management Research Center, Sep/Oct '99*

"... provides reliable mainstream medical information ... belongs on the shelves of any library with a consumer health collection." — *E-Streams, Sep '99*

"Recommended reference source."
— *Booklist, American Library Association, Feb '99*

■

Diabetes Sourcebook, 3rd Edition

Basic Consumer Health Information about Type 1 Diabetes (Insulin-Dependent or Juvenile-Onset Diabetes), Type 2 Diabetes (Noninsulin-Dependent or Adult-Onset Diabetes), Gestational Diabetes, Impaired Glucose Tolerance (IGT), and Related Complications, Such as Amputation, Eye Disease, Gum Disease, Nerve Damage, and End-Stage Renal Disease, Including Facts about Insulin, Oral Diabetes Medications, Blood Sugar Testing, and the Role of Exercise and Nutrition in the Control of Diabetes

Along with a Glossary and Resources for Further Help and Information

Edited by Dawn D. Matthews. 650 pages. 2003. 0-7808-0???-?. $78.

■

Diet & Nutrition Sourcebook, 1st Edition

Basic Information about Nutrition, Including the Dietary Guidelines for Americans, the Food Guide Pyramid, and Their Applications in Daily Diet, Nutritional Advice for Specific Age Groups, Current Nutritional Issues and Controversies, the New Food Label and How to Use It to Promote Healthy Eating, and Recent Developments in Nutritional Research

Edited by Dan R. Harris. 662 pages. 1996. 0-7808-0084-2. $78.

"Useful reference as a food and nutrition sourcebook for the general consumer." — *Booklist Health Sciences Supplement, American Library Association, Oct '97*

"Recommended for public libraries and medical libraries that receive general information requests on nutrition. It is readable and will appeal to those interested in learning more about healthy dietary practices."
— *Medical Reference Services Quarterly, Fall '97*

"An abundance of medical and social statistics is translated into readable information geared toward the general reader." — *Bookwatch, Mar '97*

"With dozens of questionable diet books on the market, it is so refreshing to find a reliable and factual reference book. Recommended to aspiring professionals, librarians, and others seeking and giving reliable dietary advice. An excellent compilation." — *Choice, Association of College and Research Libraries, Feb '97*

SEE ALSO *Digestive Diseases & Disorders Sourcebook, Gastrointestinal Diseases & Disorders Sourcebook*

Diet & Nutrition Sourcebook, 2nd Edition

Basic Consumer Health Information about Dietary Guidelines, Recommended Daily Intake Values, Vitamins, Minerals, Fiber, Fat, Weight Control, Dietary Supplements, and Food Additives

Along with Special Sections on Nutrition Needs throughout Life and Nutrition for People with Such Specific Medical Concerns as Allergies, High Blood Cholesterol, Hypertension, Diabetes, Celiac Disease, Seizure Disorders, Phenylketonuria (PKU), Cancer, and Eating Disorders, and Including Reports on Current Nutrition Research and Source Listings for Additional Help and Information

Edited by Karen Bellenir. 650 pages. 1999. 0-7808-0228-4. $78.

"This book is an excellent source of basic diet and nutrition information." — *Booklist Health Sciences Supplement, American Library Association, Dec '00*

"This reference document should be in any public library, but it would be a very good guide for beginning students in the health sciences. If the other books in this publisher's series are as good as this, they should all be in the health sciences collections."
— *American Reference Books Annual, 2000*

"This book is an excellent general nutrition reference for consumers who desire to take an active role in their health care for prevention. Consumers of all ages who select this book can feel confident they are receiving current and accurate information." — *Journal of Nutrition for the Elderly, Vol. 19, No. 4, '00*

"Recommended reference source."
— *Booklist, American Library Association, Dec '99*

SEE ALSO *Digestive Diseases & Disorders Sourcebook, Gastrointestinal Diseases & Disorders Sourcebook*

■

Digestive Diseases & Disorders Sourcebook

Basic Consumer Health Information about Diseases and Disorders that Impact the Upper and Lower Digestive System, Including Celiac Disease, Constipation, Crohn's Disease, Cyclic Vomiting Syndrome, Diarrhea, Diverticulosis and Diverticulitis, Gallstones, Heartburn, Hemorrhoids, Hernias, Indigestion (Dyspepsia), Irritable Bowel Syndrome, Lactose Intolerance, Ulcers, and More

Along with Information about Medications and Other Treatments, Tips for Maintaining a Healthy Digestive Tract, a Glossary, and Directory of Digestive Diseases Organizations

Edited by Karen Bellenir. 335 pages. 2000. 0-7808-0327-2. $78.

"This title would be an excellent addition to all public or patient-research libraries."
— *American Reference Books Annual, 2001*

"This title is recommended for public, hospital, and health sciences libraries with consumer health collections." — *E-Streams, Jul-Aug '00*

"Recommended reference source."
—*Booklist, American Library Association, May '00*

SEE ALSO *Diet & Nutrition Sourcebook, 1st and 2nd Editions, Gastrointestinal Diseases & Disorders Sourcebook*

Disabilities Sourcebook

Basic Consumer Health Information about Physical and Psychiatric Disabilities, Including Descriptions of Major Causes of Disability, Assistive and Adaptive Aids, Workplace Issues, and Accessibility Concerns

Along with Information about the Americans with Disabilities Act, a Glossary, and Resources for Additional Help and Information

Edited by Dawn D. Matthews. 616 pages. 2000. 0-7808-0389-2. $78.

"It is a must for libraries with a consumer health section." —*American Reference Books Annual 2002*

"A much needed addition to the Omnigraphics *Health Reference Series*. A current reference work to provide people with disabilities, their families, caregivers or those who work with them, a broad range of information in one volume, has not been available until now. . . . It is recommended for all public and academic library reference collections." —*E-Streams, May '01*

"An excellent source book in easy-to-read format covering many current topics; highly recommended for all libraries." —*Choice, Association of College and Research Libraries, Jan '01*

"Recommended reference source." —*Booklist, American Library Association, Jul '00*

Domestic Violence & Child Abuse Sourcebook

Basic Consumer Health Information about Spousal/ Partner, Child, Sibling, Parent, and Elder Abuse, Covering Physical, Emotional, and Sexual Abuse, Teen Dating Violence, and Stalking; Includes Information about Hotlines, Safe Houses, Safety Plans, and Other Resources for Support and Assistance, Community Initiatives, and Reports on Current Directions in Research and Treatment

Along with a Glossary, Sources for Further Reading, and Governmental and Non-Governmental Organizations Contact Information

Edited by Helene Henderson. 1,064 pages. 2001. 0-7808-0235-7. $78.

"This is important information. The Web has many resources but this sourcebook fills an important societal need. I am not aware of any other resources of this type." —*Doody's Review Service, Sep '01*

"Recommended for all libraries, scholars, and practitioners." —*Choice, Association of College & Research Libraries, Jul '01*

"Recommended reference source." —*Booklist, American Library Association, Apr '01*

"Important pick for college-level health reference libraries." —*The Bookwatch, Mar '01*

"Because this problem is so widespread and because this book includes a lot of issues within one volume, this work is recommended for all public libraries." —*American Reference Books Annual, 2001*

Drug Abuse Sourcebook

Basic Consumer Health Information about Illicit Substances of Abuse and the Diversion of Prescription Medications, Including Depressants, Hallucinogens, Inhalants, Marijuana, Narcotics, Stimulants, and Anabolic Steroids

Along with Facts about Related Health Risks, Treatment Issues, and Substance Abuse Prevention Programs, a Glossary of Terms, Statistical Data, and Directories of Hotline Services, Self-Help Groups, and Organizations Able to Provide Further Information

Edited by Karen Bellenir. 629 pages. 2000. 0-7808-0242-X. $78.

"Containing a wealth of information, this book will be useful to the college student just beginning to explore the topic of substance abuse. This resource belongs in libraries that serve a lower-division undergraduate or community college clientele as well as the general public." —*Choice, Association of College and Research Libraries, Jun '01*

"Recommended reference source." —*Booklist, American Library Association, Feb '01*

"Highly recommended." —*The Bookwatch, Jan '01*

"Even though there is a plethora of books on drug abuse, this volume is recommended for school, public, and college libraries." —*American Reference Books Annual, 2001*

SEE ALSO *Alcoholism Sourcebook, Substance Abuse Sourcebook*

Ear, Nose & Throat Disorders Sourcebook

Basic Information about Disorders of the Ears, Nose, Sinus Cavities, Pharynx, and Larynx, Including Ear Infections, Tinnitus, Vestibular Disorders, Allergic and Non-Allergic Rhinitis, Sore Throats, Tonsillitis, and Cancers That Affect the Ears, Nose, Sinuses, and Throat

Along with Reports on Current Research Initiatives, a Glossary of Related Medical Terms, and a Directory of Sources for Further Help and Information

Edited by Karen Bellenir and Linda M. Shin. 576 pages. 1998. 0-7808-0206-3. $78.

"Overall, this sourcebook is helpful for the consumer seeking information on ENT issues. It is recommended for public libraries." —*American Reference Books Annual, 1999*

"Recommended reference source." —*Booklist, American Library Association, Dec '98*

Eating Disorders Sourcebook

Basic Consumer Health Information about Eating Disorders, Including Information about Anorexia Nervosa, Bulimia Nervosa, Binge Eating, Body Dysmorphic Disorder, Pica, Laxative Abuse, and Night Eating Syndrome

Along with Information about Causes, Adverse Effects, and Treatment and Prevention Issues, and Featuring a Section on Concerns Specific to Children and Adolescents, a Glossary, and Resources for Further Help and Information

Edited by Dawn D. Matthews. 322 pages. 2001. 0-7808-0335-3. $78.

"Recommended for health science libraries that are open to the public, as well as hospital libraries. This book is a good resource for the consumer who is concerned about eating disorders." — *E-Streams, Mar '02*

"This volume is another convenient collection of excerpted articles. Recommended for school and public library patrons; lower-division undergraduates; and two-year technical program students." — *Choice, Association of College & Research Libraries, Jan '02*

"Recommended reference source." — *Booklist, American Library Association, Oct '01*

■

Emergency Medical Services Sourcebook

Basic Consumer Health Information about Preventing, Preparing for, and Managing Emergency Situations, When and Who to Call for Help, What to Expect in the Emergency Room, the Emergency Medical Team, Patient Issues, and Current Topics in Emergency Medicine

Along with Statistical Data, a Glossary, and Sources of Additional Help and Information

Edited by Jenni Lynn Colson. 494 pages. 2002. 0-7808-0420-1. $78.

■

Endocrine & Metabolic Disorders Sourcebook

Basic Information for the Layperson about Pancreatic and Insulin-Related Disorders Such as Pancreatitis, Diabetes, and Hypoglycemia; Adrenal Gland Disorders Such as Cushing's Syndrome, Addison's Disease, and Congenital Adrenal Hyperplasia; Pituitary Gland Disorders Such as Growth Hormone Deficiency, Acromegaly, and Pituitary Tumors; Thyroid Disorders Such as Hypothyroidism, Graves' Disease, Hashimoto's Disease, and Goiter; Hyperparathyroidism; and Other Diseases and Syndromes of Hormone Imbalance or Metabolic Dysfunction

Along with Reports on Current Research Initiatives

Edited by Linda M. Shin. 574 pages. 1998. 0-7808-0207-1. $78.

"Omnigraphics has produced another needed resource for health information consumers." —*American Reference Books Annual, 2000*

"Recommended reference source." — *Booklist, American Library Association, Dec '98*

Environmentally Induced Disorders Sourcebook

Basic Information about Diseases and Syndromes Linked to Exposure to Pollutants and Other Substances in Outdoor and Indoor Environments Such as Lead, Asbestos, Formaldehyde, Mercury, Emissions, Noise, and More

Edited by Allan R. Cook. 620 pages. 1997. 0-7808-0083-4. $78.

"Recommended reference source." — *Booklist, American Library Association, Sep '98*

"This book will be a useful addition to anyone's library." — *Choice Health Sciences Supplement, Association of College and Research Libraries, May '98*

". . . a good survey of numerous environmentally induced physical disorders . . . a useful addition to anyone's library." —*Doody's Health Sciences Book Reviews, Jan '98*

". . . provide[s] introductory information from the best authorities around. Since this volume covers topics that potentially affect everyone, it will surely be one of the most frequently consulted volumes in the *Health Reference Series*." — *Rettig on Reference, Nov '97*

■

Ethnic Diseases Sourcebook

Basic Consumer Health Information for Ethnic and Racial Minority Groups in the United States, Including General Health Indicators and Behaviors, Ethnic Diseases, Genetic Testing, the Impact of Chronic Diseases, Women's Health, Mental Health Issues, and Preventive Health Care Services

Along with a Glossary and a Listing of Additional Resources

Edited by Joyce Brennfleck Shannon. 664 pages. 2001. 0-7808-0336-1. $78.

"Recommended for health sciences libraries where public health programs are a priority." —*E-Streams, Jan '02*

"Not many books have been written on this topic to date, and the *Ethnic Diseases Sourcebook* is a strong addition to the list. It will be an important introductory resource for health consumers, students, health care personnel, and social scientists. It is recommended for public, academic, and large hospital libraries." — *American Reference Books Annual 2002*

"Recommended reference source." — *Booklist, American Library Association, Oct '01*

"Will prove valuable to any library seeking to maintain a current, comprehensive reference collection of health resources.... An excellent source of health information about genetic disorders which affect particular ethnic and racial minorities in the U.S." — *The Bookwatch, Aug '01*

Eye Care Sourcebook, 2nd Edition

Basic Consumer Health Information about Eye Care and Eye Disorders, Including Facts about the Diagnosis, Prevention, and Treatment of Common Refractive Problems Such as Myopia, Hyperopia, Astigmatism, and Presbyopia, and Eye Diseases, Including Glaucoma, Cataract, Age-Related Macular Degeneration, and Diabetic Retinopathy

Along with a Section on Vision Correction and Refractive Surgeries, Including LASIK and LASEK, a Glossary, and Directories of Resources for Additional Help and Information

Edited by Amy L. Sutton. 575 pages. 2003. 0-7808-0635-2. $78.

∎

Family Planning Sourcebook

Basic Consumer Health Information about Planning for Pregnancy and Contraception, Including Traditional Methods, Barrier Methods, Hormonal Methods, Permanent Methods, Future Methods, Emergency Contraception, and Birth Control Choices for Women at Each Stage of Life

Along with Statistics, a Glossary, and Sources of Additional Information

Edited by Amy Marcaccio Keyzer. 520 pages. 2001. 0-7808-0379-5. $78.

"Recommended for public, health, and undergraduate libraries as part of the circulating collection."
— E-Streams, Mar '02

"Information is presented in an unbiased, readable manner, and the sourcebook will certainly be a necessary addition to those public and high school libraries where Internet access is restricted or otherwise problematic." — American Reference Books Annual 2002

"Recommended reference source."
— Booklist, American Library Association, Oct '01

"Will prove valuable to any library seeking to maintain a current, comprehensive reference collection of health resources. . . . Excellent reference."
— The Bookwatch, Aug '01

SEE ALSO *Pregnancy & Birth Sourcebook*

∎

Fitness & Exercise Sourcebook, 1st Edition

Basic Information on Fitness and Exercise, Including Fitness Activities for Specific Age Groups, Exercise for People with Specific Medical Conditions, How to Begin a Fitness Program in Running, Walking, Swimming, Cycling, and Other Athletic Activities, and Recent Research in Fitness and Exercise

Edited by Dan R. Harris. 663 pages. 1996. 0-7808-0186-5. $78.

"A good resource for general readers." — Choice, Association of College and Research Libraries, Nov '97

"The perennial popularity of the topic . . . make this an appealing selection for public libraries."
— Rettig on Reference, Jun/Jul '97

Fitness & Exercise Sourcebook, 2nd Edition

Basic Consumer Health Information about the Fundamentals of Fitness and Exercise, Including How to Begin and Maintain a Fitness Program, Fitness as a Lifestyle, the Link between Fitness and Diet, Advice for Specific Groups of People, Exercise as It Relates to Specific Medical Conditions, and Recent Research in Fitness and Exercise

Along with a Glossary of Important Terms and Resources for Additional Help and Information

Edited by Kristen M. Gledhill. 646 pages. 2001. 0-7808-0334-5. $78.

"This work is recommended for all general reference collections."
— American Reference Books Annual 2002

"Highly recommended for public, consumer, and school grades fourth through college."
— E-Streams, Nov '01

"Recommended reference source." — Booklist, American Library Association, Oct '01

"The information appears quite comprehensive and is considered reliable. . . . This second edition is a welcomed addition to the series."
— Doody's Review Service, Sep '01

"This reference is a valuable choice for those who desire a broad source of information on exercise, fitness, and chronic-disease prevention through a healthy lifestyle." — American Medical Writers Association Journal, Fall '01

"Will prove valuable to any library seeking to maintain a current, comprehensive reference collection of health resources. . . . Excellent reference."
— The Bookwatch, Aug '01

∎

Food & Animal Borne Diseases Sourcebook

Basic Information about Diseases That Can Be Spread to Humans through the Ingestion of Contaminated Food or Water or by Contact with Infected Animals and Insects, Such as Botulism, E. Coli, Hepatitis A, Trichinosis, Lyme Disease, and Rabies

Along with Information Regarding Prevention and Treatment Methods, and Including a Special Section for International Travelers Describing Diseases Such as Cholera, Malaria, Travelers' Diarrhea, and Yellow Fever, and Offering Recommendations for Avoiding Illness

Edited by Karen Bellenir and Peter D. Dresser. 535 pages. 1995. 0-7808-0033-8. $78.

"Targeting general readers and providing them with a single, comprehensive source of information on selected topics, this book continues, with the excellent caliber of its predecessors, to catalog topical information on health matters of general interest. Readable and thorough, this valuable resource is highly recommended for all libraries."
— Academic Library Book Review, Summer '96

"A comprehensive collection of authoritative information." — Emergency Medical Services, Oct '95

Food Safety Sourcebook

Basic Consumer Health Information about the Safe Handling of Meat, Poultry, Seafood, Eggs, Fruit Juices, and Other Food Items, and Facts about Pesticides, Drinking Water, Food Safety Overseas, and the Onset, Duration, and Symptoms of Foodborne Illnesses, Including Types of Pathogenic Bacteria, Parasitic Protozoa, Worms, Viruses, and Natural Toxins

Along with the Role of the Consumer, the Food Handler, and the Government in Food Safety; a Glossary, and Resources for Additional Help and Information

Edited by Dawn D. Matthews. 339 pages. 1999. 0-7808-0326-4. $78.

"This book is recommended for public libraries and universities with home economic and food science programs." — *E-Streams, Nov '00*

"Recommended reference source."
— *Booklist, American Library Association, May '00*

"This book takes the complex issues of food safety and foodborne pathogens and presents them in an easily understood manner. [It does] an excellent job of covering a large and often confusing topic."
— *American Reference Books Annual, 2000*

Forensic Medicine Sourcebook

Basic Consumer Information for the Layperson about Forensic Medicine, Including Crime Scene Investigation, Evidence Collection and Analysis, Expert Testimony, Computer-Aided Criminal Identification, Digital Imaging in the Courtroom, DNA Profiling, Accident Reconstruction, Autopsies, Ballistics, Drugs and Explosives Detection, Latent Fingerprints, Product Tampering, and Questioned Document Examination

Along with Statistical Data, a Glossary of Forensics Terminology, and Listings of Sources for Further Help and Information

Edited by Annemarie S. Muth. 574 pages. 1999. 0-7808-0232-2. $78.

"Given the expected widespread interest in its content and its easy to read style, this book is recommended for most public and all college and university libraries."
— *E-Streams, Feb '01*

"Recommended for public libraries."
— *Reference & User Services Quarterly, American Library Association, Spring 2000*

"Recommended reference source."
— *Booklist, American Library Association, Feb '00*

"A wealth of information, useful statistics, references are up-to-date and extremely complete. This wonderful collection of data will help students who are interested in a career in any type of forensic field. It is a great resource for attorneys who need information about types of expert witnesses needed in a particular case. It also offers useful information for fiction and nonfiction writers whose work involves a crime. A fascinating compilation. All levels." — *Choice, Association of College and Research Libraries, Jan 2000*

"There are several items that make this book attractive to consumers who are seeking certain forensic data. . . . This is a useful current source for those seeking general forensic medical answers."
— *American Reference Books Annual, 2000*

Gastrointestinal Diseases & Disorders Sourcebook

Basic Information about Gastroesophageal Reflux Disease (Heartburn), Ulcers, Diverticulosis, Irritable Bowel Syndrome, Crohn's Disease, Ulcerative Colitis, Diarrhea, Constipation, Lactose Intolerance, Hemorrhoids, Hepatitis, Cirrhosis, and Other Digestive Problems, Featuring Statistics, Descriptions of Symptoms, and Current Treatment Methods of Interest for Persons Living with Upper and Lower Gastrointestinal Maladies

Edited by Linda M. Ross. 413 pages. 1996. 0-7808-0078-8. $78.

". . . very readable form. The successful editorial work that brought this material together into a useful and understandable reference makes accessible to all readers information that can help them more effectively understand and obtain help for digestive tract problems."
— *Choice, Association of College & Research Libraries, Feb '97*

SEE ALSO *Diet & Nutrition Sourcebook, 1st and 2nd Editions, Digestive Diseases & Disorders*

Genetic Disorders Sourcebook, 1st Edition

Basic Information about Heritable Diseases and Disorders Such as Down Syndrome, PKU, Hemophilia, Von Willebrand Disease, Gaucher Disease, Tay-Sachs Disease, and Sickle-Cell Disease, Along with Information about Genetic Screening, Gene Therapy, Home Care, and Including Source Listings for Further Help and Information on More Than 300 Disorders

Edited by Karen Bellenir. 642 pages. 1996. 0-7808-0034-6. $78.

"Recommended for undergraduate libraries or libraries that serve the public."
— *Science & Technology Libraries, Vol. 18, No. 1, '99*

"Provides essential medical information to both the general public and those diagnosed with a serious or fatal genetic disease or disorder." — *Choice, Association of College and Research Libraries, Jan '97*

"Geared toward the lay public. It would be well placed in all public libraries and in those hospital and medical libraries in which access to genetic references is limited." — *Doody's Health Sciences Book Review, Oct '96*

Genetic Disorders Sourcebook, 2nd Edition

Basic Consumer Health Information about Hereditary Diseases and Disorders, Including Cystic Fibrosis, Down Syndrome, Hemophilia, Huntington's Disease, Sickle Cell Anemia, and More; Facts about Genes, Gene Research and Therapy, Genetic Screening, Ethics of Gene Testing, Genetic Counseling, and Advice on Coping and Caring

Along with a Glossary of Genetic Terminology and a Resource List for Help, Support, and Further Information

Edited by Kathy Massimini. 768 pages. 2001. 0-7808-0241-1. $78.

"Recommended for public libraries and medical and hospital libraries with consumer health collections."
— *E-Streams, May '01*

"Recommended reference source."
— *Booklist, American Library Association, Apr '01*

"Important pick for college-level health reference libraries." — *The Bookwatch, Mar '01*

Head Trauma Sourcebook

Basic Information for the Layperson about Open-Head and Closed-Head Injuries, Treatment Advances, Recovery, and Rehabilitation

Along with Reports on Current Research Initiatives

Edited by Karen Bellenir. 414 pages. 1997. 0-7808-0208-X. $78.

Headache Sourcebook

Basic Consumer Health Information about Migraine, Tension, Cluster, Rebound and Other Types of Headaches, with Facts about the Cause and Prevention of Headaches, the Effects of Stress and the Environment, Headaches during Pregnancy and Menopause, and Childhood Headaches

Along with a Glossary and Other Resources for Additional Help and Information

Edited by Dawn D. Matthews. 362 pages. 2002. 0-7808-0337-X. $78.

"Highly recommended for academic and medical reference collections." — *Library Bookwatch, Sep '02*

Health Insurance Sourcebook

Basic Information about Managed Care Organizations, Traditional Fee-for-Service Insurance, Insurance Portability and Pre-Existing Conditions Clauses, Medicare, Medicaid, Social Security, and Military Health Care

Along with Information about Insurance Fraud

Edited by Wendy Wilcox. 530 pages. 1997. 0-7808-0222-5. $78.

"Particularly useful because it brings much of this information together in one volume. This book will be a handy reference source in the health sciences library, hospital library, college and university library, and medium to large public library."
— *Medical Reference Services Quarterly, Fall '98*

Awarded "Books of the Year Award"
— *American Journal of Nursing, 1997*

"The layout of the book is particularly helpful as it provides easy access to reference material. A most useful addition to the vast amount of information about health insurance. The use of data from U.S. government agencies is most commendable. Useful in a library or learning center for healthcare professional students."
— *Doody's Health Sciences Book Reviews, Nov '97*

Health Reference Series Cumulative Index 1999

A Comprehensive Index to the Individual Volumes of the Health Reference Series, Including a Subject Index, Name Index, Organization Index, and Publication Index

Along with a Master List of Acronyms and Abbreviations

Edited by Edward J. Prucha, Anne Holmes, and Robert Rudnick. 990 pages. 2000. 0-7808-0382-5. $78.

"This volume will be most helpful in libraries that have a relatively complete collection of the Health Reference Series." — *American Reference Books Annual, 2001*

"Essential for collections that hold any of the numerous *Health Reference Series* titles."
— *Choice, Association of College and Research Libraries, Nov '00*

Healthy Aging Sourcebook

Basic Consumer Health Information about Maintaining Health through the Aging Process, Including Advice on Nutrition, Exercise, and Sleep, Help in Making Decisions about Midlife Issues and Retirement, and Guidance Concerning Practical and Informed Choices in Health Consumerism

Along with Data Concerning the Theories of Aging, Different Experiences in Aging by Minority Groups, and Facts about Aging Now and Aging in the Future; and Featuring a Glossary, a Guide to Consumer Help, Additional Suggested Reading, and Practical Resource Directory

Edited by Jenifer Swanson. 536 pages. 1999. 0-7808-0390-6. $78.

"Recommended reference source."
— *Booklist, American Library Association, Feb '00*

SEE ALSO Physical & Mental Issues in Aging Sourcebook

Healthy Heart Sourcebook for Women

Basic Consumer Health Information about Cardiac Issues Specific to Women, Including Facts about Major Risk Factors and Prevention, Treatment and Control Strategies, and Important Dietary Issues

Along with a Special Section Regarding the Pros and Cons of Hormone Replacement Therapy and Its Impact on Heart Health, and Additional Help, Including Recipes, a Glossary, and a Directory of Resources

Edited by Dawn D. Matthews. 336 pages. 2000. 0-7808-0329-9. $78.

"A good reference source and recommended for all public, academic, medical, and hospital libraries."
— *Medical Reference Services Quarterly, Summer '01*

"Because of the lack of information specific to women on this topic, this book is recommended for public libraries and consumer libraries."
— *American Reference Books Annual, 2001*

"Contains very important information about coronary artery disease that all women should know. The information is current and presented in an easy-to-read format. The book will make a good addition to any library." — *American Medical Writers Association Journal, Summer '00*

"Important, basic reference."
— *Reviewer's Bookwatch, Jul '00*

SEE ALSO *Cardiovascular Diseases & Disorders Sourcebook, 1st Edition, Heart Diseases & Disorders Sourcebook, 2nd Edition, Women's Health Concerns Sourcebook*

Heart Diseases & Disorders Sourcebook, 2nd Edition

Basic Consumer Health Information about Heart Attacks, Angina, Rhythm Disorders, Heart Failure, Valve Disease, Congenital Heart Disorders, and More, Including Descriptions of Surgical Procedures and Other Interventions, Medications, Cardiac Rehabilitation, Risk Identification, and Prevention Tips

Along with Statistical Data, Reports on Current Research Initiatives, a Glossary of Cardiovascular Terms, and Resource Directory

Edited by Karen Bellenir. 612 pages. 2000. 0-7808-0238-1. $78.

"This work stands out as an imminently accessible resource for the general public. It is recommended for the reference and circulating shelves of school, public, and academic libraries."
— *American Reference Books Annual, 2001*

"Recommended reference source."
— *Booklist, American Library Association, Dec '00*

"Provides comprehensive coverage of matters related to the heart. This title is recommended for health sciences and public libraries with consumer health collections."
— *E-Streams, Oct '00*

SEE ALSO *Cardiovascular Diseases & Disorders Sourcebook, 1st Edition; Healthy Heart Sourcebook for Women*

Household Safety Sourcebook

Basic Consumer Health Information about Household Safety, Including Information about Poisons, Chemicals, Fire, and Water Hazards in the Home

Along with Advice about the Safe Use of Home Maintenance Equipment, Choosing Toys and Nursery Furniture, Holiday and Recreation Safety, a Glossary, and Resources for Further Help and Information

Edited by Dawn D. Matthews. 606 pages. 2002. 0-7808-0338-8. $78.

"As a sourcebook on household safety this book meets its mark. It is encyclopedic in scope and covers a wide range of safety issues that are commonly seen in the home." — *E-Streams, Jul '02*

Immune System Disorders Sourcebook

Basic Information about Lupus, Multiple Sclerosis, Guillain-Barré Syndrome, Chronic Granulomatous Disease, and More

Along with Statistical and Demographic Data and Reports on Current Research Initiatives

Edited by Allan R. Cook. 608 pages. 1997. 0-7808-0209-8. $78.

Infant & Toddler Health Sourcebook

Basic Consumer Health Information about the Physical and Mental Development of Newborns, Infants, and Toddlers, Including Neonatal Concerns, Nutrition Recommendations, Immunization Schedules, Common Pediatric Disorders, Assessments and Milestones, Safety Tips, and Advice for Parents and Other Caregivers

Along with a Glossary of Terms and Resource Listings for Additional Help

Edited by Jenifer Swanson. 585 pages. 2000. 0-7808-0246-2. $78.

"As a reference for the general public, this would be useful in any library." — *E-Streams, May '01*

"Recommended reference source."
— *Booklist, American Library Association, Feb '01*

"This is a good source for general use."
— *American Reference Books Annual, 2001*

Injury & Trauma Sourcebook

Basic Consumer Health Information about the Impact of Injury, the Diagnosis and Treatment of Common and Traumatic Injuries, Emergency Care, and Specific Injuries Related to Home, Community, Workplace, Transportation, and Recreation

Along with Guidelines for Injury Prevention, a Glossary, and a Directory of Additional Resources

Edited by Joyce Brennfleck Shannon. 696 pages. 2002. 0-7808-0421-X. $78.

"Practitioners should be aware of guides such as this in order to facilitate their use by patients and their families."
— *Doody's Health Sciences Book Review Journal, Sep-Oct '02*

"Recommended reference source."
— *Booklist, American Library Association, Sep '02*

"Highly recommended for academic and medical reference collections."
— *Library Bookwatch, Sep '02*

Kidney & Urinary Tract Diseases & Disorders Sourcebook

Basic Information about Kidney Stones, Urinary Incontinence, Bladder Disease, End Stage Renal Disease, Dialysis, and More

Along with Statistical and Demographic Data and Reports on Current Research Initiatives

Edited by Linda M. Ross. 602 pages. 1997. 0-7808-0079-6. $78.

Learning Disabilities Sourcebook, 1st Edition

Basic Information about Disorders Such as Dyslexia, Visual and Auditory Processing Deficits, Attention Deficit/Hyperactivity Disorder, and Autism

Along with Statistical and Demographic Data, Reports on Current Research Initiatives, an Explanation of the Assessment Process, and a Special Section for Adults with Learning Disabilities

Edited by Linda M. Shin. 579 pages. 1998. 0-7808-0210-1. $78.

Named "Outstanding Reference Book of 1999."
— *New York Public Library, Feb 2000*

"An excellent candidate for inclusion in a public library reference section. It's a great source of information. Teachers will also find the book useful. Definitely worth reading."
— *Journal of Adolescent & Adult Literacy, Feb 2000*

"Readable . . . provides a solid base of information regarding successful techniques used with individuals who have learning disabilities, as well as practical suggestions for educators and family members. Clear language, concise descriptions, and pertinent information for contacting multiple resources add to the strength of this book as a useful tool."
— *Choice, Association of College and Research Libraries, Feb '99*

"Recommended reference source."
— *Booklist, American Library Association, Sep '98*

"A useful resource for libraries and for those who don't have the time to identify and locate the individual publications."
— *Disability Resources Monthly, Sep '98*

Learning Disabilities Sourcebook, 2nd Edition

Basic Consumer Health Information about Learning Disabilities, Including Dyslexia, Developmental Speech and Language Disabilities, Non-Verbal Learning Disorders, Developmental Arithmetic Disorder, Developmental Writing Disorder, and Other Conditions That Impede Learning Such as Attention Deficit/ Hyperactivity Disorder, Brain Injury, Hearing Impairment, Klinefelter Syndrome, Dyspraxia, and Tourette Syndrome

Along with Facts about Educational Issues and Assistive Technology, Coping Strategies, a Glossary of Related Terms, and Resources for Further Help and Information

Edited by Dawn D. Matthews. 621 pages. 2003. 0-7808-0626-3. $78.

Liver Disorders Sourcebook

Basic Consumer Health Information about the Liver and How It Works; Liver Diseases, Including Cancer, Cirrhosis, Hepatitis, and Toxic and Drug Related Diseases; Tips for Maintaining a Healthy Liver; Laboratory Tests, Radiology Tests, and Facts about Liver Transplantation

Along with a Section on Support Groups, a Glossary, and Resource Listings

Edited by Joyce Brennfleck Shannon. 591 pages. 2000. 0-7808-0383-3. $78.

"A valuable resource."
— *American Reference Books Annual, 2001*

"This title is recommended for health sciences and public libraries with consumer health collections."
— *E-Streams, Oct '00*

"Recommended reference source."
— *Booklist, American Library Association, Jun '00*

Lung Disorders Sourcebook

Basic Consumer Health Information about Emphysema, Pneumonia, Tuberculosis, Asthma, Cystic Fibrosis, and Other Lung Disorders, Including Facts about Diagnostic Procedures, Treatment Strategies, Disease Prevention Efforts, and Such Risk Factors as Smoking, Air Pollution, and Exposure to Asbestos, Radon, and Other Agents

Along with a Glossary and Resources for Additional Help and Information

Edited by Dawn D. Matthews. 678 pages. 2002. 0-7808-0339-6. $78.

"Highly recommended for academic and medical reference collections."
— *Library Bookwatch, Sep '02*
[Pain SB, 2nd ed.]

"A source of valuable information. . . . This book offers help to nonmedical people who need information about pain and pain management. It is also an excellent reference for those who participate in patient education."
— *Doody's Review Service, Sep '02*

"Highly recommended for academic and medical reference collections." — *Library Bookwatch, Sep '02*

■

Medical Tests Sourcebook

Basic Consumer Health Information about Medical Tests, Including Periodic Health Exams, General Screening Tests, Tests You Can Do at Home, Findings of the U.S. Preventive Services Task Force, X-ray and Radiology Tests, Electrical Tests, Tests of Blood and Other Body Fluids and Tissues, Scope Tests, Lung Tests, Genetic Tests, Pregnancy Tests, Newborn Screening Tests, Sexually Transmitted Disease Tests, and Computer Aided Diagnoses

Along with a Section on Paying for Medical Tests, a Glossary, and Resource Listings

Edited by Joyce Brennfleck Shannon. 691 pages. 1999. 0-7808-0243-8. $78.

"Recommended for hospital and health sciences libraries with consumer health collections." — *E-Streams, Mar '00*

"This is an overall excellent reference with a wealth of general knowledge that may aid those who are reluctant to get vital tests performed." — *Today's Librarian, Jan 2000*

"A valuable reference guide." —*American Reference Books Annual, 2000*

■

Men's Health Concerns Sourcebook

Basic Information about Health Issues That Affect Men, Featuring Facts about the Top Causes of Death in Men, Including Heart Disease, Stroke, Cancers, Prostate Disorders, Chronic Obstructive Pulmonary Disease, Pneumonia and Influenza, Human Immunodeficiency Virus and Acquired Immune Deficiency Syndrome, Diabetes Mellitus, Stress, Suicide, Accidents and Homicides; and Facts about Common Concerns for Men, Including Impotence, Contraception, Circumcision, Sleep Disorders, Snoring, Hair Loss, Diet, Nutrition, Exercise, Kidney and Urological Disorders, and Backaches

Edited by Allan R. Cook. 738 pages. 1998. 0-7808-0212-8. $78.

"This comprehensive resource and the series are highly recommended." —*American Reference Books Annual, 2000*

"Recommended reference source." — *Booklist, American Library Association, Dec '98*

■

Mental Health Disorders Sourcebook, 1st Edition

Basic Information about Schizophrenia, Depression, Bipolar Disorder, Panic Disorder, Obsessive-Compulsive Disorder, Phobias and Other Anxiety Disorders, Paranoia and Other Personality Disorders, Eating Disorders, and Sleep Disorders

Along with Information about Treatment and Therapies

Edited by Karen Bellenir. 548 pages. 1995. 0-7808-0040-0. $78.

"This is an excellent new book . . . written in easy-to-understand language." — *Booklist Health Sciences Supplement, American Library Association, Oct '97*

". . . useful for public and academic libraries and consumer health collections." — *Medical Reference Services Quarterly, Spring '97*

"The great strengths of the book are its readability and its inclusion of places to find more information. Especially recommended." — *Reference Quarterly, American Library Association, Winter '96*

". . . a good resource for a consumer health library." —*Bulletin of the Medical Library Association, Oct '96*

"The information is data-based and couched in brief, concise language that avoids jargon. . . . a useful reference source." — *Readings, Sep '96*

"The text is well organized and adequately written for its target audience." — *Choice, Association of College and Research Libraries, Jun '96*

". . . provides information on a wide range of mental disorders, presented in nontechnical language." — *Exceptional Child Education Resources, Spring '96*

"Recommended for public and academic libraries." — *Reference Book Review, 1996*

■

Mental Health Disorders Sourcebook, 2nd Edition

Basic Consumer Health Information about Anxiety Disorders, Depression and Other Mood Disorders, Eating Disorders, Personality Disorders, Schizophrenia, and More, Including Disease Descriptions, Treatment Options, and Reports on Current Research Initiatives

Along with Statistical Data, Tips for Maintaining Mental Health, a Glossary, and Directory of Sources for Additional Help and Information

Edited by Karen Bellenir. 605 pages. 2000. 0-7808-0240-3. $78.

"Well organized and well written." —*American Reference Books Annual, 2001*

"Recommended reference source." —*Booklist, American Library Association, Jun '00*

■

Mental Retardation Sourcebook

Basic Consumer Health Information about Mental Retardation and Its Causes, Including Down Syndrome, Fetal Alcohol Syndrome, Fragile X Syndrome, Genetic Conditions, Injury, and Environmental Sources

Along with Preventive Strategies, Parenting Issues, Educational Implications, Health Care Needs, Employment and Economic Matters, Legal Issues, a Glossary, and a Resource Listing for Additional Help and Information

Edited by Joyce Brennfleck Shannon. 642 pages. 2000. 0-7808-0377-9. $78.

"Public libraries will find the book useful for reference and as a beginning research point for students, parents, and caregivers."
—*American Reference Books Annual, 2001*

"The strength of this work is that it compiles many basic fact sheets and addresses for further information in one volume. It is intended and suitable for the general public. This sourcebook is relevant to any collection providing health information to the general public."
—*E-Streams, Nov '00*

"From preventing retardation to parenting and family challenges, this covers health, social and legal issues and will prove an invaluable overview."
—*Reviewer's Bookwatch, Jul '00*

■

Movement Disorders Sourcebook

Basic Consumer Health Information about Neurological Movement Disorders, Including Essential Tremor, Parkinson's Disease, Dystonia, Cerebral Palsy, Huntington's Disease, Myasthenia Gravis, Multiple Sclerosis, and Other Early-Onset and Adult-Onset Movement Disorders, Their Symptoms and Causes, Diagnostic Tests, and Treatments

Along with Mobility and Assistive Technology Information, a Glossary, and a Directory of Additional Resources

Edited by Joyce Brennfleck Shannon. 650 pages. 2003. 0-7808-0628-X. $78.

■

Obesity Sourcebook

Basic Consumer Health Information about Diseases and Other Problems Associated with Obesity, and Including Facts about Risk Factors, Prevention Issues, and Management Approaches

Along with Statistical and Demographic Data, Information about Special Populations, Research Updates, a Glossary, and Source Listings for Further Help and Information

Edited by Wilma Caldwell and Chad T. Kimball. 376 pages. 2001. 0-7808-0333-7. $78.

"The book synthesizes the reliable medical literature on obesity into one easy-to-read and useful resource for the general public."
—*American Reference Books Annual 2002*

"This is a very useful resource book for the lay public."
—*Doody's Review Service, Nov '01*

"Well suited for the health reference collection of a public library or an academic health science library that serves the general population." —*E-Streams, Sep '01*

"Recommended reference source."
—*Booklist, American Library Association, Apr '01*

" Recommended pick both for specialty health library collections and any general consumer health reference collection." —*The Bookwatch, Apr '01*

Ophthalmic Disorders Sourcebook

Basic Information about Glaucoma, Cataracts, Macular Degeneration, Strabismus, Refractive Disorders, and More

Along with Statistical and Demographic Data and Reports on Current Research Initiatives

Edited by Linda M. Ross. 631 pages. 1996. 0-7808-0081-8. $78.

SEE ALSO *Eye Care Sourcebook, 2nd Edition*

■

Oral Health Sourcebook

Basic Information about Diseases and Conditions Affecting Oral Health, Including Cavities, Gum Disease, Dry Mouth, Oral Cancers, Fever Blisters, Canker Sores, Oral Thrush, Bad Breath, Temporomandibular Disorders, and other Craniofacial Syndromes

Along with Statistical Data on the Oral Health of Americans, Oral Hygiene, Emergency First Aid, Information on Treatment Procedures and Methods of Replacing Lost Teeth

Edited by Allan R. Cook. 558 pages. 1997. 0-7808-0082-6. $78.

"Unique source which will fill a gap in dental sources for patients and the lay public. A valuable reference tool even in a library with thousands of books on dentistry. Comprehensive, clear, inexpensive, and easy to read and use. It fills an enormous gap in the health care literature." —*Reference and User Services Quarterly, American Library Association, Summer '98*

"Recommended reference source."
—*Booklist, American Library Association, Dec '97*

■

Osteoporosis Sourcebook

Basic Consumer Health Information about Primary and Secondary Osteoporosis and Juvenile Osteoporosis and Related Conditions, Including Fibrous Dysplasia, Gaucher Disease, Hyperthyroidism, Hypophosphatasia, Myeloma, Osteopetrosis, Osteogenesis Imperfecta, and Paget's Disease

Along with Information about Risk Factors, Treatments, Traditional and Non-Traditional Pain Management, a Glossary of Related Terms, and a Directory of Resources

Edited by Allan R. Cook. 584 pages. 2001. 0-7808-0239-X. $78.

"This would be a book to be kept in a staff or patient library. The targeted audience is the layperson, but the therapist who needs a quick bit of information on a particular topic will also find the book useful."
—*Physical Therapy, Jan '02*

"This resource is recommended as a great reference source for public, health, and academic libraries, and is another triumph for the editors of Omnigraphics."
—*American Reference Books Annual 2002*

"Recommended for all public libraries and general health collections, especially those supporting patient education or consumer health programs."
— *E-Streams, Nov '01*

"Will prove valuable to any library seeking to maintain a current, comprehensive reference collection of health resources. . . . From prevention to treatment and associated conditions, this provides an excellent survey."
— *The Bookwatch, Aug '01*

"Recommended reference source."
— *Booklist, American Library Association, July '01*

SEE ALSO Women's Health Concerns Sourcebook

■

Pain Sourcebook, 1st Edition

Basic Information about Specific Forms of Acute and Chronic Pain, Including Headaches, Back Pain, Muscular Pain, Neuralgia, Surgical Pain, and Cancer Pain

Along with Pain Relief Options Such as Analgesics, Narcotics, Nerve Blocks, Transcutaneous Nerve Stimulation, and Alternative Forms of Pain Control, Including Biofeedback, Imaging, Behavior Modification, and Relaxation Techniques

Edited by Allan R. Cook. 667 pages. 1997. 0-7808-0213-6. $78.

"The text is readable, easily understood, and well indexed. This excellent volume belongs in all patient education libraries, consumer health sections of public libraries, and many personal collections."
— *American Reference Books Annual, 1999*

"A beneficial reference." — *Booklist Health Sciences Supplement, American Library Association, Oct '98*

"The information is basic in terms of scholarship and is appropriate for general readers. Written in journalistic style . . . intended for non-professionals. Quite thorough in its coverage of different pain conditions and summarizes the latest clinical information regarding pain treatment."
— *Choice, Association of College and Research Libraries, Jun '98*

"Recommended reference source."
— *Booklist, American Library Association, Mar '98*

■

Pain Sourcebook, 2nd Edition

Basic Consumer Health Information about Specific Forms of Acute and Chronic Pain, Including Muscle and Skeletal Pain, Nerve Pain, Cancer Pain, and Disorders Characterized by Pain, Such as Fibromyalgia, Shingles, Angina, Arthritis, and Headaches

Along with Information about Pain Medications and Management Techniques, Complementary and Alternative Pain Relief Options, Tips for People Living with Chronic Pain, a Glossary, and a Directory of Sources for Further Information

Edited by Karen Bellenir. 670 pages. 2002. 0-7808-0612-3. $78.

Pediatric Cancer Sourcebook

Basic Consumer Health Information about Leukemias, Brain Tumors, Sarcomas, Lymphomas, and Other Cancers in Infants, Children, and Adolescents, Including Descriptions of Cancers, Treatments, and Coping Strategies

Along with Suggestions for Parents, Caregivers, and Concerned Relatives, a Glossary of Cancer Terms, and Resource Listings

Edited by Edward J. Prucha. 587 pages. 1999. 0-7808-0245-4. $78.

"An excellent source of information. Recommended for public, hospital, and health science libraries with consumer health collections." — *E-Streams, Jun '00*

"Recommended reference source."
— *Booklist, American Library Association, Feb '00*

"A valuable addition to all libraries specializing in health services and many public libraries."
— *American Reference Books Annual, 2000*

■

Physical & Mental Issues in Aging Sourcebook

Basic Consumer Health Information on Physical and Mental Disorders Associated with the Aging Process, Including Concerns about Cardiovascular Disease, Pulmonary Disease, Oral Health, Digestive Disorders, Musculoskeletal and Skin Disorders, Metabolic Changes, Sexual and Reproductive Issues, and Changes in Vision, Hearing, and Other Senses

Along with Data about Longevity and Causes of Death, Information on Acute and Chronic Pain, Descriptions of Mental Concerns, a Glossary of Terms, and Resource Listings for Additional Help

Edited by Jenifer Swanson. 660 pages. 1999. 0-7808-0233-0. $78.

"This is a treasure of health information for the layperson." — *Choice Health Sciences Supplement, Association of College & Research Libraries, May 2000*

"Recommended for public libraries."
— *American Reference Books Annual, 2000*

"Recommended reference source."
— *Booklist, American Library Association, Oct '99*

SEE ALSO Healthy Aging Sourcebook

■

Podiatry Sourcebook

Basic Consumer Health Information about Foot Conditions, Diseases, and Injuries, Including Bunions, Corns, Calluses, Athlete's Foot, Plantar Warts, Hammertoes and Clawtoes, Clubfoot, Heel Pain, Gout, and More

Along with Facts about Foot Care, Disease Prevention, Foot Safety, Choosing a Foot Care Specialist, a Glossary of Terms, and Resource Listings for Additional Information

Edited by M. Lisa Weatherford. 380 pages. 2001. 0-7808-0215-2. $78.

"Recommended reference source."
— *Booklist, American Library Association, Feb '02*

"There is a lot of information presented here on a topic that is usually only covered sparingly in most larger comprehensive medical encyclopedias."
— *American Reference Books Annual 2002*

Pregnancy & Birth Sourcebook

Basic Information about Planning for Pregnancy, Maternal Health, Fetal Growth and Development, Labor and Delivery, Postpartum and Perinatal Care, Pregnancy in Mothers with Special Concerns, and Disorders of Pregnancy, Including Genetic Counseling, Nutrition and Exercise, Obstetrical Tests, Pregnancy Discomfort, Multiple Births, Cesarean Sections, Medical Testing of Newborns, Breastfeeding, Gestational Diabetes, and Ectopic Pregnancy

Edited by Heather E. Aldred. 737 pages. 1997. 0-7808-0216-0. $78.

"A well-organized handbook. Recommended."
— *Choice, Association of College and Research Libraries, Apr '98*

"Recommended reference source."
— *Booklist, American Library Association, Mar '98*

"Recommended for public libraries."
— *American Reference Books Annual, 1998*

SEE ALSO *Congenital Disorders Sourcebook, Family Planning Sourcebook*

Prostate Cancer Sourcebook

Basic Consumer Health Information about Prostate Cancer, Including Information about the Associated Risk Factors, Detection, Diagnosis, and Treatment of Prostate Cancer

Along with Information on Non-Malignant Prostate Conditions, and Featuring a Section Listing Support and Treatment Centers and a Glossary of Related Terms

Edited by Dawn D. Matthews. 358 pages. 2001. 0-7808-0324-8. $78.

"Recommended reference source."
— *Booklist, American Library Association, Jan '02*

"A valuable resource for health care consumers seeking information on the subject. . . .All text is written in a clear, easy-to-understand language that avoids technical jargon. Any library that collects consumer health resources would strengthen their collection with the addition of the *Prostate Cancer Sourcebook.*"
— *American Reference Books Annual 2002*

Public Health Sourcebook

Basic Information about Government Health Agencies, Including National Health Statistics and Trends, Healthy People 2000 Program Goals and Objectives, the Centers for Disease Control and Prevention, the Food and Drug Administration, and the National Institutes of Health

Along with Full Contact Information for Each Agency

Edited by Wendy Wilcox. 698 pages. 1998. 0-7808-0220-9. $78.

"Recommended reference source."
— *Booklist, American Library Association, Sep '98*

"This consumer guide provides welcome assistance in navigating the maze of federal health agencies and their data on public health concerns."
— *SciTech Book News, Sep '98*

Reconstructive & Cosmetic Surgery Sourcebook

Basic Consumer Health Information on Cosmetic and Reconstructive Plastic Surgery, Including Statistical Information about Different Surgical Procedures, Things to Consider Prior to Surgery, Plastic Surgery Techniques and Tools, Emotional and Psychological Considerations, and Procedure-Specific Information

Along with a Glossary of Terms and a Listing of Resources for Additional Help and Information

Edited by M. Lisa Weatherford. 374 pages. 2001. 0-7808-0214-4. $78.

"An excellent reference that addresses cosmetic and medically necessary reconstructive surgeries. . . . The style of the prose is calm and reassuring, discussing the many positive outcomes now available due to advances in surgical techniques."
— *American Reference Books Annual 2002*

"Recommended for health science libraries that are open to the public, as well as hospital libraries that are open to the patients. This book is a good resource for the consumer interested in plastic surgery."
— *E-Streams, Dec '01*

"Recommended reference source."
— *Booklist, American Library Association, July '01*

Rehabilitation Sourcebook

Basic Consumer Health Information about Rehabilitation for People Recovering from Heart Surgery, Spinal Cord Injury, Stroke, Orthopedic Impairments, Amputation, Pulmonary Impairments, Traumatic Injury, and More, Including Physical Therapy, Occupational Therapy, Speech/ Language Therapy, Massage Therapy, Dance Therapy, Art Therapy, and Recreational Therapy

Along with Information on Assistive and Adaptive Devices, a Glossary, and Resources for Additional Help and Information

Edited by Dawn D. Matthews. 531 pages. 1999. 0-7808-0236-5. $78.

"This is an excellent resource for public library reference and health collections."
— *American Reference Books Annual, 2001*

"Recommended reference source."
— *Booklist, American Library Association, May '00*

Respiratory Diseases & Disorders Sourcebook

Basic Information about Respiratory Diseases and Disorders, Including Asthma, Cystic Fibrosis, Pneumonia, the Common Cold, Influenza, and Others, Featuring Facts about the Respiratory System, Statistical and Demographic Data, Treatments, Self-Help Management Suggestions, and Current Research Initiatives

Edited by Allan R. Cook and Peter D. Dresser. 771 pages. 1995. 0-7808-0037-0. $78.

"Designed for the layperson and for patients and their families coping with respiratory illness. . . . an extensive array of information on diagnosis, treatment, management, and prevention of respiratory illnesses for the general reader." — *Choice, Association of College and Research Libraries, Jun '96*

"A highly recommended text for all collections. It is a comforting reminder of the power of knowledge that good books carry between their covers."
— *Academic Library Book Review, Spring '96*

"A comprehensive collection of authoritative information presented in a nontechnical, humanitarian style for patients, families, and caregivers."
— *Association of Operating Room Nurses, Sep/Oct '95*

■

Sexually Transmitted Diseases Sourcebook, 1st Edition

Basic Information about Herpes, Chlamydia, Gonorrhea, Hepatitis, Nongonoccocal Urethritis, Pelvic Inflammatory Disease, Syphilis, AIDS, and More

Along with Current Data on Treatments and Preventions

Edited by Linda M. Ross. 550 pages. 1997. 0-7808-0217-9. $78.

■

Sexually Transmitted Diseases Sourcebook, 2nd Edition

Basic Consumer Health Information about Sexually Transmitted Diseases, Including Information on the Diagnosis and Treatment of Chlamydia, Gonorrhea, Hepatitis, Herpes, HIV, Mononucleosis, Syphilis, and Others

Along with Information on Prevention, Such as Condom Use, Vaccines, and STD Education; And Featuring a Section on Issues Related to Youth and Adolescents, a Glossary, and Resources for Additional Help and Information

Edited by Dawn D. Matthews. 538 pages. 2001. 0-7808-0249-7. $78.

"Recommended for consumer health collections in public libraries, and secondary school and community college libraries."
— *American Reference Books Annual 2002*

"Every school and public library should have a copy of this comprehensive and user-friendly reference book."
— *Choice, Association of College & Research Libraries, Sep '01*

"This is a highly recommended book. This is an especially important book for all school and public libraries." — *AIDS Book Review Journal, Jul-Aug '01*

"Recommended reference source."
— *Booklist, American Library Association, Apr '01*

"Recommended pick both for specialty health library collections and any general consumer health reference collection." — *The Bookwatch, Apr '01*

■

Skin Disorders Sourcebook

Basic Information about Common Skin and Scalp Conditions Caused by Aging, Allergies, Immune Reactions, Sun Exposure, Infectious Organisms, Parasites, Cosmetics, and Skin Traumas, Including Abrasions, Cuts, and Pressure Sores

Along with Information on Prevention and Treatment

Edited by Allan R. Cook. 647 pages. 1997. 0-7808-0080-X. $78.

". . . comprehensive, easily read reference book."
— *Doody's Health Sciences Book Reviews, Oct '97*

SEE ALSO Burns Sourcebook

■

Sleep Disorders Sourcebook

Basic Consumer Health Information about Sleep and Its Disorders, Including Insomnia, Sleepwalking, Sleep Apnea, Restless Leg Syndrome, and Narcolepsy

Along with Data about Shiftwork and Its Effects, Information on the Societal Costs of Sleep Deprivation, Descriptions of Treatment Options, a Glossary of Terms, and Resource Listings for Additional Help

Edited by Jenifer Swanson. 439 pages. 1998. 0-7808-0234-9. $78.

"This text will complement any home or medical library. It is user-friendly and ideal for the adult reader."
— *American Reference Books Annual, 2000*

"A useful resource that provides accurate, relevant, and accessible information on sleep to the general public. Health care providers who deal with sleep disorders patients may also find it helpful in being prepared to answer some of the questions patients ask."
— *Respiratory Care, Jul '99*

"Recommended reference source."
— *Booklist, American Library Association, Feb '99*

■

Sports Injuries Sourcebook, 1st Edition

Basic Consumer Health Information about Common Sports Injuries, Prevention of Injury in Specific Sports, Tips for Training, and Rehabilitation from Injury

Along with Information about Special Concerns for Children, Young Girls in Athletic Training Programs, Senior Athletes, and Women Athletes, and a Directory of Resources for Further Help and Information

Edited by Heather E. Aldred. 624 pages. 1999. 0-7808-0218-7. $78.

"While this easy-to-read book is recommended for all libraries, it should prove to be especially useful for public, high school, and academic libraries; certainly it should be on the bookshelf of every school gymnasium." — *E-Streams, Mar '00*

"Public libraries and undergraduate academic libraries will find this book useful for its nontechnical language." — *American Reference Books Annual, 2000*

■

Sports Injuries Sourcebook, 2nd Edition

Basic Consumer Health Information about the Diagnosis, Treatment, and Rehabilitation of Common Sports-Related Injuries in Children and Adults

Along with Suggestions for Conditioning and Training, Information and Prevention Tips for Injuries Frequently Associated with Specific Sports and Special Populations, a Glossary, and a Directory of Additional Resources

Edited by Joyce Brennfleck Shannon. 614 pages. 2002. 0-7808-0604-2. $78.

■

Stress-Related Disorders Sourcebook

Basic Consumer Health Information about Stress and Stress-Related Disorders, Including Stress Origins and Signals, Environmental Stress at Work and Home, Mental and Emotional Stress Associated with Depression, Post-Traumatic Stress Disorder, Panic Disorder, Suicide, and the Physical Effects of Stress on the Cardiovascular, Immune, and Nervous Systems

Along with Stress Management Techniques, a Glossary, and a Listing of Additional Resources

Edited by Joyce Brennfleck Shannon. 610 pages. 2002. 0-7808-0560-7. $78.

"I am impressed by the amount of information. It offers a thorough overview of the causes and consequences of stress for the layperson. . . . A well-done and thorough reference guide for professionals and nonprofessionals alike." — *Doody's Review Service, Dec '02*

■

Substance Abuse Sourcebook

Basic Health-Related Information about the Abuse of Legal and Illegal Substances Such as Alcohol, Tobacco, Prescription Drugs, Marijuana, Cocaine, and Heroin; and Including Facts about Substance Abuse Prevention Strategies, Intervention Methods, Treatment and Recovery Programs, and a Section Addressing the Special Problems Related to Substance Abuse during Pregnancy

Edited by Karen Bellenir. 573 pages. 1996. 0-7808-0038-9. $78.

"A valuable addition to any health reference section. Highly recommended." — *The Book Report, Mar/Apr '97*

". . . a comprehensive collection of substance abuse information that's both highly readable and compact. Families and caregivers of substance abusers will find the information enlightening and helpful, while teachers, social workers and journalists should benefit from the concise format. Recommended." — *Drug Abuse Update, Winter '96/'97*

SEE ALSO *Alcoholism Sourcebook, Drug Abuse Sourcebook*

■

Surgery Sourcebook

Basic Consumer Health Information about Inpatient and Outpatient Surgeries, Including Cardiac, Vascular, Orthopedic, Ocular, Reconstructive, Cosmetic, Gynecologic, and Ear, Nose, and Throat Procedures and More

Along with Information about Operating Room Policies and Instruments, Laser Surgery Techniques, Hospital Errors, Statistical Data, a Glossary, and Listings of Sources for Further Help and Information

Edited by Annemarie S. Muth and Karen Bellenir. 596 pages. 2002. 0-7808-0380-9. $78.

■

Transplantation Sourcebook

Basic Consumer Health Information about Organ and Tissue Transplantation, Including Physical and Financial Preparations, Procedures and Issues Relating to Specific Solid Organ and Tissue Transplants, Rehabilitation, Pediatric Transplant Information, the Future of Transplantation, and Organ and Tissue Donation

Along with a Glossary and Listings of Additional Resources

Edited by Joyce Brennfleck Shannon. 628 pages. 2002. 0-7808-0322-1. $78.

"Recommended for libraries with an interest in offering consumer health information." — *E-Streams, Jul '02*

"This is a unique and valuable resource for patients facing transplantation and their families." — *Doody's Review Service, Jun '02*

■

Traveler's Health Sourcebook

Basic Consumer Health Information for Travelers, Including Physical and Medical Preparations, Transportation Health and Safety, Essential Information about Food and Water, Sun Exposure, Insect and Snake Bites, Camping and Wilderness Medicine, and Travel with Physical or Medical Disabilities

Along with International Travel Tips, Vaccination Recommendations, Geographical Health Issues, Disease Risks, a Glossary, and a Listing of Additional Resources

Edited by Joyce Brennfleck Shannon. 613 pages. 2000. 0-7808-0384-1. $78.

"Recommended reference source."
— *Booklist, American Library Association, Feb '01*

"This book is recommended for any public library, any travel collection, and especially any collection for the physically disabled."
— *American Reference Books Annual, 2001*

Vegetarian Sourcebook

Basic Consumer Health Information about Vegetarian Diets, Lifestyle, and Philosophy, Including Definitions of Vegetarianism and Veganism, Tips about Adopting Vegetarianism, Creating a Vegetarian Pantry, and Meeting Nutritional Needs of Vegetarians, with Facts Regarding Vegetarianism's Effect on Pregnant and Lactating Women, Children, Athletes, and Senior Citizens

Along with a Glossary of Commonly Used Vegetarian Terms and Resources for Additional Help and Information

Edited by Chad T. Kimball. 360 pages. 2002. 0-7808-0439-2. $78.

Women's Health Concerns Sourcebook

Basic Information about Health Issues That Affect Women, Featuring Facts about Menstruation and Other Gynecological Concerns, Including Endometriosis, Fibroids, Menopause, and Vaginitis; Reproductive Concerns, Including Birth Control, Infertility, and Abortion; and Facts about Additional Physical, Emotional, and Mental Health Concerns Prevalent among Women Such as Osteoporosis, Urinary Tract Disorders, Eating Disorders, and Depression

Along with Tips for Maintaining a Healthy Lifestyle

Edited by Heather E. Aldred. 567 pages. 1997. 0-7808-0219-5. $78.

"Handy compilation. There is an impressive range of diseases, devices, disorders, procedures, and other physical and emotional issues covered . . . well organized, illustrated, and indexed." — *Choice, Association of College and Research Libraries, Jan '98*

SEE ALSO *Breast Cancer Sourcebook, Cancer Sourcebook for Women, 1st and 2nd Editions, Healthy Heart Sourcebook for Women, Osteoporosis Sourcebook*

Workplace Health & Safety Sourcebook

Basic Consumer Health Information about Workplace Health and Safety, Including the Effect of Workplace Hazards on the Lungs, Skin, Heart, Ears, Eyes, Brain, Reproductive Organs, Musculoskeletal System, and Other Organs and Body Parts

Along with Information about Occupational Cancer, Personal Protective Equipment, Toxic and Hazardous Chemicals, Child Labor, Stress, and Workplace Violence

Edited by Chad T. Kimball. 626 pages. 2000. 0-7808-0231-4. $78.

"As a reference for the general public, this would be useful in any library." — *E-Streams, Jun '01*

"Provides helpful information for primary care physicians and other caregivers interested in occupational medicine. . . . General readers; professionals."
— *Choice, Association of College & Research Libraries, May '01*

"Recommended reference source."
— *Booklist, American Library Association, Feb '01*

"Highly recommended." — *The Bookwatch, Jan '01*

Worldwide Health Sourcebook

Basic Information about Global Health Issues, Including Malnutrition, Reproductive Health, Disease Dispersion and Prevention, Emerging Diseases, Risky Health Behaviors, and the Leading Causes of Death

Along with Global Health Concerns for Children, Women, and the Elderly, Mental Health Issues, Research and Technology Advancements, and Economic, Environmental, and Political Health Implications, a Glossary, and a Resource Listing for Additional Help and Information

Edited by Joyce Brennfleck Shannon. 614 pages. 2001. 0-7808-0330-2. $78.

"Named an Outstanding Academic Title."
— *Choice, Association of College & Research Libraries, Jan '02*

"Yet another handy but also unique compilation in the extensive Health Reference Series, this is a useful work because many of the international publications reprinted or excerpted are not readily available. Highly recommended."
— *Choice, Association of College & Research Libraries, Nov '01*

"Recommended reference source."
— *Booklist, American Library Association, Oct '01*

Teen Health Series
Helping Young Adults Understand, Manage, and Avoid Serious Illness

Diet Information for Teens
Health Tips about Diet and Nutrition
Including Facts about Nutrients, Dietary Guidelines, Breakfasts, School Lunches, Snacks, Party Food, Weight Control, Eating Disorders, and More

Edited by Karen Bellenir. 399 pages. 2001. 0-7808-0441-4. $58.

"Full of helpful insights and facts throughout the book. ... An excellent resource to be placed in public libraries or even in personal collections."
—American Reference Books Annual 2002

"Recommended for middle and high school libraries and media centers as well as academic libraries that educate future teachers of teenagers. It is also a suitable addition to health science libraries that serve patrons who are interested in teen health promotion and education."
—E-Streams, Oct '01

"This comprehensive book would be beneficial to collections that need information about nutrition, dietary guidelines, meal planning, and weight control. ... This reference is so easy to use that its purchase is recommended."
— The Book Report, Sep-Oct '01

"This book is written in an easy to understand format describing issues that many teens face every day, and then provides thoughtful explanations so that teens can make informed decisions. This is an interesting book that provides important facts and information for today's teens."
—Doody's Health Sciences Book Review Journal, Jul-Aug '01

"A comprehensive compendium of diet and nutrition. The information is presented in a straightforward, plain-spoken manner. This title will be useful to those working on reports on a variety of topics, as well as to general readers concerned about their dietary health."
— School Library Journal, Jun '01

Drug Information for Teens
Health Tips about the Physical and Mental Effects of Substance Abuse
Including Facts about Alcohol, Anabolic Steroids, Club Drugs, Cocaine, Depressants, Hallucinogens, Herbal Products, Inhalants, Marijuana, Narcotics, Stimulants, Tobacco, and More

Edited by Karen Bellenir. 452 pages. 2002. 0-7808-0444-9. $58.

Mental Health Information for Teens
Health Tips about Mental Health and Mental Illness
Including Facts about Anxiety, Depression, Suicide, Eating Disorders, Obsessive-Compulsive Disorders, Panic Attacks, Phobias, Schizophrenia, and More

Edited by Karen Bellenir. 406 pages. 2001. 0-7808-0442-2. $58.

"In both language and approach, this user-friendly entry in the *Teen Health Series* is on target for teens needing information on mental health concerns." *— Booklist, American Library Association, Jan '02*

"Readers will find the material accessible and informative, with the shaded notes, facts, and embedded glossary insets adding appropriately to the already interesting and succinct presentation."
—School Library Journal, Jan '02

"This title is highly recommended for any library that serves adolescents and parents/caregivers of adolescents." *—E-Streams, Jan '02*

"Recommended for high school libraries and young adult collections in public libraries. Both health professionals and teenagers will find this book useful."
— American Reference Books Annual 2002

"This is a nice book written to enlighten the society, primarily teenagers, about common teen mental health issues. It is highly recommended to teachers and parents as well as adolescents."
— Doody's Review Service, Dec '01

Sexual Health Information for Teens
Health Tips about Sexual Development, Human Reproduction, and Sexually Transmitted Diseases
Including Facts about Puberty, Reproductive Health, Chlamydia, Human Papillomavirus, Pelvic Inflammatory Disease, Herpes, AIDS, Contraception, Pregnancy, and More

Edited by Deborah A. Stanley. 400 pages. 2003. 0-7808-0445-7. $58.

Health Reference Series

WITHDRAWN

MAY 0 2 2024

DAVID O. McKAY LIBRARY
BYU-IDAHO